EVERYMAN, I will go with thee,

and be thy guide,

In thy most need to go by thy side

GIORGIO VASARI

Born at Arezzo in 1511
Died in Florence 1574

GIORGIO VASARI

The Lives of the
Painters, Sculptors
and Architects

IN FOUR VOLUMES · VOLUME THREE

TRANSLATED BY
A. B. HINDS

EDITED WITH AN INTRODUCTION BY
WILLIAM GAUNT, M.A.

Dent London Melbourne Toronto
EVERYMAN'S LIBRARY
Dutton New York

No 786   Hardback ISBN 0 460 00786 6

CONTENTS OF VOLUME THREE

PART III—*continued*

GIORGIO VASARI

PART III—*continued*

Morto da Feltro, Painter, and Andrea di Cosimo of Feltro
(c. 1474 – after 1522; 1490 – 1554)

Morto was as eccentric in his life as in his invention, and in the grotesques which made his name. He went to Rome in his youth, when Pinturicchio was painting the papal chambers for Alexander VI. and the loggia and apartments in the great tower of the Castle of St. Angelo. Being a melancholy man he was always studying antiquities, and on seeing some arabesques which pleased him, he devoted his attention to them, while in his treatment of foliage in the ancient style he was second to none. He made earnest search in Rome among the ancient caves and vaults. In the villa of Hadrian at Tivoli he remained many months, designing all the pavements and grottoes both above and below ground. Hearing that at Pozzuolo, ten miles from Naples, there were walls full of grotesques in relief, with stuccos and ancient paintings, he went to study there for several months. At Campana, hard-by, a place full of old tombs, he drew every trifle, and at Trullo, near the sea, he drew many of the temples and grottoes. He went to Baia and Mercato di Saboto, places full of ruins, endeavouring thus to increase his skill and knowledge. Returning to Rome he worked there many months studying figures, in which he did not think himself so expert as in arabesques. Hearing of the renown of the cartoons executed by Lionardo and Michelagnolo at Florence, he at once went thither, and when he saw their works he realised that he could not surpass them, and resolved to return to his arabesques.

At that time Andrea di Cosimo de' Feltrini, a Florentine painter, was living in the city. He took Morto into his house, gave him a very friendly welcome, and being pleased with his

work, resolved to try it himself. He succeeded well, surpassing
Morto, and was much esteemed in Florence, as will be said
hereafter. He succeeded in obtaining a commission for Morto
to paint the chambers of the palace with arabesques for Pier
Soderini, then gonfalonier. They were much admired, but were
destroyed when Duke Cosimo restored the apartments. For
Maestro Valerio, a Servite friar, he did a beautiful staircase,
and painted several curious arabesques for Agnolo Doni. Being
still fond of figures, he did some Madonnas, to see if he could
win fame by them. Becoming tired of Florence, he proceeded
to Venice, where he helped Giorgione at the Fondaco de'
Tedeschi, doing the ornamental decoration. He remained several
months in the city, attracted by the pleasures and bodily
delights. He then went to Friuli to work, and before he had
been there long he took the money of some Venetian lords and
became a soldier, when he was made a captain of two hundred
men, although he had no experience of his duties. The Venetian
army being transported to Zara in Sclavonia, Morto went
valorously forward in a skirmish there one day, hoping to
win a greater name than he had possessed as an artist, but he
was killed, at the age of forty-five. However, his fame will
never die, as his works will preserve his memory, their merits
having been celebrated by good writers. Indeed, it is a great
spur to artists that their works may be celebrated in writings
which assure them immortality. In his arabesques Morto
approached more nearly to the ancient style than any other
painter, and therefore he deserves great praise. What he began
was continued by Giovanni da Udine and other artists with
great beauty. But their success does not dim the renown of
Morto, who was the originator, and devoted all his study to
such work, most of his examples being taken from the ruins
of Rome; and everyone knows that it is easy to add to things
once found. The succession in Florence was taken up by Andrea
Feltrini, called Il Cosimo, from being a pupil of Cosimo Rosselli
for figures, as he was of Morto for arabesques. He possessed
naturally great invention and grace in this style, and rendered
his friezes larger and fuller and with a different style than
those of the ancients, accompanying them with figures, a thing
not previously seen in Rome or anywhere except Florence,
where he did a great number, so that no one surpassed him in
this work. An example is in a painted ornament in S. Croce,
Florence, the predella with small arabesques round Perugino's
Pietà at the altar of the Serristori, on a red and black ground

mixed, relieved by various colours, made easily with the utmost grace and boldness. He introduced the method of doing the façades of houses and palaces by stencilling. On an intonaco of lime mixed with pounded black charcoal or burnt straw he afterwards laid a coating of white, and he then made perforated cartoons of the arabesques to be executed. He next hatched the outline on the intonaco with an iron tool, with which he drew the whole design, and this he afterwards shaded with dark water-colour, producing a rich effect. The method is treated theoretically in Chapter xxvi. on Stencelling.[1] The first façades done by him in this style were in Borgo Ognissanti, one done for the Gondi, being very light and graceful; one on lung' Arno between the Ponte S. Trinità and that of la Carraia towards S. Spirito, and one for Lanfredino Lanfredini, very ornate and varied. For S. Michele of the Piazza Padella he did the house of Andrea and Tommaso Sertini, in a broader style than the others. He painted the façades of the church of the Servite friars in grisaille, doing an Annunciation in two niches for Tommaso di Stefano the painter.[2] In the courtyard containing the scenes of St. Philip and the Virgin, by Andrea del Sarto, he made the arms of Pope Leo X. between the two doors. On the coming of that pope to Florence he did some fine arabesques for the façade of S. Maria del Fiore for Jacopo di Sansovino, who gave him his sister to wife. He made the Pope's canopy, with a sky full of beautiful arabesques and draperies with the Pope's arms, and other devices of the Church. This was afterwards given to the church of S. Lorenzo in Florence, where it may still be seen. He did many standards for that entry, and in honour of the knights created by the Pope and other princes, which are placed in different churches of the city. He served the Medici for the marriages of Dukes Giuliano and Lorenzo, making trophies with ornaments and arabesques, and was also employed for the obsequies of those princes, and by Franciabigio, Andrea del Sarto, Pontormo and Ridolfo Ghirlandai, and in triumphs and other things by Granaccio, as they could do nothing without him.

Andrea was the best man who ever took up the brush. His diffidence made him unwilling to take up any work, as he dared not ask for his pay. He loved to work all day without any relaxation. He associated with Mariotto di Francesco Mettidoro,

---

[1] The reference is to Vasari's Introduction to the three arts of design, usually preceding the Lives in the Italian editions of his works.
[2] In 1510.

one of the most skilful masters of his profession, and a good man of business. They also took Raffaello di Biagio Mettidoro into partnership, sharing the gains between them; the association lasting till their deaths, Mariotto surviving longest.

To return to Andrea. For Gio. Maria Benintendi he made all the escutcheons of his house and the decorations of the antechambers containing the paintings of Franciabigio and Jacopo da Pontormo. He went with Francia to Poggio and did the scenes there in clay. None better can be seen. For the knight Gridotti he did a façade in the via Larga in *sgraffito*, and a very fine one for Bartolommeo Panciatichi on his house in the Piazza Degli Agli, now Roberto dei Ricci's. The city being full of his friezes, chests, ceilings and other things, I forbear to mention them. He also left many medallions of arms, and at every marriage his shop was filled with one thing or another for citizens. No brocades or cloths of gold were woven except from his design, for he gave them grace, variety and beauty, with spirit and vitality. If he had realised the talent he possessed he would have made a large fortune, but he was content to live and love his art.

In my youth I served Duke Alessandro de' Medici when Charles V. came to Florence, and I was employed to make the banners of the citadel, where there was a standard, eighteen braccia by forty, of crimson cloth, bearing the emperor's arms and those of the Medici, surrounded by a gold border, 45,000 gold leaves being employed. I asked Andrea to help me with the border and Mariotto to put on the gold, and I then learned many things from the worthy man, so good and kind to students of art. Andrea's skill was such that, besides helping me in making triumphal arches for his majesty's entry, he assisted both myself and Tribolo with the trophies which I made in the honour of Ottaviano de' Medici the Magnificent of S. Marco, at the coming of Charles's daughter Margaret to marry Duke Alessandro. They were adorned with arabesques by his hand, with statues by Tribolo, and with figures and scenes by me. Employed on the obsequies of Duke Alessandro, Andrea had far more to do at the wedding of Duke Cosimo, as described by M. Francesco Giambullari, painting all the devices of the court. Being a melancholy man, Andrea made several attempts to take his life, but was so carefully watched by his companion Mariotto that he reached the good old age of sixty-four leaving a name as an excellent master of arabesques, whose style every artist has imitated in Florence and elsewhere.

Marco Calavrese,[1] Painter
(1486 – ?1542)

WHEN the world possesses a great luminary in any science, every
part is illuminated, and the miracle is greater or less according
to the situation and the environment. Some provinces are
adapted to one thing and some to another, and some cannot
produce what the others put forth, no matter what efforts they
make. But we marvel when we see fruit come out of a district
such as we have not been accustomed to expect from it, and
rejoice at finding a genius in a country destitute of men of such
professions. Such was Marco Calavrese, the painter, who left
his native land and chose Naples for his home as a pleasant place,
although he had started for Rome to attain the end there that
is reached by the study of painting. But he loved the song of
the siren and the playing of the lute, the pleasant waters of the
Sebeto melted him, and he remained rooted to the spot till his
death. He produced a quantity of works in oils and fresco,
excelling all the men of that country, as we see by his work at
Aversa, ten miles from Naples, and especially in the church of
S. Agostino, the oil-painting at the high altar with a very large
ornamental border and various scenes and figures, St. Augustine
disputing with the heretics, surrounded by stories of Christ and
saints in various attitudes.[2] His manner is flowing, with a ten-
dency towards the modern style, including beautiful and skilful
colouring. This was one of his many labours in the kingdom. He
lived merrily and enjoyed life. He had no rivals in painting, was
a great favourite with the nobles, and received good payment
for his work. At the age of fifty-six he died a natural death.
He left behind his pupil, Gio. Filippo Crescioni, painter of
Naples, who in conjunction with his brother-in-law Lionardo
Castellani did many paintings. They are still alive and at work,
so that I need not say more. The paintings of Maestro Marco
were between 1508 and 1542. He was joined by another Calabrian, whose name I do not know, who long worked at Rome
with Giovanni da Udine, doing many works there, chiefly
façades in grisaille. He also painted in fresco the chapel of the
Conception in the church of la Trinità with great diligence and
skill. At the same time there flourished Niccolo, usually known
as Maestro Cola dalla Matrice,[3] who did many remarkable works

---

[1] Marco Cardisco.   [2] Now in Naples Museum.
[3] Niccola (Cola) di Mariano Filotesio.

in Ascoli, Calabria and Norcia, earning the reputation of being
the best master ever produced by those countries. He also studied
architecture, and erected all the buildings put up in Ascoli in
his time. Without caring to see Rome, he remained steadfastly
at Ascoli, living happily with his wife, a woman of good family
and singular virtue. When dissensions broke out in Ascoli in
the time of Paul III., she was pursued with Cola for her beauty
by some soldiers, and seeing no way of escape she threw herself
down a cliff and was killed, in order to save her own honour and
her husband's life, for she was very beautiful. Her husband was
left uninjured and returned to Ascoli, passing the rest of his
days in sorrow. Not long after, Alessandro Vitelli, being made
lord of la Matrice, brought Cola, then an old man, to Città di
Castello to decorate his palace with frescoes and other works.
This done, Cola returned to complete his days at Matrice. He
would have been much improved by rivalry, which would have
caused him to devote more study to painting and to cultivate
his natural abilities.

FRANCESCO MAZZUOLI,[1] Painter of Parma
(1504 – 1540)

AMONG the numerous Lombards endowed with grace and
vivacity of invention in painting and the power of making
beautiful landscapes, the first place must be conceded to Francesco Mazzuoli, who was liberally endowed with the richest
gifts of a painter, giving his figures a certain sweetness and
lightness of pose peculiar to him. His heads possess every
necessary quality, so that his style has been much imitated for
its charm, and his works will always be valued and himself
honoured by students of design. God intended him for a painter,
and if he had not conceived the whim to solidify mercury and
so make himself rich, he would have been a unique artist. But
he wasted time in seeking for what could never be found, and
neglected his art to the detriment of his life and reputation. He
was born at Parma in 1504, and having no father, he was left
when a little child to the care of two uncles, his father's brothers,
both painters, who brought him up with care as becomes a
Christian and a gentleman. When somewhat older, the moment
he had a pen in his hand to learn to write, his nature, which had

[1] Known as Parmigiano or Parmigianino.

formed him for design, led him to do marvels. His writing master, perceiving his bent, persuaded his uncles to make him learn design and painting. Although they were old, and painters of no great fame, yet they possessed good judgment, recognising that God and Nature were the first masters of the boy, and they did not hesitate to put him to study design with excellent masters, so that he should acquire a good style. Seeing that he was, so to speak, born with the brush in his hand, they sometimes took him away, fearing lest he should ruin his health by too much study. At length, at the age of sixteen, after having accomplished miracles in design, he did a panel of St. John baptising Christ [1] so fine that all must marvel that a boy could produce such work. The picture was placed in the Nunziata at Parma, where the bare-footed friars are. Not content with this, Francesco wished to try his skill in fresco, and being allotted a chapel in S. Giovanni Evangelistà a house of the black monks of St. Benedict, he succeeded so well that he did seven. At this time Pope Leo was sending Prospero Colonna to Parma with the army, and Francesco's uncles, fearing lest he should waste his time, sent him with his cousin Jeronimo Mazzuoli, also a young painter, to Viandana,[2] a place of the Duke of Mantua. Remaining there during the war, he painted two panels in tempera, one of which, a St. Francis receiving the stigmata and St. Clare, was placed in the church of the bare-footed friars, and the other, a Marriage of St. Catherine with several figures, in S. Piero. No one would have supposed these to be the work of a young beginner, but rather of an old and experienced master. On the conclusion of the war [3] Francesco returned with his cousin to Parma, and finished some paintings which he had left on his departure. He then painted in oils a Madonna and Child, between St. Jerome and the Blessed Bernardino da Feltro,[4] one head being a portrait of the donor, lacking breath only. All these things he completed before attaining the age of nineteen.

Being anxious to go to Rome after hearing the praises of the masters, especially of Raphael and Michelagnolo, he expressed his wish to his uncles, who thought his notion admirable, and gave their consent, at the same time advising him to take a specimen of his work in order to obtain an introduction to the patrons and artists. Thinking the advice good, Francesco did two small pictures and a fairly large one of a Madonna and Child, who is taking fruit from an angel's lap, and an old man with

---

[1] In 1522.   [2] About 1520.   [3] In 1522.
[4] Now in the Ducal Palace, Parma.

hairy arms, executed with art and judgment and beautifully coloured. One day he began to paint himself[1] with the help of a concave barber's mirror. Noticing the curious distortions of the buildings and doors caused by the mirror he conceived the idea of reproducing it all. Accordingly he had a ball of wood made, and cutting it out to make it of the same size and shape as the mirror he set to work to copy everything that he saw there, including his own likeness, in the most natural manner imaginable. As things near the mirror appear large while they diminish as they recede he made a hand with wonderful realism, somewhat large, as the mirror showed it. Being a handsome man, with the face of an angel rather than a man, his reflection in this ball appeared divine. He was most successful with the lustre of his glass, the reflections, shadows and lights, in fact human ingenuity could go no farther. The work when completed was greatly admired by his seniors and connoisseurs, and being packed in a case with the other pictures it was taken to Rome by one of his uncles. Upon the datary seeing the pictures and recognising their value, the youth and his uncle were immediately introduced to Pope Clement. When His Holiness saw the youth of Francesco he was amazed, as well as all his court. After heaping many favours on the youth he said that he would like Francesco to paint the Hall of the Popes, where Giovanni da Udine had already decorated the ceiling with stucco and painting. When Francesco had given the pictures to the Pope and received gifts and favours beyond what had been promised, he did a most beautiful Circumcision, remarkable for three curious lights, the first figures being illuminated by the glory of Christ's face, the second taking their light from some who are bringing gifts to the sacrifice, and are carrying torches in their hands, and the last from the dawn, which discloses a graceful landscape and countless buildings. He gave it to the Pope, who did not treat this like the others; he had given the Madonna to his nephew, Cardinal Ippolito de' Medici, and the mirror portrait to M. Pietro Aretino, the poet, his attendant, but he kept the Circumcision for himself, and it is thought that the emperor received it afterwards. I remember when quite young seeing the portrait at Arezzo in the house of M. Pietro Aretino, where it was exhibited to strangers passing through as a curiosity. It afterwards came, I do not know how, into the hands of Valerio Vincentino, a carver of crystals, and is now owned by Alessandro Vittoria, a Venetian sculptor and pupil of Jacopo Sansovino.

[1] Vienna, Kunsthistorisches Museum.

But to return to Francesco. At Rome he studied ancient and modern works of art both in painting and sculpture, especially those of Raphael and Michelagnolo, which he held in the greatest veneration. His own beautiful works and graceful manners led to the saying that the spirit of Raphael had passed into him, and he endeavoured to imitate the master in everything, especially in painting, and not in vain. His numerous pictures done in Rome, most of which ultimately came into the hands of Cardinal Ippolito de' Medici, were truly marvellous, as for example a lovely Annunciation, round in shape, done for M. Agnolo Cesis, now treasured in their house. He also painted a Madonna and Christ, some small angels and a St. Joseph of extreme beauty in the heads and colouring, executed with grace and diligence. It was in the possession of Luigi Gaddi whose heirs should now have it.

Hearing of Francesco's fame, Lorenzo Cibo, the handsome captain of the Pope's guard, got him to do his portrait,[1] which may be called life itself. Francesco then did a panel for Madonna Maria Bufalina of Città di Castello, to be placed in a chapel near the door in S. Salvatore del Lauro, representing the Virgin in the air reading, with a Child between her knees. A fine St. John kneels on one knee, and turns to greet the Christ-child. Lying on the ground is a St. Jerome in penitence, asleep.[2]

The sack of Rome in 1527 prevented the completion of this work, as it banished all the arts for a time, and caused the death of many artists. Francesco had a narrow escape, as when the sack began he was at work; and when some German soldiers entered the house he continued unmoved by the disturbance. When they came in and saw him thus, they were dumbfounded at his work, but like worthy fellows, they let him go on. Whilst these barbarians were destroying the wretched city and all profane and sacred things without regard for God or man, Francesco was protected from all injury by the Germans, and greatly esteemed. The sum of his discomfort at that time was that he had to make a quantity of designs in water-colours and with the pen, which constituted his ransom, one of the soldiers being very fond of painting. But on the soldiers being changed he nearly came off badly, for on going to find some friends he was taken prisoner by other soldiers, and forced to pay some crowns for his ransom. His uncle, grieving at the destruction which interrupted Francesco's studies, and seeing Rome desolate and the

[1] Probably the one at Windsor Castle.
[2] Painted in 1527; now in the National Gallery.

Pope a prisoner of the Spaniards, determined to take him back
to Parma. He remained a few more days in Rome, leaving the
panel done for Madonna Maria Bufalina with the friars of
la Pace. This, after being some years in their refectory, was
taken by M. Giulio Bufalini to their church at Città di Castello.

On reaching Bologna, Francesco was entertained by his
friends, especially by an intimate one, a saddler of Parma,
whose house pleased him so much that he remained some
months in the city, where he did engravings in grisaille, including a beheading of St. Peter and St. Paul and a large Diogenes.
He prepared designs for copper engravings, Maestro Antonio
da Trento [1] being ready to execute them, but gave it up, being
obliged to paint some pictures and other things for nobles of
Bologna. His first painting there was a large St. Roch in the
Monsignori Chapel in S. Petronio, of fine expression and great
beauty, represented as somewhat relieved from the plague,
lifting his head and thanking God, as good men do, even in
adversity. It was done for Fabrizio da Milano, whose life-like
half-length figure he drew, with a dog and a fine landscape, a
branch of art in which Francesco excelled. For Albio, a physician
of Parma, he did a Conversion of St. Paul, with many figures
and a remarkable landscape. For his friend the saddler he did
another of remarkable beauty, with a Madonna, turning sideways with a graceful pose, and several other figures. For Count
Giorgio Manzuoli he did another picture,[2] and painted two
canvasses in water-colour, containing graceful little figures, for
Maestro Luca dai Leuti.

At this time Antonio da Trento, who accompanied Francesco
to engrave, one morning while Francesco was still in bed,
broke open a chest and robbed him of all his copper and wood
engravings and designs, and disappeared, never being heard
of again. Francesco recovered the prints, which were left with
a friend at Bologna, but the drawings had gone for ever. In his
despair he turned to painting, making the portrait of some
Bolognese count to earn money, and then he did a Madonna with
Christ holding a globe.[3] The Madonna has a beautiful expression,
and the Child is very natural, for he always imparted a child-
like vivacity to his infants, showing the keen and mischievous
intelligence often possessed by the young. The Madonna wears
a remarkable mantle, the sleeves of a yellow gauze and as
if striped with gold, and very graceful, showing her delicate

[1] Antonio Fantuzzi.   [2] Now in the Corsini Gallery, Rome.
          [3] Madonna della Rosa, Dresden Gallery.

skin, while it is not possible to see better hair. This picture
was painted for M. Pietro Aretino, but as Pope Clement came to
Bologna at that time, Francesco gave it to him. It afterwards
passed into the hands of M. Dionigi Gianni, and is now owned
by his son M. Bartolommeo, who has had fifty copies taken,
so highly is it valued. For the nuns of S. Margherita, at Bologna,
Francesco did a panel of the Virgin, St. Margaret, St. Petronius,
St. Jerome and St. Michael,[1] greatly valued, as it deserves to be,
for the air of the heads and the other parts. He also did many
designs, notably some for Girolamo del Lino, and charming ones
for Girolamo Fagiuoli, goldsmith and engraver, who wanted it
to make a copper engraving. He painted a portrait of Bonifazio
Gozzadino and one of his wife, left unfinished. He also sketched
a Madonna, afterwards sold at Bologna to Giorgio Vasari of
Arezzo, who has it in the new houses he has built at Arezzo,
with many other noble paintings, sculptures and ancient marbles.
When the Emperor Charles V. came to Bologna to be crowned
by Clement VII., Francesco went to see him at table, and did
a large portrait of him in oils, with Fame crowning him with
laurel and an infant Hercules offering him the world. He showed
the work to Pope Clement, who was so pleased with it that
he sent Francesco with it to the bishop of Vaison, then the
emperor's datary[2]; his majesty was greatly pleased, and signified
that it should be left, but Francesco, being badly advised by a
faithless or ignorant friend, said that it was not finished, so the
emperor did not have it, and the painter did not receive he
reward he would doubtless have obtained. The picture afterwards came into the hands of Cardinal Ippolito de' Medici,
who gave it to the cardinal of Mantua, and it is now in the
duke's wardrobe, with other beautiful and noble paintings.

After a long absence from his home, winning friends but no
riches, and gaining experience in art, Francesco returned to
Parma to gratify his friends and relations. Immediately he was
set to paint a large vault in S. Maria della Steccata in fresco.[3]
He began on an arch which was in front of the vault, and
followed its curve, doing six figures, two coloured and four in
grisaille, surrounded by copper bosses in half-relief, a fancy of
his own, done with great labour. At the same time he did a
Cupid making a bow, for the Knight Baiardo, a nobleman of

---

[1] Now in the Pinacoteca, Bologna.
[2] Charles was crowned at Bologna on 24 Feb., 1530; this datary was
Jerome Scledus, bishop of Vaison, 1523-33.
[3] In 1531.

Parma, a great friend,[1] with two seated infants at his feet, one taking the other by the arm and laughing, trying to touch Cupid, and one is afraid and weeps, indicating that he does not wish to warm himself at the fire of Love. It is beautiful in colouring, ingenious in invention, and graceful in style, and consequently much valued by artists and connoisseurs. It now rests in the studio of Sig. Marc Antonio Cavalca, the knight's heir, with many designs by the same hand of great beauty and variety. There are also some fine drawings by Francesco in our book on several sheets, notably a Beheading of St. Peter and St. Paul, of which, as has been said, he circulated wood and copper engravings while at Bologna. For the church of S. Maria de' Servi he did a panel of the Virgin and sleeping Child,[2] with some angels at the side, one holding a crystal urn, reflecting a cross regarded by the Virgin. As this work did not greatly please him, he left it unfinished, though it is in his admirable and graceful style.

Meanwhile he began to neglect the work of the Steccata, or at least to progress so slowly as to show that something was wrong and this was because he had begun to study alchemy, neglecting painting in the hope of enriching himself quickly by congealing mercury. Thus, instead of conceiving beautiful ideas and plying his brush he wasted his days in manipulating coal, wood, furnaces and other things, which involved him in more expense in a day than he gained in a week at his work in the Steccata Chapel. He had no other resources, and his furnaces continually consumed more and more. What is worse, the members of the company of the Steccata, perceiving that he had altogether abandoned the work, and possibly having overpaid him, brought an action against him, but he escaped by night with some friends to Casal Maggiore. Here he rid his head of alchemy, and did a Madonna in the air for the church of S. Stefano, with St. John the Baptist and St. Stephen beneath.[3] His last painting was a Lucretia, one of his best works, but it has disappeared. By his hand also are some nymphs, now in the house of M. Niccolo Bufalini, at Città di Castello, and a group of infants for Signora Angiola de' Rossi of Parma, wife of Sig. Alessandro Vitelli, also at Città di Castello. As Francesco still doted on his alchemy, over-

[1] It should be Francesco Boiardi. The picture, painted in 1536, was in the Vienna Gallery.
[2] The Madonna del Collo lungo, painted in 1534, and now in the Pitti Gallery.
[3] Now in the Dresden Gallery.

powered by its infatuation, he allowed his beard to grow long and disordered, which made him look like a savage instead of a gentleman. He neglected himself and grew melancholy and eccentric. Being attacked by a malignant fever, he died after a few days' illness, thus concluding his troubles in a world which for him had always been full of worry and vexation. He desired to be laid in the church of the Servites, called la Fontana, a mile from Casal Maggiore, and was buried at his request naked, with a cypress cross on his breast. He died on 24th August, 1540, his death being a great loss to art for the singular grace with which he endowed his paintings. He was fond of playing the lute, and was as skilful in this as in painting. Had he but put aside the follies of alchemy, he would have been one of the rarest masters of our age. I do not deny that it is good to wait for inspiration, but I blame him for wasting his time on things which he could never accomplish, as this often leads to the loss of what can be done. If Francesco had steadily worked on day by day, with his graceful style and bright spirit he would have surpassed all others in the perfection and excellence of his design. He left behind him Jeronimo Mazuoli,[1] his cousin, who successfully imitated his style, as we see by his works in Parma and Viandana, where he fled with Francesco on account of the war. Although quite young, he did a lovely Annunciation in S. Francesco, a house of the bare-footed friars, and another in S. Maria ne' Borghi. At Parma he did the high-altar picture for the friars of S. Francesco, representing Joachim driven from the Temple, and in S. Alessandro, a nunnery of the city, he did a Madonna and the Christ-child offering a palm to St. Justina,[2] some angels drawing a curtain, St. Alexander the Pope and St. Benedict. In the church of the Carmelite friars he did a beautiful picture for the high altar, and another large panel in S. Sepolcro.[3] In S. Gio. Evangelistà, a church of nuns in the city, there are two panels by his hand of considerable beauty, but not so fine as the organ doors or the high-altar picture, which is a lovely Transfiguration,[4] very carefully finished. In the refectory of the nuns he painted a perspective in fresco, and did a picture in oils of the Last Supper, and the chapel of the high altar of the Duomo in fresco. For Madame Margherita of Austria, Duchess of Parma, he painted the por-

[1] His right name was Girolamo Bedolo.
[2] In 1540.
[3] The former in 1556 and the latter in 1543.
[4] Painted in 1555.

trait of her son Don Alessandro in armour, with his sword above
a globe, and a Parma armed and kneeling before him. At la
Steccata of Parma he painted [1] a chapel in fresco of the Apostles
receiving the Holy Spirit, and in an arch, like that of Francesco,
he did six sibyls, two coloured and four in grisaille. In a niche
opposite the arch he painted, but did not quite finish, a Nativity,
and the shepherds adoring, a very beautiful picture.[2] At the
Certosa, outside Parma, he did the Magi for the high-altar
picture, and in S. Piero, at Pavia, an abbey of the St. Bernard
monks, he did a panel, and another for the cardinal for the
Duomo of Mantua. In S. Giovanni, in the same city, he did
another panel of Christ in glory, surrounded by the Apostles
and St. John, of whom he says, *Sic eum volo manere*,[3] etc. The
picture is surrounded by the six principal miracles of St. John
the Evangelist. On the left-hand of the church of the bare-
footed friars there is a large picture by him of the Conversion
of St. Paul, a lovely work; and in S. Benedetto, at Pollirone,
twelve miles from Mantua, is a panel of Christ in the Manger
adored by the shepherds, with angels singing. He also did five
cupids in a fine picture, but I do not know exactly when; the
first is sleeping, and the others are stripping him, taking his
bow, arrows and torch. This picture belongs to Duke Ottavio,
who highly values it for Jerome's skill, for he is not inferior
to Francesco as an excellent painter and courteous man. He
still lives, and is constantly engaged upon his beautiful works.

A great friend of Francesco was M. Vincenzio Caccianemici,
a nobleman of Bologna, who painted and, as far as possible,
imitated Francesco's style. He coloured well, and some of the
things which he did for pleasure and to give to friends and
lords are really very praiseworthy, especially a panel in oils in
the chapel of his family in S. Petronio, containing the Beheading of St. John the Baptist. This talented nobleman died in
1542. There are some fine designs by him in our book.

[1] In 1546.
[2] Begun in 1553.
[3] From the Vulgate, John xxi. 22: "If I will that he tarry till I come
what is that to thee."

JACOPO PALMA and LORENZO LOTTO,
Venetian Painters
(1480 – 1528; 1480 – 1556)

THE art and beauty of one or two single works, however small,
compel artists and connoisseurs to praise their author, and
writers to celebrate him, as I now praise Palma of Venice,
who, although not excellent or rare in the perfection of painting,
was yet so polished, diligent and laborious that his things
possess at any rate some good parts, faithfully imitating Nature
and man. His colouring was harmonious, vaporous and patient,
though his designs lacked boldness, and he worked with the
utmost grace and polish, as we see from numerous pictures and
portraits at Venice, done for various nobles. I will say nothing
of any of these with the exception of some panels and a divine
and marvellous head. One of the panels he did for S. Antonio of
Venice,[1] near Castello, and the other at S. Elena, near the Lido,
where the monks of Monte Oliveto have their monastery. In this
at the high altar he represented the Magi offering their gifts to
Christ,[2] with a number of figures, including some admirable heads,
and draperies falling in beautiful folds. For the altar of the bom-
badiers in S. Maria Formosa he made a St. Barbara of life-size
with two smaller figures at the sides, namely St. Sebastian and
St. Anthony, but the St. Barbara is one of the best figures he
ever did. In the church of S. Moise, near the piazza of S. Marco,
he did another panel of the Virgin in the air and St. John at her
feet. For the meeting room of the Scuola of S. Marco, on the
piazza of S. Giovanni e Paolo, he made a beautiful scene in
competition with some already done by Gian Bellino, Giovanni
Mansueti, and other painters. It represents a ship conveying
the body of St. Mark to Venice, and a terrible storm at sea,
with boats toiling against the fury of the winds, executed with
great judgment and fine ideas. So also are a group of figures
and various demons in the air, blowing the ships like winds,
while the mariners endeavour by rowing to break through the
high waves which threaten to submerge them.[3] The work is so

---

[1] In 1521.

[2] Painted in 1525; now in the Brera.

[3] The *Tempestà di Mare*, now in the Accademia, Venice, represents a
legend which tells how Venice was saved from a terrible storm (on 25 Feb.,
1341) by St. Nicholas, St. George and St. Mark. Sansovino attributes the
canvas to Palma, Zanotto gives it to Paris Bordone; Berenson considers it
the work of Giorgione, finished by Paris Bordone.

fine that no hand, however excellent, could possibly approach more nearly to Nature in representing the force of the winds, the strength and skill of the men, the movements of the waves, the lightning, the water broken by the oars, the oars bent by the waves, and the efforts of the rowers. I cannot remember a more striking picture, displaying so much observation, design, invention and colouring, so that the panel seems palpitating with life, as if it was all real. For this work Jacopo deserves the highest praise, and a place among those who have made art their own, and who have the power to express the difficulties of their conceptions in painting. However, in such difficult things many painters sketch out their work in the first ardour of inspiration, thereby obtaining excellence and power which is lost in the finished work because they consider the parts rather than the whole, and as their ardour cools they lose their vigour. But Palma has maintained the same high level throughout, and therefore deserves the highest praise both then and always. Though his works are many and highly valued, this is undoubtedly the best of all and really prodigious. He has introduced himself wearing camel's hair, with locks of hair hanging about his head, exceedingly life-like. This marvellous and extraordinarily beautiful work is shown every year at the Ascension. In truth it merits praise for its design, art, colouring, and in fine every perfection, more than any work of a Venetian painter produced up to that time. Among other things the treatment of the eyes is not inferior to Lionardo or Michelagnolo. But it is better not to attempt to describe the grace and gravity of this portrait, for I cannot possibly overrate its merits. If Palma had died on completing it he would have been renowned above all those whom we have celebrated as rare and divine spirits. But subsequently he did not maintain this high level, falling away from it when many had expected him to advance. However, one or two perfect achievements silence the blame which the other works deserve. He died at Venice at the age of forty-eight.

Lorenzo Lotto, painter of Venice, was the companion and friend of Palma, and after imitating the style of Bellini for some time, he adopted that of Giorgione, as we see by several pictures and portraits in the houses of Venetian noblemen. The house of Andrea Odoni contains a fine portrait of him by Lorenzo,[1] and in the house of Tommaso da Empoli of Florence there is a lovely Nativity of Christ, at night-time, the glory

[1] Painted in 1527; now at Hampton Court.

of the Christ lighting the picture.[1] The Madonna is kneeling, and there is a full-length figure of M. Marco Loredano adoring Christ. In the Carmelite friary he did a St. Nicholas in the clouds in his pontificals, with three angels, and St. Lucy and St. John at his feet, with a lovely landscape beneath and many small figures and animals in various places.[2] On one side is St. George on horseback killing the serpent, and hard-by stands the damsel, with the city and an arm of the sea. In the chapel of St. Antonino, Archbishop of Florence, in S. Giovanni e Paolo, he did the saint seated, with two priests and much people beneath.[3]

While still young, and at a time when he partly followed Bellini and partly Giorgione, Lorenzo did the high-altar picture of S. Domenico at Ricanati in six compartments.[4] The middle contains the Virgin and Child giving the habit to St. Dominic by means of an angel, as he kneels before her. Two infants play a lute and a rebec respectively; another has Popes St. Gregory and St. Urban. In the third is St. Thomas Aquinas and another saint, bishop of Ricanati. Above these are three other pictures in the middle, a dead Christ supported by an angel, His mother kissing His arm, and the Magdalene. Over St. Gregory are St. Mary Magdalene and St. Vincent, and above St. Thomas Aquinas are St. Sigismund and St. Catherine of Siena. The beautiful predella of small figures represents S. Maria of Loreto carried by angels from Sclavonia to its present site, with St. Dominic preaching on one side, with the most charming little figures, and Pope Honorius confirming the Dominican rule on the other. The same church contains a St. Vincent the monk, by the same hand, in fresco. In the church of S. Maria di Castel Nuovo is a Transfiguration[5] in oils, with three scenes of small figures in the predella: Christ taking the Apostles to Mount Tabor, Christ in the Garden, and His Ascension. Lorenzo then went to Ancona, where, in S. Agostino, Mariano da Perugia had just done the high-altar picture with a magnificent frame, which, however, did not afford much satisfaction. Here he did a panel for the middle of the same church, of the Virgin and Child and two angels in the air, with foreshortened figures, crowning the Virgin.[6] When old and having all but lost his voice, Lorenzo, after doing some unimportant works in Ancona, went to the

---

[1] Possibly the picture now in the Accademia, Venice.
[2] Painted in 1529.
[3] Painted in 1542.
[4] Now in the Municipio, Recanati, painted 1506–08.
[5] Also in the Municipio, Recanati.
[6] c. 1546. Now in the Pinacoteca, Ancona.

Madonna of Loreto,[1] where he had already painted a panel in oils, which is in a chapel on the right on entering the church. Here he resolved to end his days, living in the holy house and serving the Virgin. So he began scenes about the choir above the seats of the priests, with figures of a braccia and less. One was a Nativity, the second the Adoration of the Magi; then followed the Presentation to Simeon, and next the Baptism by John; then the Woman taken in Adultery, executed with grace. He did two other scenes full of figures, one of David sacrificing,[2] and the other St. Michael fighting Lucifer after driving him from heaven. Not long after finishing these Lorenzo died, a good Christian, as he had lived. His last years were happy and very peaceful, probably winning for him eternal life. He might not have obtained this had he always been immersed in the affairs of the world, which do not permit men to raise their minds to the true benefits of the other life, and to the highest happiness and joy.

At this same time Rondinello,[3] an excellent painter, flourished in Romagna. He was mentioned in the Life of Giovan Bellino as a pupil and imitator of that master. After leaving Giovan he took such pains in art that he produced many admirable works, as, for example, the finely executed high altarpiece of the Last Supper in the Duomo of Forli. In an arc above he made a dead Christ, and in the predella he painted the acts of St. Helena, the mother of the Emperor Constantine, in finding the Cross, executed with great diligence. He did a beautiful single figure of St. Sebastian for the same church. For the altar of St. Mary Magdalene in the Duomo of Ravenna he painted a single figure of the saint in oils, with a predella of small figures beneath representing Christ appearing to the Magdalene as a gardener, Peter walking on the water to Christ, and between them the Baptism of Christ, all of great beauty. In S. Giovanni Evangelistà, in the same city, he did two panels, one of St. John consecrating the church,[4] and the other of there martyrs, S. Cancio, S. Canciano and S. Cancianilla, very beautiful figures. In S. Appollinare, in the same city, he did two much-admired pictures, with figures of St. John the Baptist and St. Sebastian in each. In the church of S. Spirito there is a panel by him of the Virgin between St. Catherine, virgin and martyr, and St. Jerome.[5] In S. Francesco he painted two panels, one of St. Catherine and St.

---

[1] In 1554.
[2] Apparently it represents the sacrifice of Melchisidec.
[3] Niccolò Rondinello, fl. 1480–1500.
[4] Now in the Brera, Milan.
[5] Correctly, St. John; the picture is now in the Ravenna Gallery.

Francis, and the other a Madonna with several figures, including St. James the Apostle and St. Francis. He did two other panels of S. Domenico, one on the left of the high altar of the Virgin and several figures, the other on a wall of the church of considerable beauty. For the Augustinian Church of S. Niccolo he did another panel of St. Laurence and St. Francis. These works won him a great reputation not only in Ravenna, but throughout the Romagna. Rondinello attained the age of sixty, and was buried in S. Francesco at Ravenna.

He left behind him Francesco da Codignuola,[1] a painter of considerable repute in that city, who painted many works, notably a Resurrection of Lazarus, with numerous figures, for the Abbey di Classi at Ravenna. Opposite this, in 1548, Giorgio Vasari did a Deposition from the Cross with a great number of figures for Abbot Don Romualdo of Verona. Francesco did a large panel of the Nativity in S. Niccolo, two panels of various figures in S. Sebastiano, a panel of the Virgin with St. Catherine, and several other figures in the hospital of S. Caterina, and a panel for S. Agata of Christ on the Cross with the Virgin and several other figures at the foot, all of which won him praise. In S. Apollinare there he did three panels, a Virgin, St. John the Baptist, St. Apollinarius, St. Jerome, and other saints for the high altar; another of St. Peter and St. Catherine for the Madonna, and a Christ bearing the Cross, which his death prevented him from completing. His colouring was charming, but in design he was inferior to Rondinello, though the people of Ravenna esteemed him highly. He desired to be buried in S. Apollinare, where he had painted his figures, hoping thus to rest on the scene of his labours.

FRÀ GIOCONDO, LIBERALE, and other Veronese
(?1433–1513; c.1445–1536)

IF historians lived a year or so longer than the common term of human life, I doubt not they could add to what they have written, for it is not possible for one man, however diligent, to ascertain the exact truth of what he is writing in so short a time. It is as clear as the sun that Time, which is called the father of Truth, is daily disclosing new things to the studious. If some years ago, when I wrote the Lives of the painters then published,

[1] Francesco Zaganelli.

I had known those particulars of that rare and universal genius, Frà Giocondo, that I now have, I should doubtless have given him an honourable notice, such as I now propose to write for the benefit of artists, when I will also write of many other distinguished Veronese. Let no one wonder that I preface this with the portrait of only one of them, because I had no choice, being unable to obtain all. But so far as I am able not one of them shall be deprived of what is due to his talents. Chronological order demands that I shall speak first of Frà Jocondo, who, when he took the Dominican habit, was called Frà Giovanni Jocondo. How he dropped the Giovanni I do not know, but he was always known as Frà Jocondo. Literature formed his chief study, and he was an excellent philosopher and theologian, and a good Greek scholar, a rare thing in that day, when the revival of letters in Italy had only begun. He was also an excellent architect, delighting chiefly in that art, as related by Scaliger in writing against Cardano, and by the learned Budæus in his books *De asse*, and his Observations on the Pandects. Frà Jocondo remained for many years with the Emperor Maximilian, and was Latin and Greek master of the learned Scaliger, who writes that he heard him dispute before Maximilian upon some most abstruse matters. Men still living remember how, when the bridge of la Pietra at Verona was being rebuilt under Maximilian,[1] and the middle pile was to be constructed, which had frequently fallen, Frà Jocondo showed how to lay the foundations so that it should not fall. He arranged that the central pier should be surrounded with a double row of piles to protect it, so that the river should not hollow away underneath, the bed being so soft that there was no place upon which to lay secure foundations. Frà Jocondo's advice has proved to be the best, because the bridge has since stood without moving a hair's breadth, and it is hoped that it will endure for ever. In his youth Frà Jocondo spent many years in Rome, studying ancient things, not only buildings, but inscriptions on tombs and other antiquities. Going also into the surrounding country and every part of Italy, he filled a book with such inscriptions, and presented it, as the Veronese declare, to Lorenzo de' Medici the Magnificent, whom he and his companion and compatriot, Domicio Calderino, always served, as the patron of all men of genius. The book is mentioned by Poliziano in his *Mugellane*, where he quotes it as an authority, referring to Frà Jocondo as a distinguished antiquary. Frà Jocondo also wrote notes on the Commentaries

[1] About 1512. It was rebuilt in stone in 1520.

of Cæsar,[1] which have been printed, and he was the first to draw
the bridge built by Cæsar over the Rhone, described in the
Commentaries, and little understood in Frà Jocondo's time.
Budæus acknowledged the friar as his master in architecture,
thanking God for having had such a learned and diligent teacher
upon Vitruvius. The Frà discovered numerous errors in that
author not previously noted, for he was skilled in all learning,
and versed in Greek and Latin. Budæus adds that through the
Frà the greater part of Pliny's epistles were discovered in an old
library at Paris, and were printed by Aldus Manutius, as we read
in a Latin letter printed with them. While in Paris, in the service
of King Louis XII., Frà Jocondo made two superb bridges over
the Seine,[2] full of shops, a work worthy of the magnificence of
the king, and of the marvellous genius of Frà Jocondo, so that,
in addition to the inscription which may still be seen on those
works, he deserved the fine distich in which that rare poet
Sannazzaro honoured him:

> *Jocundus geminum imposuit tibi, Sequana, pontem:*
> *Hunc tu jure potes dicere Pontificem.*

Besides this he did countless works for that king in his kingdom,
but as I am only speaking of the principal works, I pass them
over. Being in Rome when Bramante died, he was given the
care of S. Pietro[3] in conjunction with Raphael of Urbino and
Giuliano da San Gallo to continue the building, as it threatened
to fall in many parts, because it had been hastily built, and for the
reasons given elsewhere. So, by the advice of the three architects,
the foundations were relaid in the main in the following manner,
seen by some who are still alive. Many holes of square shape
were dug out at regular intervals under the foundations, and
then filled with masonry. Upon these pilasters were built connected by strong arches, so that the whole building was made
to rest upon new foundations without being pulled down, thus
avoiding the danger of further damage.

But a more praiseworthy work, as it seems to me, was one
for which the Venetians and all the world owe Frà Jocondo
an eternal debt. Seeing that the preservation of the republic of
Venice chiefly depended upon the impregnable position of the
lagoons, among which the city is almost miraculously built, and
that if the lagoons became dry the air would become pestilent

---

[1] Published by Aldus Manutius in 1513.
[2] The Pont Notre Dame was his work, 1507-12; restored in 1660.
There is no authentic record of his having designed another bridge.
[3] He was made architect there in 1514.

and the city uninhabitable, or at any rate exposed to the perils of a city on the mainland, he devised a means of preserving the lagoons and the site on which the city was originally founded. He then took an opportunity of warning the Signoria that if they did not speedily take steps to meet the danger they would be lost in a few years, as could be seen from what had already happened in part, and would realise their mistake when it was too late. Being thus awakened, the Signoria listened to Frà Jocondo's able arguments, and collecting the best engineers and architects of Italy, they obtained a number of suggestions and designs. But Frà Jocondo's was considered the best and was carried out. Thus they began to divert through a great channel two-thirds or at least a half of the water brought down by the River Brenta, which, after making a long detour, was made to discharge into the lagoons of Chioggia. Thus the river has not filled up the lagoons of Venice as it has done at Chioggia, where many possessions and towns have grown up on spots once under water, to the great advantage of Venice. Thus many declare, and notably M. Luigi Cornaro, a Venetian noble of great experience and knowledge, that had it not been for Frà Jocondo's warning the filling up of the lagoons would have taken place at Venice, to the incalculable damage and ruin of the city. He also declares that his city is under a great debt to Frà Jocondo, who, like all men of genius, was his great friend, and might reasonably call him her second founder, deserving more honour for preserving that noble, wealthy and powerful city than the original founders in the time of her weakness and insignificance, because the device has been and will ever be of incalculable advantage to Venice.

Not long after Jocondo had completed this blessed work the Venetians suffered the loss of the Rialto by fire,[1] the place containing the most important depots of wares, and indeed it might almost be called the treasury of the city. This happened at a time when the republic, after long and ceaseless warfare, had lost almost all her possessions on the mainland, and was much reduced, so that the Government felt doubtful what to do. But as the rebuilding was a matter of great importance, it was resolved that it should be done on a more splendid style worthy of the greatness of the republic. The work was entrusted to Frà Jocondo, of whose skill in architecture the Venetians had already received ample proofs. He designed it as follows: He wished to occupy the entire space between the canal of the Beccherie di Rialto and the Rio del Fondaco delle Farine, taking

[1] In 1513.

enough land on both sides to make a perfect square, so that the space should be as far as the distances between the openings of those Rivi on to the Grand Canal. He then arranged that the two Rivi should open into a common canal leading from one to the other, so that his construction should be surrounded by water on every hand thus: the Grand Canal being on one side, the two Rivi on two sides, and the newly constructed Rio on the fourth side. He wished to have a large open space for a piazza between the water and the bridge, for the sale of vegetables, fruit, fish and other things coming from several parts to the city. About this, shops were to be constructed facing the piazza for the sale of all manner of eatables. In these four fronts Frà Jocondo proposed to make four principal gateways; in the middle of each and opposite each other; but before entering the piazza, there was to be a street on the right- and left-hand about the square, with shops on either side, and handsome manufactories, and magazines above to supply them, for the sale of drapery, such as fine woollen cloth and silk, which are the two principal industries of the city, containing all the shops called after the Tuscans and silk dealers. This street, with its double row of shops, was to be in a line with his structure, and pass through the middle of the piazza for the convenience of the merchants and those who traffic in that city, which is the customs house of Italy and of all Europe. Under the loggias were to be the shops of the bankers, goldsmiths and jewellers, and in the middle a fine church dedicated to St. Matthew, where the nobles might attend divine service in the morning. Some, however, say that Frà Jocondo changed his mind about the church and intended to make two, but under the loggias in order not to obstruct the piazza. This superb structure was also to have every requisite and embellishment, and those who have seen the fine plan made by Frà Jocondo declare that it is impossible to imagine anything more fine and magnificent. To complete this work he was of opinion that the Rialto bridge should be built in stone and furnished with shops, which would have been remarkable. Two causes operated against the carrying out of this work: one the exhaustion of the republic on account of the expenses of the war, and the other the favour bestowed by an influential nobleman, said to have been of the Valeresso family, but of no judgment in such matters, perhaps from some private interest, upon Maestro Zanfragnino,[1] who is still alive, I am told, who had served him in his own

---

[1] His real name was Antonio Scarpagni. The true reason for adopting his plan in preference to that of Frà Giocondo was lack of funds.

buildings. This Zanfragnino, a very appropriate name for such a master, designed the hotch-potch, which was carried out and may be seen to-day. This foolish choice caused great sorrow to many who are still living. Frà Jocondo was so angered at this evidence of the greater power of favour than merit among the great, when such a sorry design was preferred to his, that he left Venice and would never return, though frequently pressed to do so. His design, with others of the master, remained in the Bragadini house, opposite S. Marina, with Frate Angelo of that family, a Dominican friar, whose merits obtained for him the see of Vicenza.

Frà Jocondo was very versatile, and besides the things mentioned he also delighted in simples and agriculture. M. Donato Giannotti of Florence, his great friend in France, relates that he once tended a peach-tree in a pot while he was living in France, until this tiny tree became so full of fruit that it was a wonder to behold; some friends advised him to put it where the king would see it, but the courtiers passing by, acting after their kind, took all the fruit, to the chagrin of Frà Jocondo, ate a part, and scattered the rest along the way. When the king heard of this he thanked the friar and consoled him with a rich gift, after he had laughed over the matter with his courtiers.

Frà Jocondo was a man of saintly life and much loved by the men of letters of his age, especially by Domizio Calderino, Matteo Bosso and Paolo Emilio, who wrote the French history, all three his compatriots. Among his other close friends were Sannazzaro, Budæus, Aldus Manutius, and all the academy of Rome. Julio Cesare Scaligero, a very learned man of our day, was a pupil of his. He died very old, but I do not know exactly when or where, nor the place of his burial.

The city of Verona closely resembles Florence in its site, customs and other particulars, and many great minds in all the noble professions have always flourished in one as in the other. I have no concern with men of letters, but to speak of artists only, they have always found an honoured refuge in that most noble city. Liberale Veronese, a pupil of Vincenzio di Stefano, who is mentioned elsewhere and who did an admirable Madonna in the Benedictine church of Ognissanti at Mantua in 1463, was much admired in his day and imitated the style of Jacopo Bellini, under whom he studied design as a boy when Jacopo was engaged upon the chapel of S. Niccolo at Verona, so that he forgot Vincenzio's teaching, and always retained Bellini's manner. His first paintings were in the chapel of the

Monte della Pietà in S. Bernardino, in his native city, where he
did a Deposition from the Cross, and angels, some holding the
mysteries of the Passion in their hands, the faces of all betraying
their grief at the Saviour's death. They are indeed very natural,
like his other things. He was fond of representing weeping
figures, as for example, in S. Nastasia at Verona, the church of
the Dominicans, where he did a dead Christ, lamented by Mary,
at the front of the Buonaveri Chapel. In the same style he did
several paintings scattered about the houses of various noblemen of Verona. In the same chapel he made a God the Father
surrounded by angels playing and singing with three figures on
each side; St. Peter, St. Dominic and St. Thomas Aquinas on
one, and on the other St. Lucy, St. Agnes and another, the first
three being better executed and more in relief. On the wall of
the chapel he did a Virgin and the Child espousing St. Catherine,
virgin and martyr, introducing a portrait of M. Piero Buonanni,
patron of the chapel. About them are angels presenting flowers,
and some smiling heads, showing him as successful in representing this emotion as that of weeping. For the altarpiece of the
chapel he painted St. Mary Magdalene supported in the air by
angels, with St. Catherine beneath, considered a beautiful work.[1]
At the altar of the Madonna in the Servite church of S. Maria
della Scala he did an Adoration of the Magi, on two shutters
enclosing the Madonna, much valued in the city. However, it
did not remain there long as it suffered so much from the
smoke of the candles that it was removed and placed in the
sacristy, where Veronese painters think very highly of it. In
the chapel of the company of the Magdalene in the church of
S. Bernardino he painted the Purification, with an admirable
figure of Simeon and the little Christ, whom the old man holds
and kisses. A priest beside him raises his eyes to heaven and,
opening his hands, seems to be thanking God for the salvation
of the world. Beside this chapel is an Adoration of the Magi
by Liberale, with the death of the Virgin at the base of the
altar, in much-admired small figures. He was indeed very fond
of doing small figures, devoting such labour to them that they
resemble miniatures. There is an example in the Duomo of an
Adoration of the Magi, containing a quantity of small figures,
horses, dogs and various other animals, witn a group of cheru-
bim, painted red, forming a support for the Virgin. In this
work the heads and everything else are finished with the same
minute care, like a miniature. For the chapel of the Madonna

[1] Dated 1512.

in the Duomo he painted a small predella with equal care with stories of the Virgin. This was subsequently removed by M. Giovan Matteo Giberti, bishop of Verona, and placed in the palace chapel of the Vescovado, where the bishops reside and where they hear Mass every morning. It is there associated with a lovely crucifix in relief, made by Giovan Battista, sculptor of Verona, who now lives in Mantua. In the Allegni Chapel in S. Vitale Liberale painted a panel of S. Mestro, confessor of Verona, a man of much sanctity, between St. Francis and St. Dominic. In S. Vittoria, church and convent of some hermit friars, he painted a panel in the chapel of St. Jerome for the Scaltritegli family, of Jerome as cardinal, St. Francis and St. Paul,[1] much admired. On the screen of S. Giovanni in Monte he painted a Circumcision and other things, which were destroyed not long since, because the screen was thought to mar the beauty of the church. Being invited to Siena by the general of the monks of Monte Oliveto, Liberale illuminated many books for the order, and his success led to his employment to illuminate others in the Piccolomini library. He also did some for the Duomo of the city for plain-song, and would have done more there had he not been driven out by envy and persecution. He returned to Verona with 800 crowns which he had gained, and which he entrusted to the monks of S. Maria in Organo of Monte Oliveto, drawing an income from them for his daily needs. He spent the remainder of his life in illuminating. At Bardolino on the lake of Garda he did a panel for the Pieve, and another for the church of S. Tommaso Apostolo, and one for the chapel of St. Bernard in S. Fermo, a Franciscan convent, representing the saint, and some scenes from his life in the predella. In the same place and elsewhere he did several other pictures, one being in the house of M. Vincenzio de' Medici in Verona, of the Virgin and the Child espousing St. Catherine. At a corner of the Cartai house at Verona, on the way from the Ponte Nuova to S. Maria in Organo, he painted a much-admired Madonna and St. Joseph. He wished to paint the Rivi chapel in S. Eufemia, erected in honour of Giovanni Rivi, captain of the men-at-arms at the battle of the Taro, but it was given to some foreigners, as his sight was said to be impaired by age. The chapel on being unveiled disclosed many errors, so that Liberale declared the Rivi had even worse sight than he.

Having attained the age of eighty-four and more, Liberale

[1] Now in the Museo Civico, Verona.

allowed himself to be ruled by his relations, especially by a
married daughter, who like the rest treated him very badly.
Accordingly Liberale made his ward Francesco Torbido, called
Il Moro, the heir of his house and garden in S. Giovanni in
Valle, a very pleasant part of the city, and went to live with
the youth, who was very fond of him, and a diligent painter,
saying that he preferred his property to go to one who improved
his talents, rather than to those who despised their relations.
But before long he died on St. Clare's day 1536, and was buried
in S. Giovanni in Valle, aged eighty-five. His pupils were Giovan
Francesco and Giovanni Caroti, Francesco Torbido, called Il
Moro, and Paolo Cavazzuola, really excellent masters, who will
be dealt with in their places.

Giovan Francesco Caroto [1] was born at Verona in 1470, and
after having learned the elements of letters, and being inclined
towards painting, he gave up grammar and went to Liberale to
learn painting, promising to relieve him of his labours. Young
as he was, he studied design with such devotion and application
that, with that and colouring, he soon proved of great assistance
to Liberale. His judgment increasing with his years, he saw
the works of Andrea Mantegna in Verona not long after, and
rightly judging them to be in a style superior to his master's,
he prevailed upon his father, with Liberale's consent, to allow
him to join Mantegna. Accordingly he went to Mantua, and
made such progress that Andrea sent abroad Caroti's works as
his own, and before many years he had become a skilful artist.
His first works after leaving Mantegna were in Verona at the
altar of the Magi in the church of the hospital of S. Cosimo,
where he did the altar shutters, representing the Circumcision
and the Flight into Egypt, with other figures. In S. Girolamo,
a Jesuit church, he did the Virgin and the annunciating Angel
in two corners.[2] For the prior of the friars of S. Giorgio he did
a manger on a small panel, which exhibits considerable improve-
ment in style, the heads of the shepherds and all the other
figures having a beautiful and sweet expression, so that the
work was deservedly praised, and it would have kept his
memory green among his fellow-citizens, only it has cracked
owing to the intonaco being badly tempered. The men of the
company of the Angel Raphael then allotted to him their chapel
in the church of S. Eufemia, where he did two stories of Raphael,
and three large angels on a panel in oils, namely Raphael
between Gabriel and Michael,[3] all well designed and coloured,

[1] c. 1470–1546.   [2] Dated 1508.   [3] Now in the Museo Civico, Verona.

though the legs were criticised as too slender and not beautiful.
But he wittily replied that angels, having wings and celestial
bodies, might well have light and slender legs like birds, to
enable them to fly the more readily. For the altar where Christ
is bearing the cross in S. Giorgio, he painted St. Roch and St.
Sebastian with some scenes of small figures on the predella.
For the company of the Madonna in S. Bernardino, he painted
the Nativity of the Virgin on the predella of the altar, and a
Massacre of the Innocents, with varied postures of the murderers, and groups of infants strenuously defended by their
mothers. The work is highly esteemed, and is covered to preserve it. It led the men of the brotherhood of St. Stephen to
employ Caroti to do three similar stories of the Virgin for their
altar, representing her Marriage, the Birth of Christ and the
Adoration of the Magi. Thinking he had made sufficient name
in Verona, Giovan Francesco proposed to go and seek other
countries, but his friends and relations prevailed upon him to
marry a noble lady, daughter of M. Braliassarti Grandoni. He
married her in 1505, but after they had lived together a year,
and had had a child, the wife died in child-birth. Being thus
set free, Giovan Francesco left Verona and went to Milan,
where Sig. Anton Maria Visconte took him to his house and
employed him to decorate it.

At that time a Fleming brought to Milan a head of a youth
painted in oils, which was much admired by all. But when
Giovan Francesco saw it he laughed and said he would make
a better. The Fleming mocked, but Giovan Francesco wagered
his picture and 25 crowns against the portrait of the Fleming
and 25 crowns. So Giovan Francesco set to work with all his
might, making the portrait of an old, clean-shaven gentleman
with a sparrow-hawk in his hand; however, although it was a
good likeness, the head of the Fleming was judged better. But
Giovan Francesco was unfortunate in his choice of a subject,
for if he had taken a handsome youth and had done it as well as
he did the old man, he would have surpassed, or at least
equalled, his adversary. However, his head was admired, and the
Fleming courteously refused the 25 ducats, contenting himself
with the painting. It afterwards came into the hands of Madonna
Isabella da Este, Marchioness of Mantua, who paid the Fleming
well for it, and placed it in her studio as a rare thing, with
quantities of beautiful marble things, medals, paintings and casts.

After serving the viscount, Giovan Francesco received a
summons from Guglielmo, Marquis of Montferrat, and went

readily. On his arrival a good provision was assigned to him, and, setting to work, he filled a chapel of the marquis at Casale with paintings of scenes from the Old and New Testaments, very carefully finished, as was the principal panel. For the chambers of the castle he did many things which brought him great fame. In S. Domenico he decorated the whole of the principal chapel by order of the marquis, to adorn a tomb in which he was to be laid. For this Giovan Francesco deservedly received liberal rewards from the marquis, who made him one of his chamberlains, as we see by an instrument in the possession of his heirs at Verona. He painted the portraits of the marquis and his wife, many pictures to be sent to France, the portrait of Guglielmo their first-born, then a child, and those of their children and all the ladies in the service of the court. On the death of the Marquis Guglielmo,[1] Giovan Francesco sold his goods, left Casale and went to Verona, where he so managed his affairs that he found himself possessed of over 7000 ducats, and gave his son a wife. However, he did not abandon painting, but worked harder than ever, not being troubled with the necessity of earning his bread.

Whether through envy or for other reasons, he obtained the reputation of being able to paint small figures only. To prove the falsehood of this he made his figures larger than life when doing the chapel of the Madonna in the Franciscan convent of S. Fermo, and acquitted himself so well that they were the best he ever did. In the air is the Virgin sitting on St. Anne's lap; above, angels rest upon clouds, and at her feet are St. Peter, St. John the Baptist, St. Roch and St. Sebastian, with a St. Francis receiving the stigmata, in a beautiful landscape.[2] The work is highly esteemed by artists. In S. Bernardino of the bare-footed friars, in the chapel of the Cross, he did a Christ kneeling to His Mother, in which he endeavoured to surpass the many notable paintings there by other masters, acquitting himself well and winning great praise, except from the warden, who blamed him with bitter words, like the pompous fool he was, for having made Christ too irreverent, because he was kneeling on one knee only. Giovan's answer was: "Father, be so good as to kneel and rise and I will give you my reasons." The warden being at length persuaded to comply, knelt first on his right knee and then on his left, and in rising, lifted first the left and then the right. Then Giovan said, "Did you observe that you did not move both knees together? My Christ also may

[1] In 1518.   [2] Dated 1528.

be said to be in the act of kneeling or of rising." The warden, though unable to reply, went away muttering.

Giovan Francesco was very sharp at retorts, and it is related that when a priest accused him of making his figures too lascivious, he replied, "If painted things move you so, how can you be trusted with living flesh and blood?" For the church of the bare-footed friars at Isola on Lake Garda he painted two panels, and in Malsessino on the same lake he did a beautiful Virgin over the door of a church, and some saints inside, at the request of Fracastoro the famous poet, and his friend. For Count Francesco Giusti, at his suggestion, he painted a naked youth, in an attitude between rising and not rising, with a beautiful maiden at his side, representing Minerva, who points up to Fame and incites him to pursue her, while Ease and Slothfulness, behind him, strive to hold him back. Underneath was a figure with a face more like a base man's than a noble's, with two large snails at his elbows and seated on a crab, with another figure hard-by, the hands full of poppies. This composition, which contains other beautiful ideas, was executed by Giovan Francesco with extreme diligence, and serves as a bed-curtain in that count's pleasant seat at S. Maria Stella, near Verona. For Count Raimondo della Torre, Giovan Francesco decorated an entire room with various scenes of small figures. Being fond of making things in relief, not only models for things he needed, but to please his fancy, he did some which are in the house of his heirs, notably a scene in half-relief of considerable merit. He did portraits on medals, some of which exist still, like that of Guglielmo, Marquis of Montferrat, with Hercules killing the . . . on the reverse, and the legend *Monstra domat*. He painted the portraits of Count Raimondo della Torre, Giulio his brother, and M. Girolamo Frascatoro. Becoming old, he began to lose his skill, as we see by the organ-shutters of S. Maria della Scala, in the Deposition of the Cross done for the Movi family, and in St. Anastasia in the chapel of St. Martin.

He valued himself highly, and would not on any account have copied others. Thus, when Bishop Giovan Matteo Giberti had the scenes of the Virgin painted in the chapel in the Duomo, he obtained designs from Rome from his friend Giulio Romano, being the datary of Clement VII., but when the bishop returned to Verona, Giovan Francesco refused to carry out those designs, so that the bishop was offended and entrusted the task to Francesco il Moro. Giovan Francesco was of opinion that varnishing damages pictures, making them age quicker, and he therefore employed a dark varnish and some purified oils. He was the first in Verona to make good landscapes, those by him there being very beautiful. At the age of seventy-six Giovan Francesco died like a good Christian, leaving good provision for his nephews and his brother Giovanni Caroti, who, after passing some time at Venice, studying art under his brother, returned to Verona just as Giovan Francesco died, being present to see the legacy of art bequeathed to him. It included a portrait of an old man in armour, beautifully executed and coloured, and the best work of its author, and a small Deposition from the Cross, which was given to Signor Spitech, a man of great influence with the King of Poland, who had come to the baths near Verona. Giovan Francesco was buried in his chapel of St. Nicholas, in the Madonna dell' Organo, adorned by him with pictures.

Giovanni Caroti, the brother,[1] although he followed his style, practised painting with less reputation. He painted the altar-piece of the chapel of St. Nicholas, of the Virgin above the clouds, introducing portraits of himself and his wife Placida beneath. At the Schioppi altar in S. Bartolomeo he did some smaller figures of saints and the portrait of Laura degli Schioppi, the donor, a lady much celebrated by the writers of the time for her beauty and virtues. In S. Giovanni in Fonte, next the Duomo, Giovanni did a small panel of St. Martin and a portrait of M. Marcantonino della Torre as a youth, who afterwards became a literary man and gave public lectures in Padua and Pavia, and also of M. Giulio, both heads being in the possession of their heirs at Verona. For the prior of S. Giorgio he painted a Virgin, which has always been kept in the prior's chamber for its excellence. He painted the transformation of Actæon into a stag for Brunetto, the organ master, who gave it to Girolamo Cicogna, an excellent embroiderer and engineer of Bishop Giberti, and it is now owned by his son, M. Vincenzio Cicogna. Giovanni drew the plans of all the antiquities of Verona, including the triumphal arches and the Coliseum, required by Falconetto, architect of Verona, for the book on the antiquities of Verona, written and published by M. Torello Saraino.[2] It was sent by Giovanni Caroti to me at Bologna, where I was engaged upon the refectory of S. Michele in Bosco, together with the portrait of Don Cipriano

---

[1] Born about 1489; died between 1562 and 1567.
[2] *De Origine et amplitudine Urbis Veronæ,* by Torello Saraina, published in 1540.

ot Verona, twice general of the monks of Monte Oliveto, so that
I might make use of it in one of the pictures. The portrait is now
in my house at Florence, with other paintings by various masters.
Giovanni, being about sixty, having passed his life without
children, without ambition and with plenty of property, died,
rejoicing at the success of some of his pupils, namely Anselmo
Canneri and Paolo Veronese, who is now working at Venice and
is considered a good master. Anselmo has done many works in
oils and fresco, notably at Soranza on the Tesino, at Castelfranco, in the palace of the Soranzi and in many other places,
but chiefly in Vicenza. To return to Giovanni. He was buried
in S. Maria dell' Organo, where he had painted the chapel.

Francesco Torbido,[1] called Il Moro, painter of Verona, learned
the first principles of art, while still young, of Giorgione of
Castelfranco, whose colouring and tone he imitated. Just as he
had almost mastered it he had a dispute with some individual
and thrashed him so soundly that he was forced to leave Venice
and return to Verona, where he gave up painting because it was
too manual, and associated with noble youths like one of good
birth. Among them were the Counts Sanbonifazi and Giusti,
illustrious families of Verona, whose houses he frequented as if
he had been born into them. It was not long before Count
Zenovello Giusti gave him a natural daughter of his to wife,
and an apartment in his own house for himself and his wife and
children. It is said that while Francesco was in the service of
the nobles he always carried his pencils in his pouch, and
wherever he went he painted a head or something on a wall
whenever he had an opportunity. Count Zenovello, seeing him
so fond of painting, generously relieved him of other affairs,
so that he might devote himself entirely to art. As he had
nearly forgotten everything, he put himself under Liberale with
the Count's permission, and by steady practice recovered the
ground he had lost and more. But though he always copied
Liberale's style, he adopted the tone and colour of Giorgione,
his first teacher, for he considered Liberale's things somewhat
dry, though good in other respects. Liberale, recognising his
ability, became so fond of him that he made him his heir, and
loved him like a son.

After Liberale's death Francesco did many things for private
houses; but his best works are in Verona. The first is the principal
chapel of the Duomo, coloured in fresco, the vaulting, in four
divisions, decorated with the Birth of the Virgin and the Presen-

[1] c. 1483–1561.

tation in the Temple.[1] In the middle are three angels hovering
in the air, foreshortened from below, holding a crown of stars
for the Virgin, who is in a niche surrounded by angels. As she
is being taken up to heaven, the Apostles look up in various
attitudes, their figures being double life-size. All these paintings
were done by Il Moro from designs by Giulio Romano for Bishop
Giovan Matteo Giberti, who was a great friend of Giulio, as has
been said. Il Moro next painted the front of the Manuelli house,
built on a pier of the Ponte Nuovo, and a façade for Dr. Torella
Saraina, who wrote the book on the antiquities of Verona
already mentioned. In Friuli he painted in fresco the principal
chapel of the abbey of Rosazzo for the Bishop Giovan Matteo,
who had it *in commendam*, and restored it like a truly religious
noble, for it had been left in ruins by the previous beneficiary,
who, as frequently happens, drew the revenues without spending
a groat on the service of God and the Church. In Verona and
Venice, Il Moro painted many things in oils. He did the figures
in fresco on the façade of S. Maria in Organo, except the Angels
Michael and Raphael, which are by Paolo Cavazzuola, and
painted the picture of the chapel in oils with the portrait of M.
Jacopo Fontani, the donor, as St. James, the Virgin, and other
beautiful figures. Above the picture in a semicircle, occupying
the entire width of the chapel, he did a Transfiguration and the
Apostles, considered one of his best efforts. In the chapel of the
bombardiers in S. Eufemia he did a St. Barbara in the air, with
St. Anthony below, his hand to his beard, a magnificent head,
and on one side he did a fine St. Roch, the whole composition
being most carefully finished in harmonious colouring. At the
altar of the Sanctification in the Madonna della Scala he did a
St. Sebastian in competition with Paolo Cavazzuola, who painted
a St. Roch, and he then did a panel which went to Bagolino,
in the Brescian mountains. Il Moro painted many portraits, his
heads being marvellously beautiful and excellent likenesses. In
Verona he did that of Count Francesco Sanbonifazio, called the
Long Count because he was so tall, and a marvellous head of one
of the Franchi. He also painted M. Girolamo Verita, but as he
was rather slow it was left unfinished, though it is kept by that
nobleman's heirs. He painted Monsignor de' Martini, a Venetian
knight of Rhodes, and sold him a marvellously beautiful head
which he had done many years before, of a Venetian noble, son
of a captain in Verona. He had kept it because he never received
any payment for it. Monsignor Martini had it converted into a

[1] Painted in 1534.

shepherd, and it is now in the house of his heirs and highly valued, for it is a rare work. At Venice, Il Moro painted the portraits of M. Alessandro Contarino, procurator of S. Marco and provveditore of the fleet, and of M. Michele Sanmichele for an intimate friend, who took the portrait to Orvieto. He is said to have done another of M. Michele, the architect, now owned by M. Paolo Ramusio, son of M. Gio. Battista. He painted a portrait of the celebrated poet Frascatoro at the instance of Monsignor Giberti. He sent it to Giovio, who put it in his museum. Il Moro did many other things which I need not mention, although all are admirable, for he was a more diligent colourist than any of his contemporaries, devoting much time and labour to his work. He was even too diligent, for he accepted everything, taking money in advance, and finished his works God knows when. If this was the case in his youth, it may be imagined what he became in his last years with the natural slowness of age, and this tardiness involved him in more disputes and vexation than he cared for. So M. Michele Sanmichele had compassion on him, and took him to Venice, treating him like a friend. Being recalled by his old patrons the Counts Giusti to Verona, Il Moro died there in their beautiful palace of S. Maria in Stella, and was buried in the church of that town, being accompanied to the tomb by all the nobles, for they loved him like a father, most of them having been born while he was living in their house. Il Moro as a youth was dexterous and courageous, skilful in the use of every kind of weapon. He was faithful to his friends and patrons, and spirited in his actions. Among his intimate friends were M. Michele Sanmichele, the architect, Il Danese of Carrara, an excellent sculptor, and the learned Frà Marco de' Medici, who frequently after his studies called on Il Moro to see him work and have a friendly conversation to recreate his mind when he was weary.

Battista d'Agnolo, afterwards called Battista del Moro, was a pupil and son-in-law of Il Moro, for he had two daughters. Although he vexed Il Moro greatly about his inheritance, he did many tolerable works. In the church of the nuns of S. Guiseppe at Verona he did a St. John the Baptist and the history of St. Paul in fresco on his altar on the screen of S. Eufemia, including his conversion and visit to Ananias, which was much admired, although he was quite young when he did it. For the Counts Canossi he painted two chambers and two fine friezes of battles in a hall, much praised by all. In Venice he did the façade of a house near the Carmine, not very large, but much admired, representing Venice crowned and seated on a lion, the device of the republic. For Camillo Trevisano he painted the façade of his house at Murano, and the courtyard in fine scenes in grisaille, aided by his son Marco. In the same house he painted a room in competition with Paolo Veronese, which brought him much honour and advantage. He did many illuminations, and a fine St. Eustace adoring the Christ between the stag's horns, and two dogs of surpassing beauty, with a landscape full of trees gradually diminishing as they recede. This sheet has won loud praises from all who have seen it, and especially from Danese da Carrara, who saw it at Verona and made use of it in doing the Fregosi Chapel, which is one of the rarest things in Italy. Il Danese was amazed at the beauty of the sheet, and persuaded Frà Marco de' Medici, his old and valued friend, not to part with it on any account, but to keep it among his treasured possessions. Battista, learning that the father wanted it, was impelled by friendship to give it to him, all but forcing him to accept it, though the good father was not ungrateful. But as Battista and Marco, his son, are still alive and at work, I will say no more of them at present.

Il Moro had another pupil called Orlando Fiacco, who has become a good master skilled in portrait-painting. He drew Cardinal Caraffa on his return from Germany, taking him by torchlight as he supped in the Vescovado of Verona. As a likeness it could not be improved upon. He also drew the Cardinal of Lorraine when he passed through Verona to Rome on his way from the Council of Trent[1]; also the two Bishops Lipomanni of Verona, Luigi the uncle, and his nephew Agostino, now in a chamber of Count Giovan Battista delle Torre. He drew M. Adamo Fumani, a learned canon and noble of Verona, M. Vincenzio de' Medici of Verona, and his wife Madonna Isotta as St. Helena, and their nephew M. Niccolo. He also made portraits of Count Antonio delle Torre, Count Girolamo Canossi, and Count Ludovico and Count Paolo, his brothers, and Sig. Astor Baglioni, captain-general of the Venetian light horse and governor of Verona, in beautiful white armour, with Signora Ginevra Salviati, his consort. He drew Palladio, that rare architect, and many others, endeavouring to make himself a reputation in painting equal to that of his namesake, the first great paladin of France.

After the death of Frà Jocondo a great impetus was given to design in Verona, where masters in painting and architecture

[1] Cardinal Louis of Lorraine, in 1563.

have flourished in every age, as we shall now see in the Lives of Francesco Monsignori,[1] Domenico Moroni and Francesco his son, Paulo Cavazzuola, Falconetto the architect, and Francesco and Girolamo, illuminators. Francesco Monsignori, son of Alberto, was born in Verona in 1455, and when he was grown his father advised him to study design, for he himself had always loved painting, though he only practised it for pleasure. Proceeding to Mantua, where Mantegna was working, Francesco took such pains that before long Francesco II., Marquis of Mantua, being charmed with his work, gave him a house to live in there, in 1487, granting him a pension. Grateful for such favours, Francesco always served the marquis with fidelity, and received great marks of favour from him, so that the marquis could not leave the city without having Francesco behind him, and he was once heard to say that he loved Francesco as much as his crown. He painted many things for the marquis in the palace of S. Sebastiano at Mantua, in Gonzaga outside, and in the fine palace of Marmitolo, where in 1499, after he had finished a number of paintings of triumphs and portraits of nobles of the court, the marquis gave him 100 fields at la Marzotta, with a noble's house, garden, meadows and other conveniences on Christmas Eve, the day on which he completed the work. Being excellent at portraits he did several for the marquis of himself, his sons and others of the Gonzaga house, which were sent as presents to various princes of France and Germany. There are many fine ones still in Mantua, such as that of the Emperor Frederick Barbarossa, the Doge Barbarigo of Venice, Francesco Sforza, Duke of Milan, Massimiliano, Duke of Milan, who died in France, the Emperor Maximilian, Sig. Ercole Gonzaga, afterwards cardinal, his brother Duke Federigo as a youth, Sig. Giovan Francesco Gonzaga, M. Andrea Mantegna the painter, and many others, of which he preserved copies in grisaille, now owned by his heirs at Mantua. Over the pulpit of the bare-footed friars' church of S. Francesco there he did St. Louis and St. Bernardino holding a circle containing the name of Jesus.[2] In the refectory of those friars, covering the top wall, is a large picture on canvas of Christ in the midst of the twelve Apostles, in perspective, of great beauty. Among them is the traitor Judas, his face quite different from the others, and in a strange attitude, while the rest hang on the words of Jesus, then nearing His Passion. On the right is a beautiful life-size figure of St. Francis, his face

[1] Bonsignori, c. 1445–1519.   [2] Now in the Brera, Milan.

being holiness incarnate, such as befitted him. He is presenting to Christ the Marquis Francesco, who is kneeling and wearing a long cloak—a fashion of the day—embroidered with white crosses, perhaps because he was then captain of the Venetians. Before him is his eldest son, afterwards Duke Federigo, then a handsome child, with his hands joined together. On the other side is St. Bernardino, as finely done as the St. Francis, presenting to Christ Cardinal Sigismondo Gonzaga, brother of the marquis, a portrait like the others, in his rochet, and kneeling. Before the cardinal is Signora Leonora, the marquis's daughter, then a child, afterwards Duchess of Urbino. The work is considered a marvel by the best painters. He also painted a St. Sebastian, afterwards placed in the Madonna delle Grazie, outside Mantua, finishing it most carefully and copying from Nature. It is said that one day, when the marquis was watching him doing this work, as he frequently did, he said: "Francesco, you should have a good model to sit for that saint." The artist replied: "I am copying a stalwart porter, who is what I want." The marquis added: "The limbs of your saint are not true, and do not show the fear of a man bound and shot at; if you will allow me, I will show you what you ought to do." "I beg you to do so," said Francesco. The marquis then said: "When you have bound your porter, send for me and I will show you." On the following day Francesco adopted this advice and sent secretly for the marquis, without, however, knowing his purpose. The marquis came out as if infuriated, holding a loaded crossbow, and ran to the model crying aloud, "Traitor, you are a dead man, but I have caught you as I wished," and similar things, on hearing which the poor porter gave himself up for lost and tried to break the ropes, his contortions showing the fear of a man who expects to be shot, and the horror of death. Then the marquis said to Francesco: "That is the way, you can do the rest yourself." By this means the painter was enabled to give his picture the utmost perfection.

Besides many other things Francesco painted the creation of the first lords of Mantua, in the Gonzaga palace, and the jousting on the piazza of S. Piero, represented in perspective. The Grand Turk having presented the marquis with a magnificent dog, a bow and a quiver, he caused Francesco to draw them with the Turk who had brought them. Wishing to prove if the dog was life-like, he brought one of his own dogs, the mortal enemy of the Turkish dog, to see the painting. No sooner did the animal perceive it than he flew at it so furiously that he struck his head

against the wall and broke it. It is related by eye-witnesses that
Benedetto Baroni, Francesco's nephew, having a picture, hardly
larger than two palms, of a bust of the Madonna, in oils, and the
Child's head and shoulders, raising an arm to caress the mother;
it is related, I say, that when the emperor was patron of Verona,
Don Alonso of Castile and Aragon, a favourite captain of his
majesty and of the Catholic king, being in the house of Count
Ludovico da Sesso of Verona, expressed a great desire to see that
picture. It was sent for, and one evening they were standing
and admiring it in a good light, when Signora Caterina, his wife,
came with one of his children holding one of those green birds
called *terrazzi* at Verona, because they make their nests on the
ground (*terra*), and perch on the hand like sparrow-hawks. As
she was looking at the picture with the others, the bird flew to
perch on the Child's extended hand, but not being able to lodge
on the picture it fell thrice, returning each time, just as if it had
been a live child on whose hand it was accustomed to perch.
Amazed at this, they offered Benedetto a great price for the
picture, but he would not part with it. Not long after they came
back to steal it, on the feast of St. Blaise, in S. Nazzaro, but the
owner was warned and the plan failed.

In S. Polo, at Verona, Francesco painted a beautiful panel,
and another in the Bandi Chapel in S. Bernardino. In Mantua he
did a panel for Verona, now in the chapel where St. Blaise is
buried, in the church of S. Nazzaro of the black monks, with
two beautiful nudes, a Madonna and Child in the air, and some
marvellous angels. Francesco was a man of holy life, the enemy
of every vice, and he would never paint lascivious things,
although the marquis often asked him to. His brothers resembled him in character, as I shall relate presently. Suffering
from his kidneys and being old, Francesco obtained the permission of the marquis to go to the baths of Caldero, as advised by
the physicians, whither he took his wife and servants. After
taking the water one day he fell into a heavy sleep and his wife
let him lie. But this sleep is most injurious to those who take
the water, and it brought on a severe fever, of which he died on
2 July, 1519. When the marquis received the news he sent a
courier to have the body brought to Mantua, and this was done
against the will of the Veronese. It was buried in S. Francesco,
in the tomb of the secret company. Francesco lived sixty-four
years, and there is a portrait of him at the age of fifty in the hands
of M. Fermo.[1] Many compositions were written in his praise,

[1] Fermo Ghisoni, a painter of Mantua.

and he was lamented by all who knew him as a virtuous and holy man. He married Francesca Gioacchini of Verona, but had no children.

The eldest of his three brothers, called Monsignore, and a lettered man, received good positions from the marquis, out of favour for Francesco. He lived eighty years, and left children to perpetuate the Monsignori family. The second brother, Girolamo, called Frà Cherubino among the bare-footed friars, was a beautiful scribe and illuminator. The third, a Dominican friar called Frà Girolamo, would only be a lay brother. He was a man of holy life, and could paint tolerably, as we see in the convent of S. Domenico at Mantua, in the refectory of which he did a fine Last Supper and Crucifixion, left unfinished at his death, as well as other things. He painted the beautiful Last Supper in the refectory of the rich abbey of the Benedictines in the Mantuan. In S. Domenico he did the Rosary altar, and in the convent of S. Nastasia at Verona he did in fresco the Virgin, St. Remigius the bishop and St. Anastasia. In the tympanum over the second door of the tower in the second cloister he did a Madonna, St. Dominic and St. Thomas Aquinas with great skill. He was a simple man, careless of worldly matters. To avoid noise and disturbance he lived on a farm belonging to the brotherhood, and he kept the money sent for his work, which he used to buy colours and other things, in a pouch without a cover, hung from the ceiling in the middle of his room, so that anyone could help himself; that he might not have the trouble of seeing what he had to eat every day, he cooked on Monday a pot of haricots for all the week. When the plague reached Mantua, and those affected were abandoned by all, as is usual in such cases, Frà Girolamo, out of pure charity, would not leave the sick, but ministered to them himself not valuing his life out of love for God. He thus took the plague and died at the age of sixty, to the grief of all who knew him. But to return to Francesco Monsignori. I forgot to mention that he drew a life-size portrait of Count Ercole Giusti of Verona in a golden robe, a fine thing,[1] now in the house of Count Giusto, his son.

Domenico Moroni,[2] born in Verona about 1430, learned the art of painting from some pupils of Stefano, and from works and copies of that master, of Jacopo Bellini, Pisano and others. Passing over many of his works in monasteries and private houses, I may say that he painted in chiaroscuro of *terretta verde*

---

[1] Possibly the National Gallery portrait of a Venetian Senator, dated 1487.
[2] 1442–after 1503.

the façade of a house of the community of Verona on the Piazza de' Signori, containing many friezes and ancient scenes with figures and habits of bygone days, very well disposed. But his best work is in S. Bernardino there, namely a Christ led to the cross with a crowd of men and horses, on the wall above the chapel of the Monte della Pietà, where Liberale did his Deposition and weeping angels. He was employed to decorate the chapel near this with gilt, at great cost, by M. Niccoli de' Medici, knight, reputed the wealthiest man in Verona, who spent much on other pious works, such being his nature. In addition to building many monasteries and churches, he hardly left a place in the city on which he did not expend something in honour of God. He chose this chapel for his tomb, employing Domenico to decorate it as being the most famous painter in the city, for Liberale was at Siena. In the interior Domenico painted the miracles of St. Anthony of Padua, to whom the chapel is dedicated, introducing the knight's portrait, as an old man, white haired, clean shaven, without a cap, and dressed in a long gold vest such as the knights of the day wore, the work being admirably designed and executed for a fresco. In the vaulting, which is all gilded, he did the four Evangelists in circles and figures of saints on the pilasters, comprising St. Elizabeth of the third order of St. Francis, St. Helena, and St. Catherine, beautiful figures, much admired for their design, grace and colouring, well fitted to display the powers of Domenico and the magnificence of the knight. Domenico lived to a good old age and was buried in S. Bernardino, which contained these works. He left his son Francesco Morone [1] the heir of his property and ability. He learned the first principles from his father, and in a short time surpassed him, as is clearly shown by the works he did in competition with him. Under his father's work at the Monte altar in S. Bernardino, Francesco painted the shutters of Liberale's panel, with a Virgin and St. John the Baptist of lifesize, beautiful in the weeping expression, the draperies and every other part. In the same chapel, at the base of the wall joining the screen, he did the Miracle of the Loaves and Fishes, with many fine figures and portraits, particularly a slender St. John turning his back to the people. In the same place in an empty wall space he did St. Louis the bishop and another figure, with some foreshortened heads in the vaulting, works much admired by the Veronese painters. At the altar of the Cross, between this chapel and that of the Medici in the same church, containing

[1] 1473–1529.

many pictures, he did the middle one of Christ on the Cross, the Virgin and St. John, while on the left-hand, above Caroti's picture, he did Christ washing the disciples' feet.[1] They stand in various attitudes, and he is said to have painted himself as the man serving Christ in carrying the water. In the Emili Chapel in the Duomo he did St. James and St. John with Christ bearing the Cross between them, the two figures being of the utmost beauty and excellence. He did several things at Lonico, an abbey of the monks of Monte Oliveto, much resorted to because of an image of the Virgin that works miracles. Francesco becoming afterwards so intimate with Girolamo dai Libri, painter and illuminator, that they were like brothers, they did together the organ doors of S. Maria in Organo [2] of the friars of Monte Oliveto. On the outside of one of these Francesco did a St. Benedict dressed in white, and St. John the Evangelist, and on the inside he painted the prophets Daniel and Isaiah, with two angels in the air, and backgrounds of lovely landscapes. He next painted the altar-picture of la Muletta,[3] representing St. Peter and St. John, more than a braccia high, so carefully finished that they are like illuminations. The carving for these works was done by Frà Giovanni da Verona, a master of marquetry and carving. In the same place Francesco painted two scenes in fresco on the choir walls: Our Lord entering Jerusalem on an ass, and the Agony in the Garden, with the armed men led by Judas coming to take him. Most beautiful of all is the vaulting of the sacristy, the whole being his except St. Anthony beaten by devils, said to be by his father Domenico. Besides the Christ and some angels foreshortened from below, he made some Benedictine popes in the lunettes, arranged in pairs in niches, and dressed in their pontificals. Beneath these lunettes he made a frieze about the sacristy, four feet deep, divided into pictures containing emperors, kings, dukes and other princes who abandoned their state and became monks. Among these Francesco has painted the portraits of many of the monks then living in the monastery, including novices and some of every condition, most beautiful heads, executed with great diligence. Indeed, thanks to this decoration, the sacristy was rendered the finest in Italy, as, in addition to the paintings, the building is well proportioned and of considerable grandeur. It also possesses a row of inlaid

[1] Now in the Verona Gallery; attributed by Crowe and Cavalcaselle to Morando, painted 1498.
[2] Begun in 1515.
[3] La Muletta is a mediæval carved wooden statue of Christ on the ass's colt, preserved in the same church.

benches, containing perspectives unequalled at the time and probably even in our own days one would not see much better. Frà Giovanni da Verona, who did them, was an excellent workman, as I said in the Life of Raphael, and as we see by his numerous works for the houses of his order, at Rome in the Pope's palace, at Monte Oliveto near Siena, and other places. But those of the sacristy are his best, for in them he surpassed himself, as he had surpassed his rivals in the others, For this place Frà Giovanni carved in walnut a chandelier, more than fourteen feet high, for the paschal taper, with incredible diligence, and probably the best work of its kind.

But to return to Francesco. In the same church he painted the picture of the chapel of the Counts Giusti, doing the Virgin, St. Augustine and St. Martin in pontificals,[1] and in the cloister he did a Deposition from the Cross with the Maries and other saints, much praised as frescoes in Verona. In the church of la Vettoria he painted the Fumanelli Chapel below the screen erected by M. Niccolo de' Medici, knight. In the cloister he did a Madonna in fresco, and painted the portrait of M. Antonio Fumanelli, a physician, famous for his works on medicine. On a house on the way from the Ponte delle Navi to S. Polo, he did a Madonna with many saints,[2] considered very beautiful for its design and colouring. In Bra he painted a similar one over the Sparvieri house opposite the garden of the friars of S. Fermo. He painted many other things which I need not mention, these being the best. He endowed his works with grace, design, harmony, and bright and charming colouring. He attained the age of fifty-five, dying on 16 May, 1529, and was buried in S. Domenico beside his father. He desired to be carried to burial dressed as a Franciscan friar. So religious and gentle was he that he was never heard to utter an evil word.

Paolo Cavazzuola[3] of Verona was a pupil of Francesco, and knew more than his master. He did many works in Verona, but I know of none elsewhere. In S. Nazzario, a house of the black monks, he did several frescoes near those of his master, which all perished at the time when the church was rebuilt by the magnanimity of Don Mauro Lonichi, a noble Veronese and abbot of the monastery. Over the old house of the Fumanelli in the via del Paradiso, Paolo painted in fresco the sibyl showing the Virgin and Child to Augustus, of considerable beauty for one of his first efforts. In the Fontani Chapel in S. Maria in Organo

---

[1] Dated 1503.   [2] Now in the Verona Gallery.
[3] Paolo Morando, 1486-1522.

he painted St. Michael and St. Raphael in fresco. In S. Eufemia, in the street leading to the chapel of Raphael, he painted the angel with Tobias [1] over a window lighting the staircase of the chapel, a most beautiful little work. Over the belfry door of S. Bernardino he painted a St. Bernardino in fresco in a circle, and lower down on the same wall, over the opening of a confessional, he did a St. Francis, which is equally well executed. These are all his works in fresco. In oils he did a picture of St. Roch [2] for the altar of the Sanctification in the Madonna della Scala, in competition with the St. Sebastian of Il Moro opposite. But his best figures are in S. Bernardino, where he did all the large paintings about the altar of the Cross, except the Madonna and St. John by the Cross of his master Francesco, which is above all the others. Beside this Paolo did two large pictures: one is Christ at the Column, and the other, His Coronation, in figures somewhat larger than life-size. Lower down he did a Deposition from the Cross, the Virgin, the Magdalene, St. John, Nicodemus and Joseph,[3] introducing his own portrait as a figure near the cross, a young man with a red beard, and a hood on his head such as was then worn. On the right is an Agony in the Garden, and on the left Christ bearing His cross to Mount Calvary. These works surpass those done by his master in the same place, and secure him a position among the best artists. At the bottom he did some saints, head and shoulders, all portraits. The first, in the Franciscan habit, representing a Blessed, is Frà Girolamo Recalchi, a Veronese noble. The next, representing St. Bonaventura, is Frà Bonaventura Recalchi, Frà Girolamo's brother; the St. Joseph is an agent of the Marquis Malaspini, then charged to direct this work by the company of la Croce. All these heads are very fine. Paolo did the picture for the chapel of St. Francis in the same church, surpassing himself in this, his last work. It contains six figures larger than life: St. Elizabeth of the third order of St. Francis, a beautiful figure of smiling and graceful aspect, her lap full of roses, seeming to rejoice at the miracle wrought in turning the bread she was carrying to the poor into roses as a sign that her charity was acceptable to God. This figure is the portrait of a noble widow of the Sacchi family. The other figures are St. Bonaventura the cardinal, St. Louis the bishop, both Franciscans, St. Louis, King of France, St. Eleazar in a dark habit, and St. Ivo in the sacerdotal habit. The Madonna

[1] Dated 1520.
[2] Now in the National Gallery, London, formerly dated 1518.
[3] Dated 1522; now in the Museo Civico, Verona.

is above in a cloud with St. Francis, and the other figures surrounding them are said to be by a friend of Paolo, who helped
him with this picture.[1] The figures indeed are not of the same
excellence as those below. The picture also contains a portrait
of Madonna Caterina de' Sacchi, the donor. The extraordinary
efforts of Paolo to make himself great and famous brought on
a sickness, and he died at thirty-one, when only beginning to
show his worth and what might be expected of him in riper
years. Otherwise he would doubtless have risen to the highest
possible rank in painting. His loss caused great sorrow to his
friends and to all who knew him, the more so because he was a
man of admirable rectitude, unspotted by any vice. He was buried
in S. Polo, rendered immortal by the beautiful works he left.

Stefano of Verona, that rare painter, had a natural brother
called Giovan' Antonio, whom he taught to paint, though with
little success, for he only became mediocre, as we see by his
works, which are not worth mentioning. He left a son, also a
painter of rubbish, called Jacopo, who begat Gio. Maria, called
Falconetto,[2] whose Life I am now to write, and Giovan' Antonio.
The latter studied painting and did many things in Rovereto,
an important place near the Trentino, and painted many others
in Verona for private houses. In the valley of the Adige above
Verona he did several things, and painted a panel at Sacco
opposite Rovereto, of St. Nicholas with animals, and several
others, going finally to die at Rovereto. He excelled especially
in animals and fruits, many drawings of which were taken to
France by Mondella of Verona, and many given by his son
Agnolo to M. Girolamo Lioni, a cultivated nobleman of Venice.
His brother Giovanmaria learned the principles of painting
from his father, and, making steady progress, he became an
artist of great reputation. We may see his works in the Chapels
of the Maffei and Emili in the Duomo of Verona,[3] in the upper
part of the cupola of S. Nazzaro and elsewhere. But recognising the imperfection of his painting and being most fond of
architecture, he began to draw all the antiquities of his native
Verona. He next went to Rome to learn architecture of the
marvellous remains there, which are the real teacher, and he
spent twelve years in the city, chiefly engaged in seeing and
drawing antiquities, making plans and noting measurements,
there being nothing that he did not draw to scale. He further
drew all the sculptures discovered at the time, and returned

[1] Now in the Verona Gallery, dated 1522.   [2] 1458–1534.
[3] Painted in 1493.

home enriched by the treasures of art. Not content with the treasures of Rome itself, he drew all that was beautiful in the Campagna of Rome, in Naples, in the duchy of Spoleto and other places. Being too poor to support himself at Rome, he would employ two or three days in every week in doing some painting, on the profits of which he lived, for masters were well paid then, while he devoted the remainder of the week to his architectural studies. He thus studied carefully all the antiquities, making careful measurements. Returning to Verona he had no opportunity of essaying his skill in architecture, as the city was disturbed by a change of government.[1] Accordingly he took to the brush and painted several pictures. Above the house of the della Torre he did their arms, surmounted by trophies, and for some German councillors of the Emperor Maximilian he did on the front of the little church of S. Giorgio some scriptural subjects, making life-size portraits of the German lords kneeling on either side. At Mantua he did several things for Sig. Luigi Gonzaga and some others at Osimo in the March of Ancona. While the emperor held Verona[2] he painted the imperial arms on the public buildings, receiving good provision and privileges from his majesty. Being a brave and fearless man, he could serve the emperor as well in arms as in art, especially as he had great influence with the inhabitants of the populous quarter of S. Zeno, where he was born and had taken his wife, of the Provali family; indeed, he was only known in the city as Il Rosso of S. Zeno. Thus, when the city again fell into the hands of its ancient masters the Venetians, Giovanmaria was forced to leave to save his life. He went to Trent, painting a little, but matters becoming settled he proceeded to Padua, where he first made the acquaintance of Monsignor Bembo, who greatly esteemed him and introduced him to M. Luigi Cornaro, a Venetian noble of high spirit and royal intellect, as proved by his numerous activities. These men being, above all, fond of architecture, as every great prince should be, and well versed in the works of Vitruvius, Leonbattista Alberti and others, and being anxious to put their principles into practice, became very fond of Falconetto, seeing his designs and observing his thorough knowledge of the subject and how he cleared away all difficulties which arose from the variety of the orders of

[1] After the Venetian defeat at Ghiaradda by the forces of the League of Cambrai, Verona declared for the Emperor Maximilian in May 1509 and remained under imperial rule for nearly eight years.

[2] 1509-17.

architecture, so that they kept him with them for the remaining twenty-one years of his life. During this time he did many things with M. Luigi, who, being anxious to see the antiquities of Rome in fact as well as in Falconetto's designs, went with him to Rome to examine everything in his company. Returning to Padua,[1] he employed Falconetto to design the beautiful loggia for the Cornaro house near the Santo, for the palace afterwards built from the model of M. Luigi himself. On this loggia Giovanmaria's name is carved on a pilaster. He also did a large and magnificent Doric gateway for the palace of the captain there, much admired by all for its purity. He also did two fine gates for the city, one called S. Giovanni, towards Vicenza, convenient for the soldiers who guard it, and the Savonarola gate, which was very well conceived.[2] He also designed the Dominican church of S. Maria delle Grazie, and began it, so fine a work, as we see from the model, that it is probably unequalled for grandeur. He also made the model of a superb palace for Sig. Girolamo Savorgnano at his strong castle of Usopo in Friuli, but it was not proceeded with owing to that noble's death, though it would have been marvellous.

At this time Falconetto went to Pola in Istria simply to see and sketch the theatre, amphitheatre and arch in that ancient city. He was the first to make plans of theatres and amphitheatres, those which exist, notably that of Verona, coming from him, and they were engraved by others from his design. He had a lofty spirit and desired nothing better than the opportunity of carrying into practice things of like grandeur to the antiquities he had copied; accordingly, he was always making plans with as much diligence as if the work was immediately to be executed, and thus lost a good deal, because he would not deign to design private houses for nobles, although much pressed to do so. He frequently visited Rome, besides the occasions mentioned, becoming so familiar with the journey that he would undertake it on the slightest occasion when he was young and strong. Some who are still living relate how he once met a foreign architect at Verona, with whom he engaged in a dispute upon the dimensions of some ancient cornice at Rome. At last he said, "I will soon clear up this question," and off he went to Rome. He designed two beautiful tombs for the Cornaro house, to be executed in S. Salvadore at Venice, one for the Queen of Cyprus, a member of the family, and one

[1] In 1524.
[2] The three gates were done in 1532, 1528 and 1530 respectively.

for Cardinal Marco Cornaro, the first in the family to obtain
that dignity. For the execution of these designs a quantity of
marble was excavated at Carrara and sent to Venice, where
it still remains in the rough in the Cornaro house.

Giovanmaria was the first to bring the true method of building
and good architecture to Verona, Venice and the neighbourhood, where no one had previously been able to make a cornice
or capital or to understand the true proportions of the columns,
or the orders, as is shown by the buildings. The knowledge
imparted by him was supplemented by his contemporary Frà
Jocondo, and had its complement in M. Michele Sanmichele,
so that the men of those parts are under a perpetual obligation
to the men of Verona, where these three great artists were born
and flourished together. To them succeeded Sansovino, who
brought sculpture to the aid of architecture, so firmly established by them, whereby buildings received a fitting decoration,
all this being due, if I may say so, to the destruction of Rome,
for, through the masters being scattered in many places, the
beauties of the art were communicated to all Europe. Giovanmaria did some works in stucco at Venice, giving instruction
in the art, and some assert that in his youth he employed
Tiziano da Padoa to decorate the vaulting of the chapel
of the Santo at Padua with stucco, and much more
stucco-work, including some at the Cornaro house, of great
beauty. He taught his two sons, Ottaviano, who became
a painter, and Provolo. Alessandro, his third son, studied the
trade of an armourer in his youth, and, becoming a soldier, he
was thrice conqueror in the lists, and at length died, an infantry
captain fighting valiantly near Turin in Piedmont, from an
arquebus wound. Giovanmaria being tortured by gout, died at
Padua in the house of M. Luigi Cornaro, who loved him like a
brother. In order that their bodies might not be separated in
death after being united in so close a friendship, M. Luigi had
planned that he should be laid in his tomb, which was also to
contain the comic poet Ruzzante, another great friend who
lived and died in his house. But I do not know if this was
carried out. Giovanmaria talked well and wittily, being of
amiable and pleasant conversation, so that Cornaro declared
that his sayings would fill a book. He lived a jocund life, in spite
of the gout, to the age of seventy-six, and died in 1534. He had
six daughters, five of whom he married himself, the sixth being
married after his death by her brothers to Bartolommeo Ridolfi
of Verona, who did many things in stucco with them, and was

a much better master than they. We see this by works in many places, but especially in the house of Fiorio della Seta at Verona on the new bridge, where he did some chambers beautifully, and some marvellous ones in the house of the Counts Canossi, with others in the house of the Murati near S. Nazzaro for Sig. Gio. Battista della Torre and Cosimo Moneta, banker of Verona, at his beautiful villa, with many others in various places, all of great beauty. That rare artist Palladio declares that he knows no one with better invention or who can better adorn apartments with stucco. Ridolfi was not many years ago taken to the King of Poland by Spitech Giordan, a great lord of the country, receiving a large pension. There he did several works in stucco, portraits, medals and many designs for palaces and other buildings, aided by his son, who is not a whit inferior to his father.

Francesco dai Libri the elder,[1] of Verona, came shortly before Liberale, though the exact date of his birth is unknown. He owed his name to his skill in illuminating books (libri)—for printing had not been discovered, or was very little in use. Books were sent to him to illuminate from every hand, and he had a quantity of work, for those who incurred the heavy expense of writing also desired to have their books illuminated as much as possible. Thus he did many books for the choir in S. Giorgio, S. Maria in Organo and S. Nazzaro in Verona, all beautiful, but his best production is two small pictures shutting up like a book, with a very delicately finished St. Jerome on one side and St. John on Patmos on the other, writing the Apocalypse. This work was left to Count Agostino Giusti by his father, and is now in S. Lionardo of the regular canons, where Don Timoteo Giusti, the count's son, has a part. After making a countless number of works for various lords, Francesco died, contented and happy, for he had lived a good life, and he left a son called Girolamo, who excelled him greatly in art, even before his own death.

This Girolamo[2] was born in Verona in 1472, and at sixteen he did the altarpiece in the Lischi Chapel of S. Maria in Organo, which when uncovered excited such wonder that the whole city ran to greet and congratulate his father. It represented a Deposition from the Cross, with many figures and beautiful, sorrowful heads. The best figures are the Virgin and St. Benedict, much commended by artists. The landscape comprised a part of Verona excellently drawn. Encouraged by praise, Girolamo

[1] Born in 1452. [2] 1474-1556.

skilfully painted the altar of the Madonna in S. Polo, and in
the church of la Scala he did a Madonna and St. Anne, between
the St. Sebastian and St. Roch of Il Moro and Cavazzuola.[1] In
the church of la Vettoria he did the high-altar picture of the
Zoccoli family, and near it the picture of S. Onofrio of the
Cipolli family, considered his best work for design and colouring.
In S. Lionardo nel Monte near Verona he painted the high-
altar picture of the Cartieri family, a large work with many
figures, greatly esteemed by all. Above all it contains a beautiful
landscape. An event which has frequently occurred in our own
day has increased the reputation of this work. It contains a
tree, apparently a laurel, against which is a large seat on which
the Virgin rests. The branches extend well beyond the seat,
and as the fine clear light shows through the spaces, which
are not numerous, it looks real; and birds have frequently
come into the church and gone to perch on the tree, especially
the swallows who make their nests in the roof. This is avouched
by credible testimony such as Padre Don Giuseppo Mangiuoli
of Verona, twice general of the order, and a man of holy life,
incapable of falsehood, Padre Don Girolamo Volpini of Verona
and many others. In S. Maria in Organo, where he did his
first work, Girolamo painted one of the organ shutters, the
other having been done by his companion Francesco Morone,
representing two saints on the outside and the manger inside.[2]
He then did the Nativity opposite, with charming shepherds,
landscapes and trees. Especially natural are two rabbits whose
hairs might be counted. He did another panel in the Buonalivi
chapel of a Madonna seated between two other figures and
angels below singing.[3] At the altar of the Sacrament in the
decoration of Frà Giovanni of Verona, he did three small
illuminations. The middle one is a Deposition from the Cross
with two angels, and there are three martyrs on each side
kneeling towards the Sacrament. The bodies of these saints
rest beneath the altar. They are Canzius, Canzianus and Can-
zianellus, nephews of the Emperor Diocletian; and Protus,
Grisogonus and Anastasius, martyred *ad aquas gradatas* near
Aquileia. The figures are very beautiful, as Girolamo excelled
all in Lombardy and the Venetian state as an illuminator. He
illuminated several books for the monks of Monte Scaglioso
in the kingdom of Naples, some at S. Giustina of Padua and
many others in the abbey of Praia on the Po, some at Can-

---

[1] Now in the National Gallery, London.
[2] Now in the Verona Gallery.   [3] Dated 1503.

diana, a wealthy monastery of regular canons of S. Salvadore, whither he went to work, a thing he never did for any other place. While there he taught the elements of illuminating to Don Giulio Clovio, a friar of the house, who has become the best exponent of the art in Italy. At Candiana, Girolamo illuminated a sheet with the *Kyrie*, a lovely thing, and also the first sheet of a psaltery for the choir. In Verona he did several things for S. Maria in Organo and the friars of S. Giorgio. For the black monks of S. Nazzario at Verona he did other beautiful illuminations. But the best of these divine works was an illuminated sheet representing Adam and Eve expelled from Paradise by the angel, who holds a sword in his hand. It is impossible to describe the beauty and variety of the trees in this work, the fruits, flowers, animals, birds and other things. It was done for Don Giorgio Cacciamale of Bergamo, then prior of S. Giorgio, Verona, who besides many other favours gave Girolamo sixty gold crowns. This work of the friar was afterwards given at Rome to a cardinal, protector of the order, who showed it to several lords there, and it came to be considered the best illumination that had ever been seen there. Girolamo made his flowers with such care, so true, beautiful and natural, that they looked real, and he depicted small cameos and other carved stones and jewels with wonderful fidelity. Some of his figures, for example those in the representations of cameos, are no bigger than a small ant, yet all the members and muscles are incredibly clear. In his extreme old age Girolamo said that he knew more of his art than ever, but that his eye and hand failed him in using the brush. He died in 1555 on 2 July, aged eighty-three, and was buried in the tomb of the company of St. Biagio in S. Nazzario. He was an amiable man and never quarrelled with anyone, his life being remarkably spotless.

Among other children he had a son called Francesco,[1] who learnt art from him, and while still young did miracles of illumination, so that Girolamo declared he had never known so much as his son. But he was taken away by a maternal uncle who was wealthy and had no children of his own, and who made him study glass-blowing in Vicenza, where he had set up a factory. After spending his best years upon this, his uncle's wife being dead, he gave up all hope, perceiving that he had been wasting his time, for his uncle married again and had children, and so Francesco was not his heir as he had expected

[1] Born in 1500.

to be. After an interval of six years, therefore, he returned to art, and among other things he did a great hollow ball four feet in diameter, covering the wooden exterior with a glue made of ox nerves, so strong that no break need be feared. After dividing it out as a globe in the presence of Frascatoro and Beroldi, both physicians and rare cosmographers and astrologers, he coloured it for M. Andrea Navagero, a Venetian noble and a learned poet and ambassador, who wanted to present it to King Francis of France, to whom he was accredited by the republic. But hardly had he reached France than he died, and the work was left unfinished, though it would have been remarkable. Even what had been done was allowed to spoil while Francesco was away, and in this state it was bought by M. Bartolommeo Lonichi, who will not part with it to anyone, though frequently pressed to and offered a high price. Francesco had previously made two smaller globes, one being in the possession of Mazzanti, arch-priest of the Duomo of Verona, and the other was owned by Count Raimondo della Torre, and is now in the hands of his son Count Gio. Battista, who values it highly, for it was made with the help of Frascatoro, a great friend of Count Raimondo. Francesco, becoming tired of the great care demanded by illuminations, took up painting and architecture, displaying great skill and doing several things in Venice and Padua. At that time the Bishop of Tournay,[1] a great, noble and very wealthy Fleming, came to Italy to study letters and see those parts. Being very fond of building and much delighted with the Italian methods which he saw at Padua, he resolved to transport them to his own country. Recognising the worth of Francesco, he retained him by a good salary to take him to Flanders, where he proposed to undertake works of importance. But when the time came to go, when he had already designed the best and most famous buildings there, poor Francesco died, though young and of good promise, to the sorrow of his patron. He left an only brother, but as he was a priest, the family died out after producing three distinguished artists in succession. They left no pupils to keep the art alive except Don Giulio Clovio, mentioned above, who learned it of Girolamo and who has attained to an excellence reached by few and surpassed by none.

I knew some particulars of these great artists of Verona, but I should not have accumulated so many facts if I had not received a great deal of information from the reverend and learned Frà

[1] Charles de Croy, bishop of Tournai, 1539-64.

Marco de' Medici of Verona, a man skilled in all the noble arts
and sciences, and from Il Danese Cataneo da Carrara, an
excellent sculptor, both friends of mine; I have written this
for the benefit of my readers, having been much assisted by the
courtesy of many friends who have made researches for my
sake and to benefit the public. This is the end of the Lives of
these Veronese. I have not been able to give portraits of all
of them, because this fuller information did not come into my
hands until I had almost finished the work.

Francesco Granacci, Painter of Florence
(1477-1543)

GREAT is the fortune of those artists who in childhood are born
or associated with men whom Heaven has chosen out for dis-
tinction in art, for they have unusual opportunities of acquiring
a good style by seeing the methods of great men, while emula-
tion exercises a great influence, as I have said elsewhere. Francesco was one of those who worked in the garden of Lorenzo
de' Medici the Magnificent, and while still a child he recognised the talent and skill of Michelagnolo and how in time he
would produce the greatest fruits, so that he could never leave
him, always following in the steps of that mighty genius with
wonderful submission and devotion. Thus Michelagnolo could
not help loving him more than all his other friends, and confided to him, more readily than to any other, his knowledge
of art. While they were both in the workshop of Domenico
Grillandai, where Granacci was considered the best of the
apprentices in design and graceful colouring in tempera, he
assisted Davitte and Benedetto Grillandaio, Domenico's brothers,
with the high-altar picture of S. Maria Novella, left unfinished
by Domenico's death, in which work Granacci learned a great
deal. He next did several panels in the same style for private
citizens, and others to be sent abroad. As he was most obliging
and very clever in arranging little things for the carnivals in
the city, Lorenzo de' Medici kept him constantly employed in
such things, and especially in the masquerade representing the
triumph of Paulus Emilius. Although very young, Granacci
introduced so many beautiful inventions into this that he won
loud praises. I may remark that Lorenzo was the first inventor

of the masquerades called Canti at Florence, in which some action is represented. In 1515 Granacci was employed upon the sumptuous preparations for the coming of Pope Leo X. by Jacopo Nardi, a learned and ingenious man, who represented the triumph of Camillus, the Eight having decreed a masquerade. The painting for this was entrusted to Granacci, and he carried it out with the utmost beauty. The words of the canzone, written by Jacopo, being:

> *Contempla in quanta gloria sei salita*
> *Felice, alma Fiorenza,*
> *Poiche dal ciel discesa, etc.*

In the same celebrations Granacci painted a quantity of scenery for a comedy. In conjunction with Grillandaio he did standards, banners and ensigns of knights, with gilt spurs, for their public entry into Florence, all at the cost of the captains of the Guelph party, as was then customary, and has been continued almost up to our own day. When the Powers [1] and tournaments were exhibited, he devised many beautiful inventions for costumes and head-dresses. These pleasant festivities, peculiar to the Florentines, were all arranged for the coming of Leo, when men practically standing on horses, with very short stirrups, would break lances as easily as warriors firmly seated in the saddle. Among other things, Granacci made a fine triumphal arch opposite the door of the Badia, full of beautiful scenes in grisaille. It was much admired for its architecture, and for a representation of the door of the Badia leading to the via del Palagio, with the stairs and everything else. To decorate the arch he made some clay figures in relief, and on the top he wrote in large letters:

LEONI X PONT. MAX. FIDEI
CVLTORI.

To come to the actually existing works of Granacci. Having studied Michelagnolo's cartoons while working with him on the great hall of the palace, he made such progress that, when Michelagnolo was summoned to Rome by Julius II. to paint the vaulting of the chapel of the palace, Granacci was one of the first invited by the master to help colour that work in fresco after the cartoons. It is true that, being dissatisfied with the style and methods of all of them, Michelagnolo managed,

---

[1] i.e. representations of royalties and their suites.

without actually dismissing them, to shut the door on all, and
so they returned to Florence. Here Granacci decorated a room
for Pierfrancesco Borgherini in his house in Borgo S. Apostolo,
where Jacopo da Pontormo, Andrea del Sarto and Francesco
Ubertini had done scenes from of the life of Joseph,[1] one of
them on a large bed in oils, of small figures, executed with
great diligence and in beautiful colouring, as well as a scene
of Joseph serving Pharaoh of unsurpassable beauty. For the
same patron he did a round Trinity,[2] God sustaining the crucifix. In S. Pier Maggiore he did an Assumption on a panel, with
many angels, and a St. Thomas, on whom the Virgin bestows
her girdle. It is a graceful figure, so vigorous that it might be
by Michelagnolo, and so is the Virgin. The design for these
two figures is in our book, with other things of Granacci. At
the sides of this picture are St. Paul, St. Laurence, St. James and
St. John, considered beautiful figures, and indeed this is reputed
to be Granacci's best work. If he had done nothing else it would
suffice to establish his reputation as an excellent painter. In
the church of S. Gallo of the Eremite friars of St. Augustine,
outside the gate, he did the Virgin and two infants, St. Zanobius,
bishop of Florence, and St. Francis,[3] for the Chapel of the
Girolami family, to which St. Zanobius belonged, now in S.
Jacopo tra' Fossi. Michelagnolo had a niece, a nun in S. Apollonia at Florence, and so he designed the decoration and picture
for the high altar. Here Granacci painted scenes of large and
small figures in oils, which greatly pleased the nuns, and
artists also. Lower down he did another panel, which
was burned by the altar-lights one night, with many valuable
properties, a great loss, because the work was much admired
by artists. For the nuns of S. Giorgio in sulla Costà, he did
the high-altar picture, with the Virgin, St. Catherine, St. John
Gualbert, St. Bernardo Uberti, the cardinal, and St. Fedele.[4]
He did many pictures for noblemen, and several cartoons for
stained-glass windows, afterwards executed by the Jesuit friars
of Florence. He was very fond of painting cloth by himself and
with others, and did many hangings. As art was a pastime with
him rather than a necessity, he worked at his ease, avoiding
discomfort as much as possible. He kept his own without
coveting the possessions of others, and, being without care, he

[1] Two of these scenes are in the Uffizi Gallery, by Granacci.
[2] Probably the one in the Berlin Gallery.
[3] Now in the uffizi, Florence.
[4] Accademia, Florence.

was agreeable and happy. He lived sixty-seven years, and was carried off by a fever, being buried in S. Ambruogio, at Florence on St. Andrew's day, 1543.

BACCIO D'AGNOLO,[1] Architect of Florence
(1462 – 1543)

IT is always a great delight to me to trace the rise of an artist from the depths to the heights, especially in architecture, which for several years now has only been practised by carvers and persons ignorant even of the technical terms, without an elementary knowledge of perspective. But architecture can only attain perfection in the hands of those who possess the highest judgment and good design, and who have had great experience in painting, sculpture and wood-carving. For in it men measure the bodies of their figures, such as columns, cornices, basements, and all the orders which are made solely for the purpose of embellishing their figures, and thus carvers in the process of time become architects by constant practice. Sculptors also, in making ornaments for tombs and other things, come to understand that art, while the painter in his perspectives, the variety of inventions, and the buildings drawn by him cannot fail to make plans, for no steps or surfaces of figures are ever prepared without some architecture being first introduced. In his early youth Baccio did some excellent marquetry for the choir stalls of S. Maria Novella, in the principal chapel, containing a St. John the Baptist and a St. Laurence, of great beauty. He carved the decoration of this chapel and that of the high altar of the Nunziata, the ornament of the organ of S. Maria Novella, and countless other public and private things in his native Florence. He then went to Rome, where he carefully studied architecture, and on his return made wooden triumphal arches in various places for the coming of Pope Leo X. At the same time he did not abandon his workshop, where many citizens and the foremost artists assembled. Here, especially in winter, remarkable discussions and important disputes took place. The principal figure at these reunions was Raphael, then a young man, and after him came Andrea Sansovino, Filippino, Maiano, Cronaca, Antonio and

[1] His surname was Baglioni.

Giuliano Sangalli, Granaccio, and on rare occasions Michelagnolo, with many Florentine youths and foreigners.

Having studied architecture to good purpose, and gained some experience, Baccio began to have such a reputation in Florence that the most magnificent structures of the time were allotted to him. When Piero Socerini was gonfaloniere, Baccio, Cronaca and others, as already said, were present at the discussions upon the great hall of the place, and Baccio did the wooden frame for the large picture, designed by Filippino and sketched by Frà Bartolommeo. In their company he did the steps leading to the hall [1] with a very beautiful stone ornament and columns of variegated marble, and marble doors of the hall now known as that of the Two Hundred. On the piazza of S. Trinità he made a palace for Giovanni Bartolini,[2] with a highly decorated interior, and many designs for its garden in Gualfonda. This palace was the first structure decorated with square windows with a portal, the columns of the door bearing an architrave frieze and cornices. The Florentines loudly blamed these things in their conversation, in sonnets, and by putting rows of branches there like a feast day at church, saying that it was more like the front of a church than a palace, and that Baccio was going mad. However, he took no notice, confident that the work was good and formed on a good model. It is true that the cornice is too large, as already stated, nevertheless the work has always been much admired in other respects. He built the house of the Lanfredino Lanfredini, lung' Arno, between the Ponte S. Trinità and the Ponte alla Carraia, and on the Piazza de' Mozzi he began but did not finish the house of the Nasi,[3] on the banks of the Arno. He also made the house of the Taddei for Taddeo Taddei,[4] which was considered beautiful and very convenient. For Pierfrancesco Borgherini he designed the house [5] which he built in Borgo S. Apostolo, making the decoration of the doors at great cost, beautiful chimneypieces, and the walnut chests, carved with infants with great diligence, impossible to equal in these days. He designed the villa which he erected on the hill of Bellosguardo, a structure of great beauty and convenience, and very costly. For Gio. Maria Benintendi he did an antechamber and an ornamental frame for some paintings by great masters. He did the model of the church of S. Giuseppo at S. Nofri, building the

[1] In 1501.   [2] In 1520: now the Hotel du Nord.
[3] Now Torrigiani.   [4] Now Pecori Giraldi, via de' Ginori.
[5] Now Rosselli.

door, which was his last work. He superintended the building of the campanile of S. Spirito at Florence, leaving it unfinished. It has been recently completed from his design by the order of Duke Cosimo. He also built the campanile of S. Miniato di Monte,[1] which though bombarded by the artillery was not destroyed, and thus won no less renown for its resistance to the enemy than for the beauty and excellence of its workmanship. Owing to his eminence and his favour with the citizens, Baccio was appointed architect of S. Maria del Fiore, and designed the balcony encircling the cupola, which Filippo Brunelleschi had been prevented by death from doing, though he had prepared designs, lost by the negligence of the ministers of the building. Baccio, after designing the whole, carried out the part on the Bischeri side, but Michelagnolo on returning from Rome, on seeing that in carrying out the work they were cutting away the projections purposely left by Filippo, made such a disturbance that the work was stopped. He said that Baccio seemed to him to have made a cage for crickets, whereas such a great monument required something larger, possessing design, art and grace, such as were entirely lacking in Baccio's plan, and that he would show them what to do. Accordingly he made a model, and the matter remained a long time in discussion between expert artists and citizens before Cardinal Giulio de' Medici, and ultimately neither model was put into execution. Baccio's design was blamed in many particulars as being too small for the structure, and for these reasons the gallery has never been completed. Baccio afterwards devoted himself to making the pavement of S. Maria del Fiore and several other structures. He had charge of all the principal monasteries and convents of Florence, and of many private houses both within and without the city. At length, when nearly eighty-three, and in possession of all his faculties, he passed to a better life in 1543, leaving three sons, Giuliano, Filippo and Domenico, who buried him in S. Lorenzo.

All these sons practised carving and joinery. The second, Giuliano, during his father's life and after, carefully studied architecture, and by the favour of Duke Cosimo he succeeded to Baccio's place at the work of S. Maria del Fiore, not only taking up what his father had begun, but all the building left unfinished at his death. At that time M. Baldassarre Turini had to set up a picture by Raphael in the principal church of Pescia, of which he was provost, and for this, comprising a

[1] 1524-7.

stone ornamentation, as well as an entire chapel and a tomb, Giuliano made designs and models, and restored M. Baldassarre's house at Pescia with all its conveniences. At Montuoghi, outside Florence, he built a very ornate house next the church for M. Francesco Campana, chief secretary in succession of Dukes Alessandro and Cosimo, with a beautiful view of all Florence and the surrounding plain. At Colle, Campana's native place, a convenient and beautiful house was built by Giuliano, who soon after began a magnificent palace for M. Ugolino Grifoni, lord of Altopascio, at S. Miniato al Tedesco. For Ser. Giovanni Conti, one of the secretaries of Duke Cosimo, he decorated his house in Florence, although in making the two windows looking on the street Giuliano departed from his usual manner, breaking the front up with projections, brackets and interruptions which approach more closely to the German style than to the true antique and the good modern. Architecture indeed should be virile, solid and simple, to be afterwards enriched with the grace of design and varied composition, which must not deviate too greatly from its order or the purpose of the designer.

When Baccio Bandinello returned from Rome, where he had finished the tombs of Leo and Clement, he persuaded the young Duke Cosimo to decorate one end of the great hall of the palace, with columns and niches and rich marble statues, and with marble and macigno windows looking out on to the piazza. The duke decided upon the work, and Bandinello began a design, but finding, as related in the Life of Cronaca, that the hall was out of the square, and having never practised architecture, which he despised, laughing at its professors, he was forced to show his designs to Giuliano and ask his advice. In this way all the masons and carvers of Florence were set to work, and the building was begun, Bandinello, by Giuliano's advice, deciding to follow the walls. Thus it was necessary to make all the stones of irregular shape, doing them with the pifferello, an instrument of irregular sides, rendering the work so awkward that it became difficult to make it fit the rest, as is related in Bandinello's Life. This would not have occurred if Bandinello had been as conversant with architecture as he was with sculpture. The great niches towards the front are dwarfed, even the middle one suffering. After the work had been carried on for ten years, it was put aside, and so it has been left for some time. It is true that the cornice stones and columns, whether of quarried stones or marble, were carefully cut under Giuliano's direction, and so well built that the joints are invisible, so that Giuliano deserves the greatest praise. The work was finished in five months with an addition by Giorgio Vasari of Arezzo.

Meanwhile Giuliano and his brothers maintained their workshop and busied themselves with many things, including the pavement of S. Maria del Fiore. Being architect and director here, he was asked by Bandinello to make plans and wooden models for some figures and other ornaments for the high altar of that church. Giuliano, being an amiable man, readily agreed, for he loved architecture as much as Bandinello despised it, and besides, Bandinello promised him great profit and honour. Accordingly he began the model, following the simple arrangement of Brunellesco, only making it richer, doubling the arch above with columns. The model with many designs being taken by Bandinello to Duke Cosimo, his excellency royally decided[1] to do not only the altar but the marble ornamentation about the choir with eight sides, following the old disposition, and richly decorated. This was subsequently done in a style befitting the grandeur and magnificence of the church. Thus Giuliano, assisted by Bandinello, began the choir without changing anything but the principal entrance opposite the altar, which he wished to have the same arch and decoration as the altar. He made two similar arches, forming a cross with the entrance and the altar, to serve two pulpits, like the old ones, the music and other requirements of the altar and choir. About the choir Giuliano made an octagonal Ionic order, half filling each corner with a pilaster, and one on each face. The pilasters diminished towards the centre, being curved and narrow inside, and sharp and broad on the outside, a device not greatly admired by the judicious. If Bandinello did not appreciate or understand architecture, he ought in such a place and in so costly a work to have obtained the best advice among his contemporaries. Giuliano should be excused, because he did what he knew, and that was not a little, although it is only too true that those who do not possess design or great invention are always poor in grace, perfection and judgment in great architectural compositions. Giuliano made a wooden bed in walnut for Filippo Strozzi, which is now at Città di Castello, in the house of the heirs of Sig. Alessandro Vitelli. He also did a rich frame for a picture of Giorgio Vasari for the high altar of the abbey of Camaldoli in Casentino, from Giorgio's design. In the church of S. Agostino of Monte Sansavino he did another carved frame for a large panel

[1] In 1555.

of Giorgio. In the Camaldolite abbey of Classi at Ravenna he did yet another frame for a panel of Vasari, and for the monks of the abbey of S. Fiore, at Arezzo, he did the setting for the paintings by Giorgio in their refectory. Behind the high altar of the Vescovado there he made a beautiful walnut wood choir,[1] from Giorgio's design, where they had to bring the altar forward. Shortly before his death he made the rich and beautiful ciborium for the Sacrament over the high altar of the Nunziata, and the two wooden angels on either side. It was his last work, as he died in 1555.

His brother Domenico possessed equal judgment, and in addition to much wood-carving, he showed himself a skilful architect in the house he made in the via de' Servi, from the design of Bastiano da Montaguto, which also contains much of his woodwork. For Agostino del Nero he made a fine corner-piece on the Piazza de' Mozzi, and a beautiful terrace for the houses of the Nasi begun by his father Baccio. If he had not died so soon, it is thought he would have far surpassed his father and his brother Giuliano.

VALERIO VINCENTINO, GIOVANNI DA CASTEL BOLOGNESE, MATTEO DAL NASARO, of Verona, and other excellent Engravers of cameos and gems.

(1468–1546; 1496–1553; ?–?1548)

SINCE the Greeks were so divine in engraving Oriental stones and made perfect cameos, I have thought it proper to mention their imitators in our own age; although none of the moderns have surpassed them in delicacy and design, unless it be those whom I am about to mention. Before I begin, I will say a few words on the art of carving hard stones and gems, which was lost after the fall of Greece and Rome. At Rome, cameos, the sardonyx and other fine intaglios are found daily among the ruins. For many years no one of any account studied the art, and so far as is known no progress was made until the time of Martin V. and Paul II., after which there was a steady advance, so that Lorenzo de' Medici the Magnificent, who was very fond of intaglios, and his son Piero, collected a great quantity engraved

[1] In 1554.

in various fashions, especially of chalcedony and cornelian. This gave an impulse to the art in that city, and many masters arrived there from various countries, who, besides setting stones, could engrave them marvellously. Through Lorenzo's instrumentality, a young Florentine called Giovanni delle Corniole learned this art, earning his name for his excellent workmanship, testified by his countless works, great and small, but especially a large one with the portrait of Frà Girolamo Savonarola,[1] the idol of Florence for his preaching.

He had a rival, Domenico de' Cammei of Milan, who hollowed out a large portrait of Duke Ludovico il Moro in a ruby larger than a Julius, one of the best modern intaglios produced. The art advanced under Leo X. by the abilities of Piermaria da Pescia, a great imitator of the antique. His rival, Michelino, was of equal excellence, and considered a graceful master. He prepared the way for the difficult intaglios used for seals in which the use of wax is necessary from time to time, to see what one is doing, rendering possible the beautiful works of Giovanni da Castel Bolognese, Valerio Vincentino, Matteo dal Nasaro and others. Giovanni, during three years that he spent with Alfonso, Duke of Ferrara, did many small things for him which I need not mention. His first larger work was the action of Bastia[2] engraved in a crystal and of great beauty. In steel he engraved the duke's portrait for medals, with a Christ taken by the multitudes on the reverse. Going afterwards to Rome and being stimulated by Giovio, he had the opportunity of making the portrait of Clement VII., by means of the Cardinals Ippolito de' Medici and Giovanni Salviati, with Joseph declaring himself to his brethren on the reverse. For this His Holiness rewarded him with the office of a Mazza, which he sold for 200 crowns in the time of Paul III. For Clement he made the four Evangelists in four round crystals, which were much admired, and secured him the friendship of many prelates, notably the Cardinals Salvati and Medici referred to, the latter being the patron of all men of ability. Giovanni did a steel medal of Ippolito, and in crystal the presentation of the wife of Darius to Alexander the Great. When Charles V. came to be crowned at Bologna Giovanni made his portrait on steel, and struck a gold medal which he took to the emperor, who gave him 100

---

[1] Now in the Uffizi. His name signifies Giovanni of the Cornelians.
[2] La Bastia di Geniolo near Ferrara. Taken by the Spaniards and retaken by the Duke of Ferrara the same day, the 31 Dec., 1511. Celebrated by Ariosto, *Orlando Furioso*, Canto XLII. stanzas 3-5.

gold doubles and invited him to Spain. He refused, saying that he could not leave the service of Clement and Cardinal Ippolito, for whom he had begun some things. On returning to Rome Giovanni did the Rape of the Sabines for Ippolito, a very beautiful thing. The cardinal heaped favours upon him, and when he left for France, accompanied by lords and nobles, he turned to Giovanni, and taking from his neck a small chain, by which a cameo was attached alone worth 600 crowns, gave it to him, telling him to keep it until his return. On the cardinals's death the cameo came into the hands of Cardinal Farnese, for whom Giovanni did many things in crystal, notably a crucifix with God the Father above, the Virgin, St. John and the Magdalen at the foot. In a triangle at the foot of the cross he did three scenes of the Passion, one on each angle. For two silver candelabra he did six circles in crystal: the centurion praying Christ to heal his son; the pool of Bethesda; the Transfiguration; the miracle of the five loaves and two fishes; the driving of the money-changers from the Temple; and the resurrection of Lazarus, all of rare beauty.

Being desirous of having a rich silver shrine, Cardinal Farnese entrusted the work to Marino, a goldsmith of Florence, mentioned elsewhere, and employed Giovanni to fill the spaces with crystals. He occupied them with scenes in marble in half-relief. He made his silver figures and ornaments with great diligence, producing a work of unequalled perfection. There are some ovals on which he has carved with marvellous art the chase of Meleager and the Calydonian boar; the Bacchantæ and a naval battle; the combat of Hercules with the Amazons, and other fancies of the cardinal, Perino del Vaga and other masters being employed to make the designs. In a crystal he afterwards did the capture of the Goletta, and in another the Turkish war. For the same cardinal he carved in crystal a Nativity, Christ in the Garden taken by the Jews, led before Annas, Herod and Pilate, scourged and crowned with thorns, bearing the cross, crucified and raised again, a work of great beauty executed with astonishing rapidity. From a design by Michelagnolo for the Cardinal de' Medici of a vulture eating the heart of a Tityus, Giovanni carved a lovely crystal, and from another design of Buonarotto he did a Phæthon driving the horses of the Sun and falling into the Po, his weeping sisters being converted into trees. He made portraits of Margarita of Austria, daughter of the Emperor Charles V. and wife of Duke Alessandro de' Medici and then of Duke Ottavio Farnese, in competition with

Valerio Vincentino. For these works Cardinal Farnese rewarded
him with the office of a Janissary, from which he drew a good
sum of money, and he received many favours from that prelate.
The cardinal never passed the commodious house which Giovanni
had built for himself at Faenza without going to stay there.
Giovanni went there to rest from his work and made it his
regular abode. On the death of his first wife, who was childless,
he took a second, who bore him two boys and a girl, and as he
possessed an income of more than 400 crowns, he lived content
to the age of sixty, when he rendered his soul to God on
Whitsunday 1555.

Matteo dal Nassaro, born at Verona, his father, Jacopo dal
Nassaro, being a shoemaker, studied both design and music
in his early childhood, having as masters in the latter Marco
Carra and Il Tromboncino of Verona, who were then in the
service of the Marquis of Mantua. In carving he was much
assisted by two Veronese of good family; one was Niccolo
Avanzi, who did cameos, cornelians and other stones privately
at Rome, which were sent to various princes. Some remember
a lapis lazuli of his, three fingers across, of a Nativity containing many figures, sold to the Duchess of Urbino as a rarity.
The other was Galeazzo Mondella, who designed beautifully,
besides being an engraver of gems. From these two Matteo
learned all he knew. A fine piece of jasper coming into his
hands, he carved on it a Deposition from the Cross, making
the red spots of the stone serve as blood, thus winning great
commendation. This jasper was sold to the Marchioness Isabella
da Este. Proceeding to France with many of his works to obtain
an introduction to the court of Francis I., he was presented to
the king, who valued all men of genius. After accepting many
of his intaglios, the king took him into his service, providing
him with a good pension, and not valuing him less as a good
musician, for he performed beautifully on the lute, than as a
carver of gems. There is no greater incentive to ability than the
rewards bestowed by princes and nobles in the way the illustrious
house of the Medici has always signalised itself as well as the
magnanimous King Francis. Matteo therefore did many rare
things for the king and for all the noblest lords and barons of
the court, almost all employing him, as cameos and similar
gems were much worn in caps and at the throat. For the high
altar of the king's chapel he did a panel full of gold figures,
some in full and some in half-relief, with many jewels distributed
about it. He also engraved many crystals, squeezes of which

may be seen in several places, but chiefly at Verona, where there are some excellent planets, and Venus with a Cupid turning his back, of unsurpassable beauty. In a fine chalcedony found in a river he engraved a head of a Deianira in the lion's skin, employing a red vein in the stone in the inside of the lion's skin so finely that it looked newly flayed. On another mark he arranged the hairs, and the face and breast on the white. It is now in the possession of the King of France, while Matteo's pupil, Zoppo, a goldsmith, has a squeeze at Verona. Matteo was a liberal and spirited man, so that he would rather give away his works than sell them cheaply. Thus, having done a cameo for a baron of importance, and being offered a wretched sum, he begged him to accept it as a gift. But as the baron declined, and still offered his miserable payment, Matteo became angry, and smashed the gem then and there with a hammer. For the same king Matteo did many drawings for arras, and in conformity with the king's wish he went with them to Flanders, remaining there while they were being woven in silk and gold. When they were brought to France they were considered most beautiful. Like nearly everyone, Matteo ultimately returned home, bringing with him several curiosities, notably woven material of Flanders, beautifully worked, which are still preserved at Verona in memory of him by Signor Luigi and Sig. Girolamo Stoppi. At Verona Matteo lived in a cave under a rock, over the garden of the Jesuits, which, besides being cool in summer and warm in winter, possesses a beautiful view. But he could not enjoy this house of his fancy as he desired, because, when King Francis was released from prison,[1] he sent a post to recall him to France and pay him his pension for his time at Verona. When he returned he was made master of the mint. Accordingly he took a wife and settled down in France, where the king was, and had some children, but so unlike him that they caused him little gratification. He was a gentle and courteous man, cordially welcoming all who were staying in France, not only Veronese, but all Lombards. His great friend there was Paulo Emilio of Verona, who wrote French history in Latin. Matteo had many pupils, among others a Veronese, brother of Domenico Brusciasorzi, his two nephews, who went to Flanders, and many others, Italian and French, whom I need not mention. He died not long after King Francis.

I now come to the excellent Valerio Vincentino.[2] He did quantities of intaglios, large and small, with incredible delicacy

[1] In March 1526.   [2] Valerio Belli of Vicenza.

and ease, and if Nature had made him as excellent in design as he was diligent and patient in execution, he would have far surpassed the ancients, whom he equalled. However, he used the designs of others, or copied ancient intaglios. For Pope Clement VII. he did a crystal casket,[1] executed with wonderful mastery, for which he received 2000 gold ducats. In the crystals he engraved the Crucifixion from designs by others. The casket was afterwards presented by Pope Clement to King Francis at Marseilles, as he was going to marry his niece to the Duke of Orleans, afterwards King Henry. For the same Pope Valerio did some lovely Peaces, a marvellous crystal cross, and dies for money with Clement's portrait, the reverses being very handsome. This led to a great increase in the professors of the art, so that the number had become marvellous before the sack of Rome, whither they flocked from Milan and other places. Valerio made the medals of twelve emperors with their reverses, copied from the antique but more beautiful, and numerous Greek medals. He carved so many crystals that the goldsmiths' shops and all the world are full of squeezes of them, whether of scenes, figures or heads. His skill was so extraordinary that no one ever produced more than he in that trade. For Pope Clement he also did numerous crystal vases, some being given to various princes and some placed in S. Lorenzo in Florence, with vases from the Medici palace, formerly the property of Lorenzo de' Medici the elder, and other members of that illustrious house, to preserve the relics of the numerous saints presented by Clement to the Church. The vases are of extraordinary variety, of sardonyx, agate, amethyst, lapis lazuli, crystals, cornelians, and others of inestimable value and beauty. For Pope Paul III. Valerio did a cross and two candelabra of crystal, carving in them the Crucifixion, introducing such a number of large and small stones that it would take too long to record them. Cardinal Farnese possessed many things by his hand, for he did not leave fewer works than Giovanni. At the age of seventy-eight he performed miracles with his eyes and hands, and taught the art to a daughter of his who worked very well. He was utterly regardless of expense in procuring ancient and modern squeezes and modern antiquities, and paintings and designs by great masters, so that his house at Verona was full of such things and a marvel. We see indeed that a man who really loves ability never stops short at the threshold, and so he wins praise in life and immortality after

[1] In 1532; now in the Uffizi (Cabinet of Gems).

death. Valerio was richly rewarded for his labours, receiving numerous offices and benefits from the princes whom he served, so that his successors were enabled to maintain an honourable position. When no longer able to work, and worn out by old age, he rendered his soul to God in 1546.

Somewhat earlier Il Marmita lived in Parma, who, after studying painting for a while, turned to intaglio, closely imitating the ancients. Many beautiful works of his exist. He taught the art to his son Ludovico, who long remained at Rome with Cardinal Giovanni de' Salviati, for whom he did four oval crystals of great excellence, carved with figures and set in a beautiful silver casket, which was given to Leonora di Toledo, Duchess of Florence. Among many other things he did a fine head of Socrates on a cameo, and he was very skilful in imitating ancient medals, an occupation which brought him much profit.

In Florence, Domenico di Polo was an excellent master of engraving. He studied under Giovanni delle Corniole, and in our own day made a divine portrait of Duke Alessandro de' Medici, for steel dies and beautiful medals, the reverse being Florence. He also made a portrait of Duke Cosimo the year he was elected to the government of Florence, with the sign of Capricorn on the reverse. He did many other intaglios of small things which I need not mention, and died aged sixty-five.

Domenico, Valerio, Marmita and Giovanni da Castel Bolognese being all dead, many remained who far surpassed them. In Venice, Luigi Anichini of Ferrara was remarkable for his delicate engraving. But the foremost in grace, perfection and universality was Alessandro Cesari,[1] called Il Greco, who has made such beautiful things in cameos and rounds, both raised and hollowed, and has chiselled steel dies, so fine in every detail, that it is impossible to imagine better. Those who wish to admire his miracles should examine a medal of Pope Paul III., who seems alive, and on the reverse Alexander the Great throwing himself at the feet of the high priest of Jerusalem, figures which excite amazement and cannot be surpassed. When Michelagnolo saw them in the presence of Giorgio Vasari, he said that the death hour of the art had come, for it could not go farther. For Pope Julius III. Cesari made the medal of 1550, the reverse representing the prisoners who were anciently released at a time of Jubilee, a beautiful and rare work. For many years he was kept busy in making dies and portraits

[1] Cesati.

for the mint at Rome. He portrayed Pierluigi Farnese, Duke of Castro, Duke Ottavio his son, and for Cardinal Farnese did his portrait on a medal, a gold head on a silver ground. For this cardinal he made a head of King Henry of France, larger than a Julius, hollowed in a cornelian, one of the best modern intaglios for design, grace, excellence and finish. He also carved many cameos, a nude woman being perfect. So are others with a lion, an infant, and many small ones which I need not mention. But the best of all was the head of Phocion the Athenian, a miraculous work, and the best cameo to be seen.

Gio. Antonio de' Rossi of Milan also carves cameos, and is an excellent master. Among many others, both large and small, he did a large cameo for Duke Cosimo, a third of a braccia each way, containing two half-length figures, the duke himself and the Duchess Leonora, each holding a circle containing Florence. Near them are portraits of Prince don Francesco, Don Giovanni the cardinal, Don Garzia, Don Ernando, Don Pietro, Donna Isabella and Donna Lucrezia, their children, the work being stupendous, surpassing all his smaller works, so that I will not mention them, for they may be seen.

Cosimo da Trezzo did many works worthy of this profession, and his merits have earned him a position with King Philip of Spain, who rewards and honours his ability. For portraits he has no equal, and in other respects he is extraordinarily clever. I need not say much of Fillipo Negrolo of Milan, who has carved arms with leaves and figures, as his published copper engravings have won him a great reputation. Gasparo and Girolamo Misuroni of Milan made beautiful crystal vases and cups, notably two for Duke Cosimo, which are marvellous. From a piece of *Elitropia* they made a vessel of marvellous size, wonderfully carved, as well as a great and admirable vase of lapis lazuli. Jacopo da Trezzo does the like in Milan, having rendered the art very beautiful and easy. I could tell of many more who have done medals, heads and reverses, surpassing the ancients, such as Benvenuto Cellini, who, when acting as goldsmith at Rome under Pope Clement, made two medals with a life-like portrait of Clement, and on the reverse Peace, who has bound Fury and is burning her arms, while the other contains Moses striking the rock and making water flow for the thirsty people, a triumph of his art, as were the coins and medals which he did for Duke Alessandro in Florence. I speak elsewhere of the knight Lione Aretino, who has done the like, and of the works which he is still producing.

Pietro Paolo Galeotto of Rome made medals for Duke Cosimo with his portrait, and dies for money and marquetry-work, imitating the processes of Maestro Salvestro, who was an excellent master of the profession at Rome and did marvellous things. Pastorino da Siena excelled in heads, and may be said to have made the portrait of every man of importance, both great lords and artists. He found a stucco for making portraits, which took natural colours, with the tints of beard, hair and flesh, giving a life-like appearance. But his steel things are much more admirable, and he made excellent metal dies. It would take too long to speak of all those who make portraits on medals and in wax, as in these days every goldsmith does some and many nobles practise the art; for example Gio Battista Sozzini at Siena, Il Rosso de' Giugni at Florence, and countless others. In conclusion, I turn to the engravers on steel, such as Girolamo Fagiuoli of Bologna, who did copper things, and in Florence Domenico Poggini, who makes dies for the mint with the medals of Duke Cosimo, and does marble statues, imitating as far as possible the distinguished men of the profession.

MARCANTONIO BOLOGNESE[1] and other Engravers
(1487 – 1539)

THE treatise on the theory of painting contains little with regard to copper engraving, as it sufficed then to explain the method of engraving silver with the burin, which is a square iron, cut diagonally, with a fine point, and I will take this opportunity to say what I consider to be enough on the subject in connection with this Life. Engraving was invented by Maso Finiguerra of Florence about 1460. Of every work engraved by him in silver to be filled with niello, he took an impression in clay on which he poured liquid sulphur, so that it was blackened by the fumes and showed in oil the subject engraved on the silver. He did the like with a damp sheet with the same tint, going over it with a round cylinder, which made it look like a pen-and-ink drawing. He was followed by Baccio Baldini,[2] goldsmith of Florence, who, not having much design, copied the drawings of Sandro Botticello. The process becoming known to Andrea Mantegna at Rome,

[1] Marcantonio Raimondi.   [2] 1436–1515.

he began to engrave many of his works, as was said in his Life. The invention then passed to Flanders, and one Martin[1] at Antwerp, considered an excellent painter, did a great many engravings and sent them to Italy, all signed M. C.[2] The first were the five foolish virgins with their lamps out, and the five prudent ones with their lamps lighted; a Christ on the cross, with St. John at his feet, so well done that Gherardo, a Florentine illuminator, began to copy it with the burin, and proved very successful, but went no farther, as he did not live long. Martin then issued the four Evangelists, and small sheets of Christ and the Apostles, Veronica with six saints, and the arms of some German lords supported by nude and draped men and women. He also issued St. George slaying the serpent, Christ before Pilate—who washes his hands—and the Passing of the Virgin, rather large, with all the Apostles, this being one of his best achievements. In another he did St. Anthony beaten by devils, and carried into the air by a swarm of them, of the most curious forms imaginable, a sheet which so pleased Michelagnolo when young that he began to colour it.

Martin was followed by Albert Dürer[3] at Antwerp, who displayed more design, better judgment and finer inventions, seeking to imitate life and to approach the Italian style, which he highly esteemed. While quite young he did many things which were considered as beautiful as those of Martin. He engraved them with his own hand and signed his name. In 1503 he issued a small Madonna, surpassing both Martin and himself. He then did horses, two on a sheet, drawn from life and very beautiful. The next was the prodigal son, kneeling with his hands crossed, looking up, while the swine are feeding in a trough, and fine old German cottages embellish the landscape. He did a small St. Sebastian, with his arms bound above his head, and a Madonna and Child, with a window behind, unsurpassed for a small work. He did a Flemish woman on horseback with a squire on foot. On copper and larger he did a nymph carried off by a marine monster, while other nymphs are bathing. Of the same size he did a Diana chastising a nymph, who has fled to a satyr for refuge, done with a masterly delicacy, attaining the perfection and goal of his art, and intended to show that he understood the nude. Though these masters were praised in their own country, they are only commended in

1 Martin Schongauer, c. 1430-91.
2 This signature is that of Martin van Cleef.
3 1471-1528; he was born at Nürnberg.

Italy for their diligent engraving. I believe that Albert could not have done better, considering that he did not enjoy proper advantages, and was compelled to draw his own pupils when he did nudes. These formed bad models, like most Germans, though they appear fine men enough when clothed. He did many costumes of Flemish peasants, in various engravings, who are playing the bagpipes and dancing, some selling fowls and so forth. One sleeps in a hot bath while Venus tempts him in a dream, a Cupid on stilts plays about him and the devil blows into his ear with the bellows. He did two different St. Christophers carrying the Christ-child, the polished hairs and other parts being beautifully executed. Finding that copper engraving took so long, and having a quantity of drawings, Albert began to engrave on wood, which offers a much wider scope to men of invention. He issued two small wood-engravings in 1510, one of the Beheading of St. John, the other his head presented on a charger to Herod. In others he did St. Christopher, St. Sixtus the Pope, St. Stephen and St. Laurence. Finding this much easier than copper engraving, he did a Mass of St. Gregory, with his deacon and sub-deacon. Still further encouraged, he did a part of a Passion of Christ on a large sheet in 1510, completing four pieces and intending to do the rest: the Last Supper, the Seizure in the Garden, the Descent into Limbo to rescue the holy Fathers, and the Resurrection. He did a beautiful oil-painting of the second subject, now in Florence, owned by Sig. Bernardetto de' Medici. Although the remaining eight parts were printed with his signature, I do not think they can be his, as they are badly executed and do not resemble his style in heads, draperies or anything. They were probably done by others after his death for the sake of gain, without a thought for his reputation. In 1511 he did the life of the Virgin in twenty sheets, of the same size, incomparable for invention, composition, perspective, buildings, costumes, and young and old heads. If this rare, diligent and versatile man had been born in Tuscany instead of Flanders, and could have studied the things of Rome as we have done, he would have been the best painter of our land, as he was the most eminent artist whom the Flemings have ever produced. The same year he endeavoured on fifteen sheets to represent the tremendous vision of St. John on the isle of Patmos, described in the Apocalypse. Accordingly he set to work, and his fantastic imagination being well adapted to such a subject, he represented heavenly and earthly things so well, and with such variety in the animals and monsters, that it has been a great light to many of our artists, who have copied them frequently. By the same hand is a naked Christ surrounded by the mysteries of His Passion, and weeping for our sins with His hands to His face, very admirably executed, though small. His ability and courage increasing from finding that his things were valued, Albert did some copper engravings which amazed the world. On a half sheet he did a Melancholia surrounded by all the instruments which render men melancholy, and nothing could be more delicately carved with the burin. On a small sheet he did three different women, most delicately engraved. But it would take too long to enumerate all Albert's works. For the present I will say that, having designed and engraved a Crucifixion in thirty-six plates, he arranged with Marcantonio of Bologna to publish them.[1] Their appearance in Venice gave an extraordinary impulse to engraving in Italy, as will be related below.

While Francesco Francia was painting at Bologna, one of the best of his pupils was a youth called Marcantonio, who, from remaining many years with his master, acquired the cognomen de' Franci. Being a better designer than his master and skilful in manipulating the burin, he made borders in niello of great beauty, those things being much in use. Desiring afterwards to go into the world and examine various things and the methods of other artists, he was permitted by Francia to go to Venice, where he was well received by the artists of the city. Meeting some Flemings with wood and copper engravings of Albert Dürer on the Piazza S. Marco, he was amazed at Albert's methods and style, and spent all the money he had brought from Bologna on those sheets, acquiring among other things the Passion of Christ engraved on thirty-six pieces of wood, quarto size, just printed by Albert, beginning with the sin of Adam and the expulsion from Paradise, and continuing to the sending of the Holy Spirit. Feeling what honour and profit might be acquired by that art in Italy, Marcantonio determined to study it diligently and carefully. He began by imitating the things of Albert, studying all the prints which he had bought, which, for their novelty and beauty, were sought after by everyone. Having engraved on copper, as thick as the wood used by Albert, all the Passion and life of Christ in thirty-six sheets, with the A. D. with which Albert signed his works, Marcantonio succeeded in making them so like that no one could tell the difference who did not know, and they were sold and bought as

[1] The Melancholia belongs to 1514, the Crucifixion to 1511.

Albert's works. On being informed of this, one of the counterfeits being sent to Flanders, Albert flew into such a rage that he left Flanders and came to Venice, and complained of Marcantonio to the Signoria. But all he obtained was that Marcantonio should no longer use his signature. Marcantonio next went to Rome and devoted himself to design, while Albert, on returning to Flanders, found another rival who had begun to make many delicate engravings. This was Lucas of Holland,[1] who, although unequal to Albert in design, was his peer with the burin. Among his numerous works, the first, in 1509, were two circular prints, one of Christ bearing the cross, and the other a Crucifixion. He afterwards issued a Sampson, David on horseback, and Peter Martyr with his persecutors. He next did a copper engraving of David playing before Saul. Not long after he had so far progressed as to make a large and delicate engraving of Virgil hung out of a window in a basket, with some heads and figures, which led to Albert issuing some printed sheets of incomparable excellence. Wishing to show his full ability, he made an armed man on horseback to represent human strength, beautifully finished, with lustrous armour, and the glossy black coat of the horse, a difficult achievement in drawing. Near the man is Death, an hour-glass in his hand, and the devil behind. There is also a hairy dog, most delicately done. In 1512 Albert issued sixteen small scenes in copper engraving of the Passion of Christ, of the utmost beauty, sweetness and grace, the figures standing out in high relief.

Incited by this competition, Lucas did twelve similar pieces of great beauty, but not so well engraved or designed. He also did a St. George comforting the girl who weeps because she is to be devoured by the serpent, a Solomon worshipping idols, the Baptism of Christ, Pyramus and Thisbe, Ahasuerus and Queen Esther kneeling. On the other hand, Albert, being determined not to be surpassed by Lucas in either the quantity or the quality of his work, did a nude figure on the clouds, and Temperance with wonderful wings and a gold cup in her hands, a bridle and a minute landscape. By her is St. Eustace kneeling before the stag with the crucifix between its horns, a marvellous sheet, especially for some fine dogs in various attitudes, which could not be surpassed. Among the children which he did for ornaments of arms and devices, Albert made some holding a shield on which is a death's head and a cock for a crest, the feathers of which are most finely wrought. Finally, he issued a St. Jerome writing,

[1] Lucas van Leyden, born 1494.

in his cardinal's hat, the sleeping lion at his feet, in a room with
glass windows, through which the sun's rays are reflected to
where the saint is writing, done with marvellous truth. There
also are books, clocks, writings and all the other articles of that
profession. Soon after, in 1523, he did a Christ with the twelve
Apostles, almost his last work. Many portraits by him were
printed, among them Erasmus of Rotterdam, Albert of Branden-
burg, the cardinal, elector of the Empire, and one of himself.
Although he engraved so much he did not abandon painting,
but continued to do panels, canvases and other valuable
things. He further left works on engraving, painting, perspective and architecture.

But to return to engravings. Albert's works incited Lucas
to renewed efforts, and he next did four copper engravings of
the acts of Joseph, the four Evangelists, the angels appearing
to Abraham in the plain of Mamre, Susannah at the bath, David
praying, Mordecai triumphing on horseback, Lot intoxicated by
his daughters, the creation of Adam and Eve, the command of
God not to eat the apple, Cain killing Abel, all issued in 1529.[1]
But the thing that most increased Lucas's fame was a large
sheet of the Crucifixion and an *Ecce Homo*, containing a great
number of figures and much valued. So also is a Conversion of
St. Paul, and his being taken to Damascus. These things secure
for Lucas a place among the best engravers with the burin. His
compositions are very right, so clear and free from confusion,
that it seems as if his ideas could not be expressed otherwise,
and more in conformity with the rules of art than Albert's. He
also showed discretion, the more distant objects gradually fading
from sight as they do in nature, and they are very softly toned,
considerations which have opened the eyes of many painters. He
made many small prints, various Madonnas, the twelve Apostles
with Christ, numerous saints, arms, crests and the like. Very fine
is a peasant having a tooth out, in such great pain that he is not
aware a woman is emptying his purse. All these things of Albert
and Lucas have induced numerous Flemings and Germans to
have similar beautiful works printed. To return to Marcantonio.
Arrived at Rome, he made a beautiful copper engraving of
a drawing of Raphael, representing Lucretia killing herself,
executed with such finish and beauty that, when it was shown
to Raphael, he was disposed to issue some prints himself from
his own designs. An earlier design by Raphael of the Judgment

[1] This is wrong: the Joseph belongs to 1512, the Susannah to 1508
the Mordecai to 1515 and the Lot to 1530.

of Paris into which he had capriciously introduced the chariot
of the sun, wood, water and river nymphs, vessels, prows and
other things was boldly engraved by Marcantonio, to the
wonder of Rome. He then did the drawing of the Innocents,
with magnificent nudes, women and children; the Neptune
with small scenes of Æneas about it, the beautiful Rape of
Helen, also designed by Raphael, and the Death of St. Felicita
in boiling oil, her children being decapitated, all of which
brought Marcantonio such fame that his things were more
valued than those of the Flemings for their good design, and
the merchants found them very profitable.

For many years Raphael had kept a boy called Il Baviera to
mix his colours, and, as he was intelligent, Raphael directed that
Marcantonio should engrave and Il Baviera print that all the
scenes might be finished, to be sold, wholesale or retail to all
who might want them. In this way countless prints were made
and considerable profit realised, all the sheets being marked
R. S. for Raphael Sanzio and M. F. for Marcantonio. The works
were Venus embraced by Love, drawn by Raphael; God blessing
the seed of Abraham, with a maid and two children; then all
the medallions drawn by Raphael in the chamber of the papal
chamber; Calliope with her horn; Prudence and Justice; a small
drawing of the Mount Parnassus with Apollo, the Muses and
Poets; Æneas carrying Anchises while Troy burns, this being a
design of Raphael for a picture; they next printed Raphael's
Galatea on a car drawn by dolphins, with Tritons carrying off
a nymph. This done, he did many single figures of Raphael in
copper, Apollo with the lyre, Love offering an olive branch to
Peace, the three Theological Virtues and the four moral ones;
of the same size, Christ and the twelve Apostles, and on a half-
sheet the Madonna painted by Raphael in the Araceli picture,
and the one that went to S. Domenico at Naples, with the
Virgin, St. Jerome, Raphael and Tobias, and a small sheet of the
Virgin embracing a half-clothed Christ as she sits on a chair.
Many other Madonnas painted by Raphael were similarly done.
He next engraved a youthful St. John the Baptist seated in the
desert, and then the St. Cecilia done by Raphael for S. Giovanni
in Monte, with other saints, a much-admired sheet. Raphael
having made cartoons for the arras of the Pope's chapel, afterwards woven in silk and gold, with stories of St. Peter, St. Paul
and St. Stephen, Marcantionio engraved the preaching of St.
Paul, the stoning of St. Stephen and the healing of the blind man,
prints equally beautiful, for Raphael's invention and grace of

design and the finished engraving of Marcantonio which is indeed unsurpassable. He next engraved a fine Deposition from the Cross, after Raphael's, with a marvellous fainting Virgin, and not long after he did Raphael's picture of Christ bearing the cross, which was sent to Palermo, and is a very fine print, and a design by Raphael of Christ in the air with the Virgin, St. John the Baptist, and St. Catherine kneeling and St. Paul standing, a large and beautiful print. But this, like the others, was spoilt by too many impressions, and it was carried away by the Germans in the sack of Rome. He engraved in profile the portrait of Pope Clement VII., clean shaven, as on a medal, and Charles V. the Emperor as a young man, and subsequently when older; as well as Ferdinand, King of the Romans, afterwards emperor. He made the portrait at Rome of M. Pietro Aretino, the famous poet, and this was his finest work. Not long after he did the twelve emperors of antiquity on medals, some of which Raphael sent to Flanders to Albert Dürer, who greatly praised Marcantonio and sent Raphael his own portrait, considered very good, as well as many other sheets.

Marcantonio's fame being thus grown, and his prints being much valued, many came to him to learn. Among these Marco da Ravenna[1] made great progress, using Raphael's signature, R. S., and Agostino Viniziano, who signed A. V.; these two printed many designs of Raphael, namely a Virgin and the dead Christ, with St. John, the Magdalene, Nicodemus and the other Maries; and another, of larger size, of the Virgin, with arms open, and her eyes turned piously upwards, the Christ lying dead. He did a large Nativity, with shepherds and angels, and God above; and about the cottage he did many vessels, both ancient and modern, and a censer, with perforated top, held by two women. He did a scene of a man transformed into a wolf as he is going to a bed to kill a sleeping man. He then did Alexander presenting a royal crown to Roxana, some cupids flying in the air, and others decking themselves out in Alexander's armour. Agostino and Marco engraved the Last Supper, an Annunciation, both from Raphael's designs, and two scenes of the marriage of Psyche, painted by Raphael not long before. Agostino and Marco between them engraved almost all the things that Raphael ever drew or painted, and paintings of Giulio Romano, copied by them, and they also did the scenes painted by Giulio in the loggia from Raphael's design, whose works they had almost exhausted. Some of their first sheets,

[1] Marco Dente of Ravenna, born 1496.

signed M. R. for Marco Ravignano, and others, A. V. for Agostino
Viniziano, have been repeated by others, such as the Creation,
God making animals, the sacrifice of Cain and Abel and Abel's
death, Abraham sacrificing Isaac, Noah's ark and the Flood, the
animals saved, the passage of the Red Sea, the giving of the laws
from Mount Sinai by Moses, the manna, David killing Goliath,
already engraved by Marcantonio, Solomon building theTemple,
his judgment, the visit of the Queen of Sheba; and from the New
Testament, the Nativity and Resurrection of Christ, the sending
of the Holy Spirit, all printed during Raphael's lifetime. After
his death Marco and Agostino separated, the latter being retained
by Baccio Bandinello, sculptor, of Florence, who employed him
to engrave a skeleton made by him of dried bones, and also a
Cleopatra, both considered very good. Encouraged by this,
Baccio designed and had engraved a Massacre of the Innocents,
one of the largest sheets done up to that time, filled with
draped women, and nude men murdering the innocent children
by Herod's command. Marcantonio meanwhile engraved the
twelve Apostles in various ways, and many saints, of which poor
painters unskilled in design can make use at their need. He also
engraved a nude figure, with a lion at his feet, and a great
banner, filled out by the wind, against the youth's will;
another carrying a pedestal on his back, and a small St. Jerome
regarding a death's head, with one finger in the cavity, an idea
and design of Raphael. He then did Justice, taken from the
chapel arras, and Dawn, drawn by two horses, bridled by the
Hours. In the antique style he did the Three Graces and a scene
of Our Lady mounting the steps of the Temple. Giulio Romano,
whose modesty would not allow anything of his to be printed
during Raphael's life, to avoid the appearance of competition,
after his death got Marcantonio to do two cavalry fights of considerable size and great beauty, and all the legends of Venus,
Apollo and Hyacinth, painted by him in the study at the villa
of M. Baldassarre Turini of Pescia. He also did four scenes of the
Magdalene and the four Evangelists on the vaulting of Trinity
Chapel, erected by a courtezan, though now the property of
M. Agnolo Massimi. He drew and had engraved similarly a fine
ancient sarcophagus from Maiano, now in the court of S. Pietro,
representing a lion hunt and one of the ancient marble bas-
reliefs under the arch of Constantine; and finally numerous
designs of Raphael for the corridors and loggias of the palace,
afterwards engraved again by Tommaso Barlacchi, together
with the hangings done by Raphael for the public consistory.

Giulio next got Marcantonio to engrave twenty of his sheets of the commerce of evil men and women, for each of which M. Pietro Aretino wrote an extremely lewd sonnet, so that I cannot say which is worse, the drawings or the words. This work was strongly condemned by Pope Clement, and if Giulio had not already set out for Mantua, he would have been severely punished. The designs were afterwards found in the most unexpected places, and were finally prohibited, Marcantonio being imprisoned. He would have come off badly had not the Cardinal de' Medici and Baccio Bandinello, who was serving the Pope in Rome, got him released. The gifts of God ought certainly not to be employed, as they so often are, upon such utterly abominable things.

On coming out of prison Marcantonio finished a large sheet for Baccio Bandinello, begun before, full of nudes, of S. Laurence on the gridiron, considered very beautiful, and engraved with great care, although Bandinello complained to the Pope that many faults had been committed. However, Baccio was repaid for his lack of courtesy, for Marcantonio finished it unknown to Baccio, and having heard all, went to the Pope, who was exceedingly fond of designs, and showed him Baccio's original, and then the print, by which the Pope perceived that he had not made any errors, but had corrected many of Baccio's of no small importance, and his engraving was more skilful than Baccio's drawing. So the Pope commended him highly, received him graciously, and would probably have conferred many favours upon him, but the sack of Rome well-nigh reduced him to beggary, as, besides losing everything, he had to ransom himself from the Spaniards. This done, he left Rome never to return, and few things of his subsequent to that time are to be seen. Our art owes much to him for introducing engravings into Italy to the benefit of art and of all men of ability, others following in his steps, as I shall relate.

Agostino Viniziano, mentioned above, came to Florence intending to join Andrea del Sarto, who was considered the best painter in Italy after Raphael. Persuaded by him to have his works engraved, Andrea designed a dead Christ supported by three angels, but as it did not prove so successful as he hoped Andrea would never have anything engraved again. But after his death they issued the Visitation, and St. John baptising, taken from Andrea's scenes painted in grisaille, in the Scalzo at Florence. Marco da Ravenna also worked in company with Agostino, and did many admirable things by himself, to be recognised by his signature. Many who succeeded them have engraved well, so that every province has seen the work of excellent men. Some have had the courage to make wood-engravings that look like pen drawings, a most ingenious and difficult thing. Such a one was Ugo da Carpi,[1] who, though a mediocre painter, was very ingenious in other fantasies. In the thirtieth chapter of the theory[2] he is mentioned as the first to succeed in making two impressions, one for the shadows and the other for colour tints, cutting deep, and leaving the lights so white that they seemed to be done with white lead when printed. In this style he did a design of Raphael, in grisaille, of a sibyl seated reading, and a draped child holding a torch. The success of this encouraged Ugo to make things in three impressions, the first for the shadows, the second for the half-tints, and the third for the lights. This also succeeded in a drawing of Æneas carrying Anchises during the burning of Troy. He then did a Deposition from the Cross, the story of Simon Magus, done by Raphael for the hangings of the chapel, and David slaying Goliath, and the flight of the Philistines, designed by Raphael to be painted on the papal loggia. After that he did many things in grisaille, including a Venus playing with cupids. Being also a painter, he painted in oils, with his finger and other curious tools, not using the brush, a panel at the altar of Volto Santo at Rome. One morning, as I was hearing Mass at the altar with Michelagnolo, I saw the inscription stating that Ugo had done it without the brush, and smilingly pointed it out to him. He laughed and replied, "Better if he had used a brush and done it less badly." This method of wood-engraving discovered by Ugo was adopted by many, who produced numerous beautiful sheets.

After him Baldassare Peruzzi, painter of Siena, did a sheet in grisaille of Hercules driving Avarice laden with gold and silver vessels from Mount Parnassus, the Muses being in fine and varied postures, and Francesco Parmigiano engraved a Diogenes, more beautiful than anything of Ugo. Parmigiano, after explaining the method of engraving with three plates to Antonio di Trento,[3] got him to do a large Decollation of SS. Peter and Paul in grisaille, and then did with two plates only the Tiburtine Sibyl showing Christ and the Virgin to Augustus, and a nude seated with his back turned. In an oval he did a Madonna lying down, and several others, painted after his death by Joannicolo Vincentino. But the finest were made after Parmigiano's death

[1] Born 1486.
[2] i.e. Vasari's own technical introduction to his Lives.
[3] Antonio Fantuzzi, born 1520.

by Domenico Beccafumi of Siena, as will be related at length
in Domenico's Life. His new method of engraving more easily
than with the burin was a most praiseworthy invention, namely
with *acqua forte*, although the things are not so clear. He first
covered the copper with wax, varnish, or oil colour, and traced
the design on this with a sharp point, acid was thrown on the
plate, and ate into the copper, which was then ready for printing.
In this way Francesco Parmigiano did many small things with
much grace, such as a Nativity, a dead Christ lamented by the
Maries, one of the chapel hangings designed by Raphael, and
many others. Battista, a painter of Vicenza, and Battista del
Moro of Verona afterwards did fifty sheets of various landscapes.
In Flanders, Jerome Cock did the Liberal Arts, and in Rome
Frà Bastiano Viniziano did the Visitation of La Pace,[1] and that
of Francesco Salviati of the Misericordia. In Venice the Feast
of Testaccio, as well as many works, were engraved by Battista
Franco, the painter, and other masters.

But to return to simple copper engravings. After Marcantonio
had published his prints Rosso was in Rome, and was persuaded
by Il Baviera to print some of his things. Accordingly he induced
Gian. Jacopo del Caraglio of Verona,[2] who then was a good and
industrious worker, imitating Marcantonio, to do a person with
a skull in its hand and sitting on a serpent, while a swan sings.
This proving successful, he had the Labours of Hercules engraved, the slaying of the Hydra, the fight with Cerberus, the
killing of Cacus, the breaking the bull's horn, the battle of the
Centaurs, Nessus carrying away Deianira, all very successful.
Then Jacopo did Rosso's design of the Pierides, who wished to
compete with the Muses in singing and were turned into magpies.
Then Il Baviera got Rosso to design for a book twenty gods in
niches, with their attributes, Gian. Jacopo engraving them all
with grace and style, and afterwards he did their transformations. Of these Rosso only designed two, because he had a
difference with Il Baviera, who got Perino del Vago to do ten.
Rosso's were the Rape of Proserpine and Philyra transformed
into a horse, both engraved with great diligence and much
valued. Caraglio next began the Rape of the Sabines for Rosso,
which would have been remarkable, but the sack of Rome
prevented its completion, for Rosso went away and all the
prints were lost. It afterwards came into the hands of the
printers, but in a bad state, because in order to gain money
more was engraved than was intended. For Francesco

[1] i.e. the Visitation by Frà Bartolommeo.   [2] Born 1512.

Parmigiano Caraglio engraved a Marriage of the Virgin and
other things of his, and then another Nativity for Titian from a
painting by him. After making many copper engravings Caraglio
began to carve cameos and gems, becoming equally excellent in
this. He then went to the King of Poland, doing jewels and
architecture, and giving up engraving as base work. Receiving
much money from the king, he invested it in the Parmesan in
order that he might enjoy his old age there with his friends
and pupils after his prolonged labours. After him came Lam-
berto Suave,[1] an excellent engraver on copper; he did thirteen
sheets of Christ and the Apostles, perfectly engraved, and they
would have been marvellous if the design had displayed equal
care, diligence and knowledge. We remark the same in a small
sheet of St. Paul writing, and a larger one of the Resurrection
of Lazarus, containing many fine things, notably the cave in
which Lazarus is buried, and the light shed on some figures,
done with beautiful invention. Gio. Battista of Mantua,[2] pupil
of Giulio Romano, has also shown skill in this, doing, among
other things, a Virgin with the moon under her feet and the
Child in her arms, containing some beautiful heads with crests,
and two sheets, one of a captain on foot and one on horseback.
Another sheet of Mars, armed, sitting on a bed, while Venus
suckles a Cupid, possesses many good points. Very charming also
are two large sheets of his of the Burning of Troy, done with
extraordinary invention, design and grace. He signed I. B. M.
No less excellent than any of these was Enea Vico[3] of Parma,
who engraved on copper the Rape of Helen by Rosso, and did
a Vulcan with some cupids forging thunderbolts, while the
Cyclops work, from another design. In another he did Michelagnolo's Leda and an Annunciation designed by Titian, the History
of Judith, painted by Michelagnolo, in the chapel, and the portrait of Duke Cosimo de' Medici when young, in armour, from
the design of Bandinello, the portrait of Bandinello himself,
the combat between Cupid and Apollo in the presence of the
gods. If Enea had been properly treated by Bandinello and had
received recognition for his labours, he would have engraved
many other beautiful things for him. Francesco, pupil of Salviati, an excellent painter, being in Florence, induced Enea to
engrave the large sheet of the Conversion of St. Paul, full of
horses and soldiers, assisted by the liberality of Duke Cosimo,
considered a beautiful thing, which brought great fame to

---

[1] Lambert Suterman of Liège; fl. 1550.
[2] G. B. Ghisi, born about 1500.   [3] Born about 1512.

Enea. He then did the portrait of Sig. Giovanni de' Medici, father of Duke Cosimo, with an ornamentation full of figures. He also engraved the portrait of the Emperor Charles V., with a border made of victories and spoils, for which he received rewards from his majesty and praise from everyone. In another sheet he did the emperor's victory on the Elbe.[1] For Doni he made some heads like medals with beautiful ornaments, Henry, King of France, Cardinal Bembo, M. Ludovico Ariosto, Il Gello of Florence, M. Ludovico Domenichi, Signora Laura Terracina, M. Capriano Morosino and Il Doni. For Don Giulio Clovio, a rare illuminator, he did a St. George on horseback killing the serpent, succeeding remarkably well, as these were practically his first engravings. Being a man of spirit and anxious to make progress, Enea studied antiquity and especially ancient medals, of which he issued several printed books containing the heads of many emperors and their wives, with inscriptions and reverses of all kinds, to delight those who like knowledge and clearness in the representations, for which he deserves great praise. Those who blame him for his books of medals are wrong, because we may well forgive minor slips when we consider his labours and their utility and beauty; his errors, which only arise from bad information or from being too credulous, or from having a different opinion from others, are very excusable, for such errors have been made by Aristotle, Pliny, and many beside. Enea also designed for the general satisfaction and benefit fifty costumes of various nations, namely Italy, France, Spain, Portugal, England, Flanders and other parts of the world, men and women, country and city folk, an ingenious, beautiful and fanciful idea. He also did a tree of all the emperors. At length, after many labours, he now rests under the shadow of Alfonso II., Duke of Ferrara, for whom he has made a genealogical tree of the Marquises of Este. He did many other things, and is still at work, and I have decided to include him among these able men.

Many others have engaged in copper engraving, but have not attained such perfection. However, they have benefited the world, and brought to light many works of great masters, giving those who cannot go to see the original works an opportunity of seeing the various inventions, and showing the ultramontanes many things which they did not know. Although many sheets have suffered by the carelessness of the printers, impelled more by the desire of gain than of honour, yet some are good, as for example the larger design of the Judgment of Michelagnolo

[1] The Battle of Mühlberg, 1547.

for the Pope's chapel, engraved by Giorgio Mantoano,[1] the crucifixion of St. Peter and the Conversion of St. Paul, painted in the Pauline chapel at Rome, and engraved by Gio. Battista de' Cavalieri,[2] who afterwards did copper engravings of St. John the Baptist in meditation, the Deposition from the Cross, painted by Daniello Ricciarelli of Volterra, in the Trinità at Rome, a Virgin with angels and countless others. Various artists have engraved many things of Michelagnolo at the request of Antonio Lanferri, who kept printers for such work, who have issued books of all manner of fishes, and the Phæthon, Tityus, Ganymede, Archers, Baccanalia, Dream, Pietà and Crucifixion of Michelagnolo, done for the Marchioness of Pescara. The four prophets of the chapel were also issued, but done so badly that I prefer not to mention the engravers and printers. But I must not forget Antonio Lanferri[3] and Tommaso Barlacchi, as they have greatly assisted engraving, keeping many youths engaged, with the designs of masters too numerous to mention, issuing in this way arabesques, ancient temples, cornices, bases, capitals and similar things, to scale. Seeing everything done very badly, Sebastiano Serlio, of Bologna, architect, has engraved two books of architecture, comprising, among other things, thirty rustic doors and twenty delicate ones. The book is dedicated to King Henry of France. Antonio Labbaco has issued in a good style all the antique and notable things of Rome, to scale, well engraved by . . . of Perugia. Jacopo Barazzo of Vignola,[4] architect, has been equally industrious, his book showing easy rules for enlarging and diminishing, according to the proportions of the five orders, a most valuable work for art, and for this we owe him a great debt, being equally bound to Giovanni Cugini of Paris[5] for his engravings and writings on architecture.

In Rome, Niccolo Beatricio of Lorraine[6] has also done much with the burin, producing many admirable sheets, such as two sarcophagi with cavalry fights, and others full of animals; one scene of the raising of the widow's daughter by Christ, boldly executed from a design by Girolamo Mosciano,[7] painter of Brescia. From a design of Michelagnolo he also engraved an Annunciation, and printed Giotto's Navicella. Many beautiful sheets have come from Venice: landscapes of Titian, a Nativity, a St. Jerome and a St. Francis in wood and on copper, Tantalus, Adonis and others, engraved by Julio Bonasone of Bologna,[8]

[1] Giorgio Ghisi, 1520-82.   [2] 1530-90.   [3] Lanfrery.
[4] Barozzi, 1507-37.   [5] Jean Cousin, 1530-90.
[6] Beautrizet.   [7] Muziano.   [8] Born 1498.

with some others of Raphael, Giulio Romano, Parmigiano and every other master from whom he could get designs. Battista Franco, painter of Venice, has engraved and etched works of various masters, a Nativity, Adoration of the Magi, Preaching of St. Peter, some scenes from the Acts of the Apostles and many from the Old Testament. The designers were thus kept constantly employed by the engravers, and after Rosso's death everything of his that could be found was engraved, such as Clelia and the Sabines crossing the river, the Masks of the Fates done for King Francis, a curious Annunciation, ten women dancing, King Francis alone at the Temple of Jove, having behind him Ignorance and other like figures. These were done by Rene,[1] a copper engraver, during Rosso's lifetime, and many others were done after his death, comprising the history of Ulysses, and the vases, lamps, candles, salt-cellars and countless other silver things done from Rosso's designs. Luca Perini [2] published two Satyrs giving drink to Bacchus, and Leda taking Cupid's arrows, Susannah at the bath, and others from designs by Rosso and Francesco Bologna Primaticcio, now abbot of St. Martin's in France. They comprise a Judgment of Paris, Abraham sacrificing Isaac, a Virgin, Christ espousing St. Catherine, Jove converting Callisto into a bear, the Council of the Gods, Penelope weaving with her women, and numerous other wood-engravings, mostly done with the burin, the small figures being executed with the greatest imaginable fineness. Who can see without wonder the works of Francesco Marcolini of Forli? Among other things he printed *il Giardino de' Pensieri*, with a frontispiece of an astrologer's sphere and his head, designed by Giuseppo Porta of Castelnuova della Garfagnana. The book contains Fate, Envy, Calamity, Timidity, Praise and many others, considered most beautiful. Very admirable also were the figures of Gabriel Giolito in the *Orlando Furioso*, done in excellent style, as were the eleven anatomical drawings done for Andrea Vessalio, and designed by John de Calcar,[3] an excellent Flemish painter. They were afterwards copied on to a smaller sheet and engraved by Valverde, who wrote on Anatomy, following Vessalio.

Among the numerous prints issued by the Flemings during the last ten years, there are some fine ones by Michele,[4] a painter, who worked for many years in two chapels in the German church at Rome; these sheets are the Brazen Serpent of Moses and thirty-two scenes of Psyche and Cupid, considered very beauti-

[1] René Boivin, 1530–98.   [2] Penni.
[3] Johannes Calcar, 1499–1546.   [4] Michael Coxcie, 1497–1592.

ful. Jerome Cock, also a Fleming, has done on a large sheet a
Delilah cutting Sampson's hair, from the design of Martin
Hemskerk. Not far off is the temple of the Philistines, where
we see the dead and the terrified fugitives among the ruins. In
three smaller sheets he did the creation of Adam and Eve, the
eating of the apple, the expulsion from Paradise; and in four
other sheets of the same size, the devil imprinting avarice and
ambition in the heart of man, and all the effects thus produced.
By him also are twenty-seven scenes of the Old Testament of
the same size, from the expulsion of Adam from Paradise,
boldly and skilfully designed by Martin, very like the Italian
style. Jerome next engraved the history of Susannah in six
round pictures and twenty-three scenes from the Old Testament,
like the first of Abraham, namely the acts of David in six, those
of Solomon in eight, Balaam in four, and Judith and Susannah
in five. Of the New Testament he did twenty-nine sheets from
the Annunciation to the Passion and Death of Christ. From
Martin's designs he did the Seven Works of Mercy, the story of
the Rich Man and Lazarus, the parable of the Good Samaritan
in four sheets, and the parable of the Talents in four, from
Matthew, chapter xviii. Meanwhile Lie Frynch,[1] in competition,
did the life and death of St. John the Baptist in ten sheets, and
the Twelve Tribes in that number of sheets, Reuben on his pig
for luxury, Simeon with the sword for homicide, and so forth.
He afterwards engraved in more delicate style subjects of the
acts of David, from his anointing by Samuel to his going before
Saul, in ten sheets, and in six others he did Amnon and Tamar,
with the death of the former. Not long after he did ten scenes
of Job, and five from the Proverbs of Solomon. He also did the
Magi, and then in six sheets the invitation to the wedding feast
and the man without the wedding garment, from St. Matthew.
In six sheets of like size he did the Acts of the Apostles, and in
eight others he did eight women of perfect beauty, six from the
Old Testament: Jael, Ruth, Abigail, Judith, Esther and Susannah; and the Virgin and Mary Magdalene from the New. He next
did six sheets of the Triumph of Patience; in the first, Patience
in a chariot holds a standard with a rose among thorns; the
second shows a red-hot heart on an anvil, beaten by three
hammers, the car drawn by two figures, a Desire with wings,
and Hope with an anchor, while behind comes Fortune as a
prisoner, her wheel broken. The third has Christ on a car with
the standard of the Cross and his Passion, at his side are the

[1] Hans Liefrink of Leyden.

Evangelists represented as animals; the car is drawn by two angels, and behind are four prisoners, the Devil, the World or flesh, Sin and Death. The next is Isaac naked upon a camel, his banner having a pair of manacles and behind are the altar with the sheep, the knife and the fire. In the next, Joseph on another car is mounted on an ox with a garland of ears of corn and fruit, and a standard with a box of peaches; his prisoners are Anger and Envy eating a heart. The next is David on a lion holding a sceptre and a standard and grasping a bridle. Behind him is Saul as a prisoner and Shimei with his tongue out. Then comes Tobias on an ass, his standard has a fountain, and his prisoners are Poverty and Blindness. The last is St. Stephen on an elephant, on his standard is Charity, and his persecutors are his prisoners. All these ingenious fancies were engraved by Jerome Cock with a bold hand. He also engraved Fraud and Avarice, and a Bacchanal with dancing children. In another he did Moses crossing the Red Sea, after the painting of Agnolo Bronzino the Florentine, painted in the upper chapel of the Duke's palace at Florence. In competition with him, Giorgio Mantovano engraved a beautiful Nativity, also from Bronzino's design. Jerome then engraved for the designer twelve sheets of the victories, battles and exploits of Charles V. For Verese,[1] the painter and eminent perspectivist, he did twenty different buildings, and for Jerome Bos [2] he did St. Martin in a boat full of curiously shaped devils and an alchemist wasting his substance, and coming at length to the hospital with his wife and children. This was designed by a painter who got him to engrave the seven mortal sins with various demons, a fantastic and laughable thing, the Last Judgment, and an old man with a lantern seeking quiet amid the turmoil of the world and not finding it. He also did a large fish eating small fish, and a Carnival rejoicing at table with others and driving away Lent, while in another Lent expels the Carnival, with many other fancies which it would be tiresome to recount.

Many other Flemings have carefully imitated the style of Albert Dürer, especially Albert Aldegraf,[3] who engraved four scenes of the creation of Adam, four of Abraham and Lot and four of Sussannah, all very beautiful. G. P.[4] also engraved the Seven Works of Mercy, in small circles, eight scenes from the Book of Kings, Regulus put in the tub full of spikes, and a

[1] Possibly Jan Cornelis Vermeyen is meant.   [2] Jerome Bosch.
[3] Albrecht Aldegrever, c. 1502–62.
[4] Georg Pencz, c. 1500–50.

lovely Artemis. I. B.[1] did the four Evangelists, wonderfully minute, and five other beautiful sheets; a young girl led by Death to the grave; Adam; a peasant, a bishop and a cardinal all led away by Death. He also did some Germans going with their mistresses to pleasures, and some fine Satyrs. By . . . we have the four Evangelists, not less fine, and twelve scenes of the Prodigal Son, executed by M. with much diligence.

Finally Francis Floris,[2] a famous painter of those parts, did a great number of designs and works, mostly engraved by Jerome Cock, such as the Labours of Hercules in ten sheets, and a large sheet of all the acts of life, another of the combat between the Horatii, the Judgment of Solomon, the fight between the Pygmies and Hercules, and Cain killing Abel, with Adam and Eve lamenting. Also Abraham sacrificing Isaac, with countless others marvellous for their various fancies.

Our book contains portraits of painters, sculptors and architects, designed by Giorgio Vasari and his pupils, and engraved by Maestro Cristofano Coriolano,[3] who is still doing many notable things at Venice. The ultramontanes have derived great advantages from prints which have enabled them to see the style of the Italians, as the Italians have from seeing those of foreigners and ultromontanes, and for this they are chiefly indebted to Marcantonio of Bologna, who, besides being among the earliest engravers, has not since been really surpassed, although a few have equalled him in some things. Not long after leaving Rome he died at Bologna. Our book contains some pen drawings of angels by him, and other very beautiful sheets copied from the chambers painted by Raphael. In these Marcantonio was drawn by Raphael as one of the bearers of Pope Julius II., in the scene where Onias the priest is praying. This is the conclusion of the notice of Marcantonio and the other engravers, of whom I have spoken at this necessary length to satisfy the students of art and all those who take delight in such works.

[1] Hans Beham.
[2] Franz Floris, 1520–70.
[3] Born at Nuremberg in 1540; his name was Lederer.

ANTONIO DA SAN GALLO, Architect of Florence
(1485–1546)

WHAT great fame many illustrious princes would leave behind
them if, in addition to the gifts of Fortune, they possessed a
high spirit, and one inclined to the things which not only
embellish the world, but are of the utmost benefit to all men.
What works perpetuate the fame of princes and great men
more than great and magnificent structures, because they endure
practically for ever? Of all the lavish expenditure incurred by
the Romans when at the height of their power, what has come
down to us, to their eternal glory, except those remains of
buildings which we honour as sacred, and as the only things
which we care to imitate? The interest of some princes in these
things will appear in the Life of Antonio San Gallo, architect
of Florence, which I am now writing.

He was the son of Bartolommeo Picconi of Mugello, a cooper,
and having learned the trade of a carpenter as a child, he left
Florence, hearing that his uncle Giuliano da San Gallo was
employed at Rome with Antonio his brother. As he was much
inclined to architecture, he gave promise of future eminence,
displayed in later years in so many things all over Italy. When
Giuliano, suffering from the stone, was forced to return to
Florence, Antonio became known to Bramante the architect,
helping the paralytic old man with his drawings, as he could
not use his hands. Antonio did these with such finish that
Bramante, finding the measurements correct, gave him the
care of many things, supplying him with the necessary inventions and compositions. Antonio showed such judgment, quickness and diligence that, in 1512, Bramante gave him the charge
of the corridor leading to the moat of the Castle of St. Angelo,
which he began with a provision of 10 crowns a month, but the
work was interrupted by the death of Julius II. Antonio, however, had already acquired the reputation of being a skilful
architect, and his excellent walls led Alessandro Farnese, the
first cardinal of the house, afterwards Pope Paul III., to think
of restoring his old palace in the Campo di Fiore, where he lived
with his family. Antonio, being anxious to win a position by
this work, made various designs, one of which, arranged in two
apartments, was adopted by the cardinal after consulting his
sons Pier Luigi and Ranuccio, whom he expected to accommo-

date in this structure. The work was therefore begun [1] and
advanced steadily every year. At this time a church dedicated
to S. Maria da Loreto at the Macello de' Corbi at Rome, near
the Trajan Column, was beautifully decorated by Antonio.
Then M. Marchionne Baldassini built a palace near S. Agostino
from Antonio's model, which, though small, is considered the
first and most convenient house in Rome, the stairs, court,
loggias, doors and rooms being most graceful. M. Marchionne was
delighted, and determined that Perino del Vaga, painter of
Florence, should decorate a hall, as will be related in his Life,
the decorations possessing much grace and beauty. Antonio
finished the house of the Centelli, near the Torre di Nona,
which is small but very convenient. Before long he went to
Gradoli, a place on the estate of Cardinal Farnese, where he built
a beautiful and convenient palace for him, and restored the
fortress of Capo di Monte with a circuit of low, well-designed
walls, designing also the fortress of Capraruola. The cardinal,
seeing himself so well served, became very fond of him, and
favoured him as far as possible in every undertaking. Cardinal
Alborense, wishing to leave a memorial of himself in the church
of his nation, employed Antonio to erect a marble chapel and
tomb for him in S. Jacopo degli Spagnuoli. The chapel, standing
between the pilasters, was painted by Pellegrino da Modana,
while Jacopo del Sansovino made a fine marble St. James for the
altar. This work of architecture was considered most praiseworthy, the marble vault being decorated with octagons. Soon
after M. Bartholommeo Ferratino, for his own convenience and
that of his friends, and to leave an honourable memorial,
employed Antonio to build him a palace [2] on the piazza of
Amelia, a beautiful construction which brought Antonio no
small fame and profit. Antonio di Monte, cardinal of S. Pras-
sede, being at Rome at this time, wished Antonio to build him
a palace, where he afterwards lived, on the street leading to
Agone, where the statue of Maestro Pasquino stands, and having
a place for a tower in the middle, constructed on three floors
with fine pilasters and windows. Francesco dell' Indaco did in
clay the figures and scenes, inside and out. Having intimate
relations with the cardinal of Arimini, Antonio built him a
palace in Tolentino della Marca, for which the cardinal rewarded
him, remaining always in his debt.

Meanwhile, as Antonio's fame was increasing and spreading,
Bramante, being very old, was summoned to another world.

[1] In 1534.   [2] Now Patrignani.

Pope Leo therefore appointed three architects for the building of S. Pietro: Raphael, Giuliano da San Gallo, Antonio's uncle, and Frà Giocondo of Verona. Before long Frà Giocondo left Rome, and Giuliano, being old, obtained permission to return to Florence. Antonio, being in the service of Cardinal Farnese, begged him to get Pope Leo to appoint him to his uncle's place. This he easily obtained,[1] because his ability merited the appointment, and he was supported by the influence of the Pope and Cardinal Farnese, and so the building was continued in a very dilatory fashion by him and Raphael. When the Pope went to fortify Civitavecchia, accompanied by numerous lords, including Gio. Paolo Baglioni and Sig. Vitello, and by Pietro Navarra and Antonio Marchisi, architect of fortification who had come from Naples by the Pope's command, various designs were submitted, but Antonio's was accepted by the Pope and the others as being the finest and strongest, and so he won great credit at the court. After this Antonio's skill was able to repair a great error. In making the papal loggia and apartments, Raphael had left a number of spaces to please some people, to the detriment of the structure, as, the weight being too great, the building would certainly have fallen if Antonio had not supported it with props, making new foundations and leaving it more firm than it had ever been.

The Florentine nation having begun their church in the Strada Giulia behind the Banchi from the designs of Jacopo Sansovino, it was set too far back to the river. Accordingly they were involved in an expenditure of 12,000 crowns for foundations in the water. This was excellently carried out by Antonio, who had succeeded in doing what had baffled Jacopo, and several bracchia were built over the water, Andrea making a remarkable model, and if the work had been completed it would have been stupendous. However, it was a disgrace, and showed great want of foresight in the head of the nation at Rome, to permit the architects to found so large a church in so formidable a river, in order to gain 20 braccia in length and throw so many crowns away on foundations involving a continual struggle with the river, when the church might have been brought farther forward on the land, if shaped differently, and could have been completed at the same cost. If they trusted in the wealth of the nation, time proved their calculations to be false, for the church remained and still is in the same condition,[2] during all the years of Popes Leo and Clement, both

---

[1] In 1517.   [2] It was finished between 1832 and 1838.

Medici, Julius III. and Marcellus, all Florentines, and in spite
of the greatness of numerous cardinals and the riches of merchants; and architects ought to look to the end before putting
their hands to a work of importance.

But to return to Antonio. One summer he accompanied the
Pope to Monte Fiascone and restored the fortress there erected
by Pope Urban, and did two small temples in the Viscentina
island on the Lake of Bolsena for Cardinal Farnese; one of
them octagonal outside and round within, the other square
outside and octagonal within, with a niche at each angle
outside. Both were excellent, showing Antonio's resources in
architecture. While they were building, he returned to Rome
and began the palace of the Bishop of Cervia at the corner of
S. Lucia, where the new mint is, but it was left unfinished.
Near the Corte Savella he did the church of S. Maria di Monferrato, considered very beautiful, and the house of Marrano,
behind the Cibo palace, near the house of the Massimi.

On the death of Leo all the fine arts revived by him and
by Julius II. languished under Adrian VI. who succeeded, who
treated them so badly that if his pontificate had lasted longer
a ruin would have overtaken them, such as befel when the Goths
came, all statues being condemned to the flames, good as well as
improper ones. Adrian might perhaps have followed this example
of his predecessors, and had already begun to talk of pulling
down Michelagnolo's chapel which he called a stew of nudes,
and contemptuously classified all good pictures and statues as
lascivious and abominable. Thus all good artists, including
Antonio, stopped work, and the building of S. Pietro was
almost at a standstill during this pontificate, though he might
have cared for this even if hostile to other worldly things.
Antonio therefore only did small things, restoring the aisles
of the church of S. Jacopo degli Spagnuoli, and making some
fine windows in the façade. He did the Tabernacle of the Imagine
di Ponte in travertine, which is very graceful though small, and
here Perino del Vaga did a beautiful little work in fresco. The
unfortunate arts were thus badly circumstanced under Adrian,
when Heaven by the death of one revived a thousand. He made
way for one more deserving of the station, and who would deal
otherwise with worldly affairs. Clement VII. followed in the
footsteps of Leo and the other members of his illustrious house,
feeling that, as he had made such fine memorials as cardinal, he
ought as Pope to advance all buildings and decorations. His
election encouraged the artists and restored life to the timid,

who afterwards produced the beautiful works which we now see. By the Pope's commission Antonio began a court in the palace before the loggias already painted by Raphael. Antonio greatly enhanced its convenience and beauty by enlarging some narrow and tortuous ways and giving them a better form. But it has since been altered, as Julius III. removed the granite columns to decorate his villa, and changed everything. In Banchi Antonio did the façade of the old mint, with a most graceful rounded corner, of great difficulty, putting the Pope's arms there. He made new foundations for the remainder of the loggias, left uncompleted by Leo's death, and untouched under Adrian, completing them as Clement desired. His Holiness resolved to fortify Parma and Piacenza,[1] and after many plans had been prepared by various people, Antonio was sent thither with Giuliano Leno, the supervisor. Arrived there with his pupil Antonio l'Abbaco, Pier Francesco of Viterbo, a clever engineer, and Michele da S. Michele, architect of Verona, they together perfected the designs of these fortifications. This done, while the others stayed, Antonio returned to Rome, where Pope Clement directed him to begin the apartments over the Ferraria, where the public consistories are held, there being only scanty accommodation in the palace. The execution of the work gave great satisfaction to the Pope, who next had his chamberlains' apartments constructed. Above these Antonio made others of great convenience, the work being dangerous because of the foundations. In this respect Antonio showed great skill, as his buildings have never moved a hair's breadth, no modern architect being so safe as he.

In the time of Paul II. the little church of the Madonna of Loreto, the roof of which rested on rough brick pilasters, was restored upon its present plan by Giuliano da Maiano, being afterwards raised by Sixtus V. and others, as has been said. But in the time of Clement, after having stood perfectly firm, it cracked in 1526 so that the arches of the tribune were endangered, and the church also in many places, because the foundations were weak and the walls leaning out. Being sent by Clement to repair these defects, Antonio proceeded to Loreto, propped up the arches like a determined and judicious architect, and made new foundations. He thickened the walls and the pilasters within and without, rendering it beautiful in form and proportion, and capable of bearing any strain. He continued this arrangement for the crossing and aisles, with superb mould-

[1] In 1525.

ings upon the arches, friezes and cornices. Especially fine were the bases of his four large pilasters at the eight sides of the tribune bearing the four arches, namely the three of the crossing where the chapels are, and the large one of the nave. This was considered his best work, and with good cause, because those who erect buildings from the beginning can fashion them as they please, whereas those who restore things begun by others and ill-designed or spoiled by misfortune, do not enjoy this advantage; so that Antonio may be said to have raised the dead, and to have achieved what was all but impossible. He directed that it should be roofed with lead, and showed how the remainder of the work was to be done, thus endowing that famous sanctuary with form and grace greater than it had possessed before, and giving it the hope of a long life.

Returning to Rome after the sack, the Pope being at Orvieto and the court being in great want of water, Antonio built a stone well there,[1] at the Pope's desire, 25 braccia across, with two spiral staircases cut in the sides, one above the other, so that the animals descending for water by one should come back by the other without turning at the bottom, and should come out of the well by a different door. This ingenious and convenient work, of marvellous beauty, was almost completed before Clement died. The mouth was finished under Paul III., but not as ordained by Clement and designed by Antonio. The ancients certainly never did anything to equal it in industry and art, the opening being so spacious that light penetrated to the very bottom by means of windows on the staircases. In the meantime Antonio directed the fortification of Ancona, which was completed later.

Pope Clement decided, while his nephew Alesandro de' Medici was Duke of Florence, to build an impregnable fortress in that city.[2] This was completed by Sig. Alessandro Vitelli, Pier Francesco da Viterbo and Antonio, between the Prato and S. Gallo gates, with more expedition than had been displayed in any such construction, whether ancient or modern. In a large tower called il Toso, the first to be built, many inscriptions and medals were placed with great ceremony. The fort has a world-wide fame, and is considered impregnable.

Antonio took Il Tribolo, the sculptor, to Loreto, and also Raffællo di Monte Lupo, Francesco di S. Gallo, then a youth, and Simone Coli, who finished the marble bas-reliefs begun by

---

[1] Pozzo di S. Patrizio, begun in 1527.
[2] The Castel S. Giovambatista, begun 1534.

Andrea Sansovino. In the same place a stone chimneypiece was constructed for the heirs of Pelligrino da Fossombrone by Antonio il Mosca of Florence, an excellent carver of marble, as I shall relate in his Life, this work being very fine. At Loreto he did most divine festoons, so that the decoration of the chamber of Our Lady was completed with speed and diligence, although Antonio had five works of importance on his hands at the same time in places far distant from each other. But he managed all, sending his brother Battista when he could not go himself. They were the fortress of Florence, that of Ancona, the work at Loreto, the Pope's palace, and the well at Orvieto.

On the death of Clement and the election of Paul III., Antonio's credit rose, for he had been the Pope's friend in the days when he was cardinal. The Pope, therefore, having created his son, Sig. Pierluigi, Duke of Castro, sent Antonio to design the fortress that the duke began, the palace called l'Osteria on the piazza, and the mint, built of travertine there, like that at Rome. Antonio did yet other designs for palaces and other buildings there for various natives and foreigners, who incurred incredible expenses, without reserve, all these structures being ornate and most convenient. No doubt many acted thus to please the Pope, hoping to obtain favours, a very praiseworthy thing, when it produces such results for the universal convenience and delight.

In the year that the Emperor Charles V. returned victorious from Tunis,[1] magnificent triumphal arches were erected in Messina, Apulia, and Naples to celebrate his success. For his reception at Rome, Antonio made a wooden triumphal arch at the palace of S. Marco, by the Pope's commission, to serve two streets, more beautiful than anything of its kind, and if it had been executed in marble with equal study, art and diligence, it might well have been enumerated among the seven wonders of the world. It was placed at the end corner of the principal piazza, and had four circular Corinthian columns covered with silver on each side, the capitals being carved with beautiful foliage and overlaid with gold. Magnificent architraves, friezes and cornices rested with projections on each column, two scenes being in each, making four on each side and eight in all, containing the acts of the emperor, as I shall relate in speaking of the painter. As a finish, two figures of four and a half braccia were placed above the arch, one for Rome, and the two emperors of the House of Austria, Albert and Maximilian, were put in front, and Frederick and Rudolph on the other side. At the corners were four

[1] In 1535.

prisoners, two at each, and a great number of trophies, with the arms of the Pope and Emperor, all executed under Antonio, by the best sculptors and painters then in Rome. He also designed all the apparatus for the festivities for receiving the emperor. For the Duke of Castro he next did the fortress of Nepi[1] and the defence of all the city, which is impregnable and magnificent. Here also he planned several streets, designing houses and palaces for the citizens. For the Pope he then made the bastions of Rome, of great strength, including the S. Spirito gate, with rustic ornaments in travertine, very solid, and of such magnificence that it equals the ancients. After Antonio's death a great effort was made to destroy it, chiefly through envy, but this was not permitted. He also made new foundations for the apostolic palace, which threatened to fall in several places, including one side of the Sistine Chapel, where the works of Michelagnolo are, and the façade, a work involving more danger than it promised glory. He enlarged the great hall of the Sistine Chapel, making two large windows in two lunettes with stucco ornament, which rendered the hall the most beautiful and richest in the world. He also made some steps leading to S. Pietro as convenient as anything seen among the ancients and moderns. He did the Paulina Chapel, where the Sacrament is placed, most beautifully proportioned, graceful and attractive. During the dissensions between the Perugians and the Pope he made the fortress of Perugia,[2] pulling down the Baglioni houses, finishing it with marvellous speed and making it very beautiful. He also built the fortress of Ascoli, rendering it defensible in a few days, a thing the Ascolians did not expect for many years, so that the people were amazed at a garrison being placed there so soon. In Rome he made new foundations for his house in Strada Giulia to protect it when the Tiber was swollen, and he began and made considerable progress with the palace near S. Biagio, now owned by Cardinal Riccio da Montepulciano, who completed it at great cost, and with sumptuous rooms, in addition to the thousands of crowns which Antonio had expended.

But none of Antonio's works is to be compared with the stupendous fabric of S. Pietro at Rome, begun by Bramante, but extraordinarily enlarged and rearranged by him, as he gave it proportion, composition and decoration in every part, as we see by the completed wooden model made by his pupil Antonio Labacco, which gave Antonio a great name. This

<hr>

[1] In 1537.   [2] 1540.

model and the plans were published by Labacco after his death, who wished to show his master's skill, and that men should know his views. Michelagnolo, however, made other dispositions, which were much contested, as I shall relate. He and many others who saw Antonio's model thought the composition too dwarfed by projections and members, which are small, as are the columns, arches being placed upon arches and cornices above cornices. He condemned the finish or garland of numerous small columns of the two campanili, the four small tribunes and the great tribune, nor did he like the numerous pyramids, which he thought approached the German style more than the good antique observed by the best architects.

Labacco having finished the models, that of S. Pietro cost 4184 crowns for the carpenters and joiners only. Labacco did his part well, for he possessed a good knowledge of architecture, as we see by his fine printed book on Rome. The model is now in the principal chapel of S. Pietro, and is 35 palms long, 26 broad and 20½ high, so that the complete work would have been 1040 palms or 104 canne long, and 360 broad or 36 canne, the Roman canna being 10 palms. For the labours on this model and the designs Antonio was granted 1500 crowns, but he only received 1000 before his death. He thickened the pilasters of S. Pietro to bear the weight of the tribune and filled the foundations with solid materials, making it so strong that it could not move as it had done in Bramante's time. If that masterpiece were above ground instead of being hidden beneath, it would dismay the most formidable intelligence, and for it this admirable artist must always retain a place among the rarest intellects.

From the days of the ancient Romans there has been continual enmity between Narni and Terni, because the lake of Marmora does harm to one or the other, so that when Narni wishes to open it Terni will not consent, and thus there have been disputes under both emperors and popes. Cicero was sent by the Senate to compound such a difference, but did not succeed. In 1546 ambassadors were sent to Paul III. on the matter, and he dispatched Antonio to settle the dispute. He decided that the lake ought to discharge on the side where the wall is, and with great difficulty he cut it. But the weather was very warm, and Antonio being an old man fell sick of the fever at Terni, and died soon after, to the sorrow of his friends and relations, and the loss of many buildings, chiefly the Farnese palace near the Campo di Fiore.

When a cardinal, Paul III. had advanced the palace to a good state, and had begun the front windows, the inside hall, and cleared a part of the court, though it was not sufficiently advanced to show its perfections. After the Pope's election Antonio entirely changed the design for something befitting a pope and not a cardinal. Pulling down some houses and the old staircases, he made new and more pleasant ones, enlarged the court in every sense and the whole of the palace, making larger salons, more numerous rooms, and finer ceilings, with beautiful carving and other decoration. He completed the second windows, and it only remained to set up the surrounding cornice. The Pope, being a man of spirit and of good judgment, wished to have a finer cornice, the richest possible, and better than that of any other palace, so in addition to the plans prepared by Antonio all the best architects in Rome made theirs though Antonio was to superintend the work. One morning, as the Pope was driving in Belvedere, all the designs were brought to him in the presence of Antonio. They were by Perino del Vaga, Frà Bastiano del Piombo, Michelagnolo Buonarotti and Giorgio Vasari, then young and in the service of Cardinal Farnese, with whose commission and the Pope's he had prepared two designs for the cornice. Buonarotti did not bring his, but sent it by Giorgio, who took his own and excused his friend as being indisposed. The Pope examined the designs carefully, and praised all as being ingenious and beautiful, but especially that of Michelagnolo. Antonio did not like all this, as he wished to be the chief, and he was even more dissatisfied at seeing the favour bestowed by the Pope on one Jacopo Melighino of Ferrara, although he had no design and not much judgment, in employing him upon the work of S. Pietro and in giving him the same salary as Antonio had for all his labours. This was because Melighino had served the Pope for many years without any reward, and the Pope chose to reward him in this way, and moreover he had given him charge of the Belvedere and some other buildings. After examining the designs, the Pope said, perhaps to test Antonio: "These are all fine, but I should like to see one by our Melighino." Antonio rather resented this, and thinking the Pope was jesting he said, "Holy Father, Melighino is an architect *pour rire*." On hearing this the Pope, who was seated, almost bent his head to the ground, and turning to Antonio he said, "Be good enough to remember that we consider Melighino a serious architect, as you may see by his provision," and then departed, dismissing them all; for he wished to show that princes, more than merit, often bring men to greatness. The cornice was ultimately made by Michelagnolo, as will be said in his Life, and he practically rebuilt the whole palace in another form. Antonio left a brother, Battista Gobbo, an ingenious man, who devoted all this time to his brother's buildings, though Antonio did not treat him very well. He survived Antonio many years, and at his death left all his property to the company of the Misericordia of the Florentines at Rome, on condition that they should print his book of observations upon Vitruvius, which has never appeared. It is supposed to have been a good work, because he thoroughly understood art and possessed judgment and intelligence.

But to return to Antonio. He died at Terni and was taken with great pomp to be buried at Rome, followed by all artists and many others. His body was afterwards laid in a vault near the chapel of Pope Sixtus in S. Pietro, with this epitaph:

Antonio Sancti Galli Florentino Urbe munienda ac publ. operibus, præcipueque D. Petri templo ornan. architectorum facile principi, dum Velini lacus emissionem parat, Paulo pont. max. auctore, interamne intempestive extincte. Isabella Deta uxor mæstiss. posuit 1546 III. Kalend. Octobr.

Indeed, for his excellent works Antonio merits no less praise than any other architect, ancient or modern, no matter who.

GIULIO ROMANO,[1] Painter
(1492–1546)

AMONG the countless pupils of Raphael, who mostly became excellent, no one imitated him more closely in style, invention, design and colouring than Giulio Romano, nor was anyone of them more profound, spirited, fanciful, various, prolific and universal; he also was an agreeable companion, jovial, affable, gracious and abounding in excellent qualities, so that Raphael loved him as if he had been his son, and employed him on all his principal works. Thus, when Raphael had designed the building, decoration and scenes for the loggias for Leo X., he charged Giulio to do many of the paintings, and amongst others the creation of Adam and Eve, that of the animals, the building

[1] Giulio Pippi.

of Noah's ark, the sacrifice, and many others recognisable by the style, such as Pharoah's daughter finding Moses in the ark, a marvellous work with a finely executed landscape. He also helped Raphael to colour many things in the chamber of the Borgia tower containing the burning of the Borgo, notably the bronze-coloured basement, the Countess Matilda, King Pepin, Charlemagne, Godfrey of Bouillon, King of Jerusalem, and other benefactors of the Church, all excellent figures. A part was issued as prints not long ago from Giulio's design. He also did most of the scenes in fresco in the loggia of Agostino Ghigi, and a fine St. Elizabeth in oils, done by Raphael and sent to King Francis of France with another of St. Margaret, almost entirely by Giulio from Raphael's design, who sent to the same king a portrait of the vice-queen of Naples,[1] in which Raphael only did the head, the rest being by Giulio. These works greatly pleased the king, and they are still in the royal chapel at Fontainebleau. In this way Giulio learned the difficulties of art, taught to him with great patience by Raphael, and before long he became skilled in drawing perspectives, measuring buildings and making plans. Sometimes Raphael would sketch his ideas and Giulio would enlarge them for use in architecture, in which he began to take such delight that with practice he became an excellent master. On Raphael's death Giulio and Giovanfrancesco, called Il Fattore, were left his heirs and charged to finish his works, a task which they honourably fulfilled in most cases.

Cardinal Giuliano de' Medici, afterwards Clement VII., acquired a site in Rome under Mt. Mario, with a beautiful view, flowing water, well wooded, and extending along the Tiber from Ponte Molle to the S. Piero gate. Here on the flat ground at the top of the bank he resolved to erect a palace furnished with convenient rooms, loggias, gardens, fountains, woods and other things of beauty, and gave the work to Giulio. He took it readily, and erected the palace then known as the Vigna de' Medici, and now as the Vigna di Madama, with great perfection. Accommodating himself to the site and to the cardinal's wishes, he designed a semicircular façade with niches and windows of the Ionic order, so much admired that many believed Raphael had designed them, and that Giulio had but elaborated his sketches. Giulio decorated the chambers and other parts with pictures, notably a fine loggia beyond the first vestibule, adorned with large and small niches containing a quantity of ancient statues comprising a Jupiter of rare beauty, afterwards sent

[1] The "St. Margaret" and "Joan of Aragon," now in the Louvre.

by the Farnesi to King Francis of France, with many other
beautiful statues. The walls and vaulting are, moreover, covered
with arabesques by Giovanni da Udine, and the loggia is
decorated with stucco. At the top Giulio painted a great Polyphemus in fresco, with infants and satyrs playing about him,
for which he won great praise. His other designs there were
equally admired, of fisheries, pavements, rustic fountains, woods
and other things, all of great beauty and executed with judgment. But the work was interrupted by the death of Leo, as,
on the election of Adrian and the departure of the Cardinal
de' Medici for Florence, all public works begun by Leo were
discontinued. Meanwhile Giuliano and Giovanfrancesco finished
many of Raphael's incomplete works, and prepared to carry out
the cartoons he had done for the great hall of the palace, representing four scenes of the acts of the Emperor Constantine. Before
his death Raphael had prepared the surface of one wall to receive
the oils. But Adrian, who cared nothing for painting, sculpture,
or anything fine, did not want it done. Thus, while Adrian lived,
Giulio, Giovanfrancesco, Perino del Vaga, Giovanni da Udine,
Bastiano Veniziano and other excellent artists came near dying
of hunger. But while the court, nourished on the greatness of
Leo, had come to this pass, and the best artists were at their
wits' end, their abilities being no longer valued, Adrian died,
by God's will, and Cardinal Giulio de' Medici was elected pope
as Clement VII. Thus in one day all the arts of design revived
with the other talents, and Giulio and Giovanfrencesco immediately and joyfully set about finishing the Hall of Constantine
by the Pope's order. They threw down the wall prepared for the
oils, leaving, however, two figures, which they had previously
painted as a decoration about some popes, of Justice and
another virtue. The hall being low, the dispositions had been
judiciously arranged by Raphael. At the corners over the doors
he put some large niches decorated with infants holding various
devices of Leo X., such as lilies, diamonds, feathers and the
like. In the niches were seated popes in their pontificals, each
one having a shadow. About them were cherubs holding books
and other suitable things. On either side of each pope was an
appropriate Virtue. Peter had Religion and Charity or Piety,
and the others had the like, the popes being Damasus I.,
Alexander I., Leo III., Gregory, Silvester and some others,
all well executed by Giulio, who devoted his best energies to
the task. His labour and diligence are shown by a fine drawing
of St. Silvester by him, probably more graceful than the painting,

for he was always happier in expressing his ideas in drawing than in painting, obtaining more vivacity, vigour and expression, possibly because a design is made in an hour in heat, while a painting takes months and years. Thus he became tired, losing his first ardour, and it is no wonder that the paintings are inferior.

But to return to the scenes. On one of the walls Giulio painted Constantine addressing his soldiers, a cross appearing in the air with some cherubs, and the letters IN HOC SIGNO VINCES. A dwarf at Constantine's feet, putting on a helmet, is made with great art. On the largest wall is a cavalry fight near Ponte Molle, where Constantine routs Maxentius, an admirable work for the wounded and dead and the varied and curious attitudes of the infantry and cavalry fiercely engaged. There are also many portraits, and if it did not contain too much black, of which Giulio was always fond, it would be perfect, but this greatly detracts from its beauty. He did the whole landscape of Monte Mario, and Maxentius drowning in the River Tiber on his horse. This scene[1] has proved of great assistance to those who have since represented battles. Giuliano studied the ancient columns of Trajan and Antoninus at Rome, making great use of them for the dresses of the soldiers, the armour, ensigns, bastions, stockades, rams and other implements of war represented there. Below this he painted many admirable things in bronze colour. On the other wall he did St. Silvester the Pope baptising Constantine, representing the very bath made by that emperor, now at St. John Lateran. St. Silvester is a portrait of Pope Clement, and many assistants and others are present. Among the Pope's servants he drew the Pope's favourite, M. Niccolo Vespucci, knight of Rhodes, the little cavalier, and below in bronze colour he painted Constantine building S. Pietro, an allusion to Pope Clement, with portraits of Bramante and Giulian Lemi, who hold the plan of the church, making a very beautiful scene. On the fourth wall over the chimneypiece he represented S. Pietro in perspective, with the papal residence as it stands, the Pope singing Mass with the cardinals and other prelates of the court, and the chapel of the choristers and musicians. The Pope is seated, as St. Silvester, with Constantine kneeling at his feet and presenting to him a golden Rome as it is shown on ancient medals, to indicate the gift which Constantine made to the Church. Giulio here introduced many beautiful women kneeling to view the ceremony, a poor man asking alms,

[1] Begun in 1524.

a boy playing with a dog, and the lances of the Pope's guard making the people stand back in the usual way. Among the numerous portraits are those of Giulio himself, his friend Count Baldassare Castiglione, author of *Il Cortigiano*, Pontano, his great friend, Marullo and many other men of letters, and courtiers. About the windows Giulio painted many designs and poetic fancies of great beauty, greatly delighting the Pope, who richly rewarded him.

While this hall was being painted, Giulio and Gio. Francesco did an Assumption[1] of great beauty, which was sent to Perugia, and placed in the monastery of the nuns of Montelucci. Giulio alone did a Madonna with a cat,[2] so natural that it was called the picture of the cat. In another large picture he represented Christ at the Column, which was placed over the high altar of S. Prassedia at Rome. Not long after M. Gio. Matteo Giberti, afterwards bishop of Verona, and then datary of Pope Clement, employed his friend Giulio to design some apartments, built of brick, near the door of the Pope's palace, on the piazza of S. Pietro, near where the trumpeters stand when the cardinals go to the consistory, with convenient steps, which can be mounted on horse or foot. For the same friend Giulio did a Stoning of St. Stephen,[3] with remarkable invention, grace and composition, and while the Jews are stoning him young Saul is seated on their clothes. Giulio never did a finer work than this, representing the vigour of the assailants and the patience of Stephen, who really seems to see Christ on the right hand of the Father in a lovely sky. M. Gio. Matteo gave this work to the monks of Monte Oliveto, together with the benefice, which they have converted into a monastery. For Jacopo Fugger, a German, Giulio did a panel for a chapel in S. Maria *de Anima* at Rome of the Virgin, St. Anne, St. Joseph, St. James, the little St. John, and St. Mark kneeling, with a lion at his feet, and a book. This was a difficult task, as the lion has wings, with soft, plumy feathers, an extraordinary imitation of nature. He also made a building, round like a theatre, with statues of inexpressible beauty, finely disposed. Among them is a woman spinning, and looking at a hen with her chickens, wonderfully natural. Above the Virgin are some cherubs, holding a graceful canopy, but unfortunately this picture also contained too much black, which goes far to neutralise the labour bestowed on it, for the black always contains some carbon or other acid which

---

[1] In 1525; now in the Vatican Gallery.   [2] Naples Museum.
[3] In 1523, in S. Stefano, Genoa.

eats into the material. Among the numerous pupils of Giulio who assisted him with this work were Bartolommeo da Castiglione, Tommaso Paparello[1] of Cortona, Benedetto Pagni of Pescia, and Giovanni da Lione and Raffaello dal Colle of Borgo S. Sepolcro, both much employed in the Hall of Constantine and the other works mentioned. Being dexterous painters who had carefully observed Giulio's methods, they coloured from his designs the arms of Pope Clement VII., near the old mint in Banchi, with a figure on either side. Not long after Raffaello, from a design of Giulio, painted in fresco, in the lunette of the door of the palace of the Cardinal della Valle, a Virgin covering the sleeping Child, between St. Andrew the Apostle and St. Nicholas, considered an excellent work. Giulio being friendly with M. Baldassarre Turini of Pescia, made a model and built him a palace on Mount Janiculum,[2] where he has a fine view, of the utmost grace and convenience. The rooms were adorned with stucco and painting, as Giulio himself painted stories of Numa Pompilius, who was buried there. In the bath-room Giulio painted stories of Venus and Cupid, Apollo, Hyacinth, being helped by his apprentices, all of which scenes are engraved. On separating from Gio. Francesco, he did various works in architecture at Rome, such as the design for the Alberini house in Banchi, attributed by some to Raphael, and a palace on the Piazza della Dogana at Rome, since engraved because of its good arrangement. He also did a fine range of windows at a corner of the Macello de' Corbi, where his birthplace was, which, though small, is very graceful. After Raphael's death Giulio's excellent qualities gave him the reputation of being the best artist in Italy, and Count Baldassarre Castiglione, then ambassador at Rome of Federigo Gonzaga, Marquis of Mantua, and his friend, being requested by the marquis to procure him an architect for his palace, he succeeded by prayers and promises in getting Giulio to go if he could obtain the permission of Pope Clement. That done, the count, on going to Mantua with a message from the Pope to the emperor, took Giulio with him.[3] He presented him to the marquis, who received Giulio graciously, gave him a well-furnished house, and ordained a provision for him and for Benedetto Pagni and another youth. He also sent him several ells of velvet and smooth cloth to dress himself, and, understanding that he had no horse, gave him a favourite of his own called Ruggieri. On this creature Giulio rode a bow-shot out of the S. Bastiano gate, where the marquis had a place

---

[1] Papacello. [2] Villa Lante. [3] In 1524.

and stables, called the T, in the middle of a meadow, where he
kept his stud. When he arrived there, the marquis said that he
wanted, without destroying the old building, to have a place
where he could resort for amusement and take refreshment.
Giulio, after examining the site, set to work and, using the old
walls, made the first hall in a larger part, as may be seen on
entering, with the chambers on either side. As there is no good
stone there for building or carving, he used bricks and tiles,
with stucco, and of this material he made columns, bases,
capitals, cornices, doors, windows and other things in fine
proportion, with new and extraordinary decoration for the
vaulting, and richly decorated the interior, and this led to the
marquis deciding to make the present fine palace there from a
humble beginning. Giulio prepared a fine model in the court of
rustic-work, which greatly pleased the marquis, who gave him a
provision and, Giulio bringing many builders to the place, the
work was speedily completed.[1] The building is rectangular, with
an open court in the middle for a piazza, upon which four ways
open, in the form of a cross. The first passes to a large loggia,
which leads through another into the garden. Two others lead
to various apartments, decorated with stucco and painting. The
vaulting of the hall, which is entered from the first, is painted
in fresco, and the walls contain representations of all the best
horses of the marquis's breed, and the dogs also, which are marked
like the horses, each with its name, all being designed by Giulio,
and coloured in fresco by his pupils, Benedetto Pagni and
Rinaldo Mantovano, so well that they seem alive. From here
one enters a room at the corner of the palace, the vaulting of
which is finely decorated with stucco and various cornices, gilt
in some places. These form four octagons, which surround a
square in the highest part, where a cupid stands before Jove,
who is surrounded by a celestial light, and espouses Psyche in
the presence of the gods, a most graceful design, the figures
being so well foreshortened, as seen from beneath, that some,
not more than a braccia long, look three; indeed, Giulio has made
the illusion complete, the figures are in such relief. The octagons
contain the other stories of Psyche, of the wrath of Venus
against her, executed with the same beauty and perfection. The
other angles contain cupids, and there are others in the windows
with various expressions according to the spaces. The ceiling is
coloured in oils by Benedetto and Rinaldo. The remainder of
the scenes on the lower walls represent Psyche taking her bath,

[1] Palazzo del Te. Between 1525 and 1535.

attended by the cupids, while we see the banquet of Mercury, with the Bacchantæ playing, and the Graces beautifully embellishing the picture, Silenus supported by satyrs with his ass, and a goat, with two infants sucking her dugs; and near him is Bacchus, with two tigers at his feet; he leans on a sideboard on one arm, and has a camel on one side, and an elephant on the other. This sideboard is semicircular, and covered with festoons and flowers, full of vines and grapes. Beneath are three tiers of curious vases, basins, cups and such things in various forms, and so lustrous that they actually seem silver and gold, though he has used simple yellow colour, an instance of Giulio's genius and ability, which was rich, varied and prolific in invention and art. Not far off is Psyche, surrounded by women serving her, and in the distance is Phœbus guiding the four horses of his chariot, and a naked Zephyr reclining on clouds and blowing soft breezes through a horn, making a pleasant atmosphere about Psyche. These designs were engraved soon after by Battista Franco of Venice, who made them uniform with the large cartoon of Giulio done by Benedetto and Rinaldo, who executed these scenes, except the Bacchus, the Silenus and the two children suckled by the goat. The work was indeed retouched by Giulio, and is therefore his. He learned this method from Raphael, and it is very useful for the young men employed, because they become excellent masters, and although some think they are better than those who direct the work, they soon recognise that without such guidance they would find themselves blind in a sea of infinite errors. But to return to the rooms of the T. The Psyche room led into another, full of friezes of figures in bas-relief in stucco from Giulio's design, by Francesco Primaticcio of Bologna,[1] then a youth, and by Gio. Battista Mantovano, containing all the soldiers on the Trajan Column at Rome, done in fine style, the ceiling of an ante-chamber being painted in oils, representing Icarus directed by his father Dædalus, who, through wishing to fly too high, comes in sight of Cancer and the chariot of the sun, drawn by four horses, near Leo, and is left without wings, the wax being melted by the heat. He is next seen falling, his face deathly pale, a fine idea of Giulio, and very truthful, as we notice the sun's heat withering the wings, the smoke of the fire, the splitting of the feathers and the death agony in the face of Icarus, with passion and grief in that of Dædalus. I have the original design for this beautiful scene in my book. In the same place Giulio did the Months, with

[1] He was at Mantua between 1525 and 1531.

the usual occupations of each, a work of delightful imagination, carried out with judgment and diligence.

Passing the great loggia, decorated with stucco, arms and other curious ornaments, we come to some rooms full of such various fancies that the mind is bewildered, for Guilio being very imaginative and ingenious, to show his ability, intended to make a room similar to the Psyche room, the walls of which should correspond with the painting and create an illusion. As the place was marshy he laid the foundations deep and double, building a round room with thick walls so that the four external angles should be strong enough to bear a double barrel-vault. He then made the windows, door and chimneypiece of rustic stone, so twisted that they looked as if they leaned to one side and would fall. In this strangely built place he began to paint the most curious idea imaginable: Jove fulminating the giants. On the vaulting is the throne of Jove foreshortened, and a round Ionic temple on perforated columns, with a canopy over the seat in the middle. His eagle is there, the whole being on the clouds. Lower down angry Jove is fulminating the giants, with Juno assisting; lower still, while the strange-faced winds blow on the earth, the goddess Ops turns at the noise with her lions, as do the other gods and goddesses, especially Venus, who is next to Mars and Momus, who with wide-open arms seems to be expecting the heavens to fall, and yet remains immovable. The Graces stand in fear with the Hours near them, and each goddess is fleeing in her chariot. The Moon, with Saturn and Janus, move towards an opening in the clouds to get away from the noise and fury, and so does Neptune, who, with his dolphins, seems to be trying to rest on his trident, while Pallas and the nine Muses wonder what this portends. Pan embraces a nymph who is trembling with fear, and he wishes to take her away from the tumult and lightnings which fill the heavens. Apollo stands on the chariot of the sun and some of the Hours attempt to stop the horses. Bacchus and Silenus, with satyrs and nymphs, exhibit the utmost fear, and Vulcan, with his huge hammer on his shoulder, looks towards Hercules, who is speaking of the matter to Mercury. Near them stands the trembling Pomona, while Vertumnus and all the other gods exhibit the emotion of fear, which is presented with indescribable force both in those standing and in those fleeing. On the lower part, that is to say on the walls below the arching of the vault, are the giants, some under mountains and huge rocks, which they are carrying on their strong shoulders to mount to heaven. But Jove fulminates and all heaven is incensed against them, so that it not only strikes terror into the rash daring of the giants, hurling mountains at them, but all the world seems overturned and the end of all things at hand. We see Briareus in a dark cavern almost covered by the huge masses of rock, the other giants lying crushed and some killed under the fragments. Through the cleft of a dark cave many giants may be seen fleeing, struck by the thunders of Jove and about to be crushed like the others. Elsewhere Giulio did other giants with temples, columns and parts of mountains falling, making a great slaughter among them. Between these falling walls is the fireplace, and when a fire is lighted the giants seem to be burning. Pluto in his car is drawn by shrivelled horses, and flees to the centre accompanied by the Furies, and thus Giulio decorated the chimneypiece most beautifully with this idea of fire. To make the work more terrible, he represented huge giants struck in various ways by the lightning and thunderbolts, falling to earth, some killed, some wounded, and some crushed beneath mountains and ruins. No more terrible work of the brush exists, and anyone entering the room and seeing the windows, doors and other things so twisted that they appear about to fall, and the tumbling mountains and ruins, will fear that all is about to come about his ears, especially as he sees the gods fleeing hither and thither. A marvellous feature is that the painting has neither beginning nor end, and is not interrupted in any way, so that objects near the buildings seem very large, and those in the distant landscape are gradually lost, and the room, which is not more than fifteen braccia long, looks like an open country, and the floor being of small round stones set with a knife and the walls at the junction being painted like them, there seem to be no corner stones, and the place looks extremely large. The judgment and art here displayed by Giulio place artists under a great debt to him. In this work Rinaldo became a perfect colourist, as he completed it from Giulio's designs, as well as the other apartments. If he had not died young he would have brought great honour to Giulio in after years. Besides this palace, in which Giulio did many admirable things, which I pass over in order not to be too long, he restored many rooms of the duke's castle at Mantua, and made two large spiral staircases, richly decorated with stucco throughout. He decorated one hall with the history of the Trojan war, and did twelve scenes in oil in an ante-chamber under the heads of the Roman emperors by Titian, considered rare. At Marmiruolo, five miles from Mantua, he designed a convenient

structure and large paintings not less fine than those of the
castle and palace of the T. In the Chapel of Signora Isabella
Buschetta in S. Andrea, at Mantua, he did an oil-panel of the
Virgin adoring the Child Jesus lying on the ground, while
Joseph, the ass and the ox are near a manger. On one side is
St. John the Evangelist and on the other St. Longinus, larger
than life-size.[1] On the walls of the same chapel Rinaldo did two
fine scenes from his designs, a Crucifixion with the thieves,
some angels in the air, and the executioners, the Maries and
many horses below (for he loved to paint horses, and made them
marvellously beautiful) and many soldiers in various attitudes.
The other was the Finding of the Blood of Christ in the time of
the Countess Matilda, a most beautiful work. For Duke Federigo
Giulio next did with his own hand a Virgin washing the Christ-
child, who is standing in a basin while St. John empties water
out of a jug, both figures, which are life-size, being very beautiful.[2] In the distance are half-length figures of women coming
on a visit. This picture was afterwards given by the duke to
Signora Isabella Buschetta. Giulio made a fine portrait of this
lady in a small Nativity, a braccia high, now in the possession
of Sig. Vespasiano Gonzaga, with another of Giulio's given him
by Duke Federigo, representing a youth and maiden embracing
on a bed,[3] while an old woman secretly observes them at a door,
the figures being rather less than life-size and very graceful. In
the same house there is a very fine St. Jerome by Giulio. Count
Niccolo Maffei has a life-size Alexander the Great holding a
Victory in his hand, copied from an ancient medal, and a very
beautiful thing. Giulio next painted for his friend, M. Girolamo,
organist of the Duomo at Mantua, a Vulcan forging arrows, in
fresco. He holds the bellows in his hand and grasps a piece of
red-hot iron with pincers, while Venus cools some of the arrows
in a vase and puts them in Cupid's quiver.[4] This is one of Giulio's
most beautiful works, and there is very little else of his in fresco.
In S. Domenico he did a dead Christ for M. Ludovico da Fermo,
and Joseph and Nicodemus preparing to carry him to the tomb,
with the Virgin, the Maries and St. John the Evangelist nearby.
He did another dead Christ, now at Venice, in the house of Tommaso da Empoli of Florence. About this time Sig. Giovanni de'
Medici, being wounded by a musket, was taken to Mantua,

[1] Now in the Louvre, formerly in the collection of Charles I.
[2] The Madonna della Catina, Dresden.
[3] Berlin Gallery.
[4] Probably the Venus and Vulcan of the Louvre.

where he died. M. Pietro Aretino, his faithful servant and a friend of Giulio, desired the artist to take a death mask, from which he made a portrait which remained in Aretino's possession for many years.

When Charles V. came to Mantua,[1] Giulio, by the duke's order, made many fine arches, scenes for comedies and other things, in which he had no peer, no one being like him for masquerades, and making curious costumes for jousts, feasts, tournaments, which excited great wonder in the emperor and in all present. For the city of Mantua at various times he designed temples, chapels, houses, gardens, façades, and was so fond of decorating them that, by his industry, he rendered dry, healthy and pleasant places previously miry, full of stagnant water, and almost uninhabitable.

While he was serving the duke, the Po one year broke its banks, so that in some parts of Mantua the water was nearly four braccia deep, and frogs lived there almost all the year. Giulio considered how he would make this good, and he succeeded in restoring the former state and in preventing the recurrence of the accident, causing the streets to be raised on that side, by the duke's command, so that the buildings were above the level of the water. He directed that the small houses there should be pulled down, rebuilding larger and finer ones. When some opponents told the duke that Giulio was destroying too much, he refused to hear them, making Giulio master of the work and directing that no one should build except under him. This led to many complaints and threats, which reached the duke's ears, and he spoke out, letting it be known that he would consider any wrong done to Giulio as an injury to himself. The duke loved the talents of Giulio so that he could not live without him, and Giulio cherished the utmost reverence for the duke. He asked for no favour that he did not receive, and at his death he was found to have an income of over 1000 ducats owing to the duke's liberality. Giulio built himself a house at Mantua opposite S. Barnaba, with a fantastic façade in coloured stucco, the inside being similiarly decorated, and furnished with numerous antiquities brought from Rome and received from the duke, to whom he gave many of his own. Giulio designed an incredible number of things for foreign parts and Mantua, for no palaces or other important buildings could be erected there without his designs. He rebuilt the church of S. Benedetto there near the Po, a large and rich house of the black monks, upon the old walls, and he

[1] In 1530.

embellished the building with fine paintings and pictures. As his things were highly valued in Lombardy, Gian. Matteo Giberti, bishop of Verona, wished to have the tribune of the Duomo there painted by Moro Veronese from Giulio's designs. For the Duke of Ferrara Giulio prepared many designs for arras, afterwards executed by Maestro Niccolo and Gio. Battista Rosso, Flemings, in silk and gold. These were engraved by Giovan. Battista Mantovano, who thus treated several of Giulio's designs, and besides three battle-scenes engraved by others, he did a physician putting leeches on a woman's back, a Flight into Egypt, Joseph leading the ass, and angels bending a palm-tree to permit Christ to gather the fruit. He also engraved from Giulio's design the Tiber wolf suckling Romulus and Remus, and four scenes of Pluto, Jove and Neptune dividing the heavens, the earth and the sea by lot. He did the goat Alfea held by Melissa and nourishing Jove, and men tortured in prison, on a large sheet. Other prints were the parley between the armies of Scipio and Hannibal on the banks of a river; the Nativity of St. John the Baptist, engraved by Sebastiano da Reggio, and many others printed in Italy. In Flanders and France also many were printed, which I need not mention, beautiful as they were, as he produced them in the mass. Everything in art came so easy to him, especially design, that no one is known to have done more than he. He was universal and could discuss everything, but especially medals, upon which he spent much time and money. Although he spent most of his time on great things, yet he also did the smallest to oblige his patron and friends, and no sooner had they opened their mouth to express an idea than he had grasped it and made a sketch. Among the numerous treasures in his house there was a portrait of Albert Dürer, by himself, on fine cambric, sent by him to Raphael, diligently executed in water-colours, and finished without using white lead, the fabric itself serving for the whites and the fine threads being used to represent the hairs of the beard, and when held up to the light it was transparent all over. Giulio, who valued it highly, showed it to me himself as a miracle once when I was on business at Mantua.

The death of Duke Federigo,[1] whom Giulio loved beyond all imagining, affected him so deeply that he would have left Mantua if the cardinal, the duke's brother, regent during the minority of Federigo's sons, had not detained him. Giulio, indeed, had there his wife, children, houses, estate, and all

[1] In 1540.

the other requirements of a gentleman of position. The cardinal also wished to consult Giulio on the restoration of the Duomo. To this Giulio put his hand,[1] executing it in a beautiful style.

At this time Giorgio Vasari a great friend of Giulio, though they only knew each other by report and by letters, passed through Mantua on his way to Venice to see him and his works. On meeting, they recognised each other as though they had met a thousand times before. Giulio was so delighted that he spent four days in showing Vasari all his works, especially the plans of ancient buildings at Rome, Naples, Pozzuolo, Campagna, and all the other principal antiquities designed partly by him and partly by others. Then, opening a great cupboard, he showed him plans of all the buildings erected from his designs in Mantua, Rome and all Lombardy, so beautiful that I do not believe that more original, fanciful or convenient buildings exist. When the cardinal afterwards asked Giorgio, in Giulio's presence, what he thought of Giulio's work, he answered that he deserved a statue to every corner of the city and half the state would not suffice at reward his labours. The cardinal answered that Giulio was much more the master of the state than himself, and as Giulio was a most amiable man, especially to his friends, he loaded Giorgio with caresses.

Vasari left Mantua for Venice, and returned to Rome at the time when Michelagnolo uncovered his Last Judgment. He sent to Giulio by M. Nino Nini of Cortona, secretary of the cardinal of Mantua, three drawings of the seven mortal sins represented in that Judgment, which Giulio greatly welcomed for the author, and because he was about to do a chapel for the cardinal in the palace, and this incited him to greater things than he had purposed. Accordingly he made every effort to produce a fine cartoon,[2] and represented the call of Peter and Andrew to become fishers of men. It was the finest cartoon he ever did, and was executed by Fermo Guisoni, his pupil, now an excellent master. Not long after, the chiefs of the building of S. Petronio at Bologna desired to begin the façade of that church,[3] and sent for Guilio and a Milanese architect called Tofano Lombardino, a man then much esteemed in Lombardy for numerous buildings. They made several designs and, those of Baldassare Peruzzi being lost, one of Giulio's proved so fine that he deserved the greatest praise from that people and a rich reward on returning to Mantua.

[1] In 1544.   [2] The original is in the Louvre.   [3] In 1543.

Antonio Sangallo having died at Rome,[1] and the trustees of S. Pietro being in no small difficulty, not knowing to whom they should entrust the completion of so great a structure, they thought no one was better fitted than Giulio, whose qualities they all knew. Accordingly they endeavoured to tempt him with a large provision and by means of his friends, but all in vain, for although he would willingly have gone, two things detained him, the cardinal would not let him go, and his wife, friends and relations dissuaded him in every way. Perhaps neither cause would have prevailed, only he was not in good health. He thought of the honour to himself and his children, and began to make preparations, intending to ask the cardinal's permission, but the trouble grew worse. It was decreed that he should not go to Rome, and the end of his life was near, for he died in a few days at Mantua, in grief and pain, not being allowed to adorn his native Rome as he had adorned that city. He was fifty-four and left only one son, named Raffaello, after his master. This boy, having mastered the elements of the arts and shown considerable promise, died not long after, and so did his mother. A daughter named Virginia alone survives as the wife of Ercole Malatesta, and is living at Mantua. The death of Giulio caused deep sorrow to all who knew him. He was buried in S. Barnaba, where they intended to raise an honourable memorial. But his children and wife kept putting it off till at last there remained none. It is a shame that a man who did so much for the city has not received any recognition except from those who made use of him, who often remembered him in their needs. But the talents which adorned him through life and which are displayed in his works form a perpetual memorial which neither time nor years will destroy.

He was of medium stature, rather plump than thin, dark skinned, a handsome face, black and laughing eyes, most amiable, of courtly manners, a small eater, and elegant in his dress and bearing. Among his numerous pupils the best were Gian. dal Lione, Raffaello dal Colle Borghese, Benedetto Pagni of Pescia, Figurino da Faenza, Rinaldo and Gio. Battista Mantovani and Fermo Guisoni, who is still in Mantua and does him honour, being an excellent master. So also has Benedetto, who has done many things in his native Pescia, and a panel in the Opera of the Duomo at Pisa, a picture of the Virgin with a Florence presenting to her the dignity of the Medici house, a picture now owned by Sig. Mondragone, a Spaniard, highly favoured

[1] In 1546.

by the illustrious Prince of Florence. Giulio died in 1546 on
All Saints' Day, and the following epitaph was placed on
his tomb:

> Romanus moriens secum tres Julius arteis
> Abstulit (haud mirum) quatuor unus erat.

SEBASTIANO VINIZIANO,[1] Friar of the Piombo and Painter
(1485–1547)

PAINTING was not, as many affirm, the first profession of
Sebastiano, but music, as besides singing he delighted in playing
various instruments and especially the lute, on which he could
render all the parts without accompaniment. It was an exercise
of which the Venetian nobles were very fond, and he always
enjoyed intimate relations with them. While still young he turned
to painting, learning the elements from Giovan. Bellini, then
an old man. Then Giorgione da Castlefranco introduced a more
modern style, more harmonious and the colours better toned,
so that Sebastiano left Giovanni and joined Giorgione, whose
style he in great part acquired. He did many good portraits in
Venice, among others that of Verdelotto, an excellent French
musician then chapel-master in S. Marco, and in the same picture
Uberto, his fellow-singer. Verdelotto took this picture to Florence,
where he became chapel-master in S. Giovanni, and it is now in
the house of Francesco Sangallo, the sculptor. At that time
Sebastiano did a panel with some figures in S. Giovanni Grisos-
tomo at Venice, so like Giorgione's work that many people,
not experts, have been deceived. It is a fine picture, the colouring
giving it great relief. Sebastiano's fame spreading, Agostino
Chigi, a wealthy Sienese merchant, having affairs at Venice
and hearing him greatly praised in Rome, tried to induce him
to go thither, being pleased also with his lute-playing and
pleasant conversation. The task was not a hard one, for Sebastiano knew that city to be the home of all lofty spirits. When
Sebastiano arrived there [2] Agostino gave him work, the first
thing being the arches of the loggia in the palace of Agostino
in Travestevere,[3] opening on the garden where Baldassare of

---

[1] Sebastiano Luciani.   [2] About 1512.   [3] The Farnesina.

Siena had painted the vaulting. Here Sebastiano did some
poetical fancies in a style he had brought from Venice, very
unlike that in use among the prominent painters then at Rome.
After this, Raphael having done a scene of Galatea there,
Sebastiano, at Agostino's request, painted Polyphemus beside
it, doing his utmost, spurred by the competition of Baldassare
of Siena and of Raphael. He then painted some things in oils
much valued in Rome for the method of colouring he had
learned from Giorgione. While he was at work at Rome, Raphael
had become so famous that his friends said his paintings were
superior to those of Michelagnolo for beauty of colour, excellence
in design and grace, and they judged Raphael superior or at
least equal to him in painting, but absolutely superior in colouring. These things, being spread abroad by many artists who
thought more of Raphael's grace than of Michelagnolo's profundity, had made many more favourable to the former than the
latter. Sebastiano, however, was not among these, as his exquisite
judgment showed him the precise worth of each. Michelagnolo
therefore turned to him, being attracted by his colouring and
grace, and took him under his protection, thinking that if he gave
his assistance to Sebastian in design he might succeed in confounding his rivals under cover of a third person. While matters were in
this state and some things of Sebastiano being greatly appreciated
by the praises bestowed by Michelagnolo, besides being beautiful
and admirable of themselves, some one from Viterbo, in high
favour with the Pope, employed Sebastiano to decorate a chapel
for him in S. Francesco at Viterbo, with a dead Christ lamented
by His Mother.[1] This was diligently completed by Sebastiano,
who introduced a much-admired shaded landscape, but the
invention and cartoon were Michelagnolo's. The work was
considered most beautiful by all who saw it, and Sebastiano
acquired great credit and confirmed the reports of those who
favoured him. Piero Francesco Borgherini, a Florentine merchant, having taken a chapel in S. Pietro a Montorio on the
right on entering the church, it was allotted to Sebastiano by
Michelagnolo's influence, because Piero thought Michelagnolo
would prepare the design, as he did. Sebastiano executed it with
such diligence that it was rightly considered very beautiful.
From Michelagnolo's small design he made some larger ones
for his own use, a particularly good one being in our book.
Sebastiano thought he had discovered a method of colouring
in oils on a wall, and so he prepared the surface of the walls of

[1] In 1525.

this chapel with an incrustation which he thought would serve his purpose, and did the part with Christ at the Column in oils. Many thought that Michelagnolo outlined the Christ as well as doing the design, as there is a great difference between it and the other figures, and if Sebastiano had made no other figures he would deserve everlasting fame for this. The heads are excellent, and some of the hands and feet very beautiful, and though his style is somewhat hard, owing to the pains he took in copying, he may be counted among the good artists. Above this fresco he did two prophets and a Transfiguration in the vaulting. St. Peter and St. Paul stand on either side of the scene below, very life-like figures. He took six years over this little thing, but when works are so perfectly executed it is thankless to ask if they were done quickly or slowly, although those who work quickly obtain most praise, and those whose work does not please excuse themselves for their haste, though if this was not necessary they only accuse themselves in so doing. When Sebastiano uncovered the work it silenced the slanderers, for it was well done, and he had taken great pains. When Raphael did for the Cardinal de' Medici the picture of the Transfiguration intended for France, but placed at the principal altar of S. Pietro a Montorio after his death, Sebastiano did another of a Resurrection of Lazarus,[1] as it were in competition, very carefully finished, in part from Michelagnolo's design. Both were put together in the consistory when finished and received great praise, and although Raphael's was unequalled for grace and beauty, that of Sebastiano was universally admired. Cardinal Giulio de' Medici sent one of them to his bishopric at Narbonne, and the other was placed in the chancery until it was taken to S. Pietro a Montorio with the ornamental frame made by Giovan. Barile. When the cardinal became pope he richly rewarded Sebastiano, who rendered him a great service by this picture.

On the death of Raphael, Sebastiano, thanks to Michelagnolo, was universally admitted to hold the first place in painting above Giulio Romano, Gio. Francesco of Florence, Perino del Vaga, Polidoro, Maturino, Baldassare of Siena and the others. Thus Agostino Chigi, who got Raphael to design his tomb and chapel in S. Maria del Popolo, arranged that Sebastiano should paint it. But it remained covered till 1554, when Agostino's son Luigi wished to see it, a thing his father had not been able to. Accordingly he allotted the picture and the chapel to Francesco Salviati, who soon brought it to completion, which Sebastiano's

[1] 1517-19; now in the National Gallery, London.

slowness and irresolution would never have succeeded in doing, although he received far more from Agostino and his heirs than if he had completed it; but he did little, being perhaps tired of art, or too much taken up with ease and pleasure. For M. Filippo da Siena, clerk of the chamber, he began a scene in oils in la Pace at Rome on the wall over the high altar, but never finished it. The friars, in despair, were compelled to remove the obstructing scaffolding and cover the work with canvas, waiting patiently during Sebastiano's life. On his death they uncovered it, disclosing a beautiful Visitation, with many portraits of women executed with much grace.[1] It must be admitted that he took great pains in all his works, though he had not a natural facility, and he studied ceaselessly. In the Chapel of Agostino Chigi in la Pace, where Raphael had done his sibyls and prophets, Sebastiano wished to do some things on stone to surpass him, and he began by covering it with peperigno, filling the interstices with stucco; but after taking ten years to consider, he died. It is true that he made portraits with ease and excellence, but it was the contrary with scenes and other figures. Portraiture, indeed, was his forte, as we see by the excellent living likeness of Marcantonio Colonna, that of Ferdinando, Marquis of Pescara, and that of Vittoria Colonna.[2] He also portrayed Adrian VI. when he came to Rome, and Cardinal Nincofort,[3] who wanted him to decorate a chapel in S. Maria de Anima in Rome. But as he kept putting it off, the cardinal at length gave it to Michele the Fleming,[4] who painted scenes from the life of St. Barbara in fresco, imitating the Italian style very well, and introducing the cardinal's portrait into the picture.

But to return to Sebastiano. He drew Sig. Federigo da Bozzolo, some captain in armour,[5] now owned by Giulio de' Nobili, at Florence, a Roman woman,[6] now in the house of Luca Torrigiani, and an unfinished head, in possession of Gio. Battista Cavalcanti. He did a Virgin covering the Child with a cloth, a rare work now in the wardrobe of Cardinal Farnese. He sketched, but did not finish, a fine panel of St. Michael standing over

[1] The paintings were removed when Bernini's monument for the Chigi was set up; portions are now at Alnwick Castle.
[2] Possibly the "Lady as St. Agatha" in the National Gallery.
[3] Cardinal Enckenvoort: possibly the portrait in the Naples Museum, sometimes described as Pope Alexander VI.
[4] Michael Coxcie.
[5] Possibly the knight of the Berlin Gallery.
[6] This may be the picture long described as the Fornarina and attributed to Raphael.

the devil, to go to the King of France, who had previously
received a picture of his.

On the elevation of Giulio de' Medici to the papacy as
Clement VII., that pontiff told him, by the bishop of Vaison,
that the time had come when he would give him a benefice.
Sebastiano, while thus in high hope, did many portraits, among
them Pope Clement, then beardless, doing two, one for the
bishop of Vaison; and the other, a much larger picture, represented seated down to the knees, is now in Sebastiano's house
at Rome. He also drew Anton Francesco degli Albizzi of Florence,
then on business in Rome, making it most life-like, so that it was
sent to Florence as a precious jewel. The head and hands are
truly marvellous, not to mention the excellence of the velvets,
furs and other parts, and as Sebastiano was pre-eminent in
portrait-painting, all Florence was amazed at this work. He
also drew a portrait of M. Pietro Aretino, at once a good likeness
and remarkable painting for the difference between five or six
kinds of black, velvet, broadcloth, ermine, damask, cloth, and
his dark black beard, all most realistic. The figure holds a
laurel branch and a sheet, on which is written the name of
Clement VII., and two masks, a beautiful one for Virtue and
an ugly one for Vice. M. Pietro gave this to his native place,
and the Aretines put it in the public hall of their council, honour-
ing the name of their distinguished fellow-citizen. Sebastiano
next drew a remarkable portrait of Andrea Doria,[1] and the
head of Baccio Valori of Florence, of incredible beauty. Remembering the promise made by the bishop of Vaison, Sebastiano
asked for the office of the Piombo on the death of Frà Mariano
Fetti, the holder, and although Giovanni da Udine, who had
long served the Pope *in minoribus*, also demanded it, Clement
gave it to Sebastiano,[2] owing to the prayers of the bishop, and
because he deserved it for his skill, while he gave Giovanni a
pension of 300 crowns upon it.

Sebastiano accordingly became a friar, and finding that he had
enough to satisfy his desires without lifting his brush, he took
his ease, repaying himself for toilsome days and restless nights.
But when he had anything to do he went back to work like one
to execution. Thus we see how easily men err in their judgment,
as they usually desire what is most opposite to their profession,
and when they think they are crossing themselves with their

[1] Doria Gallery, Rome.
[2] In 1531. The holder of the office affixed the leaden seals to the papal
documents. Piombo, from Latin *plumbum*, lead.

finger they poke it in their eye, as the Tuscan proverb runs. It is a common opinion that rewards and honour incite men to the study of the arts for which they receive them, while the neglect of those arts leads to their abandonment, and both ancients and moderns unite to blame those princes who do not assist all kinds of able men by rewards. But to prove this rule we sometimes see such rewards produce the opposite effect, for many men are more useful to the world when poor than when they have an abundance of everything. Thus the liberality of Clement rendered the industrious Sebastiano indolent, though when poor and competing with Raphael he never rested. Prudent princes ought therefore to consider the nature of those whom they reward, so that their liberality may not turn them away from their labours. After becoming a friar, Sebastiano did a half-length Christ bearing the Cross [1] on stone for the patriarch of Aquileia, which was much admired, especially for the head and hands, at which he was excellent. Not long after, the Pope's niece came to Rome, the present Queen of France, and Frà Sebastiano began her portrait, but it was left unfinished in the Pope's wardrobe. The Cardinal Ippolito de' Medici becoming enamoured of Signora Giulia Gonzaga, then living at Fondi, sent Sebastiano thither with four light horses to take her portrait.[2] This he completed in a month, reproducing the celestial beauty of that lady, and when the picture was taken to Rome the cardinal fully recognised the artist's labours, for he perceived it to be far superior to all Sebastiano's works up to that time. It was afterwards sent to King Francis of France, who kept it at Fontainebleau. Sebastiano introduced a new method of colouring in oils on stone which greatly pleased the people, as it seemed that such works ought to last for ever and that neither fire nor worms could harm them. Accordingly he began many such paintings, framing them in ornaments of variegated stones, thus forming a fine offset when they were polished. It is true that owing to their great weight such paintings could not be moved without the utmost difficulty. Many, attracted by the novelty and beauty of the thing, gave him earnest money to do some for them, but being more fond of talking than acting, he kept putting things off. However, he did a dead Christ and the Virgin on stone for Don Ferrante Gonzaga,[3] who sent it to Spain, with a stone ornament. It was considered a very beautiful work, and Sebastiano

---

[1] Now at Madrid.
[2] In 1532, also a candidate for the National Gallery portrait.
[3] Madrid; commissioned 1533, finished 1539.

received 500 crowns for it from M. Niccolo da Cortona, the cardinal of Mantua's agent in Rome. Sebastiano certainly deserved praise because, whereas his compatriot Domenico was the first to paint in oils on a wall, followed by Andrea del Castagno, Antonio and Piero del Pollaiuolo, he succeeded in preventing his frescoes from blackening, a thing they had never achieved. Thus his Christ at the Column in S. Pietro a Montorio has never changed, possessing the same brilliancy of colour as on the first day. He used every care, employing a rich lime mixed with mastic and pitch, which he melted together on the fire and laid it on the wall, smoothing it over with red-hot lime, so that his things have stood the damp and kept their colour. He used the same mixture for work on stone, marble, porphyry, and similar materials, on which paintings last a very long time. He also showed how to paint on silver, copper, tin and other metals. He was so fond of gossiping that he would spend whole days without working, and when he did begin it cost him an effort, chiefly because he believed that his work could never be paid for adequately. For the cardinal of Aragon [1] he did a beautiful nude St. Agatha martyred, now in the wardrobe of Guidobaldo, Duke of Urbino, no whit inferior to many other fine paintings there by Raphael, Titian and others. He drew a fine portrait of Sig. Piero Gonzaga on stone, in oils, though he spent three years upon it. Michelagnolo being in Florence at the time of Pope Clement, engaged upon the new sacristy of S. Lorenzo, Giuliano Bugiardini wished Baccio Valori to paint himself and Pope Clement in one picture, and the Pope and the archbishop of Capua in another for M. Ottaviano de' Medici. So Michelagnolo sent to request Frà Sebastiano to send a painting of the Pope's head to Rome, and he did a fine one. Giuliano made use of this, and when the pictures were finished Michelagnolo presented them to his friend, M. Ottaviano. This is certainly the finest head that Sebastiano ever did, and the best likeness, as we may see in the house of M. Ottaviano's heirs. He also drew Pope Paul Farnese immediately after his election, and began his son the Duke of Castro, but like so many other things begun by him, he did not finish it.

Frà Sebastiano had a pleasant house near Popolo, which he built and where he lived at ease without thinking of painting or working. He would often say that it is very hard in old age to bridle the ardour of youthful artists to win name and

---

[1] Cardinal Ranzoni; the picture is in the Pitti Gallery, signed and dated 1520.

advantage by competition, and that it was as prudent to live peaceably as to trouble about one's reputation after death, for all works die sooner or later. He acted up to this, always sought to have the best wines and most valuable things, counting life more than art. Being a great friend of all men of genius, he often invited Il Molza and M. Gandolfo[1] to dine. M. Francesco Berni of Florence, who wrote him a piece of poetry, was another friend, and Frà Sebastiano replied with another, for, being very versatile, he could make humorous Tuscan verses. When some said that it was shameful now that he had enough to live on that he would no longer work, Frà Sebastiano answered, "I do nothing now that I have enough, because there are men now living who can do in two months what used to take me two years, and I believe if I live long enough I shall see everything painted. As these do so much, it is as well there should be some who do nothing, so that they may have the more employment." Such pleasantries and others did he indulge in, being a witty man, and indeed no one was ever better company than he. He was a great friend of Michelagnolo. But when he had to paint a wall of the Pope's chapel, where Buonarroti's Last Judgment is, some coldness arose between them, for Sebastiano persuaded the Pope to have it done in oils, while Michelagnolo did not wish to do it except in fresco. As Michelagnolo did not declare himself one way or the other, and the wall was prepared in Sebastiano's fashion, several months passed and nothing was done, but on being approached Michelagnolo declared that he would only do it in fresco, and that oil-painting was a woman's art and only fit for lazy well-to-do people like Frà Sebastiano. Accordingly he removed the incrustation made by the friar's direction, and prepared everything for work in fresco. But he never forgave Sebastiano for the injury which he conceived had been done to him. Sebastiano attained the age of sixty-two, having for long done nothing beyond attending to the duties of his office and good living. He then fell sick of a severe fever, and being rubicund and sanguine, he died in a few days. His will provided for his burial without priests, friars or lights, but that all the money for such expenses should be distributed among the poor, and this was done. He was buried in the church of the Popolo in June 1547. Art did not lose much by his death, because he was lost to it as soon as he became friar of the Piombo, though his friends and many artists grieved at the loss of a pleasant companion. Many youths came to Sebastiano to learn art, but

[1] Gandolfo Porri.

made small profit, as they learned little from his example except good living. However, Tommaso Laurato, a Sicilian, besides many other things did a beautiful Venus and Love embracing, now in the house of M. Francesco Bolognetti. He also did a much-admired portrait of Sig. Bernardino Savelli and some other works which I need not mention.

PERINO DEL VAGA, Painter of Florence
(1500–1547)

GENIUS is a great gift, and without regard for wealth or power or nobility, it is usually bestowed upon a poor man. Heaven does this to show the influence of the stars, giving some more and some less, just as some are born hot and some slow, weak or strong, fierce or mild, fortunate or unfortunate, with more or less ability. If any doubt on this subject remained, the life of Perino del Vaga would prove my contention. His father was a poor man, and while quite little he was abandoned by his parents, having art as his sole legitimate mother whom he always honoured. He fortified his natural ability by much study, enabling him afterwards to make those magnificent decorations, the glory of Genoa and of Prince Doria. We must, therefore, believe that Heaven alone raises men from the lowest depths to the summit of greatness by means of their works. Thus Perino rose by the art of design in which he displayed the utmost excellence and grace, while in stucco he equalled the ancients and all the modern artists, showing all the most desirable qualities of beauty, excellence, lightness in his colouring and other ornaments.

There was living in Florence one Giovanni Buonaccorsi who, being young, spirited and liberal, spent all his property in the wars of Charles VIII. of France in the service of that prince, in war and gaming, and finally he died. His son Piero was only two months old when his mother died of the plague. He was suckled by a goat until his father took a second wife at Bologna, whose husband and children had died of the plague. Though thus tainted she finished the weaning of Piero, who was called Perino as a pet name, and as such he was ever afterwards known. When his father went to France he left the child at Florence with some relations, who, not wishing to have the trouble of keeping him and teaching him a trade, sent him to the apothecary of the Pinadoro to learn that trade, But as he did not like it, the painter Andrea de' Ceri took him to run errands, being pleased with him, and looking to find in him genius and quickness. Andrea was but a mediocre painter, one of those who work publicly in their shop at mechanical jobs and who did some wax candles (ceri) every year on the feast of St. John to be offered with the other tribute of the city, and hence his name, which was also given to Perino for a while. Andrea kept Perino a year, teaching him the principles of his art as well as he could, but when the boy was eleven he was constrained to send him to a better master. Having close relations with Ridolfo, son of Domenico Ghirlandaio, considered a very able painter, Andrea sent Perino to him to study design and make progress in the art for which he displayed such talent. In a short time, by careful study, Perino surpassed all his fellow-pupils. Among them was one who continually spurred him on, named Toto del Nunziata, who, rising to the level of the best geniuses, left Florence and went to England with some Florentine merchants, where he did all his works. He served the king there in architecture, building his chief palace, and was highly esteemed. He and Perino competed together and soon became excellent. Perino, by dint of drawing the cartoons of Michelagnolo with the others, became the best of all, so that he aroused great expectations.

At that time Vaga, a Florentine painter, was in the city. He did some rude things in Toscanella in Roman territory, being a mediocre master, and having a great deal of work he needed help and wanted to take some youth with him to assist him in design, which he did not himself possess, and in other matters. Seeing Perino designing in Ridolfo's shop with the other youths, and observing his superiority to the rest, he was amazed, and being pleased with his appearance and methods, for he was a handsome youth, courteous, modest and well-bred, Vaga asked if he would like to go to Rome, saying he would assist him in his studies, and that he should name his own terms. Perino greatly desired to succeed in his profession and wanted to see Rome, so he said he would speak to Andrea, who, however, did not wish to lose him. But Vaga persuaded Ridolfo and Andrea, and finally took Perino to Toscanella. There, with Perino's help, they finished the work begun and many other things undertaken afterwards. But Perino, seeing that the promise to take him to Rome was neglected, to serve Vaga's interests, determined to go by himself. This led Vaga to leave all his works and take him to

Rome, where Perino returned to his loved design, his ardour being more and more kindled during a stay there of many weeks. But as Vaga wished to return to Toscanella, he introduced Perino to many ordinary painters and to all his friends, asking them to help him, and in this way the boy became known thenceforward as Perino del Vaga.

Perino remained in Rome, observing the ancient sculptures, the marvellous constructions, mostly in ruins, and was filled with admiration for the illustrious men who had produced such works. His artistic sense being thus quickened, he burned to emulate their excellence, to win a great name and wealth as they had done. Considering his own base condition and poverty, and seeing that he could not reach their level without the means to live, he agreed to work for the shops, now with one painter and to-morrow with another, like a journeyman. This proved a hindrance to his studies, and caused him infinite sorrow because he could not progress so rapidly as he had hoped. Accordingly he proposed to divide his time, giving half to jobs and the rest to design. In the latter category came all feast days and a great part of the night, robbing time from time in order to become famous and to escape from the hands of others as much as possible. He began designing in the chapel of Pope Julius, where the vaulting is by Michelagnolo, following Raphael's style and methods. He did the like with antique marbles, and studied the arabesques in the caves, learned the methods of stucco, and, begging his bread, suffered any hardship in his quest of excellence. Before long he became the best designer in all Rome, with a better understanding of the muscles and the difficulties of nude figures than any, even perhaps among the best masters. This made him known not only to artists but to many lords and prelates, especially as Giulio Romano and Gio. Francesco il Fattore, pupils of Raphael, praised him to their master, so that he wanted to know Perino and see his designs. These, and the spirit of the youth, so pleased Raphael that he predicted a brilliant future for him. Leo X. had directed that the papal loggias, built for him by Raphael, should be decorated with stucco and gilded as Raphael should see fit. For this work the master appointed Giovanni da Udine as director for the stucco and arabesques, a unique master of the craft, especially in animals, fruit and other small things. Raphael searched Rome and sent abroad for other masters, thus collecting a group of men skilled in stucco, arabesques, foliage, festoons, scenes, and so forth, and according to their success they were advanced and received higher wages. In this way many youths made progress and afterwards became excellent. Among them Perino was recommended by Raphael to Giovanni to do arabesques and scenes, as Giovanni should employ him. By working hard to prove his ability in competition with the others, Perino soon acquired the reputation of being the best of all in design, colouring, finish, and in working arabesques and figures with the lightest grace, as we see by his arabesques, figures and scenes there executed from Raphael's designs and sketches. In the vaulting in the middle of the loggia he did the Jews crossing the Jordan with the ark, the march round the walls of Jericho and the fall of the walls. Then follows the fight of Joshua with the Amorites, making the sun stand still, with bronze-coloured representations beneath of Abraham sacrificing Isaac, Jacob wrestling with the angel, Joseph receiving the twelve brethren, fire consuming the sons of Levi, and others too numerous to mention, which may be distinguished by their style. At the entrance of the loggia he did a Nativity, a Baptism of Christ, and a Last Supper of great beauty, and under the windows the best bronze-coloured scenes in all the work. These and the numerous stucco things he did, with his beautiful colouring and finish, excited great admiration. The work made him very famous, but the praise only kindled him to renewed efforts, as he felt certain that he ought to reap such fruits as he saw daily gathered by Raphael and Michelagnolo, and he was rejoiced at having the esteem of Giovanni da Udine and Raphael, and at being employed on important work. He always treated Raphael with the utmost deference, so that the master loved him like a son.

At this time the vaulting of the Hall of the Popes leading to the loggias of the rooms of Alexander VI., painted by Pinturicchio, was decorated by Gio. da Udine and Perino, by order of Pope Leo, with the stucco, arabesques, animals and other decorations, the place being divided into circles and ovals for seven planets drawn by their animals, Jupiter by the eagle, Venus by the dove, Luna by women, Mars by wolves, Mercury by cocks, the Sun by horses, and Saturn by serpents; besides the twelve signs of the Zodiac and the forty-eight images of the sky, such as the Great Bear, the Dog Star, and many others too numerous to recount, especially as the work may be seen. Most of these are by Perino's hand. In the middle of the vault is a circle with four figures, representing Victories holding the Pope's realm and the keys. They are foreshortened from below and executed with masterly art, with light, slender draperies, partially disclosing the bare legs and arms. This work has always been greatly admired for its rich beauty and delicate charm, and it is worthy of the Pope, who did not forget to reward the artists. Perino did a façade in grisaille, imitating Polidoro and Maturino, opposite the house of the Marchioness of Massa, near Maestro Pasquino, executed in a bold design, and carefully finished.[1] In the third year of his pontificate Leo went to Florence, where many triumphs were made. Perino preceded the court, to see his native place and the pomp there. He did for a triumphal arch at S. Trinità a large figure seven braccia high, in competition with his old rival Toto del Nunziata. But Perino wearied for Rome, judging the methods of the Roman artists very superior, so he left Florence and returned to take up his work in S. Eustachio dalla Dogana, doing a St. Peter in fresco, a figure in high relief with simple draperies, though designed with judgment. At that time the archbishop of Cyprus was in Rome, a great admirer of talent, especially in painting. Having a house near Chiavica, and a garden furnished with statues and other antiquities, he sent for his friend Perino, to consult him about decorating the walls of the garden with Bacchantes, Satyrs, Fauns, and other rustic things, to correspond with an ancient statue of Bacchus seated next a tigress. Perino did a small loggia here among other things, with little figures, various arabesques and landscapes, coloured with the utmost grace and diligence, and the work has always been much admired by artists. He thus became known to the Fuggers, German merchants, who, having built a house near the Banchi, on the way to the Florentine church, employed him to do a court and loggia and many figures, distinguished by his light and graceful style. At the same time M. Marchionne Baldassini had a very well planned house built by Antonio da S. Gallo, near S. Agostino, and wishing to have a hall there painted, after considering many youths he chose Perino, so that it might be well done. When the price had been settled, Perino began, never resting until he had finished it. He divided it by pilasters, with large and small niches between them, the large containing philosophers, one or two in each, and the lesser naked infants, some veiled, surmounted by women's heads, painted like marble. Above the cornice, on the pilasters, he made scenes of the deeds of the Romans from Romulus to Numa Pompilius. He represented various ornaments of different sorts of stones and marble, and a beautiful Peace above the chimney, burning arms

[1] In 1515.

and trophies. The work was much valued by M. Marchionne, and has been greatly admired by all painters. In the convent of St. Anna he did a chapel in fresco containing many figures, with his customary finish. In S. Stefano del Cacco he did a Pietà in fresco for a Roman lady, at the altar, with the lady's portrait, a work of great beauty, executed with facile dexterity. Antonio da S. Gallo had then made a very ornate tabernacle of travertine at the corner of the house in Rome called l'Imagine di Ponte, and received a commission from the donor to have a fine picture put in it. Knowing Perino to be the best of the young artists, Antonio allotted it to him. Perino accordingly did Christ crowning the Virgin, with a choir of angels and seraphim in delicate draperies, scattering flowers and beautiful infants. On the two sides he did St. Sebastian and St. Anthony, beautiful and graceful, like all his work. A protonotary had finished a marble chapel on four columns in the Minerva, and being desirous of having a picture, even if not a large one, he employed Perino, of whose fame he had heard. Perino did a Descent from the Cross, the subject chosen by the donor, most carefully, representing the body on the ground, the Maries about it weeping in gestures full of grief and Nicodemus and others in deep sorrow at seeing the innocence of the dead Christ. But most remarkable of all were the two thieves still on their crosses, with fine muscles and sinews, showing the effects of their violent death. There is also a fine landscape in darkness. If the flood that happened in Rome after the sack[1] had not half-destroyed it, its excellence would be apparent. But the water has softened the plaster and warped the wood, like the refraction of the legs when bathing, so that it gives little pleasure and one can only feel very sorry, for it must have been one of the treasures of Rome.

Jacopo Sansovino was then engaged in restoring the church of S. Marcello at Rome,[2] a convent of the Servites, left unfinished, and on completing the walls and some chapels and roofing them, the friars decided that Perino should do a Virgin adored, in the church, and St. Joseph and St. Philip, the Servite, in niches on either side. Above them he did some beautiful cherubs, one on a dado with the ends of two festoons on his shoulders, which run to the corners of the chapel, where two other cherubs hold them, their legs finely disposed, a work of the finest grace and art, the bright colouring in its freshness and beauty looking real and not painted. These may be considered the best works in fresco ever produced, because the figures live and move, the mouths

[1] 8 October, 1530.   [2] About 1519.

seem about to speak, and Art has conquered Nature, attaining her utmost limits. It brought Perino a great name, connoisseurs recognised his great talent, and he was much more highly esteemed than before. Thus Lorenzo Pucci, Cardinal Santiquattro, having taken a chapel on the left of the principal chapel in la Trinità, a convent of French and Calabrian friars of the order of St. Francesco di Paola, allotted it to Perino. Here he painted the life of the Virgin in fresco, finishing the vaulting and a wall under the arch. Over an arch outside he did two prophets, Isaiah and Daniel, 4½ braccia high, showing the excellence of his design and the beauty of his colouring. His excellence may be seen in the Isaiah, a melancholy figure reading, and seeming to desire something new; he looks at the book, with one hand to his head, as some do when studying. Daniel raises his head to heaven, to solve the doubts of his people. Between them are two infants holding the cardinal's arms on a fine shield, and they seem alive and in relief. In the four compartments of the vaulting are four scenes: the Conception of the Virgin, her birth, when she ascends the Temple steps, and her marriage. On the wall under the arch of the vaulting is a Visitation containing many fine figures, notably some who have jumped on to pedestals to see what is passing, done very naturally, while the buildings and other figures are fine in every part. Perino went no farther, for he fell sick, and when he recovered, the plague broke out in Rome in 1523 with such violence that those who wished to save their lives had to go.

At this time a goldsmith named Piloto, a great friend of Perino, was living at Rome, and as they were dining together one morning he persuaded Perino to go to Florence, for it was many years since he had been there, and it would be a good thing to make himself known and leave some trace of his gifts there. Although Andrea de' Ceri and his wife, who had brought him up, were dead, yet Perino loved his country, though he had nothing there. So one morning he and Piloto set out for Florence. Arrived there, he was delighted at seeing the works of the old masters which he had studied in his boyhood, and also those of the best living masters. His friends obtained work for him, as I shall relate.

One day a crowd of artists, painters, sculptors, architects, goldsmiths, marble and wood carvers came together, according to the old custom, some to see and hear Perino, and many to compare the differences between the artists of Rome and Florence, but most to hear the blame and praise frequently bandied about between artists. They chanced to come to Masaccio's Chapel in the Carmine, and as they examined the paintings all expressed wonder that the master should have possessed so much judgment when he had nothing but Giotto's works to see, designing and colouring in such a modern style that his facility displayed the difficulty of art, while no one had ever combined so much relief, vigour and skill. The conversation pleased Perino, and he said, "I do not deny the truth of what you say, and you might even go farther, but I will always dispute that no one can equal this style, and without disparagement I say that I know many who possess more vigour and grace, whose works are not less vivid than these and far more beautiful. I am sorry, though I am not foremost in art, that there is no place here where a figure could be made, so that, before I leave Florence, I could do one in fresco beside one of those, in order that you might be able to judge whether one of the moderns cannot equal them." A master who was considered the foremost painter in Florence, being curious to see Perino's work, and perhaps anxious to abase his pride, spoke as follows: "Though this part is filled, there is the St. Paul opposite which is as fine a figure as any in the chapel. You may readily demonstrate what you say by making another Apostle beside the St. Peter of Masolino or the St. Paul of Masaccio." The St. Peter was nearer the window, in a larger space and a better light, while it was not inferior to the St. Paul. Thus everyone pressed Perino to try, as they were curious to see the Roman style, and many declared it would be a good thing to rid them of the fancy they had cherished for so many decades; and if he did better, then all would hasten to adopt the modern style. Accordingly Perino decided to do it, being urged by the master, who said that he ought not to fail to afford so much pleasure to the men of genius there, that he could do it in fresco in two weeks, while his labours would be praised for years. The speaker, however, believed that Perino could not do much better than those who were esteemed the best artists. Perino then asked permission of M. Giovanni da Pisa, prior of the convent, to paint his figure. This was graciously accorded; and after measuring the space, they parted. Perino then drew a cartoon of St. Andrew, finishing it with great diligence. He had already put up his scaffolding, but before he began his numerous friends, who had seen his works in Rome, had procured for him a work in fresco, whereby he could leave a memorial of himself in Florence and show the beauty and brilliance of his genius, so that the rulers might possibly entrust him with some work of importance. In Camaldoli at Florence artists used then to meet in the Company de' Martiri, and they had often wished to have a wall painted there representing legends of the martyrs, their condemnation to death before the two Roman emperors, and their crucifixion after the battle on the trees of a wood. This work was entrusted to Perino, and although the place was remote and the price small, the delight in making scenes and the advice of his friends induced him to accept, for the work would earn him the consideration he deserved among the citizens and artists of Florence, who only knew him by repute. Accordingly he made a small design, which was much admired, and prepared a cartoon as large as the work, completing it and finishing the principal figures, and so his Apostle was abandoned. He made his cartoon on a white sheet, leaving the lights blank. The two emperors in their tribunal are condemning all the prisoners to the cross. Some are kneeling before the tribunal, some upright and some bent; all are naked and bound in various ways; some are writhing and trembling at the prospect of crucifixion; the heads of the old display the constancy of faith, those of the young the fear of death, others, fearful of the pain, are writhing in their bonds. We see the tension of the muscles and the cold sweat of fear. The soldiers who present the prisoners at the tribunal and then lead them to death are cruel and bold. The emperors and soldiers wear antique cuirasses, very ornate and curious clothes, their shoes, greaves, helmets, shields and other armour being covered with beautiful decoration in imitation of the antique, displaying all the resources of art. Artists and other connoisseurs declared they had never seen a more beautiful cartoon, except that designed by Michelagnolo for the hall of the council in Florence. Thus Perino acquired the highest possible fame, and while he was completing his cartoon he passed the time in arranging and mixing the oil-colours to make an admirable little picture for his friend the goldsmith Piloto of a Virgin which he half finished.

One Ser Raffaello di Sandro, a lame priest and chaplain of S. Lorenzo, a great friend of artists, had for many years been intimate with Perino. He persuaded the artist to come to his house, for Perino had no one to keep house for him, and passed the time staying first with one friend and then with another. So Perino went and stayed several weeks. Meanwhile an outbreak of the plague in some parts of Florence caused Perino to

leave. He first wished to pay his share of the expenses, but Ser
Raffaello would take nothing, saying he would be contented
to have a drawing. Perino took four braccia of coarse canvas,
and fastening it to the wall between two doors of the hall, he
did a scene in bronze colour, in a day and a night, of Moses
crossing the Red Sea, and the drowning of Pharoah, his horses
and chariots. The figures are in fine attitudes, some swimming
in armour, some naked, others holding the horses' necks, their
beards wet with the water and crying out in fear of death,
making every effort to escape. On the opposite side of the sea
are Moses, Aaron and the other Hebrew men and women
thanking God, and a number of vases of which they have
spoiled the Egyptians, all are beautifully dressed, the women's
coiffures being finely varied. This gave as much pleasure to his
good friend Ser Raffaello as if the priorate of S. Lorenzo had
been presented to him. The canvas was much prized and admired,
and on Ser Raffaello's death it passed with his other property
to Domenico di Sandro, the pork butcher, his brother.

Leaving Florence, Perino abandoned his Martyrs, of which
he was very tired, though if it had been anywhere but in
Camaldoli he would have finished it; but the officials of the
board of health having taken the place, he preferred to escape,
feeling that he had done enough to show his skill in design.
The cartoon and his other property were left to his friend
Giovanni di Goro, a goldsmith, who died of the plague, and
they then came into the hands of Piloto, who was always ready
to show these treasures to men of ability, but I do not know
what became of them after his death. Perino avoided the
plague for several months in various places, never ceasing to
design and study, and on the cessation of the scourge, he
returned to Rome and did some small things, which I will
not describe.

The election of Pope Clement VII., in 1523, revived the arts
of painting and sculpture which had suffered great depression
under Adrian VI., who took no pleasure in them, but rather
hated such things, so that no one else patronised artists. On
the election of the new Pope Perino did many things. In place
of Raphael, now dead, it was proposed to make Giulio Romano
and Giovanni Francesco called Il Fattore chiefs of the art, to share
out the work to others, as had been the custom, but Perino, who
had done the Pope's arms in fresco, with a cartoon of Giulio over
the door of Cardinal Ceserino, succeeded so well that they were
afraid he might be put over them, as although they were the pupils

and heirs of Raphael they had not fully inherited the master's art nor the gracefulness which he imparted to his figures by colouring. Accordingly Giulio and Gio. Francesco decided to make up to Perino, and so in the year 1525 they married the latter's sister to Perino to cement the intimate friendship between them which had lasted so long. In a short time the praise accorded to Perino's work in S. Marcello led the prior and certain heads of the company of the Crocofisso, which owns a chapel there, to determine to have it painted, and they allotted the work to Perino, in the hope of getting something excellent. After making his scaffolding he began in the middle of the barrel vaulting a creation of Eve. A fine nude Adam lies sleeping while a vivacious Eve, with her hands clasped, rises to receive the blessing of her Maker. The Lord is a figure of grave, majestic aspect, his garments lapping over the nude figures; on his right are St. Mark and St. John, completed by Perino, except the head and a bare arm of the latter. Between them are two cherubs embracing, as an ornament of a chandelier, with vivid flesh-tints, while the heads, draperies and arms of the Evangelists and all that he did himself are of the utmost beauty. The work was interrupted by much sickness and many misfortunes, and it is said the men of the company left him short of money. It dragged on until the sack of Rome in 1527 when many artists were killed and their works destroyed and scattered. After running from place to place with his wife and little girl, Perino was most unfortunately taken prisoner and compelled to pay a ransom, a thing sufficient to unseat his reason. After the sack he was so depressed, being unable to shake off his fear, that he put aside all matters of art, though he painted gauze cloths and other fancies for Spanish soldiers, and when he had recovered his balance he lived in poverty like the others. Il Baviera alone among the artists, who had the prints of Raphael, had not lost much. Out of friendship for Perino he got him to design for him the Metamorphoses of the Gods, to be engraved by the excellent Jacopo Caraglio. They are well done, as the engraver, in preserving Perino's outlines and style, has also endeavoured to keep their lightness and grace. While the sack had ruined Rome and driven out its inhabitants, the Pope himself being at Orvieto, and while almost nothing was going on, Niccolo Viniziano, a rare master of embroidery and servant of Prince Doria, came to Rome. Out of his old friendship for Perino and his good disposition towards artists, he persuaded him to come away from his wretched lot there and proceed to Genoa, promising to give him work with the prince, who loved painting and would employ him on important works, especially as he had often said he wished to decorate a suite of rooms. Perino in his need did not require much persuasion, as he was eager to leave Rome. After arranging to leave his wife and daughter with relations at Rome he went to Genoa, where Niccolo introduced him to the prince, who was more delighted than he had ever been in his life. After many discussions and all manner of favours, it was arranged that Perino should begin to decorate a palace with stucco, frescoes and oil-paintings. I will attempt to describe this work as shortly as possible, which is the best Perino ever did. At the entrance is a Doric door in marble, the designs and models for which are Perino's, with pedestals, bases, shafts, capitals, architraves, friezes, cornices and beautiful women sitting and holding some arms, a work carved by Maestro Giov. da Fiesole, the figures being by Silvio, sculptor of Fiesole, a bold and vivacious master. After passing the door, the vaulting is of stucco with varied scenes and arabesques, the arcades containing squires fighting on foot and on horse, showing great diligence and art. The staircases on the left are sumptuously adorned with antique arabesques, with various scenes and small figures, masks, infants, animals and other fancies done with his customary invention and judgment, in these matters truly divine. On mounting the stairs you arrive in a fine loggia, with a stone door at each extremity, over which are two figures painted, a man and a woman, turned away from each other, one looking forward, the other back. The vaulting of five arches is superbly decorated with stucco and oval compartments containing scenes of the utmost beauty. The walls are done right to the ground with seated captains, some of them portraits and some imaginary, representing the Dorias, with large gold letters above: *Magni viri, maximi duces optima fecere pro patria*. In the first hall, entered by a door on the left from the loggia, are fine stucco ornaments on the vaulting. In the middle is a large scene of a shipwreck of Æneas, containing live and dead nude figures in various attitudes, besides a good number of galleys and ships, some safe and some broken by the storm. We also remark the figures defending themselves, the terrible clouds, rolling waves, the peril of life, and a representation of all the passions aroused by the fortunes of the sea. This was the first scene begun by Perino for the prince. It is said that on Perino's arrival at Genoa Girolamo da Trevisi came to paint some things, and he did a façade facing the garden. While

Perino was beginning the cartoon for his shipwreck, working at his ease in Genoa and seeing the city, and had done a good part of his cartoon, some in grisaille, some in carbon and black crayon, some only in outline, Girolamo grumbled, saying "What is the use of cartoons? I have art at the point of my brush." His words, frequently repeated, reached Perino, who immediately, in anger, fixed his cartoon to the vault, and removing the scaffolding in many places to allow it to be seen, he opened the room. All Genoa flocked to see it, and sang the praises of Perino's great design. Among them went Girolamo, who saw what he had not expected from Perino. Accordingly, terrified by its beauty, he left Genoa without asking the prince's licence, and returned to Bologna, where he lived. Meanwhile Perino did the walls of the room in oils, considered a thing of remarkable beauty, the vaulting down to the lunettes being decorated with stucco. In the other room, entered by the right door of the loggia, he did in fresco and stucco Jupiter subduing the giants, containing many fine nudes larger than life. The gods in the sky are making gestures appropriate to their characters at the terrible thunders, while the stucco is done with the utmost diligence and the colouring could not be finer, for Perino was a perfect master in that art. He decorated four rooms of which the vaulting is done in stucco and fresco, representing the best fables of Ovid. The beauty, abundance and variety of the figures, foliage, animals and grotesques cannot be imagined. On the other side of the hall he did four other scenes, designing the stucco and the paintings, which were carried out by his apprentices. Among his assistants was Lucio Romano, who did arabesques and stucco, and many Lombards. Not a single room there but is full of friezes right up to the vaulting, of infants, curious masks and animals, while in the studies, ante-chambers and cabinets everything is painted and beautiful. From the palace to the garden one passes a terrace which has friezes in every room up to the vaulting, and the chambers, halls and ante-chambers are done similarly. Pordenone assisted here, as related in his Life, and Domenico Beccafumi of Siena showed himself not inferior to the others, although his best works are in Siena.

But to return to Perino. After finishing the prince's palace, he did a frieze in a room in the house of Giannetin Doria, containing beautiful women, and numerous works in fresco and oils for nobles, such as a fine panel in S. Francesco, beautifully designed. In S. Maria di Consolatione he did a panel for a noble

of the Baciadonne house, representing a Nativity, an admirable
work, but put in such a dark place that its perfections cannot
be seen, especially as Perino adopted a dark style which required
a good light. He made drawings of the greater part of the
Æneid, including the history of Dido, for arras, and decorations
for the poops of galleys, carved by Carota and Tasso, excellent
wood-carvers of Florence. He further did a great number of
standards for the galleys of the prince, richly decorated. The
prince became so fond of him that he would have richly rewarded
him if Perino had stayed to serve him.

While working in Genoa Perino determined to fetch his wife
from Rome. Being fond of Pisa, he proposed to live there as he
grew old, and bought a house in the city. About that time
M. Antonio di Urbano was warden of the Duomo,[1] and being
very anxious to embellish the church, he began a marble decoration for the chapels, removing some old, ill-proportioned and
clumsy work, the new being done by Stagio da Pietrasanta, a
skilful carver. He then desired to have paintings for the marble
framework, with scenes and stucco divisions by the best masters,
without caring about the expense. He had already begun the
sacristy, where he had many pictures painted in the principal
niche behind the high altar by Gio. Antonio Sogliani, painter
of Florence, the remainder being completed many years after
by M. Sebastiano della Seta, warden of the Duomo.[2] At this
time Perino arrived in Pisa from Genoa, and having seen the
beginning by means of Battista del Cervelliera, a connoisseur
and a master of marquetry, he was taken to the warden and
discussed the matter. They needed a panel for the door inside
the entry representing St. George slaying the serpent. Perino
prepared a fine design of a row of infants and other ornaments
between two chapels, and niches with prophets and scenes,
pleasing the warden so greatly that a cartoon being made for
one, he began to colour it on the opposite door, and finished
six infants. This was to have been continued all round, and
would have formed a handsome decoration. But Perino became
anxious to return to Genoa, where he had indulged in various
pleasures, and on leaving he gave a small panel in oils to the
nuns of St. Matteo, which is in their convent. He stayed several
months in Genoa, doing more things for the prince. The warden
at Pisa was very sorry for his departure, but much more so at
the work being left unfinished. So he wrote every day urging
him to return, and importuned Perino's wife, whom he had left

at Pisa. But seeing that he did not return, and receiving no answer, the warden gave the work to Gio. Antonio Sogliani, who finished it and put it in its place. When Perino returned soon after and saw the work of Sogliani, he was angry and refused to continue what he had begun, so that Gio. Antonio continued, doing four pictures. But the new warden, Sebastiano della Seta, thought them too much in the same style and rather inferior to the first. So he allotted a picture to Domenico Beccafumi of Siena, after he had done some fine pictures in the sacristy as a test, but as the panel did not please the warden, he entrusted the two remaining ones to Giorgio Vasari of Arezzo. They were placed at the two doors on one side of the façade of the church. It is not becoming of me to speak of these and numerous works scattered about Italy, but I will leave everyone to judge for himself. All this grieved Perino, as he had made designs worthy of himself, to decorate the church and render himself immortal.

Perino had grown tired of Genoa, from which he had derived so much pleasure and profit, and remembering Rome in the happy days of Leo, and his letters from Cardinal Ippolito de' Medici, he had determined to return there when the cardinal's death stopped him. His numerous friends, however, pressed him to come, for which he was more eager than any, and one morning he left Pisa without saying a word and went to Rome. Here he was introduced to Cardinal Farnese and then to Pope Paul, and remained several months inactive, first because he was continually put off, and then because he suffered from a bad arm and spent several hundred crowns before he could get it healed. Not having anyone to take him up, he was much tempted to leave, owing to the coldness of the court. However, Il Molza and many other friends advised him to have patience, saying that Rome was no longer the same, and it was necessary to experience her disdain before she courted anyone, especially those engaged in any distinguished pursuit. About this time M. Pietro de' Massimi bought a chapel in la Trinità, and had the vaulting and lunettes decorated with stucco ornaments and an oil-painting by Giulio Romano and Gio. Francesco, his brother-in-law. Wishing to have it finished, the lunettes containing four scenes of Mary Magdalene and the altarpiece a *Noli me tangere*, he first had a gilt wood frame made for the picture, which had a poor stucco one, and then gave the walls to Perino. He set up his scaffolding and completed it after several months. He made some curious arabesques, partly in bas-relief and partly

painted, and enclosed two small scenes within a stucco frame
of great diversity. One was the Pool of Bethesda, with the
sick waiting for the moving of the waters, and a fine view of
the portico foreshortened in perspective, the priests graciously
moving about, although the figures are not very large. In the
other he did the resurrection of Lazarus, who is pale as death,
while some are shuddering and some marvelling. The scene is
further adorned with some small temples diminishing as they
recede, done with great skill, as are all the parts in stucco.
Four lesser scenes, two on either side of the large one, represent
the centurion asking Christ to heal his son, the driving out of the
money-changers, the Transfiguration, and another. On the inner
side of the projections of the pilasters he did four figures dressed
as prophets, of the utmost possible beauty and proportion. This
work in its delicacy resembles a miniature rather than a painting. The colouring is very beautiful and done with great patience,
showing his true love for art. He did all this work with his own
hand, though most of the stucco was executed from his designs
by Guglielmo Milanese,[1] who had been with him in Genoa, and
of whom he was very fond, as he wished to marry him to his
daughter. In order to restore the Farnese antiquities he has
now been made friar of the Piombo, in succession to Frà Sebastiano of Venice. On one wall of this chapel there was a fine
marble tomb with a woman's figure in death, excellently done
by Il Bologna,[2] the sculptor, and two nude infants at the side.
The woman was a portrait of a famous courtezan of Rome,
and the friars removed the effigy, feeling scruples against allowing such a person to rest there. This work and numerous designs
induced Cardinal Farnese to give Perino a pension and employ
him on many things. By Pope Paul's order he removed a
chimney from the Camera del Fuoco to that of the Segnatura
containing the carved wooden beams done by Frà Giovanni,
the carver of Pope Julius. Raphael having painted in both
chambers, it was necessary to restore the bottom of those
scenes in the Segnatura representing Mount Parnassus. Perino
represented marble with festoons, masks and other ornaments,
and in certain spaces he did some things in bronze colour. In
the scene the philosophers treat of philosophy, the theologians
of theology, and so on, and although he did not do everything
himself, he retouched a secco, and did the cartoons so that they
might almost be his, but being ill of a cold he could not exert

---

[1] Guglielmo della Porta.
[2] Domenico Aimo of Bologna, called Varignana.

himself. The Pope, considering that he was deserving because of his age and on every account, made him a provision of 25 ducats a month for life, on condition that he should serve the palace and the Farnese house.

Michelagnolo had now uncovered his Last Judgment in the chapel, and only needed to paint the bottom where silk and gold arras was to be hung. The Pope arranged that they should be woven in Flanders, and with Michelagnolo's consent got Perino to begin a painted canvas of the same size, with women and infants and termini holding festoons, with curious fancies. These remained incomplete at his death in some rooms of Belvedere, the work being worthy of him and as a decoration to such a divine painting. Antonio da San Gallo having finished the Great Hall of the Kings in the Pope's palace, before the chapel of Sixtus IV., Perino did the ceiling in eight divisions, a cross and ovals sunk and in relief. He then adorned it with stucco as beautifully as he knew. In the angles he made four infants in relief, their feet towards the middle and their twisted arms forming a rose. In the remainder of the divisions are all the Farnese arms, and those of the Pope occupy the middle of the vaulting. This stucco may be considered to have surpassed the ancients and moderns in beauty, refinement and difficulty, and to be worthy of the head of the Christian religion. The stained-glass windows were made from Perino's designs by Pastorina da Siena, a skilful master, and below Perino prepared the wall for his scenes with fine stucco ornaments, afterwards continued by Daniello Ricciarelli of Volterra, the painter, who, if death had not prevented him, would have shown how moderns could not only equal the ancients, but even perhaps far surpass them.

While the stucco was being made and Perino was thinking of the designs for the scenes, the old walls of S. Pietro were being pulled down for the new church, and the builders came upon a wall containing a Madonna and other paintings by Giotto. Perino and his friend M. Niccolo Acciauioli, a Florentine doctor, seeing this, and from a feeling of respect, would not allow the picture to be destroyed, but cut out the wall, supported it with iron and wood, and put it under the organ of S. Pietro, where there was no altar or anything. Before the wall about the Madonna was pulled down, Perino copied a portrait of Orso dell Anguillara, a Roman senator, the same who crowned M. Francesco Petrarca in the Capitol, who was represented at the Madonna's feet. About it a frame was to be put

of stucco and painting in memory of Niccolo Acciauioli, a
senator of Rome. Perino made the designs and, aided by his
young men and his pupil Marcello Mantovano,[1] completed the
work with great diligence.

The Sacrament occupied a somewhat ignoble position in
S. Pietro because of the wall; accordingly the deputies of the
company directed that a chapel should be erected in the middle
of the church by Antonio da S. Gallo, partly of spoils of ancient
marble columns and partly of marble, bronze and stucco, with
a tabernacle by Donatello in the midst. Perino made a fine
overceiling with scenes from the Old Testament figurative of
the Sacrament. In the middle he did a larger scene of the Last
Supper below two prophets on either side of the body of Christ.
For the church of S. Giuseppe near Ripetta he employed his
young men to do the chapel, retouching it himself. He did the
same for a chapel in S. Bartolommeo in Isola, making the
designs and retouching it himself. In S. Salvadore del Lauro he
painted scenes on the high altar and grotesques in the vaulting,
while on the front wall his pupil Girolamo Sermoneta did an
Annunciation. He thus followed Raphael's plan at the end of
his life, partly from necessity and partly from indolence, for he
loved designing better than executing works. The dangers of
this may be seen by the works of the Chigi and those done by
others, as well as those which Perino had done. Giulio Romano
also has not won much credit from the works which are not by
his own hand. And although princes are pleased at work being
done quickly, and perhaps it benefits the artists engaged upon
them, yet they are not so interested as they would be in their own
work, and however well the cartoons may be drawn, the pupils
cannot imitate them so exactly as their designer could. He,
seeing the work being spoiled, hurries it on in desperation; and
thus all who thirst for honour should do their own work. As
an instance, I devoted much care to the cartoons of the Hall
of the Chancery in the palace of S. Giorgio at Rome, yet, as the
work had to be done in a hundred days, so many painters were
set to colour it, and deviated so much from the excellence of
the original, that from that day I have always executed my
own work. A man who wishes to obtain all the honour due to
his genius must needs take this course. Perino, owing to the
numerous tasks committed to him, was forced to employ many
men, caring more for gain than glory, as he considered that he
had squandered and had gained nothing in his youth, and he

[1] Marcello Venusti.

so disliked seeing his young men coming to the fore that he endeavoured to keep them under him so that they should not impede his path.

When Titian of Cadore came to Rome in 1546 to paint portraits,[1] he first did Pope Paul when His Holiness went to Busseto, and not being rewarded for this or for others done for Cardinal Farnese and at S. Fiore, he was honourably received by them in Belvedere. A report thus arose in the court, and spread through Rome, that he had come to do scenes in the king's hall in the palace, where Perino was to work, and had already done the stucco. This arrival displeased Perino, and he complained to his friends, not because he thought that Titian would surpass him in fresco, but because he hoped to go quietly on with the work until his death, and to do what was to be done without competition, the vaulting and walls of Michelagnolo's chapel nearby being more than sufficient to spur him on. Thus he avoided Titian during the latter's visit, and displayed much ill-humour until his departure.

Tiberio Crispo, the constable of the castle of St. Angelo and afterwards cardinal, being fond of art, wished to embellish the castle, and he rendered the loggias, rooms and halls very beautiful for the better reception of the Pope when he went there. He had many apartments decorated from designs by Raffaello da Montelupo, and finally by Antonio da S. Gallo, and got Raffaello to do a loggia and the marble angel there, six braccia high, set on the top of the last large tower of the castle. He had the loggia painted by Girolamo Sermoneta, on the side towards the open country. He gave the rest of the rooms to Luzio Romano, and the halls and other important chambers were done by Perino, partly by his own hand and partly by others from his cartoons. The hall is very charming and beautiful, decorated with stucco and full of scenes from Roman history done by his young men, and several by Domenico Beccafumi's pupil Marco da Siena, while some rooms contain fine friezes. Although Perino could have plenty of able youths to help him, yet this did not prevent him doing purely mechanical work. He frequently did the pennons of trumpets, the banners of the castle and those with the arms of the Church. He thus did cloth, overgarments and every little detail. He began some canvases for arras for Prince Doria, did a chapel for Cardinal Farnese and a scriptorium for Madama Margaret of Austria. At S. Maria del Pianto he did an ornament about the Madonna

[1] He was in Rome in 1545.

and another for the one in the Piazza Guidea, and other works too numerous to mention, for he habitually took everything that came to hand. The officials of the palace, knowing his nature, kept him constantly employed, and he was anxious to be on good terms with them because they paid him his provision and other things. Moreover, the position he had acquired brought him all the work of Rome, and he did his things for very little, thus causing considerable harm to himself and art. If he had undertaken to do the king's hall with his apprentices, several hundred crowns would have been paid him, which all went to the ministers in charge of the work, who paid the painters by the day. Having undertaken so much, and being infirm, he could not support his labour, being compelled to work day and night to satisfy the needs of the palace, designing numerous ornaments for the Farnese and other cardinals and lords. He never had an hour's quiet, his mind being constantly occupied, and he was always surrounded by sculptors, stucco-workers, wood-carvers, tailors, joiners, painters, gilders and other artisans. He sometimes sought rest at an inn with his friends, finding there true happiness and rest from toil. His health being thus disordered by his labours, his amours and his intemperance, he contracted an asthma which gradually developed into consumption, and one evening, while conversing with a friend near his house, he fell down dead of apoplexy, at the age of forty-seven. Many artists grieved for the great loss suffered by painting. He was buried by M. Joseffo Cincio, physician of Madama, his son-in-law, and by his wife, in the Rotonda at Rome, in the chapel of St. Joseph, with this epitaph:

Perino Bonaccursio Vagae florentino, qui ingenio et arte singulari egregios cum pictores permultos, tum plastas facile omnes superavit, Catherina Perini conjugi, Lavinia Buonaccursia parenti, Josephus Cincius socero charissimo et optimo fecere. Vixit ann. 46 men. 3 dies 21. Mortuus est 14 Calen. Novemb. Ann. Christ. 1547.

Perino left in his place Daniello of Volterra, who worked a good deal with him, and finished the other two prophets in the Chapel of the Crucified in S. Marcello. In the Trinità he did a beautiful chapel in stucco and painting for Signora Elena Orsina and many other works, recorded in the proper place. We see then that Perino was one of the most versatile painters of our day, assisting artists to make excellent stucco arabesques, landscapes, animals and other things of the painter's art, including colouring in oils, fresco and tempera, so that he may be called the father of these noble arts, his talents living in those who imitate him. Many of his designs were engraved after his death, such as the fulmination of the giants at Genoa, eight scenes of St. Peter from the Acts of the Apostles, designed for a cope for Pope Paul III., and many others, recognisable by their style. Perino employed many young men and taught many pupils, the best of all being Girolamo Siciolante of Sermoneta, of whom I shall speak elsewhere. Another pupil, Marcello Mantovano, did from his design a Madonna and several saints of great beauty on a wall in fresco, but his works also are mentioned elsewhere. Perino left many designs by himself and others, including a fine one of Michelagnolo's chapel by Leonardo Cungi of Borgo S. Sepolcro. All these designs were sold by his heirs, and our book contains several of his pen drawings of great beauty.

DOMENICO BECCAFUMI,[1] Painter and Maker of Casts of Siena
(1486 – 1551)

THE natural gift which we have observed in Giotto and other painters hitherto referred to was also possessed by Domenico Beccafumi. While guarding the sheep of his father Pacio, a labourer of Lorenzo Beccafumi, a citizen of Siena, he was observed, child though he was, to be occupied in drawing upon stones or in some other way. One day Lorenzo saw him drawing with a pointed stick in the sand of a little stream as he was keeping his sheep, and he asked him of his father, intending to take the boy into his service and to have him taught. Pacio granted his permission, and the little Mecherino, for that was his name, was taken to Siena, where Lorenzo made him spend all the time he could spare from service in the house in the shop of a mediocre painter hard-by. However, he taught Mecherino with the designs of some great painters which he had for his own use, as is the practice of some masters unskilful in design, and the boy soon gave promise of excellence. At that time Pietro Perugino happened to be in Siena,[2] where he did two panels, and Domenico was much attracted by his style. The boy studied the panels and copied them, and before long he acquired the

[1] Domenico Mecarino.   [2] 1508 or 1509.

style. When the chapel of Michelagnolo and the works of Raphael were uncovered in Rome, Domenico, whose one desire was to learn and who knew he was wasting time in Siena, took leave of Lorenzo,[1] from whom he took his family and surname, and went to Rome, where he joined a painter who kept him free of cost, and together they did several works, studying the things of Michelagnolo, Raphael and other great masters, as well as ancient statues and sarcophagi of wonderful workmanship. Thus before long he became a bold draughtsman of prolific invention, and a beautiful colourist. During this period of less than two years he did nothing of note except to decorate a façade in Borgo with the arms of Julius II.

At this time Gio. Antonio of Vercelli, the painter, a youth of considerable skill, was brought to Siena by one of the Spannocchi, a merchant, where he was much employed, chiefly in making portraits by the nobles of the city, which has always encouraged able men. On hearing this, Domenico, who longed to return home, went back to Siena, and perceiving that Gio. Antonio was well grounded in design, which is the essence of art, he bent all his efforts to follow him, practising anatomy and drawing nudes, not being satisfied with his work at Rome. He succeeded admirably, and had soon made a name in that noble city. He was as much beloved for his good qualities as for his art, because Gio. Antonio was a brutal, licentious man whose vices had won him the name of Sodoma, of which he was rather proud. But Domenico lived like a Christian, and spent most of his time alone. As good companions are often more esteemed by men than the virtuous, most of the youth of Siena followed Sodoma, praising his merit. He was an eccentric man, and to please the lower classes he had his house full of parrots, baboons, dwarf asses, Elba ponies, a speaking raven, barbary horses for racing, and such-like things, so that everyone was full of his follies. As he had painted in fresco the façade of the house of M. Agostino Bardi, Domenico did one in competition with him by the column of la Postierla, near the Duomo, at the house of the Borghese, over which he took great pains. In a frieze under the roof he did some much-admired little figures in grisaille, and in bronze colour he did the ancient gods and other figures, between the three rows of travertine windows, which were of considerable merit, although those of Sodoma won more praise. Both façades were done in 1512. In S. Benedetto, a house of the monks of Monte Oliveto outside the Tufi gate, Domenico did a panel of St.

[1] After 1510.

Catherine of Siena receiving the stigmata,[1] under a house, with St. Benedict on the right, and St. Jerome on the left dressed as a cardinal. This panel has always been much admired for its soft colouring and high relief. In the predella he did some small scenes in tempera with wonderful vigour and the utmost grace, without a trace of any effort. They represent St. Catherine receiving a part of the consecrated Host from an angel, Jesus Christ espousing her, the taking of the Dominican habit, and other scenes. In a large panel in S. Martino he did a Nativity and the Virgin, Joseph and the shepherds adoring, with angels dancing above the cottage. In this work, which is much admired by artists, Domenico began to show his superiority to Sodoma in soundness. In the large hospital of la Madonna he painted a very beautiful and natural Visitation,[2] and in S. Spirito he did a panel of the Virgin and the Child espousing St. Catherine of Siena, with St. Bernardino, St. Francis, St. Jerome and St. Catherine, Virgin and Martyr. In front, standing on steps, are SS. Peter and Paul, the colour of whose draperies is reflected in the polished marble with great judgment and design. This brought him much honour, as did some small figures in the predella representing St. John baptising Christ, a king casting the wife and children of St. Sigismund into a well, St. Dominic burning the books of heretics, Christ presenting to St. Catherine of Siena a crown of roses and another of thorns, and St. Bernardino preaching to a multitude on the piazza of Siena. The fame of these works procured for Domenico a commission to do a panel for the Carmine of St. Michael subduing Lucifer.[3] Being a man of ideas, he thought of a new treatment of this theme to prove his ability. Thus he began a shower of nude figures, representing Lucifer and his followers driven out of heaven, though they were rather confused owing to the labour he bestowed on them. The picture remained unfinished, and after Domenico's death it was taken to a room near the high altar at the top of the stairs in the great hospital, where it may still be seen. It is remarkable for some nude figures finely foreshortened. In the Carmine, where it was to have gone, another was placed representing God upon the clouds, surrounded by angels. In the middle is St. Michael in armour, pointing as he flies to Lucifer, who is driven to the centre of the earth amid burning walls, falling rocks and a flaming lake, with angels in various postures and nude figures swimming about and suffering torment, the whole done with

---

[1] Now in the Siena Gallery.   [2] Painted in 1512.
[3] Now in the Siena Gallery.

such style and grace that the place seems illuminated by the
fire. Baldassarre Peruzzi, the great Sienese painter, could never
praise the work enough. One day, when I was passing through
Siena, he took me to see it, and I was greatly struck by it, and
also by the beauty and judgment displayed in the five little
scenes of the predella, done in tempera. Domenico did another
panel for the nuns of Ognissanti in that city, representing
Christ crowning the glorified Virgin, with St. Gregory, St.
Anthony, St. Mary Magdalene and St. Catherine, Virgin and
Martyr, beneath. The predella contains some beautiful little
figures in tempera. In the house of Sig. Marcello Agostini,[1]
Domenico painted the vaulting of a room in fresco. There are
three lunettes on each wall and two at each end, with friezes
going all round, works of great beauty. In the middle he made
two pictures on a ground made to represent silk, one of Scipio
Africanus rendering the young wife unharmed to her husband,
the other of the great painter Zeuxis drawing several nude
women for his painting for the temple of Juno. In one of the
lunettes, in small but very beautiful figures of half a braccia, he
did the two Roman brothers who from being enemies became
friends for the good of their country. In another Torquatus
enforces the laws by having one of his own and one of his son's
eyes put out. Next follows the petition . . . when, after his
crimes against the Roman people and his country have been
read, he is put to death. The one beside it is the Roman people
deciding on the expedition of Scipio to Africa. Then in a
lunette follows an ancient sacrifice full of varied figures, and a
temple in perspective, a thing in which Domenico especially
excelled. The last is Cato's suicide, with some horses beautifully
painted. The spaces of the lunettes contain small scenes
beautifully finished.

The beauty of the work led the Government to employ
Domenico to paint the vaulting of a hall in the palace of the
Signori,[2] in which he made every effort to display his powers
and decorate that celebrated building of his native town. The
hall is twice as long as it is broad, the vaulting being shaped
like a ship, not in lunettes. Thinking it would arrange itself
better so, Domenico divided his paintings by gilded friezes and
cornices, giving them much grace and beauty, without employing any stucco or other decoration, so that it seems in relief.
At each end of the hall is a large square scene, and on each
wall are two separated by an octagon, making six squares and

[1] Palazzo Bindi Sergardi.   [2] Sala del Consistorio, painted 1529–35.

two octagons. At each corner of the vaulting is a circle, broken
by the groin of the vaulting, giving it eight semicircles, each
one containing large seated figures of men who have defended
the state and kept the laws. The plane of the vaulting at the
summit is in three sections, forming a circle above the octagons,
and two squares above the squares on the walls. One of the
octagons contains a woman surrounded by children, holding a
heart in her hand and representing patriotism. The other also
contains a woman and infants representing concord among the
citizens. Between them in the circle is Justice with the sword
and scales, foreshortened from below with marvellous boldness,
the colouring, which is dark at the feet, becoming brighter and
brighter until the head is in such glory that the figure seems
about to vanish in light. It is of a beauty impossible to describe
to those who have not seen it, and produced with more judgment and art than any work similarly foreshortened. On the
left-hand on entering the hall are Marcus Lepidus and Fulvius
Flaccus, the censors, becoming friends on their appointment to
the censorship, and putting aside their private enmity for the
good of their country. Domenico made them kneeling and
embracing, with many figures about, and buildings and temples
in perspective showing his intimate acquaintance with that art.
On the other wall is the story of Postumius Tubertus, the
dictator who, having left the care of the army to his only son,
who was only set to guard the quarters, puts him to death for
disobedience in seizing an opportunity to attack the foe and
win a victory. Postumius is represented as old and clean-
shaven, his right hand resting on his axe. With his left he points
out to the army his dead son lying on the ground, a finely
foreshortened figure. Below this fine picture is an appropriate
inscription. In the middle of the next octagon is the beheading
of Spurius Cassius, and the destruction of his house because
the Senate feared he would make himself king. His head lies
beside the executioner, and his body is finely foreshortened.
In the next square Publius Mucius, the tribune, is burning all
his colleagues who aspired to the tyranny with Spurius, the fire
being excellently done. At the other end of the hall is Codrus
the Athenian, who, after hearing from the oracle that the victory
will rest with the side that loses its king, casts off his clothes and
throws himself upon the unsuspecting enemy and is slain, thus
enabling his men to win the victory. Domenico painted him as
seated and undressing near a fine round temple, surrounded by
his captains; in the distance we see his death and his name in

an inscription. The first scene on the opposite wall is Prince
Zaleucus, who had an eye of himself and his son put out in
order not to violate the laws, several bystanders beseeching
him not to be so cruel. In the distance his son is represented
violating a girl, and below is his name in an inscription. The
octagon next this contains the casting of Marcus Manlius from
the Capitol. Marcus is a youth thrown from a terrace, the
head being finely foreshortened so that he looks alive, and so
do some figures below. In the other is Spurius Mælius, the knight,
put to death by Servilius, the tribune, because the people sus-
pected him of wishing to be tyrant. Servilius is seated and
surrounded by a multitude, and one points out the dead Spurius
on the ground. The circles mentioned above contain men famous
for defending their country. The first is Fabius Maximus in
armour, seated. On the other side is Speusippus, Dux of the
Tegeates, who when a friend pressed him to rid himself of
an adversary and rival refused to deprive his country of such
a citizen. The circle at the next corner contains the praetor
Caelius who was punished by the Senate because he fought contrary to the auspices, although he gained the victory. Beside
him sits Thrasybulus, who, with some friends, valiantly slew
thirty tyrants to free his country. He is an old, clean-shaven,
white-haired man, his name being underneath like those of the
others. At the other corner below a circle is Genutius Cippus,
the praetor, of whom, when a huge bird settled on his head with
wings in the shape of a horn, the augur prophesied that he
would be king of his country. Being old, he resolved to go into
exile to avoid it, and thus Domenico made him with a bird on
his head. Next him sits Charondas, who returned to town and
went before the Senate without disarming, contrary to the law
which imposed the penalty of death on those who entered the
Senate with arms, and who killed himself when apprised of the
error. In the last circle are Damon and Pythias, known for their
great friendship, and with them is Dionysius, tyrant of Sicily.
Nearby sits Brutus, who condemned his own sons to death
because they sought to bring back the Tarquins. This truly
remarkable work showed the Sienese the ability of Domenico,
who displayed great judgment and intelligence in every action,

On Charles V.'s first visit to Italy he was expected at Siena.
and the ambassadors of the Republic being notified of his
intention, great preparations were made for his reception.
Domenico made a horse of pasteboard, eight braccia high, supported by an iron framework, surmounted by the statue of the

emperor in armour in the antique style, holding his baton.
Below were three large conquered figures, which also supported
a part of the weight, as the horse had its forelegs in the air.
The figures represented three provinces subdued by the emperor. In this work Domenico showed that he knew as much
of sculpture as of painting. The horse was mounted on a wooden
castle four braccia high, running on wheels and moved by men
inside. Domenico intended that when the emperor entered the
city the horse should accompany him to the palace of the
Signoria and remain in the middle of the piazza. The horse only
needed gilding, but so it remained, for the emperor did not
come to Siena, but was crowned at Bologna, and then left
Italy. However, Domenico's ability was recognised, and the
excellence of his horse won him much praise. It remained in
the opera of the Duomo until the emperor's victorious return
from Africa, when he went to Messina, Naples, Rome, and
finally came to Siena,[1] and this time the horse was put in the
piazza of the Duomo and won Domenico great praise.

His fame being thus spread abroad, Prince Doria, who with
his court had seen all Domenico's works at Siena, desired him
to work in his palace at Genoa, on which Perino del Vaga,
Gio. Antonio da Pordenone and Girolamo da Trevisi had been
engaged. But Domenico could not then go because he had
undertaken to finish in a new style the marble pavement of the
Duomo, begun by Duccio. The figures and scenes were mostly
designed on the marble, and the outlines cut in the stone and
filled in with black, with an ornamental border of coloured
marble, and so was the ground for the figures. Domenico's good
judgment showed him that he could greatly improve that work.
He took dark marble to form a shadow for the white, and making
outlines with the chisel, he found he could thus obtain the effect
of chiaroscuro. The work succeeded marvellously in invention,
design, quantity of figures, and formed the most magnificent
pavement ever seen. By working steadily he completed most
of it during his life. About the high altar he made a frieze of
pictures to continue the sequence of the series begun by Duccio,
representing stories from Genesis; for example, Adam and Eve
driven from Paradise and tilling the soil, the sacrifices of Abel
and Melchisedec, and in front of the altar a large scene of Abraham
sacrificing Isaac. It is surrounded by a border of half-length
figures carrying animals to sacrifice. Descending the steps, there
is another large picture of Moses receiving the laws from God

[1] 23 April, 1536.

upon Mount Sinai, while below the people are worshipping the calf of gold, and Moses breaks the tables of the law. Opposite the pulpit, under this scene, is one with a great quantity of figures, composed with the utmost grace and design, representing Moses striking the rock and water issuing forth for the thirsty people to drink. The water flows like a river the length of the frieze, and the people are drinking most naturally in fine and graceful attitudes, some bending to the ground, some kneeling to the rock and holding up vases and cups, and some drinking with their hands. Some are bringing animals to drink amid the rejoicings of the people. Especially remarkable is a boy taking a dog by the neck and pushing his muzzle into the water to drink, and the animal when he has had enough wriggles his head in the most natural manner. This border is unequalled in its kind, although the shadows of the figures are remarkable rather than beautiful, and although the whole work is of great beauty, this part is considered the best. Under the cupola is a hexagon divided into seven hexagons and six rhombs. Of the hexagons Domenico completed four before his death, doing the sacrifices of Elias. This work remained his study and pastime, and he never entirely abandoned it for anything else.

While he was working in various places he did a large panel in oils on the right on entering S. Francesco of Christ's descent into Limbo [1] and the release of the patriarchs, including a lovely nude Eve, a thief with the cross behind Christ, a finely executed figure, and the cave of Limbo with curious demons and fires. Believing that things coloured in tempera last longer than those done in oils, for he said that the works in oil of Luca of Cortona, of the Pollajuoli and others had faded more than those of Frà Giovanni, Frà Filippo, Benozzo and others who coloured in tempera before them, Domenico determined to do in tempera his picture for the company of St. Bernardino on the piazza of S. Francesco, representing a Virgin and several saints,[2] of great excellence. The predella, also in tempera and of great beauty, contains St. Francis receiving the stigmata, St. Anthony of Padua making the ass bow to the Host, to convert some heretics, and St. Bernardino of Siena preaching to his fellow-citizens on the piazza of the Signori. On the walls he did two stories of the Virgin in fresco, in competition with some done by Sodoma there. One represents the Visitation and the other the Assumption,[3] both being much admired. At length Domenico

[1] Now in the Gallery, Siena.   [2] Painted in 1537.
[3] Painted in 1518. The Visitation is by Sodoma, painted in 1537.

went to Genoa,[1] where the Prince Doria had long been expecting him. The removal was very distasteful to him, for he was accustomed to live quietly, and required no more than his simple needs, and was not used to travelling. Moreover, a mile outside the Camollia gate of Siena he had built a little house and a villa for his pleasure, visiting it frequently, and he had never gone far from Siena. On reaching Genoa he did a scene next to that of Pordenone, doing very well, though not in his best style. But as the life of the court did not suit him, as he was accustomed to freedom, he felt dissatisfied there and seemed rather bewildered. On completing the work, therefore, he asked the prince's permission to return home. As he was passing through Pisa, Battista del Cervelliera entertained him and showed him all the most noteworthy things of the city, especially the pictures of Sogliani and those in the niches behind the high altar of the Duomo. Sebastiano della Seta, warden of the Duomo,[2] having heard from Cervelliera of the abilities of Domenico, wished him to finish the work over which Sogliani had taken so long, and allotted two of the niches to him. He did them at Siena, and sent them to Pisa. One represents Moses breaking the tables on seeing the people worshipping the calf of gold.[3] In this Domenico introduced some fine nudes. The other contains Moses, and the earth opening and swallowing a part of the people. This also contains remarkable nude figures killed by flames of fire. These pictures led to Domenico doing four more for the niche,[4] two on each side, with the four Evangelists, very fine figures. Sebastiano, being well satisfied, next employed him to do the picture of a chapel in the Duomo, where four had hitherto been done by Sogliani. Accordingly Domenico stayed in Pisa and did a Madonna on clouds surrounded by cherubs, with saints beneath,[5] a well-executed work, but not so excellent as his other pictures there. He excused himself for this to his friends, notably to Giorgio Vasari, by saying that he was away from the air of Siena and every comfort, and did not seem able to do anything. He returned home determined never to leave it again to work, and did a panel in oils behind a door for the nuns of S. Paolo, near S. Marco, of the Nativity of the Virgin, with nurses and St. Anne foreshortened in bed. A woman, lighted only by the fire, is drying clothes. The charming predella contains three scenes in tempera: the Presentation of the Virgin at the Temple, her Marriage, and the Adoration of the Magi.[6] In the

Mercanzia, a tribunal of the city, the officials have a panel of
great beauty which was done, they declare, by Domenico when
a youth. It represents St. Paul seated, and at the sides his conversion and beheading in small figures. Finally Domenico was
employed [1] to paint the great niche of the Duomo behind the
high altar, where he previously did all the decoration of foliage,
figures and two victories in the semicircular space, a rich and
beautiful decoration. In the middle he then painted the Ascension
in fresco,[2] making three pictures up to the cornice, divided by
columns in perspective. The middle one has an arch above with
the Virgin, St. Peter and St. John, and at the sides the ten Apostles
in various attitudes, regarding Christ's ascent into heaven. Over
each group of Apostles is an angel, foreshortened, representing
the two who said He had ascended into heaven. The work is
marvellous, though it is marred by a somewhat unpleasant air
of the heads, as in his old age Domenico gave them a frightened
and not very charming expression; but if the heads had been
better the work would be unequalled. The Sienese considered
Sodoma superior to Domenico in expression, although the
figures of the latter had more design and power. The heads are
an important feature in our art, and the rendering of them with
beauty and grace has saved many masters from the censure that
the rest of their work deserved. This was Domenico's last work.
Having taken the fancy to do things in relief, he began casting
bronzes, and succeeded, though with much labour, in doing the
six angels for six columns of the Duomo nearest the high altar.[3]
They are rather less than life-size, and hold a candlestick with a
light, and he was much praised for the last ones. Encouraged by
this, he began the twelve Apostles to put on the columns below,
where there are some old marble ones in a bad style. But he did
not live long enough to continue them. Being full of ideas, and
as nothing came amiss to him, he did wood blocks for engraving
to make prints in chiaroscuro, and two excellent Apostles of his
still exist, one being in our book of designs with some sheets of
his, beautifully drawn. He also did copper-engravings with the
burin, and etched some fanciful scenes of alchemy, where Jove
and the other gods, desiring to conceal Mercury, put him bound
in a crucible, while Vulcan and Pluto stir the fire, and when they
think they have him safe he escapes as smoke. Domenico did
many other works of minor importance, such as Madonnas, and
similar chamber pictures, one, for example, in the house of the
knight Donati, and a picture in tempera of Jupiter converting

[1] In 1544.   [2] Begun in 1548.   [3] In 1551.

himself into a shower of gold and raining into the lap of Danæ. Piero Castanei also has a beautiful Virgin in oils, a round. For the brotherhood of St. Lucia he painted a beautiful bier and another for that of St. Antonio.[1] Let no one wonder that I mention such works, as they are of real beauty, as all who have seen them know.

When sixty-five years of age Domenico hastened his end by working unaided a whole day and night in casting metal and in polishing, refusing all assistance. He died on 18 May 1549,[2] and was buried by Giuliano the goldsmith, his friend, in the Duomo, where he had done so many masterpieces. He was followed by all the artists of Siena, who knew how much the city had lost. This is recognised to-day more than ever, in the admiration for his works. Domenico was an honest, straight-living man, fearing God and studying art, but excessively solitary. He has well deserved the verses in the vulgar and Latin tongues written in his honour by his fellow-citizens.

Giovan Antonio Lappoli, Painter of Arezzo
(1492–1552)

It is rare that an old vine-stem does not put forth fresh shoots which in time cover the empty spot with their leaves and produce good fruit which recalls the savour of that of the first tree. The truth of this is demonstrated in the present Life. Giovan's father, Matteo, was the last notable painter of his day. On his death Giovan was left to the charge of his mother, being well provided for, until the age of twelve. He then cared for nothing but painting, wishing above all to follow in his father's footsteps. His first master was Domenico Pecori, a painter of Arezzo, who with Matteo had been a pupil of Clemente. After remaining with him for some time, and desiring to make better progress than he could under that master, and to leave a place where he could not learn by himself, in spite of his natural bent, Giovan Antonio thought of going to Florence. The circumstances were favourable, for his mother was dead and his young sister married to Lionardo Ricoveri, one of the first citizens of Arezzo. So he went to Florence, where the works of Andrea del Sarto and Jacopo da Pontormo pleased

[1] The former in 1522, the latter in 1540.   [2] Correctly, 1551.

him more than all the others. He determined to join one of them, and was hesitating as to which it should be, when Pontormo unveiled his Faith and Charity under the portico of the Nunziata. Lappoli resolved to join him, thinking the style so beautiful, as everyone did, and that one so young ought to surpass all the artists of the age. Thus, though he might have gone to Andrea, he joined Jacopo and studied design, being spurred on by competition to strenuous efforts. One competitor was Giovan Maria of Borgo a S. Sepolcro,[1] who studied design and painting under the same master, which led to his adopting the good style of Pontormo in exchange for his own, and also because Agnolo, called Bronzino, was much favoured by Jacopo for his tractability, good humour and diligence in imitating his master, and he designed and coloured in a way that was an earnest of his future perfection, seen in our own day. Giovan Antonio, being anxious to learn, spent many months in drawing and copying the works of Jacopo, and his natural ability, his desire to learn, competition, and the good style of his master would have rendered him excellent, as we see by designs in red chalk by his hand in our book. But pleasures are frequently the greatest enemies of ability in a youth and distract his attention, and those who study art or science should be doubly careful to associate only with men of good character and their own profession. Giovan Antonio, being in tutelage, was put to stay in the house of one Ser Raffaello di Sandro del Zoppo, chaplain in S. Lorenzo, paying so much a year. But he neglected his painting sadly, for the priest being a worthy man and fond of painting, music and other delights, gathered together many choice spirits in his rooms in S. Lorenzo, among them M. Antonio of Lucca, an excellent musician and performer on the lute, and then quite young, from whom Lappoli learned to play that instrument. Although Rosso the painter and other artists stayed in the same place, Lappoli attended to everything but his art, though he might have learned much from them and amused himself at the same time. These impediments largely cooled his ardour for painting, but being friendly with Pier Francesco di Jacopo di Sandro, a pupil of Andrea del Sarto, he sometimes went with him to the Scalzo to copy paintings and draw nudes. Devoting himself to colouring, he very soon did pictures of Jacopo, and then some Madonnas and portraits by himself, among them those of M. Antonio da Lucca and Ser Raffaello, which are very good.

[1] Gio. Maria Butteri.

The plague having broken out at Rome in 1523, Perino del Vaga came to Florence, and frequented Ser Raffaello's. Lappoli became very friendly with him, knowing his talent, and this revived his interest in painting, so that he proposed, when the plague ceased, to abandon his other pleasures, take up painting and accompany Perino to Rome. But the plague reached Florence just as Perino had completed in bronze colour the Drowning of Pharaoh in the Red Sea for Ser Raffaello, with whom Lappoli was still staying, and so both were obliged to leave Florence to save their lives. Giovan Antonio, returning to Arezzo, to pass the time began the Death of Orpheus, killed by the Bacchantes, on canvas, in bronze colour, imitating Perino's style, a work that was much admired. He then completed a panel begun by his former master, Domenico Pecori, for the nuns of St. Margherita, representing an Annunciation. It is still in the convent. He did cartoons for two fine half-length portraits, one of Lorenzo d'Antonio di Giorgio, a student and handsome youth, the other of Ser Piero Guazzesi, a *bon vivant*. When the plague ceased, Cipriano d'Anghiari, a wealthy Aretine, who had built a chapel in the abbey of S. Fiore, at Arezzo, with ornaments and stone columns, allotted the altarpiece to Lappoli for 100 crowns. Rosso happened to be passing through Arezzo on his way to Rome, and hearing what his friend was about to do, he made him a fine sketch of nudes when staying in his house. Lappoli therefore copied Rosso's design, and did a Visitation, with God and some cherubs in a semicircle above, drawing the draperies and other things from life. The work was much admired, especially some heads, portraits done in good style. Seeing that if he wished to make progress he must leave Arezzo, Lappoli determined to go to Rome, the plague being over, where he knew Perino, Rosso and many other friends to be engaged upon great works. He sought a convenient opportunity of going, and when M. Paolo Valdarabrini, secretary of Pope Clement VII., on returning post from France, passed through Arezzo to see his brothers and nephews, Lappoli went to visit him. M. Paolo, being anxious that his city should possess men distinguished for all talents ready to display the qualities of their native air, advised Lappoli to go with him to Rome, although he needed but little persuasion, where he would have opportunities of studying art. He did so, meeting Perino, Rosso and other old friends, and being introduced by M. Paolo to Giulio Romano, Bastiano of Venice, and Francesco Mazzuoli of Parma, who arrived in Rome at that time. This

Francesco was fond of the lute, and conceived a great friendship for Lappoli, so that they were always together. Owing to this Lappoli devoted much study to design and colouring in order to make the best of his opportunities in knowing the best painters in Rome. When he had almost completed a life-size Madonna to present to Pope Clement and make himself known, the unhappy sack of Rome took place on 6 May, 1527, as his ill-fortune willed it. M. Paolo and Lappoli fled on horse-back to the S. Spirito gate in Trastevere, by which the soldiers of Bourbon were entering, M. Paolo being killed and Lappoli made prisoner by the Spaniards. In the sack Lappoli lost his picture, his designs and everything, and after suffering many things from the Spaniards, who demanded a ransom, he escaped one night in his shirt, with other prisoners, and amid great dangers, as the roads were not safe, and at length reached Arezzo. Here he was received by his uncle, M. Giovanni Pollastra, a learned man, and recovered with difficulty from the exhaustion and shock. But the same year the plague broke out in Arezzo, so severely that four hundred persons died in a day, and Lappoli was obliged to fly once more and to remain away for some months. At the end of this run of misfortunes Frà Guasparri, of S. Francesco, superior of the convent of the city, allotted to him the picture of the high altar of his church for 100 crowns, to do an Adoration of the Magi. Hearing that Rosso was working at Borgo S. Sepolcro, having fled from Rome, doing the altarpiece of the company of St. Croce, Lappoli went to visit him, sending to Arezzo for some necessities, for he had lost all in the sack of Rome, and after showing him many courtesies he got a design for the picture to be done for Frà Guasparri. Returning to Arezzo, he set to work and finished this in a year from the time of the commission, according to the agreement, and so good that it won great praise. This design of Rosso came into the hands of Giorgio Vasari, who gave it to Don Vincenzio Borghini, master of the hospital of the Innocents at Florence, who keeps it in a book of designs by various painters. Not long after Lappoli became surety for Rosso for 300 crowns, for paintings to be done by him in Madonna delle Lacrime. But Rosso left without completing the work, and Lappoli would have been ruined if his friends, especially Giorgio Vasari, had not assisted him by estimating the work done at 300 crowns. Lappoli next did a panel in oils in S. Maria del Sasso, a Dominican house in Casentino, for the abbot Camaiani of Babbiena, of the Virgin, St. Bartholomew and St. Matthias, imitating Rosso's style with great success. This led a brotherhood in Bibbiena to employ him to do a processional banner of Christ with the cross shedding His blood into a cup, and an Annunciation on the other side, one of his best works.

In 1534 the Aretines expected Duke Alessandro de' Medici, and Luigi Guicciardini, the commissioner there, directed two comedies to be prepared in his honour. One was prepared by the noblest youths of the city, known as the Umidi, and was called *Gl' Intronati da Siena*, the scenery by Niccolo Soggi, which was much admired, and it was played very successfully. Another company of noble youths, called gl' Infiammiti, played the second, a comedy by M. Giovanni Pollastra, an Aretine poet, under his direction, the scenery being by Lappoli, who did extremely well, the comedy bringing much honour to the company and the city. I must not forget an ingenious device of this poet. While these festivals were being prepared, the two companies frequently quarrelled for various reasons and brawls occurred, leading to an inquiry. The ingenious Pollastra, when the people and the quality had assembled to hear the comedy, caused four of his young men, who had previously been attacked in the city, to come out with their naked swords and pretend to kill each other, the first going out with an apparently bloody head, crying out, "Come outside, traitors!" At this the people rose in a body, laying their hands on their swords, while the relations of the youths who pretended to deal each other terrible blows rushed to the stage. But the one who had gone out first turned to the other youths and said, "Put up your swords, sirs, I am not hurt, and the comedy will proceed, for though wounded I will begin the prologue." After this jest, which deceived every one, including the actors, excepting the four concerned, the comedy began and was so well played that, in 1540, when Duke Cosimo and the Duchess Leonora were in Arezzo, Lappoli had to make new scenery for the piazza of the Vescovado, where it was performed before their excellencies, and gave such satisfaction that the performers were invited to Florence to play it at the carnival. Lappoli did the scenes very well and was much praised. He next did a decoration for a triumphal arch, with bronze-coloured scenes, put about the altar of the Madonna delle Chiave. Lappoli established himself then at Arezzo with his wife and children, intending to remain there, living upon the income of the offices he enjoyed, without doing much work. Not long after he sought to obtain two panels to be done in Arezzo, one in the church and company of St. Rocco, the other

at the high altar of S. Domenico. But both were given to
Giorgio Vasari, whose design was considered the best of all those
submitted. For the company of the Ascension in that city
Lappoli did a Resurrection with many soldiers and an Ascension
with the Virgin in the midst of the twelve Apostles, on a processional banner, with great diligence. In the Pieve he did an
oil-painting of a Visitation, with saints, and painted a Madonna
and saints for the Pieve of S. Stefano, both being far better
than any of his previous works, for he had seen reliefs and casts
of statues by Michelagnolo and of antiques brought by Giorgio
Vasari to his house at Arezzo. He did some Madonnas for
Arezzo and other places, and a Judith putting the head of
Holofernes in a basket held by a servant, now in the possession
of M. Bernardetto Minerbetti, bishop of Arezzo, the friend of
Lappoli and of all men of talent. He received from Lappoli,
among other things, a young St. John the Baptist in the desert,
an excellent figure, almost nude, which he values highly. At
length Lappoli recognised that perfection in art consisted in
wealth of invention acquired early, a study of the nude and
the rendering of difficulties easy, and he repented that he had
wasted so much time in pleasure instead of studying, seeing
that he could not well do in age what he might have accomplished when young. He began to study, however, in his age,
and lived to see Giorgio Vasari finish in forty-two days a picture
fourteen braccia long by six and a half high for the refectory
of the abbey of St. Fiore at Arezzo, representing the wedding of
Esther and King Ahasuerus, and containing over sixty figures
larger than life-size.[1] One day Lappoli said to Giorgio: "I see
that continual study and work make men rise to eminence, and
that our art is not derived from inspiration." Lappoli did not
work much at fresco, because the colours affected his health;
however, there is a Pietà with two little nude angels over the
church of Murello of considerable merit. This artist, of good
judgment and considerable skill, died of a severe fever in 1552
at the age of sixty.

His pupil, Bartolommeo Torri, of a noble Aretine family,
went to Rome under Don Giulio Clovio, an excellent illuminator,
and studied design and the nude, but especially anatomy, becoming the best designer in Rome. Not long ago Don Silvano
Razzi told me that Don Giulio Clovio, after praising this youth,
declared to him in Rome that he had left his house owing to
his study of anatomy, because he kept limbs and fragments of

[1] Now in the Accademia Petrarca, Arezzo.

men under his bed, rendering the place unbearable. He ruined his life, living like a philosopher, dirty, without order, fleeing the conversation of men, thinking that this was the way to become immortal. But Nature cannot tolerate such treatment, and he fell sick at the age of twenty-five. Returning to Arezzo to recover, he pursued the same course, and died in four months, soon after his master. His loss caused great sorrow to the city, where his promising beginning had excited great expectations. His designs, when quite young, were marvellous, and one is filled with compassion at his early end.

NICCOLO SOGGI, Painter of Florence
(1480–1554)

AMONG the numerous pupils of Pietro Perugino none was more studious and diligent, after Raphael, than Niccolo, whose Life I now write. Born in Florence of Jacopo Soggi, a worthy man but not rich, he remained in Rome in the service of M. Antonio dal Monte, with whom Jacopo had close relations, as he had a farm at Marciano in Valdichiana, where he spent most of his time. Seeing his son inclined to painting, Jacopo placed him with Pietro, and he made such progress by continual study that before long Pietro began to make use of him in his works. This was a great advantage to Niccolo, who attained to high excellence in perspective and drawing from life. He also studied clay and wax modelling, putting on them damp cloth and parchment, a thing which rendered his style dry, a defect which he retained all his life in spite of his efforts to throw it off. His first work after Pietro's death was a picture in oils for the women's hospital of Bonifazio Lupi, in the via S. Gallo, in Florence, namely an Annunciation, behind the altar, with a building in perspective, containing arches and vaulting, in Pietro's style. In 1512, after doing several Madonnas for private citizens, and other small things, he went to Rome to improve himself. He visited M. Antonio di Monte, then a cardinal, who gladly welcomed him, and immediately set him to do the arms of Pope Leo between those of the Roman people and the cardinal on the façade of the palace, where the statue of Maestro Pasquino stands. This took place at the beginning of the pontifi-

cate. Niccolo did not acquit himself so well in some nude and
draped figures, done as an ornament to the arms, which show
the evil effects of studying models only. When this disappointing
work was uncovered, Niccolo began an oil-painting of St. Prassedia the Martyr squeezing a sponge full of blood into a vase,
doing it with such diligence that he partly recovered the honour
which he considered he had lost by the arms. This picture,
done for the cardinal, was placed in the middle of the church
of St. Prassedia above an altar, under which is a well of the
blood of the martyrs to which the painting refers. Niccolo then
did a picture in oils, three-quarters of a braccia high, for the
cardinal, of a Madonna and Child, St. John as a child, and landscapes, finished as carefully as an illumination. This picture was
one of his best works, and it remained many years in the
cardinal's chamber. The cardinal on going to Arezzo lodged in
the Benedictine abbey of S. Fiore, and for the courtesies received
there he gave this picture to the sacristy, where it still is.
Niccolo followed the cardinal to Arezzo, and while there he
made the friendship of Domenico Pecori, the painter, who was
then doing a Circumcision for the company of the Trinity.
Their friendship was so close that Niccolo did a building for
this panel, with columns and arches in perspective, supporting
a roof full of bosses, as customary then, and considered very
beautiful. He also did a Madonna with the people beneath her
for Domenico, on canvas, as a baldachino of the brotherhood
of Arezzo. It perished by fire during a festival in S. Francesco,
as related in Domenico's Life. In the second chapel on the right
on entering S. Francesco, Niccolo did in tempera a Virgin,
St. John the Baptist, St. Bernard, St. Anthony, St. Francis and
three angels in the air singing, and God the Father at the top,
almost all done with the point of the brush. His labour was
thrown away, because the strength of the tempera has caused
it to peel off. It was done as an experiment, and when Niccolo
discovered the true method of painting in fresco, he tried it at
the earliest opportunity, doing a chapel on the left on entering
S. Agostino in Arezzo, allotted to him by Scamarra, an iron-
master. Here he did the Virgin in the air with the people below,
St. Donato and St. Francis kneeling; but the best part of the
work was a St. Roch, in the roof of the chapel. Being pleased
with this, Domenico Ricciardi of Arezzo entrusted Niccolo with
the altarpiece of his chapel in the Madonna delle Lagrime.
Niccolo accordingly painted a Nativity with great diligence,
and although with effort, he succeeded in producing a beautiful

thing worthy of all praise, showing incredible diligence in every detail, a ruined building near the cottage, where Christ and the Virgin are, being admirably rendered. The St. Joseph and some of the shepherds are portraits, namely Stagio Sassoli, a painter and friend of Niccolo, and Papino della Pieve, his pupil, who would have done great credit to himself and his country if he had not died so young. Three angels singing in the air would alone suffice to show the skill and patience bestowed on the work by Niccolo. No sooner had he finished it than the men of the company of S. Maria della Neve of Monte Sansovino asked him to do a panel for them representing the snowfall at S. Maria Maggiore, at Rome, on 6 August, which led to the erection of their church. Niccolo executed this with great diligence, and then did an admirable fresco at Marciano. In 1524 M. Baldo Magini had a marble tabernacle, with two columns, architrave and cornice, executed in the Madonna delle Carceri in the Prato territory by Antonio, brother of Giuliano da S. Gallo, who persuaded M. Baldo to employ Niccolo to do the picture for it, as he had made friends with him when working at Monte Sansovino in the palace of the Cardinal di Monte. Although M. Baldo had intended to give the work to Andrea del Sarto, he followed Antonio's advice and allotted it to Niccolo, who did his utmost to produce a beautiful work. He did not succeed, for in spite of his diligence it contained no excellence of design or anything admirable, for his hard style almost invariably produced a laborious and displeasing effect. Yet no one could have worked harder or with more care, and because he knew that no one . . . he felt convinced for many years that no painters could ever surpass him. This work represents God the Father bestowing on the Madonna the crown of virginity and humility by the hands of angels, some of whom are playing various instruments. He introduced M. Baldo kneeling at the feet of St. Ubaldo, the bishop, with St. Joseph on the other side and between them the miracle-working image of the Virgin. Niccolo then made a portrait of M. Baldo, three braccia high, holding the church of S. Fabiano, which he presented to the chapter of canons of the Pieve, to be given to the chapter as a memorial of the rich gift, to be placed in their sacristy, a worthy recompense of this benefactor of the principal church of his native place called after the Girdle of Our Lady. The portrait was one of Niccolo's best paintings. Some think he did a small panel in the company of St. Pier Martire, on the piazza of St. Domenico, containing several portraits. I believe for my own part that it is anterior to all the other pictures mentioned. Niccolo then left Prato, where he had taught the elements of art to Domenico Giuntalocchi, an intelligent youth of those parts, who having acquired his master's style did not become a painter of great account. Niccolo proceeded to Florence, but perceiving that the most important works were given to better men, and that his style was very different from that of Andrea del Sarto, Pontormo, Rosso and the others, he resolved to return to Arezzo, where he had more friends, greater credit and less competition. Directly he arrived he visited M. Giuliano Bacci, one of the principal citizens, and expressed his wish to stay there, and that he would like to undertake some work to keep him employed and to display his skill to the city.

M. Giuliano, desiring to embellish his native place, induced the governors of the company of the Nunziata, who had built a large vaulting in their church, intending to have it painted, to employ Niccolo to do a front arch,[1] hoping to get him to do the rest if the first part pleased the men of the company. During two years Niccolo, in spite of great efforts, did no more than half of this arch, representing the Tiburtine Sibyl and Octavian, who was a portrait of M. Giuliano, while a young man in a red dress is his pupil Domenico, and other heads are portraits of other friends. The work did not displease the men of the city or of the company, though the slow and laborious execution disgusted them all. Nevertheless Niccolo would have obtained the rest had not Rosso, the distinguished Florentine painter, arrived in Arezzo with recommendations from Giovan Antonio Lappoli, the Aretine painter, and M. Giovanni Pollastra. Niccola was so angry at the work being given to Rosso that he would have left Arezzo immediately if he had not taken a wife the previous year, and had a son. Reconciling himself at length, he did a panel for the church of Sargiano, two miles from Arezzo, a house of the bare-footed friars, of an Assumption with cherubs bearing the Virgin, St. Thomas at her feet receiving the girdle, St. Francis, St. Louis, St. John the Baptist and St. Elizabeth of Hungary, some of the figures, especially the cherubs, being excellent, while the predella contains meritorious scenes of small figures. In the convent of the nuns of the Murate of the same order he did a dead Christ with the Maries, smoothly executed, and in the abbey of the black monks of St. Fiore he did a Christ praying in the Garden in oils on canvas, behind the crucifix on the high altar, with an angel showing Him the cup and comforting Him,

[1] In 1527; taken from him in 1529.

a really good work. For the nuns of St. Benedetto d'Arezzo, of the order of Camaldoli, he did, in a tympanum, the Virgin, St. Benedict and St. Catherine, afterwards destroyed to enlarge the church. At Marciana, in Valdichiana, where he frequently went, living on his rents there and partly on his gains, he began a dead Christ on a panel and several other things. He kept his pupil Domenico Giuntalocchi with him the while, treating him like a son, and he became excellent in art, as Niccolo taught him perspective, drawing from life and designing, in all of which he succeeded, being an intelligent youth. Niccolo did this because, as he was becoming old, he hoped to have Domenico's assistance in his last years. Niccolo was amiable to all and a sincere friend to genuine students of art, readily teaching what he knew. Leaving Marciano and returning to Arezzo, having parted with Domenico, Niccolo was employed by the company of the Corpo di Cristo to paint the high-altar picture of S. Domenico. Giorgio Vasari, then quite young, also desired this, and when Niccolo knew it, he did what few artists of our day would do, resigned his own claims and prevailed on his fellow-members of the company to give the work to Giorgio, thinking more of the advantages that the youth would derive than of his own interests. Meanwhile Domenico enjoyed a stroke of good fortune at Rome, whither he had gone, becoming known to Don Martino, ambassador of the King of Portugal, with whom he stayed, doing some twenty portraits for him on a large canvas, representing his friends, with himself in the middle, speaking. Don Martino was so pleased that he considered Domenico the first painter in the world.

Don Ferrante Gonzaga being afterwards appointed viceroy of Sicily, and wishing to have someone to design fortresses and put on paper his projects, wrote to Don Martino asking him to recommend a youth and send him for this service. Don Martino first sent designs of Domenico to Don Ferrante, including a Coliseum engraved by Girolamo Fagiuoli of Bologna for Antonio Salamanca, and an old man in a car with the legend ANCORA IMPARO, and a portrait of Don Martino. He afterwards sent Domenico, with whom Don Ferrante was much pleased. When Domenico reached Sicily, Don Ferrante provided him with a pension, a horse and a servant, and before long he was employed in making walls and fortifications, so that he abandoned painting for what was more profitable at the moment. Being an intelligent man, he employed servants inured to labour, collected beasts of burden, with men to take charge of them, to bring sand, chalk, etc., and caused furnaces to be built, so that before long he was able to buy offices in Rome for 2000 crowns, and then others. After he had become wardrobe-keeper of Don Ferrante, that lord was removed from the government of Sicily and sent to that of Milan. Domenico followed him, doing the fortifications, and being industrious and somewhat miserly he became very wealthy and, what is more, the virtual governor. Niccolo, being an old man, heard of this at Arezzo and went to meet Domenico at Milan, having nothing to do, expecting to be well received for his previous benefits, hoping that as Domenico had received many while in his service, he might assist him in his wretched old age. But those who expect too much are often deceived, as he learned to his cost, and men usually change their nature with their condition. When Niccolo reached Milan he had great difficulty in obtaining an audience. He seized the opportunity to relate his miseries, begging Domenico to help him by taking him into his service. But Domenico would not remember how Niccolo had treated him like a son, and giving him a wretched sum of money, dismissed him as soon as possible. Niccolo returned sadly to Arezzo, realising that the man he had cherished as a son was little better than an enemy. To support himself he did whatever came to hand, a course he had followed many years before. Among other things he painted for the people of Monte Sansovino a Virgin in the air between two saints, on canvas. The picture was placed on an altar in the Madonna di Vertigli of the Camaldoli monks, not far from Monte Sansovino, and here many miracles are wrought for those who recommend themselves to the Virgin.

On the creation of Julius III., Niccolo, though eighty, went to Rome to kiss the Pope's feet, as he had been intimate with the Monte family, and begged for employment on the buildings which it was said were to be erected at Monte, which the Duke of Florence had given in fee to the Pope. Julius received him kindly, and ordained that he should have sufficient provision in Rome to support him without work. Accordingly Niccolo remained there several months designing many antiquities as a pastime. When the Pope proposed to enlarge his native Monte Sansovino, making an aqueduct there, because the place suffered for want of water, Giorgio Vasari, who was commissioned to begin the works, warmly recommended the appointment of Niccolo as director. Accordingly Niccolo went there, but before many days he succumbed to the troubles of this world and to his grief at being so cruelly abandoned, and was buried in S.

Domenico. Not long after this Domenico Giuntalocchi left Milan, Don Ferrante being dead, intending to return to Prato and spend the remainder of his days in quiet. But finding neither friends nor relations there, and tardily repenting of his ingratitude to Niccolo, he returned to Lombardy to serve the sons of Don Ferrante. But before long he fell sick unto death and made his will, leaving 10,000 crowns to Prato to be invested for the maintenance of students of the city, as was done by another bequest. This was carried out, and in memory of Domenico's liberality they have erected a statue to him in their council chamber.

NICCOLO, called IL TRIBOLO, Sculptor and Architect (1500–1550)

RAFFAELLO the carpenter, called Il Riccio de' Pericoli, who lived near the corner at Monteloro in Florence, had a son in 1500, as he himself has told me, called Niccolo after his grandfather. Seeing the boy was intelligent, he first had him taught reading, writing and arithmetic. But he could never be still, proving himself a turk both in and out of school, for he was continually in trouble, and thus he obtained the nickname Il Tribolo, which always clung to him. As he grew up his father took him into his shop, hoping to bridle his spirits, but finding him unfitted for the trade and rather delicate, he sent him to do wood carving as being less laborious. Perceiving that he could not become excellent without design, the father of the arts, he made him draw cornices, foliage, arabesques, and other things necessary for his trade. Finding the child intelligent at this, Raffaello, being a wise man, saw that his son could not learn much with him, and he consulted Ciappino the carpenter, by whose advice he apprenticed the boy for three years to his good friend Nanni Unghero. To Nanni's workshop resorted Jacopo Sansovino, Andrea del Sarto, and others who afterwards became distinguished. Nanni, who had a good reputation at this time, did much joinery and carving for the house of Zanobi Bartolini outside the Croce gate at Rovezzano, for the palace of the Bartolini then built by his brother Giovanni on the piazzi of S. Trinità, and for his garden and house in Gualfonda. Niccolo was made to work without consideration, and his constitution could not stand the effort, so that he grew dissatisfied and told

Riccio that he did not think he could remain with Nanni, and asked to be put with Andrea del Sarto or Jacopo Sansovino, whom he had known in Nanni's shop, as he hoped with them to do well and enjoy better health. Riccio, advised by Ciappino, put him with Jacopo Sansovino, who welcomed his old acquaintance, whose good design and better relief he had remarked in Nanni's workshop. When Tribolo had recovered and was staying with him, Jacopo did the marble statue of St. James the Apostle in the opera of S. Maria del Fiore, in competition with Benedetto da Rovezzano, Andrea da Fiesole, and Baccio Bandinelli. Seizing this opportunity of learning, Tribolo did clay models and designs with great diligence, and made so much progress that Jacopo became daily fonder of him and encouraged him to go on first with one thing and then with another. He had in his shop Solosmeo da Settignano and Pippo del Fabro, youths of great promise, but as Tribolo far surpassed them, and also understood the management of the chisel and of clay and iron, he began to employ him on his works. On finishing the Apostle and a Bacchus for Giovanni Bartolini for his house of Gualfonda, Jacopo undertook to do a chamber and macigno stone bath for his friend M. Giovanni Gaddi for his houses at the piazza of the Madonna, and gave Tribolo some large clay infants to do for the cornice. He did them so extraordinarily well that M.Giovanni, recognising his ability, gave him two marble medallions, which were afterwards placed over doors of the same house. When an artist was required to do a tomb for the King of Portugal, Jacopo was selected by the influence of the Bartolini, as the pupil of Andrea Contucci of Monte Sansovino, with the reputation of having a finer style than his master. Jacopo made a superb model of wood, full of scenes and figures in wax, mostly done by Tribolo, which greatly increased that youth's reputation, so that when he left Jacopo to work for himself, Matteo di Lorenzo Strozzi gave him some stone infants to do, and being much pleased with them, gave him two more in marble holding a dolphin which spouts water into a lake. It is now at the villa of M. Matteo at S. Casciano, eight miles from Florence.[1]

While Tribolo was thus engaged at Florence, M. Bartolommeo Barbazzi, a Bolognese nobleman, came there on business, and recollecting that Bologna needed a young man to do the marble figures and scenes for the façade of S. Petronio, he spoke to Tribolo, whose works pleased him, as well as his good qualities. He took Tribolo to Bologna, where in a short time he did the

[1] The Villa Caserotta.

two marble sibyls afterwards placed in the decoration of the door of S. Petronio leading to the Hospital della Morte. These done, and while he was being much favoured by M. Bartolommeo and promised greater things, the plague broke out in Bologna and all Lombardy in 1525. Tribolo fled to Florence, remaining there until the plague ceased, when he was recalled to Bologna. M. Bartolommeo would not permit him to do any more for the façade, and resolved to have a tomb made for himself, his relations and friends, many of whom had died. After making a model, Tribolo went to Carrara to obtain the marble on the spot, so that it might be more easily worked, and to obtain better figures. To lose no time, he there sketched two marble infants, which were brought to Bologna as they were and placed in a chapel of S. Petronio with the other things, where they still are, on the death of M. Bartolommeo, an event which caused Tribolo to return to Tuscany. On his way to Florence Tribolo went to Pisa to visit his friend Maestro Stagio da Pietrasanta, the sculptor, who did two marble columns with perforated capitals on either side of the tabernacle of the Sacrament at the high altar of the Duomo, with a marble angel of one-and-three-quarter braccia upon each, holding a candlestick in its hand. At Stagio's invitation Tribolo undertook one of the angels, having nothing else in hand, and finished it with the utmost success and delicacy. The angel is in the act of flying while it firmly holds the light, and its graceful draperies disclose the outlines of its body and appear admirable from every point of view. Having spent some time on this, which he had done for mere pleasure, and not being rewarded by the wardens as he had expected, Tribolo determined to do no more and returned to Florence, where he met Giovanni Battista della Palla, who was busily occupied in obtaining sculpture and paintings to send to King Francis in France, and who bought all kinds of antiquities and pictures of every description, so that they were by good masters, which he packed and sent off daily. At the time of Tribolo's return Gio. Battista had a beautiful antique granite vase which he wished to adapt for use as a fountain for the king. He consulted Tribolo, who made him a Goddess of Nature who holds the vase on her head, the first row of her breasts being decorated with infants cut out of the marble, holding festoons and arranged in beautiful attitudes, the next row with quadrupeds, and the feet with divers fishes. This was sent to France with other things, where it was highly valued by the king and placed as a great treasure in Fontainebleau.

In 1529, during the siege of Florence, when Pope Clement wished to see where he could best dispose his army, he had arranged that a plan of the city should be taken and the country round at a radius of a mile, with the hills, rivers, houses, churches, piazzas, streets, bastions and other defences. The charge of this was given to Benvenuto di Lorenzo by Volpaia, a master watchmaker and excellent astrologer, who especially excelled in making plans. He wished for the help of Tribolo, who was very good at such work and in estimating the height of mountains and the depressions. It was done at no small risk, as they stayed out all night to measure the roads, the heights of campaniles and towers, using the compass and taking the cupola as a centre. This task occupied many months, when the plan was made of cork for the sake of lightness, the whole being compressed in a space of four braccia. It was then packed secretly in some bales of wool consigned to Perugia, with orders to be sent to the Pope, who made constant use of it during the siege, keeping it in his room and following the operations with great interest according to his advices, as to the site of the camp, the locality of the skirmishes, in short for all the incidents and discussions and disputes that took place during the siege. During the war Tribolo did some things in clay for his friends, as well as three figures in wax for his friend Andrea del Sarto, used by him in painting three captains in fresco in the Piazzo alla Condotta, who escaped with the money-chest and were hanged by the leg. Being summoned by the Pope, Benvenuto went to Rome to kiss the feet of His Holiness, and was put in charge of the Belvedere with a good provision. He had frequent interviews with the Pope and never lost an opportunity of singing the praises of Tribolo as an excellent sculptor, so that at the end of the siege Clement employed him. When Clement proposed to finish the chapel of the Madonna of Loreto, begun by Leo and abandoned at the death of Andrea Contucci, he directed Antonio da Sangallo, who had charge of the construction, to call in Tribolo to complete the scenes left unfinished by Andrea. Tribolo therefore took his family to Loreto, where he found Simone il Mosca, a rare carver of marble, Raffaello Montelupo, Francesco da Sangallo the younger, Girolamo Ferrarese the sculptor, Andrea's pupil, Simone Cioli, Ranieri da Pietrasanta and Francesco del Tadda,[1] assembled to complete the work. Tribolo took up, as being of the most importance, a Marriage of the Virgin, begun by Andrea, where he made a

[1] Francesco Ferrucci of Fiesole.

remarkable figure breaking his staff because it did not flower, showing his wrath very naturally. Tribolo had already made wax models of the prophets to go in the niches about the chapel, which were all ready for them, when Pope Clement, after seeing and praising the work, especially Tribolo's, proposed that they should all repair to Florence without delay to finish under Michelagnolo the figures required for the sacristy and library of S. Lorenzo, and also the façade. To prevent delay he sent Michelagnolo to Florence with Frà Gio. Agnolo the Servite, who had done some things in Belvedere, to help in chiselling the marble and making statues as Michelagnolo should direct. He was given a St. Cosmo to be placed with a Madonna, together with a St. Damian by Montelupo. Michelagnolo wanted Tribolo to do two nude statues to go on either side of his own Duke Giuliano, one representing Earth, crowned with cypress and weeping for the death of Giuliano, with extended arms, the other Heaven joyfully raising her arms at receiving the spirit of that lord. But when Tribolo was about to begin the Earth, he fell sick of the ague, through change of air, his delicate constitution, or some excesses, and he remained prostrate for many months, tormented by the grief of having lost the work while the friar and Raffaello were engaged upon it. But in order not to be distanced by his rivals, whose fame increased daily, sick as he was he made a large clay model of the Earth and then began it in marble, finishing the front. But the death of Clement, when least expected, removed the animating spirit from those men, who hoped, under Michelagnolo, to achieve immortality. This quite discouraged Tribolo, who was still sick, as he saw nothing to do either in Florence or elsewhere. But his friend Giorgio Vasari, who always assisted him as much as possible, told him not to lose heart, and promised he would get Duke Alessandro to give him something to do by means of the favour of Ottaviano de' Medici the Magnificent, in whose service he was. Somewhat encouraged, Tribolo copied in clay all the marble figures done in the sacristy by Michelagnolo, namely Dawn, Twilight, Day and Night, succeeding so well that M. Gio. Battista Figiovanni, prior of S. Lorenzo, to whom he gave the Night for admitting him to the sacristy, thought it remarkable, and presented it to Duke Alessandro, who gave it to Giorgio, who was then serving him, knowing that he was interested in such things. The figure is now at Arezzo in Giorgio's house. Having made a clay model of Michelagnolo's Madonna, in the same sacristy, Tribolo gave it to M. Ottaviano, who had a beautiful decoration made for it by Battista del Cinque, with columns, bases, cornices and other carving. By the favour of the steward of his excellency, Tribolo was employed by Bertoldo Corsini, provveditore of the fortress then building, to do two nude figures representing Victories, for the three escutcheons, which the duke directed should be placed one on each bastion. He did one of these of four braccia, with great quickness and diligence, supported by three large masks, which earned him the duke's favour.

When the duke went to Naples to defend himself before the Emperor Charles V., returning from Tunis,[1] from calumnies circulated by certain citizens, on which occasion the emperor gave him his daughter Margaret to wife, he wrote to Florence that four men should be directed to make decorations for a magnificent reception of the emperor at Florence. The task of distributing the work fell to me, and I worked with the four, who were Giovanni Corsi, Luigi Guicciarini, Palla Ruccellai and Alessandro Corsini, and gave the greatest and most difficult tasks to Tribolo. These were four great statues, one of Hercules killing the hydra, six braccia high and covered with silver, placed at the corner of the piazza of S. Felice, at the end of the via Maggio, with an inscription in silver letters: "*Ut Hercules labore et aerumnis monstra edomuit, ita Cæsar virtute et clementia hostibus victis seu placatis, pacem Orbi terrarum et quietem restituit.*" The others were two colossi, eight braccia high, one representing the River Bagradas resting on the spoils of the serpent which was carried to Rome, the other for the Ebro with the horn of Amalthæa in one hand and a rudder in the other, of bronze colour, with "*Hiberus ex Hispania*" on the pedestal under the Ebro, and "*Bagradas ex Africa*" under the other. The last was a statue of five braccia at the corner of the Medici, representing Peace with an olive branch in one hand and a lighted torch in the other, which she is putting to a pile of arms heaped on the pedestal where she stands, with the legend "*Fiat pax in virtute tua.*" He did not complete, as he had proposed, the horse, seven braccia high, done for the piazza of S. Trinità, with the figure of the emperor in armour upon it, because his friend Tasso, the wood-carver, did not make sufficient haste with the pedestal and other carved woodwork, but wasted his time in talking and jesting, so that he had hardly time to cover the horse alone with tin over the still wet clay. The pedestal contained these words: "*Imperatori Carlo Augusto victoriosissimo*

[1] In 1535.

post devictos hostes, Italiæ pace restituta et salutato Ferdin. fratre expulsis iterum Turcis, Africaque perdomita, Alexander Med. Dux Florentiæ D.D." When the emperor left Florence preparations were begun for the nuptials of his daughter. In order that she and the Vice-Queen of Naples, who was with her, might lodge conveniently in the house of M. Ottaviano de' Medici, to the amazement of all an annex was made to the old house in four weeks, Tribolo, Andrea di Cosimo the painter and I, aided by about ninety painters and sculptors of the city, doing the decorations in ten days, painting the loggias, the courts and other public places in a manner appropriate to the wedding. Among other things Tribolo did two Victories about the principal door, in half-relief, supported by termini and bearing the arms of the emperor, which hung from the neck of a fine eagle, done in full relief. He also did cherubs over the tops of doors on either side of some much-admired busts. During the festivities Tribolo received a letter from Bologna in which his friend M. Pietro del Magno besought him to go there and do a marble bas-relief of three and a half braccia for the Madonna di Galiera, where a fine marble ornament already existed. Having nothing else to do, Tribolo went and did a model of a Virgin ascending into heaven with the twelve Apostles beneath in various attitudes. He then began to work at it, but with little pleasure, for his material was saligno, a bad quality of Milanese marble, and he felt he was wasting time, without enjoying the satisfaction of those who can show a surface that looks like real flesh. He had almost finished when I persuaded Duke Alessandro to recall Michelagnolo and the others from Rome to finish the sacristy begun by Clement, and I proposed to give him work at Florence. But the duke was assassinated by Lorenzo di Pier Francesco de' Medici,[1] a circumstance that prevented this project, and caused the despair of artists. When Tribolo heard of the duke's death, he wrote sorrowing letters of comfort to me, advising me to go to Rome, as he understood I wished to do, to leave the court and pursue my studies, and that he would fall in with what I should arrange. But as it happened this was not necessary, as on Sig. Cosimo de' Medici becoming duke, who routed his enemies at Monte Murlo in his first year,[2] quiet was established. The duke used then to frequent the villa of Castello, rather more than two miles from Florence, where he began gradually to build quarters for himself and the court, being incited by Maestro Piero da S. Casciano, reputed a master of merit and a devoted servant

of Signora Maria, the duke's mother, and the builder and servant
of Sig. Giovanni. He resolved to satisfy a long-cherished desire
to bring water to that place. Accordingly an aqueduct was begun
to bring water from the hill of Castellina, about a quarter of
a mile from Castello, the work progressing bravely with many
labourers. But the duke perceived that Piero did not possess
invention or design equal to the task of preparing a work that
could later on receive decoration, such as the site and the water
required, and one day, when he was speaking of the matter there,
M. Ottaviano de' Medici and Cristofano Rinieri, Tribolo's friend
and an old servant of Signora Maria and the duke, praised
Tribolo as being a man well fitted for such a task. The duke
therefore gave Cristofano a commission to fetch him from
Bologna. This was done speedily, and Tribolo, who desired
nothing better than to serve Duke Cosimo, came immediately
to Florence and was taken to Castello, when the duke, learning
what he proposed to do, gave him a commission to make the
models. He was engaged upon this while Piero was making
the aqueduct, when the duke, who had begun to make a wall
round the bastions on the hill of S. Miniato, erected during the
siege from the design of Michelagnolo, ordered Tribolo to make
arms in *pietra forte*, with two Victories, for the corner of a
bastion facing Florence. But after Tribolo had laboriously
completed the arms and one of the Victories, four braccia high,
considered very beautiful, he was obliged to desist, because
Piero having advanced the aqueduct to the duke's satisfaction, his excellency wished Tribolo to carry out his design
and models for the decoration of the place, granting him
8 crowns a month, such as Piero had enjoyed. In order that
there may be no confusion between the aqueduct and the
decoration of the fountain, I will here say a few words of the
site of Castello.

The villa of Castello is situated at the roots of Monte Morello,
below the villa of Topaia, which is half-way up. In front of it
the plain slopes gradually to the River Arno for a mile and a
half, and at the point where the mountain begins is the palace
built with good design by Pier Francesco de' Medici. Its principal
front faces south over an extensive swamp, with two large lakes
filled with water from an ancient Roman aqueduct built to bring
water from Valdimarra to a vaulted reservoir at Florence, so
that it possesses a delightful view. In the middle of the lakes
is a bridge twelve braccia broad, leading to an avenue of the
same width, covered by mulberry-trees along its whole length

of three hundred braccia, affording a pleasant shade. It goes to
the Prato high-road, reached by a gate between two fountains,
which supply drink to wayfarers and cattle. Toward the east
are fine stables, and to the west a private garden, approached
from the court of the stables, passing through the palace between
the loggias, halls and chambers of the ground floor. From this
garden a door on the west gives access to another large garden
full of fruit-trees, and terminating in a thicket of fir-trees, hiding
the houses of the labourers and other servants. On the north
side the meadow is as large as the area of the palace, stables and
private garden together. From it one mounts to the principal
garden, surrounded by an ordinary wall, and as one gradually
ascends the garden rises clear into full sunshine, as if there was
no palace in front. From the top there is a view not only of the
palace, but of the surrounding plain as far as the city. In the
middle of the garden are high and thick cypresses, laurels and
myrtles growing wild, and forming a labyrinth surrounded by
a hedge two and a half braccia high, so regular that it looks as
if it had been produced by the brush. In the middle of the labyrinth Tribolo made a beautiful marble fountain, as the duke
desired. At the principal entrance by the lakes Tribolo wished
to extend the avenue for more than a mile, to the Arno, and
that the water from the fountains should accompany it to the
river in channels at the sides, to be filled with various fish. He
wished to make a loggia in front of the palace and, after passing
an open court, to have another palace like the old one in every
respect on the side of the stables, which would have formed
a very large palace and a fine façade. On passing the court at
the entrance to the great garden of the labyrinth, and mounting
the steps to it, one entered a clearing thirty braccia square, made
to receive a large fountain of white marble, to rise fourteen
braccia above the ornamentation, and that the water should
issue from the mouth of a statue at the summit, six braccia
high. At the end of the meadow there were to be two loggias
opposite each other, thirty braccia by fifteen, with a marble
bas-relief of twelve braccia in the middle of each, and outside
a cistern of eight braccia to receive the water from a vase held
by two figures. In the middle of the labyrinth Tribolo intended
to make the water pass through spouts, but the marble basin
afterwards put there had to be far smaller than the one of the
principal fountain, and at the top there was to be a bronze
figure spouting water. In the middle, at the end of the garden,
there was to be a door with marble cherubs spouting water in

every direction, and double niches at the corners containing statues, like those on the side walls at the junction of the avenues traversing the garden, which are covered with verdure. The door gives access by some steps to another garden as broad as the first, but not so long, at the base of the mountain. It was to contain two other loggias at the sides, and a cave in the wall opposite the side against the hill, with three cisterns to catch water, and two fountains in the wall on either side, and two others opposite with the door between, these containing as many fountains as the lower garden, the upper one receiving the water. It was to be filled with orange-trees since it is protected by the walls and the mountain from the north and other contrary winds. Two flights of steps, one on each side, led up to a wood of cypresses, mulberry-trees, yews, laurels and other evergreen trees, finely spaced out. In the middle there was to be a fine lake, according to Tribolo's design. As it narrowed to a corner, it was necessary to make a loggia with a pointed end, from which, on mounting steps, there was a view of the palace, the fountains, the gardens, and all the country round as far as the ducal villa of Poggio a Caiano, Florence, Prato, Siena,[1] and the surrounding country·for many miles. On Piero completing the aqueduct as far as Castello, taking in all the waters of la Castellina, he died of a severe fever after a few days. Tribolo therefore took up the task, and recognised that the water, although plentiful, would not suffice for what he proposed to do, and it would not rise as high as was necessary. The duke then permitted him to bring water from Petraia, more than one hundred and fifty braccia above Castello, where it is both plentiful and good. He made an aqueduct like the other, and high enough to reach the lakes and principal fountain by another channel. He then began the grotto, for the three niches and the fountains on either side, one of which was to have a large stone statue of Monte Asinaio, to spout water from its mouth into a cistern, from which the water was to pass to the fountain which is now behind the steps of the labyrinth garden, and to enter the vase on the shoulders of the River Mugnone, standing in a large niche of grey stone, beautifully decorated and covered with spungite; a representation of the fact that the Mugnone rises in Monte Asinaio. Tribolo then made his Mugnone, a figure in grey stone four braccia high, in a fine attitude, holding a vase on its shoulder and emptying it into a cistern, while the other shoulder rests on the ground, the left leg is crossed over the right.

[1] He probably means Signa.

Behind is a nude female figure representing Fiesole, rising amid
the spungite in the middle of the niche, holding the moon, the
ancient device of the city. Below the niche is a large basin
supported by two large goats, one of the duke's devices, with
festoons and masks hanging about them. The water issues from
the lips of the goats to the bottom of the basin, passes round the
walls of the labyrinth garden, where there are fountains between
the niches, and oranges and pomegranates between these. In
the second garden Tribolo had arranged for a Monte della
Falterona similar to his Monte Asinaio, from which the statue
representing the Arno was to receive its water. But as neither
figure was ever completed, I will speak of the fountain and of
the Arno which Tribolo did. The river holds a vase to its side,
and leans on a lion with a lily in its claws, the vase receiving
its water from a hole in the wall, behind which la Falterona was
to be. As the long basin is exactly like that of Mugnone, I will
say nothing except that it is a pity that such a beautiful work
is not in marble. Continuing his conduit, Tribolo brought the
water from the grotto under the orange garden, and the next
one to the labyrinth, which it encircled, and in the middle he
made the water-spout. He then united the waters of Arno and
Mugnone under the level of the labyrinth in bronze channels,
finely devised, filling the pavement with slender jets, so that by
turning a tap all those who come to see the fountain are sprinkled,
and escape is not easy, because Tribolo made a stone seat about
the fountain, supported by lions intermixed with marine monsters in bas-relief, a difficult task as it is on a slope and he had
to make a level surface and seats too. He next began the fountain
of the labyrinth, making marine monsters encircling the base,
in marble, so carved with their tails intertwined that it is a
unique work of its kind. He then did the marble basin, first
carried out at Castello, with a large marble bas-relief, from the
villa of Antella, brought by M. Ottaviano de' Medici from
Giuliano Salviati. Before making the basin Tribolo did some
cherubs dancing, to decorate this, holding festoons of marine
objects beautifully carved. He also gracefully executed the
cherubs and masks for spouting water, and proposed to erect
a bronze statue three braccia high on the top, to represent
Florence, to which the waters of Arno and Mugnone flow. For
this figure he had made a fine model, which was to wring water
out of its hair. After bringing the water to the first quadrangle
of thirty braccia beneath the labyrinth, he began the great
fountain. This was octagonal, and devised to receive all the

waters mentioned into the first basin, from the labyrinth and from the main conduit as well. Each of the eight sides forms a step of $\frac{1}{8}$ a braccia high, and at each angle is a projection with a corresponding one on the steps, which rise to the height of $\frac{2}{8}$ at the angles, so that the middle point of the steps is indented, giving them a quaint appearance, but very convenient to mount. The rim of the fountain is shaped like a vase, and the body of it is round. The pedestal is octagonal and continues in this shape almost up to the button of the tazza, forming eight pedestals on which are seated eight cherubs of life-size, in various attitudes, with entwined arms and legs, forming a rich ornament. The tazza, which was round and 8 braccia across, discharged water evenly all round into the octagonal basin, like a fine rain. Thus the cherubs are not touched, and seem to be playing and avoiding the bath in a charmingly childish manner, an idea unequalled for its simple beauty. Opposite the four sides of the crossing of the garden four bronze cherubs are lying at play in various attitudes, all made from Tribolo's design though done by others. Above the tazza another pedestal begins, at the base of which four cherubs are on projections, squeezing the necks of some geese who are spouting water brought from the principal conduit leading from the labyrinth, which rises exactly to this height. Above the cherubs is the remainder of the shaft, which is made of small tubes from which the water flows in a curious way, and assuming a square shape, it rests upon some well-made masks. Above them is a smaller basin, at the edges of which are four goat's heads tied up by the horns spouting water into the great basin, and combining with the cherubs to make the falling rain already mentioned. Another shaft followed higher up, with other ornaments and cherubs in half-relief, forming a round top, which serves as a base for a figure of Hercules crushing Antæus, designed by Tribolo and executed by others. From the mouth of Antæus water issues in a great quantity, instead of his spirit, being supplied from the great conduit of Petraia, rising sixteen braccia from the level where the steps are and falling into the larger basin. Through this aqueduct pass the waters from the lake and grotto, as well as those of Petraia, and, joined to those of Castellina, go to the fountains of Falterona and Monte Asinaio, and thence to those of the Arno and Mugnone. Reunited at the fountain of the labyrinth, they go to the great fountain where the cherubs with the geese are. They were to flow thence according to Tribolo's design by two conduits to the basins of the loggias, and thence each to its private garden.

The first of these gardens, on the west, is full of curious and medicinal herbs, and there was to be a statue of Æsculapius in the niche of the fountain behind the marble basin. This principal fountain was completed by Tribolo in marble, and so perfectly that I think it may truthfully be called the richest, best proportioned and most charming that has ever been made, great diligence having been applied to every part. After modelling the Æsculapius, Tribolo began it in marble, but, being hindered by other things, he put it aside and it was finished by Antonio di Gino, the sculptor, his pupil. In a meadow to the east of the garden Tribolo planted a holm so thickly covered with ivy that it looked like a thicket, and it was approached by convenient wooden steps, at the top of which is a resting-place, with seats about it, with backs, all of living green, and in the middle a marble table with a vase of variegated marble, into which water is brought by a pipe which spouts in the air and is carried off by another pipe. The pipes for the water are so covered by the ivy that they cannot be seen, and the water is controlled by taps. It is impossible to describe how the water is carried along the branches of this tree, to sprinkle people and to make fearful hissing sounds. The water is finally collected at the two lakes outside the palace at the beginning of the avenue, and thence goes to serve the other needs of the villa. For the ornamental statues to stand in the niches about the labyrinth gardens, Tribolo consulted M. Benedetto Varchi, a distinguished poet, orator and philosopher of our day, and intended to put the four Seasons, each one in a place most appropriate for it. Winter was to be on the right on entering, with six figures below to show the greatness of the Medici house, and that Duke Cosimo possessed all the virtues. They were Justice, Pity, Valour, Nobility, Wisdom and Liberality, virtues always possessed by the Medici, and especially by his excellency. Tribolo also intended to put the Laws, Peace, Arms, the Sciences, the Languages and the Arts opposite these virtues, because the Medici always favoured such things, the duke being just in legislation, pitiful in peace, valorous in war, noble in science, wise in his introduction of the tongues and talent, and liberal to the arts. He arranged that the statues should be on the Arno and Mugnone, to show that they honour Florence. He proposed to make each figure a portrait of a member of the Medici house, Justice being the duke; Pity, Giuliano the Magnificent; Valour, Sig. Giovanni; Nobility, Lorenzo the elder; Wisdom, Cosimo the elder, or Clement VII.; Liberality, Pope Leo; while in front other heads of the Medici family could have been placed, or of persons dependent on them. To make the arrangement clearer I show it thus:

Summer. Mugnone. Door. Arno. Spring.

Arts.	Liberality.
Tongues.	Wisdom.
Sciences.	Nobility.
Arms.	Valour.
Peace.	Pity.
Laws.	Justice.

Loggia.   Loggia.

Autumn. Door. Loggia. Door. Winter.

All these ornaments would have made it the most magnificent garden in Europe, but they were not completed, because Tribolo did not push on the work while the duke was in the mind, although he might easily have done so, as he had the men, and the duke spent freely, not being hampered as he was afterwards. Not content with the water there, the duke intended to go to Valcenni for more, and to bring it by an aqueduct from Castello to the piazza of his palace in Florence. If the work had been in the hands of a man more active and ambitious than Tribolo, it would at least have been carried much farther. But Tribolo was slow, and being occupied with other affairs of the duke, he only himself did the two fountains with the two rivers, Arno and Mugnone, and the statue of Fiesole. There was no apparent reason for this except that he was busy over other things for the duke. Among other things the duke employed him to make a bridge over the Mugnone outside the S. Gallo gate, on the high-road to Bologna. Tribolo did this, contorting the arch to fit the river, a new idea and much admired, all his stones being made awry, forming a strong and graceful bridge.

Not long before, the duke, desiring to erect the tomb of Sig Giovanni de' Medici, his father,[1] commissioned Tribolo to do it. He made a fine model in competition with one prepared by Raffaello da Montelupo, favoured by Francesco di Sandro, master of arms of his excellency. Tribolo went to Carrara for the marble, and also found two cisterns for the loggias of Castello, a slab and many other marbles. M. Gio. Battista da Ricasoli,

[1] Called Giovanni delle Bande Nere, ob. 1526.

now bishop of Pistoia, being then at Rome on the duke's affairs, was met by Baccio Bandinelli, who had just finished the tombs of Leo and Clement in the Minerva, who asked for a recommendation to the duke. M. Giovanni therefore wrote that Bandinelli desired to serve the duke, who agreed that he should fetch him. On reaching Florence, Baccio audaciously showed the duke his designs and models, and succeeded in obtaining the commission for the tomb of Sig. Giovanni allotted to Tribolo. Having taken marble of Michelagnolo in the via Mozza in Florence, without consideration for anyone, he began the work, and Tribolo, on returning from Carrara, found the work taken from him through his being too complacent and dilatory.

When Duke Cosimo and Sig. Don Pietro di Toledo, Marquis of Villafranca, then Viceroy of Naples, became united by the marriage of the duke to Leonora, the viceroy's daughter, Tribolo was commissioned to make a triumphal arch at the Prato gate, by which the bride was to enter on her way from Poggio. Tribolo made a fine one, decorated with columns, pilasters, architraves, cornices and pediments, full of scenes and figures painted by Battista Franco of Venice, Ridolfo Ghirlandajo and Michele, his pupil, the statues being by Tribolo. The principal figure, placed in the middle upon a pedestal in relief, was a female representing Fecundity, with five children, three about her legs, one in her lap and one in her arms. It stood between two figures of the same size, a Security, who leans on a column with a slender rod in her hand, and Eternity, with a ball in her arms and an old figure at her feet, for Time, while the Sun and the Moon hang at her neck. I will not speak of the paintings, because they are described in the accounts of the preparations for the wedding. For the decoration of the palace of the Medici, of which Tribolo had special charge, he did many things relating to the wedding and those of all the illustrious members of the Medici, in the lunettes of the courtyard. In the grand court he made a sumptuous trophy, full of scenes, on the one hand, of the Greeks and Romans, and on the other of the deeds of illustrious members of the Medici house, executed by the best young painters in Florence, under Tribolo's direction: Bronzino, Pier Francesco di Sandro, Francesco Bachiacca, Domenico Conti, Antonio di Domenico and Battista Franco of Venice. On the piazza of S. Marco, on a pedestal ten braccia high, over the cornice of which Bronzino had painted two fine scenes in bronze colour, Tribolo did a bronze horse twelve braccia high, rearing up and ridden by an armed figure of proportionate

size, representing Sig. Giovanni de' Medici, with dead and
wounded men lying beneath. The work was executed with
such judgment and art that it was admired by all who saw it,
and the speed with which it was produced excited astonish-
ment, Tribolo being helped by Sandro Buglioni, the sculptor,
who fell and rendered himself lame, narrowly escaping death.
Under Tribolo's direction Aristotile da S. Gallo did a marvellous perspective, and Tribolo himself designed the most
charming dresses that it is possible to imagine, which were
made by Gio. Battista Strozzi. The duke therefore employed
Tribolo in many masquerades, such as that of the bears, the
race of buffaloes, that of the crows, and others. When Don
Francesco, the duke's eldest son, was born, Tribolo had charge
of the decoration of S. Giovanni at Florence for the christening,
with an apparatus to contain the hundred youths who walked
in procession from the palace to the church. Together with
Tasso he made that ancient and beautiful building look new
and modern, surrounding it with seats richly adorned with pictures and gilding. Under the lantern he made a large octagonal
wooden vessel, carved, approached by four steps. At the angles
were large vine-stems starting from the ground, where lions'
claws are represented, and at the top are large cherubs in
various attitudes, holding the mouth of the vase and supporting festoons on their shoulders forming a garland about.
Tribolo also made a wooden pedestal, in the middle of the vase,
decorated with beautiful fancies, surmounted by Donatello's
St. John the Baptist from the house of Gismondo Martelli. Only
the principal chapel escaped decoration, containing an old
tabernacle with figures in relief by Andrea Pisano. But this
seemed to detract from the grace of the rest, everything being
renewed. So one day, when the duke went to the spot and praised
Tribolo's arrangements, for his good judgment showed him how
well Tribolo had adapted himself to this site and in other
ways, he blamed him for not touching the principal chapel.
At once, like a man of judgment, Tribolo decided that it should
be covered with a large canvas painted in grisaille, representing
St. John the Baptist baptising Christ, with people looking on,
and being baptised, some undressing and others dressing, in
various attitudes. From above God sends down the Holy Spirit,
and two springs, the JOR and the DAN, unite to form the
Jordan. When M. Pier Francesco Riccio, then the duke's major-
domo, wanted Jacopo da Pontormo to do this work, he refused,
because he only had six days, and he did not think it sufficient.

Ridolfo Ghirlandajo, Bronzino and many others also declined. Giorgio Vasari returned from Bologna at this time, being engaged on the picture for M. Bindo Altoviti in his chapel of S. Apostolo in Florence. He was not in much consideration, although he was friendly with Tribolo and Tasso, because those who were not of the party favoured by M. Pier Francesco Riccio did not enjoy the favour of the court, however skilful they might be, so that many who might have excelled if assisted by the prince were neglected, Tasso directing everything, being architect of the palace and a merry fellow who exercised complete dominion over Tribolo. Being suspicious of Giorgio, who laughed at their vanity and folly, and sought to gain more by study of his art than by favour, they did not think of him, when the duke ordered him to do that canvas. He completed it in six days, in grisaille, gracefully decorating that part of the church which most needed such an adornment.

To return to Tribolo, whom I have left I know not how. He won the greatest praise for his decorations, and the duke desired that some of them between the columns should be left, and there they still are. At the villa of Cristofano Rinieri, at Castello, Tribolo made a life-size river of grey stone, while he was doing the duke's fountains, above a pond at the top in a niche, spouting water into a very large cistern of the same stone. The figure, though made of pieces, is so well joined that it seems of one block. Tribolo then began the steps of the library of S. Lorenzo for his excellency, namely those before the door. After he had laid four steps without finding the method or measure of Michelagnolo, the duke sent him to Rome, not only to learn Michelagnolo's opinion, but to bring him to Florence. He succeeded in neither, for Michelagnolo would not leave Rome, and remembered nothing about the steps. Tribolo therefore returned to Florence, and, unable to continue the steps, he began the pavement of the library in white and red bricks, like some he had seen in Rome, adding a red clay to the white, mixed with bole, to give the effect of carving in the bricks, and making the pavement a copy of the ceiling and soffit above, bringing him much praise. He began, but did not finish, owing to a work at the fortress of the Faenza gate for Don Giovanni di Luna, the Castellan, an escutcheon, and a large two-headed eagle in wax, to be cast in bronze, but only did the shield.

Every year at the feast of St. John the Baptist it was the custom at Florence to have a *girandola*, that is to say at night, on the principal piazza, a machine full of fireworks, sometimes made like a church or a ship or rocks, a city or a hell, according to the fancy of the inventor. One year Tribolo was charged to make one, and he produced a very beautiful work, but as such fireworks are fully treated by Vannoccio of Siena,[1] I will not enlarge on the matter. But I will say something about the *girandole*. These are made of wood with wide spaces, so that the fire, when started from the bottom, may not flare up all at once, but rise gradually and evenly at regular intervals, and together fill the sky with flame, which is in the *girandola* at the top and bottom also. They are spread out in this way so that they may not burn away all in a moment, and they make a fine spectacle. It is the same with the fireworks, which are fastened to the solid parts of this *girandola* and make a merry show. Trumpets are introduced in the decoration and are usually made to issue from the mouths of masks and other similar things. But the important part consists in arranging the lights so that they shall burn all night and illuminate the piazza, the whole being regulated by a train bathed in sulphur and spirit, which burns slowly towards the various places where the fire is to be started until all is alight. Various things are represented, but they must be connected with fire. Some time ago they did Sodom with Lot and his daughters escaping. At another time Gerion ridden by Virgil and Dante, as the latter relates in the *Inferno*, and, long before, Orpheus and Eurydice, with many other things. The duke ordained that the work should not be given to blockheads who had been producing their clumsy shows for many years, but that an eminent master should do something good. Tribolo was therefore employed, and he made a beautiful octagonal temple, twenty braccia high with its ornaments, and an image of Peace setting fire to a great heap of arms at her feet. The arms, the statue and the other figures were of paper, clay and cloth, the materials being light, so that the whole thing could be suspended in the air for some time on a double rope across the piazza at some distance from the ground. But the fire caught so rapidly, the fireworks being too near each other, that all burned at once instead of lasting at least an hour, and caught the framework and ropes, with no small damage and to the disappointment of the people. But the work itself was the finest *girandola* ever made up to that time.

[1] Vannoccio Biringucci, born at Siena in 1480. His *Pirotechnia* was first printed at Vènice in 1540.

The duke wanted to make the loggia of the Mercato Nuovo for the benefit of citizens and merchants, but was unwilling to overwork Tribolo, who, as master of the captains of the party, and the commissioners of the rivers and of the sewers, rode about the territory to embank rivers which were overflowing, repair bridges and other things. The duke therefore employed Tasso[1] by the advice of M. Pier Francesco the major-domo, thus making an architect out of a carpenter. It was indeed against Tribolo's will, though he affected friendship for Tasso and refrained from pointing out many errors in his model, such as in the capitals of the columns on the pilasters at the corners. For the columns not being of the requisite length when put in their places, the crown did not fall on the top of the capitals, and it was necessary to reduce them so much that the order was spoiled. There were many other errors which I need not mention. For M. Pier Francesco Tasso did the door of S. Romolo and a low window on the Piazza del Duca in a style of his own, the capitals serving as bases, and the whole so destitute of order and proportion that it looked as if he was reviving the German style. His stairs and rooms in the palace were such that the duke had them destroyed, since they possessed no order or proportion, were lopsided and out of the square, and lacked all grace and convenience. These things troubled Tribolo, who was competent himself, and could not bear to see the duke wasting his money and disgracing himself, or witness without pain the folly of his friend Tasso. Connoisseurs well recognised the presumption of the one in practising an art of which he knew nothing, and the dissimulation of the other who declared himself pleased with what he knew to be bad. The same fate befel Tribolo as Tasso, as Giorgio Vasari had to destroy many works in the palace. Tasso left his wood carving, in which he was unequalled, to take up an art of which he knew nothing, while Tribolo abandoned sculpture, in which he was excellent, for the embanking of rivers. The one brought him honour, the other involved him in loss and shame, because he did not succeed in confining the rivers, and made many enemies, especially about Prato, because of Bisenzio, and in Valdinievole in many places.

When Duke Cosimo bought the Pitti palace he wished to adorn it with gardens, woods, fountains and ponds and suchlike things. Accordingly he directed Tribolo to lay out the rising ground as it now is, although some things have since been changed. I will take another opportunity of speaking of this

[1] About 1547.

palace, which is the finest in Europe. Tribolo was next sent by the duke to Elba to see the city and the port to be made there, and to fetch a round piece of granite, twelve braccia in diameter, to make a basin for the principal fountain in the Pitti palace garden. Tribolo had a boat made on purpose to carry this block, and after leaving instructions he returned to Florence. He found the city full of clamour against him, because the rivers which he had embanked had broken loose and done great damage, though it was not perhaps altogether his fault. However, the malignity and envy of certain officials accorded him all the blame, perhaps justly, and as he was not very bold and somewhat lacking in resource he feared that he would lose the duke's favour. He was thus in a sorry plight when he was overtaken by a severe fever on 20 August 1550. Giorgio was in Florence, engaged in taking to Rome the marble for the tomb of Julius III. in S. Pietro a Montorio. He visited his friend Tribolo and urged him to think only of his health and of finishing the work of Castello when he was better, letting the rivers alone, as they would do more harm than good to anyone. He promised and would have done so, I believe, had not death closed his eyes on 7 September in the same year. Thus his works at Castello remained incomplete, for although one thing and then another was taken up, after his time, they never showed the same diligence and alacrity over them as when Tribolo was alive and the duke was eager about the work. If great works are not pushed forward while those who have them done are willing to spend and are free from embarrassments, they will be left unfinished, depriving their designer of memory and honour, for it rarely happens that the successors of the original designer are willing to finish them according to his plan. The principal lake at Castello, however, has been modestly finished by Giorgio Vasari by the duke's commission, in accordance with the original design, as his excellency desired. Tribolo lived sixty-five years, and was laid to rest by the company of the Scalzo in their burial-place. He left a son Raffaello, who has not followed the arts, and two daughters, one of whom is the wife of Davitte, who helped in the work of Castello, being a man of judgment, well fitted for this, and who is now engaged upon the water-supply of Florence, Pisa, and other places of the dominion.

Pierino da Vinci, Sculptor
(?1520 – ?1554)

ALTHOUGH we usually extol those who have successfully accomplished something, yet if the works of a master show that he could have done much greater things had he not been prevented by some unusual bad fortune, we ought in justice to praise him also. The shortness of Vinci's life ought not therefore to deprive him of praise, considering what he did in the time, and he would have produced even more abundant fruit had not the cruel tempest destroyed both fruit and plant together.

I remember having said elsewhere that Ser Piero, father of the famous painter Lionardo, came from Vinci in the Valdarno. This Piero had a son Bartolommeo, born after Lionardo. He remained at Vinci and married a daughter of one of the best families. Bartolommeo was anxious to have a son, and often told his wife of the genius of his brother Lionardo, praying God to grant him another Lionardo, his brother being dead. In a short while a gracious child was born whom he wished to call Lionardo, but by the advice of his relatives he named him Piero, after his father. At the age of three the child displayed much grace, was beautiful with curly hair, and of a quick intelligence. When Maestro Giuliano del Carmine,[1] a noted astrologer, stayed in the house with a priest who was a palmist, both great friends of Bartolommeo, they both predicted that the child would be a genius, would make great progress in the mercurial arts, but would only enjoy a short life. Their prophecy proved only too true.

As Piero grew his father taught him letters, but unaided he practised design and made clay models, showing that the genius predicted for him was beginning to work. Bartolommeo therefore concluded that God had heard his prayer, feeling that his brother had been restored to him in his son. He resolved to take the twelve-year-old Piero to Florence, where he left him with Bandinelli, who, as a friend of Lionardo, promised to look after the child and teach him carefully, for he seemed more inclined to sculpture than painting. But on his frequent visits to Florence Bartolommeo found that Bandinelli was not fulfilling his promise, and so he took the boy away and gave him to Tribolo, who seemed more ready to take pains to help those who wanted to

[1] Frà Giuliano Ristori.

learn, to be more studious in art, and to be more devoted to the memory of Lionardo. Tribolo was engaged upon the fountains at Castello,[1] and there Piero began to design, as was his wont, being spurred by the competition of the young men with Tribolo. He studied ardently both day and night, hoping to acquire ability and honour, and spurred by the example of his fellows. In a few months his progress excited general wonder, and he began to use the iron tools to see if he was skilful enough to realise the conceptions of his mind. Tribolo perceived his dexterity, and having just finished a stone laver for Cristofano Rinieri, he gave Piero a piece of marble to make a child for it to spout water. Piero joyfully took the marble, and after making a clay model executed the work with such grace that Tribolo and the others concluded that he would become a rare master. Being set to do a ducal crown of stone above the arms of balls of M. Pier Francesco Riccio, the duke's major-domo, he made it with two infants, their legs intertwined, who hold the cap in their hands and lay it on the top of the arms, which are over the door of the house then occupied by M. Riccio, opposite S. Giuliano, beside the priests of S. Antonio. On seeing this work the artists of Florence ratified the judgment of Tribolo. Piero next did a child hugging a fish spouting water, for the fountains of Castello. From a larger piece of marble, given him by Tribolo, he carved two infants embracing and squeezing fish which spout water. These infants, with their legs, arms and hair, were done so gracefully that it was clear Piero could undertake the most difficult tasks with success. Taking courage, he bought a piece of grey stone, two and a half braccia long, took it to his house at the Briga corner, and worked at it in evenings, at night and on festivals, producing a Bacchus with a satyr at his feet and holding a cup in one hand, and in the other a bunch of grapes, and on his head a crown of grapes, copied from his own clay model. In this and in his other early works Piero displayed a marvellous facility which never offends the eye. The Bacchus was bought by Bongianni Capponi, and is now in a court of Lodovico Capponi, his nephew. While Piero was thus engaged few yet knew him to be Lionardo's nephew, but as his works made him famous they discovered his relationship. Thus ever afterwards he was known as Il Vinci, for his uncle's sake, and for his own skill.

Having frequently heard of Rome and its praises, Vinci, like everyone else, conceived a great desire to go there, hoping to

[1] About 1546.

profit by seeing the works of the ancients and of Michelagnolo, as well as that artist himself, then living there. He therefore went with some friends, and, after seeing all he desired, he returned to Florence, wisely concluding that the things of Rome were still too deep for him and that they ought to be seen and imitated, not at the beginning, but at a more advanced stage. Tribolo had then finished a model of the shaft of the labyrinth fountain, containing satyrs in bas-relief, four masks and four small infants in relief seated on vine-branches. On Vinci's return Tribolo gave him this shaft to do, and he introduced certain graceful ideas not employed by others, but which gave great delight. On finishing the marble basin, Tribolo proposed to make four children on the rim, playing in the water, to be cast in bronze. Vinci made a clay model, and they were afterwards cast by Zanobi Lastricati the sculptor, a skilful founder, and were placed upon the fountain not long since, being very beautiful to see.

Luca Martini, then proveditore of the Mercato Nuovo, used daily to visit Tribolo, and desiring to assist Vinci, whose genius and good character he extolled, gave him a piece of marble two-thirds braccia by one and a quarter braccia. With this Vinci made a Christ at the Column in bas-relief. Indeed, he made everyone marvel, for he was not yet seventeen, and in five years he had learned more than others do in a lifetime after long experience.

At this time Tribolo had taken the office of head of the sewers of Florence, and he directed that the sewer of the old piazza of S. Maria Novella should be enlarged so that it should be better able to hold all the waters which flowed into it. He commissioned Vinci to make a model of a large mask of three braccia, through the mouth of which the rain-water should pass. The work being allotted to Vinci by the officials of the Torre, he called in the help of Lorenzo Marignolli the sculptor, to finish it more quickly. He made it in a hard stone, and it adorns the piazza, to the great benefit of the city.

Vinci now thought himself qualified to go to Rome, where he expected to make great profit from association with artists, and when the opportunity offered he seized it eagerly. Michelagnolo's great friend, Francesco Bandini, had arrived from Rome, to whom Vinci was introduced and much praised by Luca Martini. He commissioned Vinci to make a wax model for a marble tomb which he wished to erect in his chapel in S. Croce, and soon after he took Vinci with him to Rome because the youth had disclosed his purpose to Luca. There Vinci stayed a year studying, and did some remarkable works. The first was a Christ on the Cross giving up the ghost, in bas-relief, copied from a design by Michelagnolo. For Cardinal Ridolfo he made a bronze bust and a much-admired marble bas-relief of Venus. For Francesco Bandini he restored an antique horse which lacked several pieces. To show his gratitude to Luca, who continually wrote to him and recommended him to Bandini, he did Michelagnolo's Moses in wax, two-thirds the size of the one on the tomb of Julius II. in S. Pietro, a work of unsurpassed beauty, and sent it as a present to Luca.

While Vinci was thus employed in Rome, the duke made Luca proveditore of Pisa, where he did not forget his friend. He wrote that he was preparing a room for him and a piece of marble three braccia high, and that Vinci might come when he pleased, for nothing would be lacking. Vinci, out of his affection for Luca, resolved to go to Pisa, where he expected to have an opportunity of showing his skill. On reaching the city he found the marble ready in the room, and began to carve a figure, when he discovered a flaw which deprived him of a braccia, and this determined him to make his figure recumbent. He made a youth, representing a river, holding a vase which spouts water. The vase is supported by three children, who help to pour out the water. At the feet of the figure is a quantity of water containing fish and water-fowl. On completing the river Vinci presented it to Luca, who gave it to the duchess. She valued it greatly, and her brother, Don Garzia of Toledo, being then at Pisa with the galleys, she gave it to him, and he took it gladly for the fountains of his garden at Chiaia in Naples. At this time Luca was writing on Dante's *Commedia*, and after he had shown Vinci the cruelty of the Pisans and Archbishop Ruggieri to Count Ugolino della Gherardesca in starving him to death with his four sons in the Torre della Fame, Vinci conceived an idea for a new work. While still engaged upon his river he began a wax model[1] for a bronze cast, more than a braccia high by three-quarters of a braccia broad, representing two sons of the count dead, one expiring and one in extremities, the blind father wretchedly groping about the prostrate bodies. In this work Vinci showed as much talent in design as Dante displayed poetical skill in his verses,[2] for the sculptor's model excites no less compassion than the poet's lines. To show the site of the event he represented the River Arno on the plinth,

---

[1] Now in the Ashmolean, Oxford.   [2] *Inferno*, Canto xxxiii.

occupying the whole breadth of the scene, because the tower is not far from the river. Above it he made a nude, shrivelled and fearful figure representing Hunger, practically as described by Ovid. He then cast the scene in bronze, which delighted the count, all men considering the work remarkable.

Duke Cosimo was then intent upon adorning the city of Pisa, and had already rebuilt the Piazza del Mercato, with numerous shops and a column ten braccia high in the middle, upon which he proposed to set up a statue of Plenty by Luca's design. Martini spoke to the duke and recommended Vinci, who was commissioned to make this statue,[1] for the duke was ever anxious to help men of ability. Vinci made the statue of travertine, three and a half braccia high, and it was much admired, as he had introduced a little child at the feet helping to hold the cornucopia, and he made the rough, hard stone seem charming and easy. Luca next sent to Carrara for a marble block five braccia by three for Vinci to make two statues of five braccia on the subject of Samson slaying a Philistine with the jawbone of an ass, for which he had seen a design by Michelagnolo. Before the marble arrived Vinci busied himself by making models, all differing from each other. At length he settled on one, and when the block came he at once set to work, imitating Michelagnolo in gradually developing his idea from the block, without impairing it or making mistakes. He made the perforations with great facility, and the style of the whole was charming; but as the work proved exacting he diverted himself with other studies of less importance. Thus he made a small marble basrelief of the Virgin and Child with St. John and St. Elizabeth,[2] a remarkable work, owned by the duchess, and now among the duke's treasures in his scriptorium. He then began a marble half- and bas-relief, one braccia high by one and a half broad, representing Pisa restored by the duke,[3] who is introduced into the scene. About him are his virtues, and notably a Minerva representing Wisdom and the arts revived by the duke in Pisa. The city is surrounded by the numerous vices and natural defects of the place, which are besieging and harassing it like enemies, while the duke relieves the city from the assault. All these virtues and vices were copied by Vinci beautifully, but he left the work unfinished, to the regret of all those who have seen the perfection of the completed parts.

The fame of Vinci being thus spread abroad, the heirs of

[1] In 1550.   [2] Now in the Uffizi Gallery.
[3] Now in the Vatican.

M. Baldassarre Turini of Pescia begged him to make a model
of a marble tomb for M. Baldassarre. He did this to their satisfaction, and it was agreed that the tomb should be made, and
Vinci sent Francesco del Tadda, a skilful marble-carver, to
Carrara for the marble. He sent a piece, and Vinci began a
figure that might have been taken for a work of Michelagnolo.
His abilities were so much admired that he was more in request
than any man of his years, when Heaven decreed that he should
go no farther, and deprived the world of the excellent works
which he would have produced had he lived. While Vinci was
engaged on this tomb, unconscious that his own was preparing,
the duke sent Luca Martini to Genoa on affairs of importance.
Being fond of Vinci, and desiring to give him a change, Luca
took him with him, and while he was busy he induced M. Adamo
Centurioni to employ Vinci to make a figure of St. John the
Baptist, for which he made the model. But he was seized with
a fever, and to double the misfortune, his friend was removed,
possibly to fulfil the fates. Luca was obliged by his affairs to
go back to see the duke at Florence, and the friends parted in
sorrow, Vinci being left in the house of the abbot Nero, although
he was very unwilling to remain in Genoa. But Vinci, growing
daily worse, resolved to leave Genoa, and sent to Pisa for a
pupil called Tiberio Cavalieri, with whose assistance he went
by sea to Livorno, and thence to Pisa in a litter. Arriving at
Pisa at ten o'clock in the evening, the fatigue of the journey
and the fever prevented him from sleeping that night, and the
following morning he died, not having reached the age of
twenty-three. His death grieved all his friends, and especially
Luca Martini, and all those who had expected so much from
him. M. Benedetto Varchi wrote the following sonnet in his
memory:

> Come potro da me, se tu non presti
> O forza o tregua al mio gran duolo interno,
> Soffrirlo in pace mai, Signor superno,
> Che fin nuova ogn'or pena mi desti?
> Dunque de' miei piu cari or quegli or questi
> Verde sen voli all'alto asilo eterno,
> Ed io canuto in questo basso inferno
> A pianger sempre e lamentarmi resti?
> Sciolgami almen tua gran bontade quinci,
> Or che reo fato nostro o sua ventura,
> Ch'era ben degno d'altra vita e gente,
> Per far piu ricco il cielo, e la scultura
> Men bella, e me col buon MARTIN dolente
> N'ha privi, o pieta, del secondo VINCI.

BACCIO BANDINELLI, Sculptor of Florence
(1493–1560)

IN the days when the arts of design, fostered by Lorenzo de'
Medici the elder, flourished in Florence, a goldsmith lived there
named Michelagnolo di Viviano of Gaiuole, who worked excellently with the chisel and in enamel, being skilful in all branches.
He was clever at setting jewels, and owing to his versatility he
became the head of all the foreign masters of his art, whom he
received, together with the youths of the city, so that his shop
was deservedly considered the first in Florence. Lorenzo and all
the Medici employed him, and for Giuliano, Lorenzo's brother,
he made all the ornaments for the helmets and swords, with
subtle mastery, for the tournament in the piazza of S. Croce.[1]
This made his name, and won him the favour of the sons of
Lorenzo, who always valued his work, their friendship proving
most useful to him, so that he became rich and highly considered
in his craft. When the Medici departed from Florence in 1494
they left him much silver and jewels, which he kept secretly until
their return, on which occasion they praised his fidelity and
rewarded him. In 1487 he had a son whom he called Bartolommeo, but who was afterwards known as Baccio, following the
Florentine custom. Michelagnolo wished to leave his son the
heir of his art and property, and took him into his shop with
other youths, who were learning to design, for a man was not
then considered a good goldsmith unless he could design
well and make good reliefs. Baccio therefore studied design,
profiting greatly by the rivalry of the other youths, among
whom was one called Piloto, who afterwards became a skilful
goldsmith. Together they would frequent the churches designing
the works of good painters, and copying in wax some things of
Donato and Verrocchio, while they often did clay works in
full relief.

While still a child, Baccio sometimes repaired to the shop of
Girolamo del Buda, a mediocre painter, on the piazza of S. Puli-
nari.[2] One winter, when there had been a lot of snow, which had
been heaped up on the piazza, Girolamo turned to Baccio and
said jestingly, "If this snow were marble, wouldn't it make a
fine giant, such as Marforius, lying down." "I am willing to do

---

[1] This took place in 1468, but Michelagnolo was only born in 1459.
[2] i.e. S. Apollonia.

it as if it were marble," replied Baccio, and laying down his
cloak, he modelled the snow with his hands, assisted by the
other children, and sketched out a recumbent figure of Marforius, eight braccia in length. The painters and others were
astonished, not so much at what he had done as at the spirit
of so small a child in undertaking such a work. Indeed, Baccio
gave many signs of being more fond of sculpture than of his
goldsmith's work. At Pinzirimonte, a villa bought by his father,
he would frequently stand before the naked workmen and draw
them, and he did the like with the farm animals. At this time
he went every morning to Prato, near the villa, and remained
there all day drawing in the chapel of the Pieve, painted by Frà
Filippo Lippi, not resting till he had drawn everything, imitating
the rare draperies of that master. He managed with skill the
stylo and pen and the red and black matita, a soft stone from
the French mountains which, when the edges are sawn off,
favours very delicate drawing. His father perceiving his son's
bent, changed his plans, and taking counsel with his friends
put the boy in the charge of Gio. Francesco Rustici, one of the
best sculptors of the city, where Lionardo da Vinci continually
practised. That master was pleased with Baccio's drawings, and
advised him to take up work in relief, praising the works of
Donato, and telling him to make some heads or bas-reliefs in
marble. Encouraged by Lionardo's advice, Baccio began to
copy an ancient marble head of a woman which he had modelled
from one in the Medici palace. For a first work it was praiseworthy, and Andrea Carnesecci, to whom Baccio's father gave
it, valued it highly, putting it in his house in the via Larga
over the middle door in the court leading into the garden. But
as Baccio continued to make clay models, his father, to afford
him an opportunity for real study, sent to Carrara for some
pieces of marble, and in his house at Pinti he erected a room
on the via Fiesolana, with the lights adapted for work. Baccio
sketched various marble figures, and completed a Hercules, two
and a half braccia high, holding a dead Cacus between his legs.
The sketches are still there in memory of him.

At this time the cartoon full of nude figures, done by Michelagnolo for Piero Soderini for the hall of the Great Council, was
uncovered, and all artists gathered together to draw it on
account of its excellence. Among them came Baccio, and before
long he surpassed them all, especially in the nudes, with his
outlines, shading and finish. Other students were Jacopo Sansovino, Andrea del Sarto, Rosso, still a youth, and Alfonso

Barughetta the Spaniard. Baccio frequented the spot more than
the others, and had the key counterfeited. At this time, in 1512,
Piero Soderini was deposed and the Medici restored. During the
consequent tumults at the palace, Baccio secretly tore the
cartoon to pieces. The cause not being known, some said he had
done it to have pieces in his possession, others supposed that
he wished to deprive the youths of the advantage of seeing it,
while some said it was out of affection for Lionardo da Vinci
whose reputation the cartoon had done much to obscure; but
some, perhaps nearer the truth, guessed it was from his hatred
of Michelagnolo, displayed by him throughout his life. The loss
to the city was great, and Baccio deservedly earned the general
reputation of being an envious and malignant man. He did
some parts of a cartoon in white lead and chalk, including a
fine nude Cleopatra, which he gave to Piloto the goldsmith.
Having acquired a reputation as a great draughtsman, Baccio
wished to learn to use colours, feeling confident that he could
surpass Michelagnolo in both professions. He made a cartoon
of Leda, with Castor and Pollux issuing from the swan's egg,
and wished to colour it in oils, to show a variety of tints with
lights and shades not taught him by others, but discovered by
himself. Accordingly he sought his friend Andrea del Sarto to
make his portrait in oils, in order that he might see the mixing
of colours and learn the secrets of painting. But Andrea perceived Baccio's intention, and felt indignant at his cunning and
mistrust, because he would readily have shown him what he
wanted if he had asked him as a friend. Accordingly he pretended
to disclose the things to him, putting all manner of tints upon
the palette, and dexterously taking now one and now another,
he represented Baccio's fresh complexion. But Andrea moved
very quickly, and Baccio was obliged to sit still, so that he could
not see or learn as he desired. It was right of Andrea thus to
punish the mistrust of a friend, and show the great skill and
experience necessary for painting. However, Baccio did not
relinquish his plan, being helped by Rosso, of whom he more
frankly asked what he wanted. He therefore began in oils thà
Patriarchs released from Hell by Christ, as well as a larger
picture of Noah's drunkenness. He experimented in painting
on a wall in fresh lime, doing on the walls of his house heads,
arms, legs and torsos, coloured variously. But perceiving that
the work involved more difficulties than he had anticipated
owing to the drying of the lime, he returned to his sculpture.
He made a marble Mercury, three braccia high, holding a flute,

to which he devoted much study and which was much admired. It was bought in 1530 by Giovanni Battista della Palla, and sent to King Francis of France, who thought highly of it. Baccio then devoted himself to the study of anatomy for many months and years. We must indeed extol his desire to excel in the arts, which he had received from Nature rather than any aptitude and dexterity in them. He spared no pains or time, being always occupied on something, and was never found idle, as he hoped in time to surpass all who had ever practised his art, and this induced him to labour hard. He issued a great number of his designs, and induced Agostino Viniziano the engraver to do a nude Cleopatra for him, and a larger sheet of anatomy, which brought him much praise. He next did a wax figure of St. Jerome in penitence, of one and a half braccia. The figure is withered, and shows the bones, muscles, nerves and dried skin, so that all artists, and especially Lionardo da Vinci, declared that nothing better of its kind had ever been seen. Baccio took it to Cardinal Giovanni de' Medici and his brother Giuliano, introducing himself as the son of Michelagnolo the goldsmith. Besides praising his work, they showed him many other favours. This was after their restoration in 1512.

At this time some marble Apostles were being done in the opera of S. Maria del Fiore, to be placed in the marble taber- nacle where the paintings of Lorenzo di Bicci are. By Giuliano's influence, St. Peter was allotted to Baccio, a figure four and a half braccia high. After a long time he completed a figure, not perfect indeed, but well designed. It remained in the opera from 1513 to 1565, when Duke Cosimo wished S. Maria del Fiore to be whitewashed for the marriage of Queen Joan of Austria, and that the four Apostles, including the St. Peter, should be set up in their places. The church had not been done since its erection.

In 1515, when Leo X. was passing through Florence to Bologna, the city erected a colossus of nine and a half braccia under an arch of the loggia of the piazza, near the palace, and gave it to Baccio. It was a Hercules, which, from what Baccio said, led people to expect that it would surpass Michelagnolo's David hard-by. But doing proved a different matter from talking, so that his boasting injured Baccio's reputation with the artists and the city considerably.

Pope Leo having allotted the marble decoration surrounding the Virgin's chamber at Loreto, as well as statues and scenes, to Andrea Contucci of Monte Sansovino, who had already done many admirable works and was engaged on others, Baccio took to the Pope at Rome a fine model of a nude David cutting off Goliath's head, which he intended to execute in marble or bronze for the court of the Medici palace at Florence, where Donato's David first stood, which was afterwards taken to the old palace of the Signori when the Medici palace was sacked. The Pope praised Baccio, but not thinking it was a time to make the David, he sent him to Loreto, for Andrea to give him a bas-relief. On arriving there he was welcomed by Andrea, who had heard of his fame and had the Pope's recommendation, and he gave Baccio a Nativity of the Virgin to do. But Baccio immediately began to criticise Andrea's works and those of the other sculptors there, saying that they had no design, so that very soon they all disliked him. When Andrea learned all that Baccio had said of him, he chided him gently, like a wise man, saying that work is done with the hands and not with the tongue, and that good design does not consist in the paper, but in the perfection of the finished work in stone. He concluded by saying that Baccio must speak of him more respectfully in future. But as Baccio replied with many abusive words, Andrea could bear no more and tried to kill him. They were separated by some who came in at the moment.

Being forced to leave Loreto, Baccio took his bas-relief to Ancona, but becoming tired of it, he left it unfinished, though it was nearly complete, and departed. It was afterwards finished by Raffaello da Montelupo, and set up with those by Andrea, but though praiseworthy it does not equal them in beauty. On returning to Rome, Baccio asked the Pope through Cardinal Giulio de' Medici, that friend of genius, to allow him to do some statues for the court of the Medici palace at Florence. Accordingly he went to Florence, where he did a marble Orpheus, who by his playing and singing pacifies Cerberus and moves Hell to pity. In this work he imitated the Apollo Belvedere of Rome, and it was deservedly praised, because, although it has not the attitude of the Apollo, yet he has very successfully imitated the style of the torso and of all the members. When it was finished, Cardinal Giulio placed the statue in the court, while he governed Florence, on a carved pedestal by Benedetto da Rovezzano the sculptor. But as Baccio never cared for architecture, not considering the genius of Donato, who had made a pedestal for his David, so that passers-by might see it through the door in the court opposite, he put his statue on a rough base, which spoils the view and occupies the door space, so that passers-by see nothing beyond the first court.

Beneath Monte Mario at Rome Cardinal Giulio had erected a beautiful villa in which he wished to have two giants, and as Baccio excelled in these, he gave them to him to do in stucco. They are eight braccia high, and stand on either side of the door leading to the wilderness, and are considered of reasonable beauty. While thus engaged Baccio did not abandon his design, and got the engravers Marco da Ravenna and Agostino Viniziano to engrave a scene designed by him on a large sheet, representing the Massacre of the Innocents, full of nudes, living and dead children, and women and soldiers in various attitudes, showing good design in the figures and a knowledge of the muscles and limbs, which brought him great fame in Europe. He made a fine wood model and wax figures for a tomb for the King of England, but this was afterwards given to Benedetto da Rovezzano, who executed it in metal.

Cardinal Bernardo Divizio of Bibbiena had then returned from a visit to France,[1] where he had observed that King Francis had no marble works either ancient or modern, though he was very fond of them, and so he had promised his majesty that he would persuade the Pope to send him something beautiful. Two ambassadors from King Francis came to the Pope later on, and after seeing the statues of Belvedere, extolled the Laocoon.[2] The Cardinals Medici and Bibbiena asked if their king would like something similar, and they replied that it would be too great a gift. Then the cardinal said that they would send the king the Laocoon or something so like it that he could not tell the difference. Desiring to make a copy, he remembered Baccio, and so sent for him, asking him if he could venture to copy the Laocoon. Baccio replied that he would produce something better, and the cardinal decided to trust him. While waiting for the marble Baccio did a wax model, which was much admired, and then made a carbon drawing of the same size as the marble. On the arrival of the marble, Baccio erected a scaffolding in the Belvedere and began on one of the larger boys, satisfying the Pope and all connoisseurs because there was scarcely any difference between his work and the antique. But he had hardly begun a second child and the father when the Pope died. On the creation of Adrian VI., Baccio accompanied the cardinal to Florence, where he studied design. When Clement succeeded Adrian, Baccio went post to Rome to assist at the coronation, making statues and half-reliefs by the Pope's order. The Pope afterwards gave him rooms and a provision, and he returned to the Laocoon, completing it in two years, and thus producing his finest work. He also restored the right arm of the ancient Laocoon, which was lost, making a large wax one, with corresponding muscles, and he caught the spirit of the antique, showing his knowledge of art. The model served him for the entire arm of his own group. The Pope considered the work so good that he changed his mind and decided to send other antiques to the king and to send this to Florence.[1] He therefore ordered Cardinal Silvio Passerino of Cortona, legate in Florence, who then governed the city, to put it in the Medici palace at the top of the second court, in the year 1525. The work brought great fame to Baccio, who next designed a scene for the Pope to be painted in the principal chapel of S. Lorenzo at Florence, of the martyrdom of SS. Cosmo and Damian on one wall and the roasting of St. Laurence on the other. Baccio did the St. Laurence scene very delicately in the treatment of the nude and draped figures and various movements of the body in those standing about the saint, and especially in Decius, who with threatening aspect hastens the fire and the death of the Martyr, who raises his arm to heaven and recommends his soul to God. The Pope was so delighted that he commissioned Marcantonio to engrave it, and he created Baccio a knight of St. Peter for his genius.

Returning to Florence, Baccio found Gio. Francesco Rustici, his first master, engaged in painting a Conversion of St. Paul. In competition with him Baccio began a cartoon of a naked St. John in the desert, holding a lamb with his left arm and raising the other to heaven. He then began to colour the picture, and when finished exhibited it in his father's shop, opposite the lane leading from Orsanmichele to the Mercato Nuovo. The design was praised by artists, but not the colouring, which was crude and in bad style. However, Baccio sent it as a present to Pope Clement, who put it in his wardrobe, where it now is.

In the time of Leo X. a piece of marble nine and a half braccia by five braccia had been quarried at Carrara with the marble for the façade of S. Lorenzo at Florence. In this piece Michelagnolo proposed to make a Hercules killing Cacus to put on the piazza beside his colossal David. He made several models and designs, and had sought the favour of Cardinal Giulio de' Medici and Pope Leo, saying that the David had many faults,

[1] It is now in the Uffizi.

caused by Maestro Andrea, the sculptor who had first sketched
it. But on the death of Leo both the façade and the statue were
abandoned. Pope Clement, however, wished to employ Michelagnolo for the tombs of the Medici in the sacristy of S. Lorenzo
so that it was necessary to quarry fresh marble. The accounts
for this were kept by Domenico Boninsegni. He endeavoured
to obtain Michelagnolo's secret co-operation to make a profit
out of the façade of S. Lorenzo, but Michelagnolo refused, as
he did not like his genius to be used for the purpose of defrauding
the Pope. Domenico was so enraged that he employed every
means to humiliate and injure Michelagnolo, though he acted
covertly. He contrived that the façade should be abandoned
and the sacristy advanced, saying that the two works would
keep Michelagnolo employed for many years. He persuaded the
Pope to give the marble for the giant to Baccio, who was then
free, saying that these two great men would stimulate each other
by competition. The Pope thought the advice good and followed
it. Baccio made a large wax model of Hercules holding the head
of Cacus with his knee between two rocks and squeezing him
with his left arm, holding him between his legs in a painful
attitude, Cacus suffering from the violence of Hercules, with
every muscle strained. Hercules, with his head bent towards
his foe, is grinding his teeth and striking his adversary's head
with his club. When Michelagnolo heard that the marble had
been given to Baccio he was very angry, but try as he would
he could not change the Pope, who was pleased with Baccio's
model. That artist boasted that he would surpass Michelagnolo's
David, while Boninsegni declared that Michelagnolo wanted
everything for himself. Thus the city was deprived of a great
ornament which Buonarrotti would undoubtedly have produced. Baccio's model is now in Duke Cosimo's wardrobe, who
values it highly, as do artists. Baccio was sent to Carrara to see
the marble, the wardens of S. Maria del Fiore giving him a commission to bring it by the Arno as far as Signa, eight miles from
Siena. But when it was being taken out it fell into the river,
which was low, and sunk so deeply in the sand owing to its
weight that the wardens could not get it out, despite all their
efforts. The Pope being anxious to recover it at all costs, employed Piero Rosselli, an ingenious old builder, to divert the
stream, and then to take out the marble with levers, a work
for which he won great praise. On this accident some satirical
verses in Tuscan and Latin were written against Baccio, who
was hated for his evil-speaking about other artists. One of

them said that the marble, after being destined for the genius of Michelagnolo, had learned that it was to be mauled by Baccio, and in despair had cast itself into the river. While it was in the water Baccio found that in height and breadth he could not carve his first model out of it. Accordingly he went to Rome, taking his measurements, to inform the Pope that he was compelled to prepare a new design. After he had made several models, the Pope selected one where Hercules has Cacus between his legs and holds him fast by the hair. Returning to Florence, Baccio found that Piero Rosselli had brought the marble to the opera of S. Maria del Fiore by means of large walnut beams, placed lengthwise beneath the block, and changed as it advanced, the block resting on rollers and being drawn by a windlass. Here Baccio began a clay model as large as the marble, following his conception made at Rome, and he finished it with much diligence in a few months. But many artists did not think it possessed the vigour and vivacity of his first model. He then began it in marble, carving up to the navel and doing the front members while he contemplated bringing out the figures, which were just like those of the clay model. At the same time he had undertaken to paint a panel of considerable size for the church of Cestello, and had made a fine cartoon of a dead Christ surrounded by the Maries, Nicodemus and other figures. But he did not paint it for reasons related below. It was also at this time that he did a cartoon of a Christ taken from the Cross, lying in the arms of Nicodemus, and His Mother weeping at the foot, while an angel holds the nails and the crown of thorns. He quickly coloured it and exhibited it in the Mercato Nuovo, in the shop of Giovanni di Goro the goldsmith, his friend, to hear the general opinion and what Michelagnolo said. The latter was brought to see it by Piloto the goldsmith, and after examining it he said that he wondered how such a good designer as Baccio could produce such a crude and ungraceful picture, that any poor painter could do better, and that it was not worthy of Baccio. Piloto reported his opinion to Baccio, who in spite of his dislike admitted the truth of the criticism. The designs of Baccio were indeed excellent, but his colouring was poor and ungraceful. He therefore resolved to paint no more himself, but engaged a youth to do this called Agnolo, brother of the famous painter Franciabigio, who had died a few years before. He wished Agnolo to do the panel of Cestello, but it remained unfinished owing to the departure of the Medici after the sack of Rome in 1527.

Baccio did not consider himself safe, as he had an enemy near his villa of Pinzerimonte, of the popular faction. He therefore buried some cameos and small antique bronze figures which belonged to the Medici, and went to live in Lucca. There he remained until Charles V. came to Bologna to be crowned. He had himself presented to the Pope and accompanied him to Rome, staying in his accustomed rooms in Belvedere. While there His Holiness resolved to fulfil a vow which he had made in the castle of St. Angelo to finish the marble tower in front of the Ponte a Castello, by placing seven bronze figures, six braccia high, lying in various attitudes and crowned by a bronze angel with a sword in its hand, to stand on a column of variegated marble. The angel was to be Michael, the custodian of the castle, who had released him from that prison. The seven figures were the seven mortal sins, to show that with the help of the angel the Pope had overcome all his impious enemies. A model was prepared, and the Pope ordered Baccio to make the figures in clay of the proper size, to be afterwards cast in bronze. Baccio completed one of the figures in Belvedere, which was much praised. To pass the time, and as an experiment in casting, he made many small figures, such as Hercules, Venus, Apollo, Leda and others, which being cast in bronze by Maestro Jacopo della Barba of Florence succeeded excellently. He gave them to the Pope and several lords, and some are now in the scriptorium of Duke Cosimo, with more than a hundred rare antiques and other modern things. At the same time Baccio did a Deposition from the Cross in bas- and half-relief, cast in bronze, a rare work, very carefully finished. He gave it to Charles V. at Genoa, who valued it highly, gave Baccio a commandery of St. James and made him a knight. He received many courtesies from Prince Doria, and the republic of Genoa allotted to him a marble statue of six braccia representing Prince Doria as Neptune, to be placed on the piazza as a memorial to the prince from whom the republic had received such benefits. The price was 1000 florins, of which he then received 500, and at once went to Carrara to the quarry of Polvaccio.

Whilst the popular Government ruled Florence, Michelagnolo was employed on the fortifications of the city, and he was shown the marble chiselled by Baccio and his model of Hercules and Cacus, so that if the marble was not too much cut away he might make two figures of his own. After considering the group, he had another idea, and took a Samson holding down two Philistines; one is dead, while he is about to slay the other with the jawbone of an ass. But, as often happens in human affairs, man proposes and God disposes, for, on the outbreak of war, Michelagnolo had other matters to think of, and from fear of the citizens he was obliged to leave the city. At the end of the war Pope Clement recalled him to finish the sacristy of S. Lorenzo, and sent Baccio to complete the giant. While engaged upon this, Baccio took rooms in the Medici palace, and, to show his devotion, wrote almost every week to the Pope, when, besides artistic matters, he gave particulars of the citizens and the Government, with odious representations calculated to render him more unpopular than before. When Duke Alessandro returned to Florence from the court of his majesty, the citizens complained to him of Baccio's sinister proceedings, and they hindered his work with the giant as much as possible. At this time, after the Hungarian war, Pope Clement and the Emperor Charles met at Bologna, where Cardinal Ippolito de' Medici and Duke Alessandro joined them. Baccio thought he would go and kiss the Pope's feet, and took with him a bas-relief, a braccia high by one and a half broad, of Christ scourged at the column by two nude figures, excellently done. He gave this to Clement, with a medal of His Holiness executed for his friend Francesco dal Prato, with Christ scourged on the reverse. The Pope accepted the gift, and Baccio told him of the hindrances and annoyances he received in finishing his Hercules, and begged him to give him the means of completing it. He added that he was envied and hated in the city, and succeeded in persuading the Pope to induce Duke Alessandro to see that the work was completed and placed on the piazza. Baccio's father was now dead, and had left in Baccio's hands a large silver cross which he had undertaken to do for the wardens of S. Maria del Fiore, full of bas-reliefs of the Passion of Christ, for which Baccio had modelled the figures and scenes in wax. He had many pounds of silver, and he asked the Pope to give the work to Francesco dal Prato, who had accompanied him to Bologna. The Pope, perceiving that Baccio wished to profit by his father's work and to gain something from Francesco, directed that the silver and the finished scenes should be given to the wardens, that the account should be paid, and that the wardens should melt down all the silver of the cross to use it for the necessities of the church, which had been despoiled of its ornaments during the siege. To Baccio he gave 100 gold florins and letters of recommendation that he should return to Florence and finish his giant.

While Baccio was at Bologna, Cardinal Doria, understanding that he was about to leave the court, came post thither and threatened him for having broken his word in not completing the statue of Prince Doria, having left it sketched at Carrara, when he had received 500 crowns, and he declared that if Andrea could lay hands on him he would send Baccio to the galleys. Baccio humbly protested that he had been hindered, but promised that he would make the figure of a block of marble of the same size which he had at Florence and he would send it to Genoa, and in this way and with other fair words he succeeded in escaping from the cardinal. Returning to Florence, he began the pedestal of the giant, and by assiduous labour completely finished it in 1534. But owing to the hostility of the citizens, Duke Alessandro did not care to put it on the piazza. The Pope had returned to Rome several months before, and as he wanted to have a tomb made in the Minerva for himself and Pope Leo, Baccio seized the opportunity to go to Rome. The Pope then decided that Baccio should do the tombs after the giant had been put on the piazza. The Pope wrote to the duke directing him to afford Baccio every facility for this, and thus a pedestal was built, an inscription in memory of Clement being put inside, with several medals stamped with the heads of the Pope and duke. The giant was then taken out of the opera, where it had been made, and placed in a framework, for convenience and safety, and secured by ropes. Ten pairs of oxen then drew it to the piazza. Two large beams, forming a base, rested on other beams similarly disposed, and these were placed on rollers as the thing advanced. The charge of this was given to Baccio d'Agnolo and Antonio da Sangallo the elder, architects of the Duomo, who afterwards set the statue firmly on its base. A great multitude occupied the piazza for two days to see the giant unveiled, various opinions being expressed, though all agreed in blaming the work and its author. Many Latin and Tuscan verses were affixed to the pedestal, much pleasant wit being displayed. But as some of the satire passed all bounds, the duke felt obliged to imprison a few of the sonnet-makers, and this soon stopped the mouths of the slanderers. When Baccio saw his work *in situ*, he thought the air favoured it but little, making the muscles appear too weak. He therefore put up a new screen, and set to work with his chisel, rendering them sharper than before. When finally unveiled the work was considered well studied, showing knowledge in every part, the figure of Cacus being admirably arranged. Michelagnolo's David beside it certainly detracted from its admiration, for that is the finest colossal statue ever made, full of grace and excellence, while the style of Baccio is utterly different. However, his Hercules, considered by itself, deserves great praise, the more so because many other sculptors have since attempted to make colossal statues without attaining the same level. Nature indeed had endowed Baccio with much grace and facility, and these advantages, added to great study, made him a perfect sculptor. Wishing to know what was said of his work, he sent a pedagogue from his house to the piazza, with instructions to report faithfully what he heard. The man, hearing nothing but ill, returned sadly, and answered Baccio's inquiries by saying that all blamed the giant. "And what do you say?" asked Baccio. "I spoke well of it to please you," he replied. "Go and speak ill of it," said Baccio, "for you know I never praise anyone. Now we are quits." He dissimulated his chagrin, and pretended, as usual, not to care for the adverse criticisms. However, it is probable that he suffered much, as it is natural that those who work for honour and only receive blame should be afflicted, even if the blame is undeserved. He was consoled by a property which Pope Clement gave him in addition to his payment. The gift was doubly dear to him, being next his villa of Pinzerimonte, and because it had originally belonged to his mortal enemy Rignadori, with whom he had been in continual conflict over the boundaries of the farm, and who had been declared a rebel.

At this time Prince Doria wrote to Duke Alessandro, asking him to see that Baccio finished his statue as he had now completed the giant, saying he would punish him if he did not do his duty, so that Baccio was afraid to go to Carrara. However, being reassured by Cardinal Cibo and the duke he went there, and with assistance continued the statue. The duke was daily informed of what Baccio was doing, and learning that the statue was not of its promised excellence, he gave Baccio to understand that if he did not serve him well he would punish him. Baccio said many ill things of the prince, who, on hearing of them, resolved to get the artist into his hands and frighten him with the galleys. But Baccio, observing some spies watching him, and being a wary and resolute man, left the work as it was and returned to Florence.

At this time a mistress of Baccio bore him a son whom he called Clemente after the recently deceased Pope,[1] who had so

[1] Clement VII. died on 25 September, 1534.

favoured him. He learned that Cardinal Ippolito de' Medici, Cardinal Cibo, Cardinal Salviati and Cardinal Ridolfi, with M. Baldassarre Turini of Pescia, were executors of the will and ought to give him the tombs of Leo and Clement in the Minerva, for which he had already made the models. These tombs had been newly promised to Alfonso Lombardi, a sculptor of Ferrara, by the favour of the Cardinal de' Medici, whom he served. He had changed the idea, by Michelagnolo's advice, and had made models, though without any definite assurance, expecting daily to have to go to Carrara for the marble. But meanwhile Cardinal Ippolito died of poison on the way to visit Charles V.[1] On hearing this, Baccio lost no time in going to Rome, and then visited Madonna Lucrezia Salviata de' Medici, sister of Pope Leo, showing her that no one could do more honour to the remains of those great pontiffs than he, adding that Alfonso possessed no design, and being without skill or judgment in marble he could not produce such good work. By these and other means he succeeded in inducing the executors to charge Cardinal Salviati to give the work to him. At this time Charles V. arrived in Naples, and Filippo Strozzi, Antonfrancesco degli Albizi and other exiles negotiated with Cardinal Salviati to approach the emperor against Duke Alessandro. They were with the cardinal at all hours, and Baccio was waiting for the contract of his tombs in the same rooms. Seeing him there regularly, they grew suspicious, thinking him a spy of the duke, and they employed some of their young men to do away with him one evening. But fortune came to his rescue in time, inducing the other executors to conclude the negotiations with Baccio. Knowing his poverty in architecture, they procured a design from Antonio da San Gallo, and ordained that all the marble-work should be given to Lorenzetti the sculptor, and the marble statues and reliefs to Baccio. The contract being thus drawn up,[2] Baccio did not appear again at Cardinal Salviati's, and the exiles thought no more of him. Baccio next made two wooden models with the statues and reliefs in wax. The pedestals were without projections and upon each were four fluted Ionic columns enclosing three spaces. The large middle one contained a pedestal for a seated figure of each Pope giving the benediction and the lesser spaces contained a niche with a figure, four braccia high in each, and saints on either side of the Pope. It resembled a triumphal arch, and over the columns bearing the cornice was a

---

[1] Poisoned at Itri by order of Duke Alessandro on 10 August, 1535.
[2] In 1536.

bas-relief three braccia high by four and a half broad, representing the visit of Francis I. to Bologna, over the statue of Pope Leo. This statue stood between two niches containing St. Peter and St. Paul, and above were two smaller reliefs, one of St. Peter raising a dead man, the other of St. Paul preaching. The corresponding relief of Pope Clement was a Coronation of Charles V. at Bologna. It stood between St. John the Baptist preaching and St. John the Evangelist raising Drusiana. The niches beneath contained figures of those saints, four braccia high, with Clement in the middle, similar to the Leo. In this work Baccio displayed scant religion or overmuch adulation, or both, as he made the saints and founders of our religion after Christ yield the pre-eminence to the Popes, and this was certainly his design. But I think our religion should command the respect of all, and however much one may desire to praise anyone, it is necessary to observe certain limits so that the praise and honour do not surpass just bounds, displeasing to the person praised if he is judicious. In acting as he did Baccio displayed his devotion to the popes, but little judgment. The models were taken by him to the garden of Cardinal Ridolfi at S. Agata, Monte Cavallo, where he had invited Cibo, Salviati and M. Baldassarre da Pescia to give the necessary finish to the tombs. While they were at table, Solosmeo the sculptor arrived, a bold and pleasant man, who loved to speak his mind, and who hated Baccio. When he was announced, Ridolfi was for admitting him and, turning to Baccio, he said, "I want to hear Solosmeo's opinion about the allotting of these tombs; get up and conceal yourself behind the portière." Baccio obeyed and Solosmeo came in. After passing the wine they discussed the tombs, and Solosmeo blamed the cardinals for giving them to Baccio, whom he taxed with ignorance, avarice and arrogance, citing many instances. Baccio would not allow him to finish, but came out in a rage and said, "What have I done that you should speak thus of me?" Dumbfounded at Baccio's appearance, Solosmeo turned to Ridolfi and said, "What is this? I will not have any of these priests' tricks," and flung out. But the cardinals laughed at them both. Then Salviati said to Baccio, "You now know the judgment of artists; let your works prove them to be slanderers."

Baccio began the statues and reliefs, but did not succeed according to his promises, using little diligence, and he left them badly finished and full of faults, being more anxious to get his money than to do good work. The cardinals, hearing of his action, reflected that the marble for the two largest statues of the two popes was still to be done, and asking him to do better, they directed him to finish them. But Baccio, who had received all his money, negotiated with M. Gio. Battista da Ricasoli, bishop of Cortona, who was in Rome on affairs of Duke Cosimo, to go to Florence to serve the duke on the fountains of Castello and the tomb of Sig. Giovanni. The duke agreed, and Baccio departed without saying a word, leaving the tombs unfinished and the statues in the hands of two apprentices. The cardinals therefore allotted the Pope Leo to Raffaello da Montelupo and the Clement to Giovanni di Baccio.[1] They ordered the work done to be put *in situ*, but the statues and reliefs, not being polished in many places, brought Baccio more blame than glory.

On reaching Florence, Baccio found that the duke had sent Tribolo to Carrara for marble for the fountains and the tomb of Sig. Giovanni, and he prevailed upon the duke to give the tomb to him, showing that most of the necessary marble was already in Florence, and he became gradually so intimate with the duke that everyone feared him for this and his overbearing character. He then suggested to the duke that the tomb should be set up in the Neroni Chapel, a dark and narrow place, not wanting to propose the erection of a new chapel, such as was due to so great a prince. He also persuaded the duke to require of Michelagnolo many marbles which he had in Florence, and among them he obtained a statue in an advanced stage, and several figures sketched. Baccio destroyed everything, hoping to avenge himself and vex Michelagnolo. He also found in the same room of S. Lorenzo, where Michelagnolo worked, a marble group of Hercules crushing Antæus, which the duke had commissioned Frà Gio. Agnolo the sculptor to do, and telling the duke that the friar had spoilt the marble Baccio broke it in pieces, though it was well advanced. At length he built the base of the tomb, which stands by itself, and is four braccia square. A socle surrounds it, and there is a frieze above carved with skulls of horses bound together by draperies, with an armed statue seated, in the antique style, four and a half braccia high, holding a general's baton, to represent Sig. Giovanni. He never finished this statue or set it up, though it was well advanced. On the front he indeed finished a marble half-relief representing, in figures two braccia high, Sig. Giovanni seated, prisoners brought before him, including soldiers and dishevelled women, with nudes, but destitute of

[1] In 1540.

design or expression. This relief contains a figure with a pig on his shoulders, said to represent M. Baldassarre da Pescia, whom Baccio considered his enemy for having allotted the statues of Leo and Clement to others, and for having compelled him to restore the money advanced to him.

Baccio had insisted to Duke Cosimo on the glory of the ancients won by statues and buildings, saying that the duke ought to make some memorial of himself and his deeds. Having nearly completed the tomb, he proposed to begin a great and costly work for the duke. Cosimo had ceased to live in the Medici palace, and had returned with his court to the palace of the Signoria, which he was embellishing every day. Having told Baccio that he required an audience-chamber to receive foreign ambassadors and citizens, Baccio and Giuliano di Baccio d' Agnolo together devised an ornament of stone and marble thirty braccia broad by eighteen high for such a room, to be in the great hall of the palace at the north end. It was to have a platform fourteen braccia broad, approached by seven steps, and enclosed with balusters in front, except the middle entrance, where there were to be three large arches at the end of the hall, two to serve as windows, each divided by four columns, two of stone and two of marble, with an arch above, and a frieze of corbels going round. These were to decorate both the exterior of the palace and interior of the hall. The middle arch, forming a niche, was to have two similar niches at the end of the hall, one east and one west, decorated with four Corinthian columns ten braccia high, with a projecting cornice. The middle wall was to have four pilasters between the arches to bear the architrave, frieze and cornice surrounding the room. Between the pilasters was to be a space of about three braccia occupied by niches for statues. Each niche was to contain three statues. They also proposed a very costly decoration for the exterior to make it four-square, by a projection of six braccia about the front of the palazzo vecchio with columns fourteen braccia high, bearing other columns joined by arches with a loggia beneath going round, where the court of pleas and the giants are, and another row of pillars above, also arched, to go round the palace windows, to make a façade about the palace and above these pilasters to make a sort of theatre, with another row of arches and pilasters, so that the battlements of the palace should form a cornice to the whole. They perceived how great the cost would be, and agreed that they would only tell the duke of their projects for the decoration of the audience-chamber and the stone front towards the piazza, twenty-four braccia long and as broad as the hall. Giuliano prepared designs and plans, and Baccio showed them to the duke, saying he wished to fill the larger niches with marble statues seated on pedestals, four braccia high, such as Leo giving peace to Italy, and Clement crowning Charles V., with two statues in the lesser niches to show the virtues of these popes. Between the pilasters he proposed to make standing statues of Sig. Giovanni, Duke Alessandro and Duke Cosimo, with many carved ornaments and a pavement of variegated marble. The duke was much pleased, and hoped that in time, by adding other ornaments and a ceiling, he would possess the finest hall in Italy, as he afterwards did. He felt so anxious for the work to be done that he gave Baccio every week as much money as he asked for. The stone was excavated and the carving begun for the basement, columns and cornices, Baccio wishing all to be done by the masons of the opera of S. Maria del Fiore. The masters certainly worked with a will, and if they had asked it they might have had all the stone decoration finished and set up. But Baccio only attended to sketching statues, finishing them and drawing his monthly salary from the duke, who paid his slightest expenses and gave him 500 crowns for a single completed statue. The work, therefore, was never finished. But if Baccio and Giuliano had made the end of the hall rectangular, as they might, for it was eight braccia out and ill-proportioned, and if they had made their columns higher to render the style grander, and if they had carried their cornice to the height of the old ceiling, they would have displayed greater ability and judgment, and the immense labour would not have been incurred in vain, as those who had to rearrange it all perceived. In the subsequent alterations it was necessary to correct many errors in the door and the corresponding niches. But, short of rebuilding, it will never be possible to remedy its not being rectangular, which appears in the floor and ceiling. They certainly endured great labour, and deserve praise for the numerous carved stones, which are diligently joined together and beautifully worked, though half is lost owing to the shape of the hall. They would, however, have done far better if Baccio, who always despised architecture, had consulted someone of better judgment than Giuliano, who, although a good worker in wood and a competent architect, was not equal to such a work, as experience showed. The work dragged on for several years, but little more than half was actually completed. Baccio finished the statues of Sig. Giovanni and Duke Alessandro, and put them in the smaller niches, and set up the statue of Pope Clement on a brick pedestal. He also finished the statue of Duke Cosimo, taking great pains with the head, though the duke and courtiers said it was not at all like him. Baccio therefore, having first made a marble one, now in the same palace in the upper chamber, the best bust he ever did, corrected his first error by its excellence. But hearing the head condemned by all, he one day broke it to atoms in his anger, intending to make another in its place, but this he never did.

Baccio had a habit of introducing small and large pieces of marble in his statues, which did not trouble him, indeed he laughed about it. He did this in the Orpheus, for one of the heads of Cerberus, and added a piece of drapery in the St. Peter in S. Maria del Fiore. To the Cacus of the piazza he added a shoulder and a leg. He did the like in many others, a proceeding much condemned by sculptors. On completing these statues he took up the Pope Leo, making considerable progress, and seeing that it promised to take a long time, that he would never finish his first design, and that much money and time had been expended, while the work was not half done and gave little general pleasure, he thought to divert the duke's attention from the palace, as he seemed tired of the work.

In the opera of S. Maria del Fiore Baccio had made enemies of the proveditore and all the masons, and as all the statues for the audience-chamber were in his style, some finished and some sketched, and the ornament in great part set up, to hide the numerous defects, Baccio represented to the duke that the opera wasted money, and no longer produced anything remarkable. He said he thought the duke would do well to divert money from this useless channel to make the octagonal choir of the church and the decoration of altars, steps, pews for the duke and magistrates, and stalls for the canons, chaplains and clerks, as befitted such a church. Brunellesco had left a model of the simple wooden framework which originally served for the choir, intending in time to do it in marble, of the same form but more ornate. Baccio thought the choir would afford him an opportunity of making statues and reliefs in marble and bronze for the high altar and about the choir, and for the two marble pulpits of the choir, and that the eight outside faces might be decorated with bronze reliefs set in the marble. Above this he proposed to make a row of columns and pilasters, to bear cornices and four arches divided according to the axes of the church. One was to form the principal entrance, corresponding with the arch over the high altar, and the other two at the sides, right and left, under which the pulpits were to be placed. Above the cornice he proposed to place a row of balusters running round the eight faces, and upon them to erect another row of candlesticks to crown the choir with lights, as was done when it was of wood. He showed all these things to the duke, saying that the income of the opera, with what his liberality supplied, would suffice to adorn the church and add to its grandeur and that of the city in a short time, and would form a noble memorial to the duke. He also said that the duke would thus afford him an opportunity of producing many good works, and of leaving a name to posterity, which should be an inducement because he had been reared by the Medici house. By such arguments Baccio so prevailed that the duke told him to make a model of all the choir, and agreed that the work should be done. Baccio then conferred with Giuliano di Baccio d' Agnolo, his architect, and after examining the spot together they decided not to depart from the form of Filippo's model, but simply to add ornaments of columns and corbels, and enrich it as much as possible. But it is not the multitude of ornaments that enrich a structure, but their quality and adaptation, and such things when done with judgment are praised. Giuliano and Baccio do not seem to have thought so, as they undertook a large, difficult, but ungraceful task, as experience showed. Giuliano's plan was to make pilasters at each of the eight angles in the Ionic order; they were not equal, being broad outside and narrow within, which is disproportionate. The lines of the centre diminish so that the two columns on either side of the pilasters make them appear slender, and render the work ungraceful, both without and within. Giuliano also made the model of the altar one and a half braccia from the ornament of the choir, over which Baccio did a dead Christ in wax with two angels, one supporting His head on its knee and holding His right arm, the other holding the mysteries of the Passion. The statue occupied almost all the altar, rendering it a difficult matter to celebrate there. He proposed to make it about four and a half braccia. Behind the altar he made a projecting pedestal, on which he placed a God the Father seated, of six braccia, giving the benediction, accompanied by two angels of four braccia, kneeling at the corners and ends of the predella, where the Almighty's feet rested. This predella was more than a braccia high, and contained reliefs of the Passion of Christ to be done in bronze. The two angels at the corners held candlesticks, with eight others, three and a half braccia high, between them to decorate the altar, and God the Father in the midst. Behind Him there was a space of half a braccia to mount to the lights. Under the arch at the choir entry he placed the Tree of Knowledge with the serpent having a human face and turned round the trunk, and two large nude figures of Adam and Eve standing by. On the outside was a space of three braccia for a bronze or marble relief of the creation of Adam and Eve, one of a series of twenty-one reliefs on Old Testament subjects. Each socket was to contain a draped or nude figure of a prophet, to be executed in marble, a great work, affording an opportunity of displaying all the art of a perfect master whose memory should be immortal. The duke saw the model and Baccio's duplicate designs, and they pleased him for their variety, number and beauty, as Baccio worked in wax with spirit and designed well. So the duke ordained that the work should be begun at once, diverting to it all the expenses of the opera, and directed that a great quantity of marble should be brought from Carrara.

Baccio began with an Adam with an outstretched arm, about four braccia high. He finished it, but, as it was narrow-sided and possessed other defects, he converted it into a Bacchus and gave it to the duke, who kept it many years in a chamber in his palace. Not long ago it was placed in a niche on the ground-floor, where the prince lives in summer. He half-finished a seated Eve of the same size, which was delayed by the Adam, and, as he began another Adam in a different pose, he had to change his Eve. The first one he changed into a Ceres, and gave it to the Duchess Leonora with a nude Apollo. It was placed in front of the lake in the Pitti garden [1] designed by Giorgio Vasari. Baccio derived much gratification from his Adam and Eve, as he expected to satisfy all artists as he had himself, and he polished them with great diligence; but when they were unveiled they experienced the same fate as his other things, being cruelly dealt with in sonnets and Latin verses. One said that just as Adam and Eve were driven out of Paradise for their disobedience, so these figures disgraced the earth, and ought to be expelled from the church. They are, however, well-proportioned and possess many good parts, and though not very graceful they merit considerable praise for their art and design. A lady being asked what she thought of these nude bodies, said that she was not qualified to speak of the man,

[1] Now known as the Boboli Gardens. The statue is now in the grotto there.

but she thought the Eve had two good qualities, being white and smooth. Thus wittily, while seeming to praise, she covertly blamed the artist, because these qualities belonged to the stone, and were not produced by art. Baccio next began a dead Christ, but as it did not come out as he intended he abandoned it in a somewhat advanced state. He began another in a different attitude, with an angel supporting Christ's head on its knee and holding an arm, but did not finish this either. When put on the altar it proved too large for the surface, allowing no room for the priest. Although fair and one of the best that Baccio did, this statue was also lampooned, and not only the people but the priests pulled it to pieces.

Recognising that by leaving his works unfinished he injured his reputation among artists and connoisseurs, Baccio resolved to make a God the Father to accompany the Christ, and fetched a beautiful piece of marble from Carrara. After working at it for some time, making it nude like a Jupiter, he left it because it did not please the duke or himself either, and so it exists in the opera. He did not mind what people said, but only desired to enrich himself and acquire property. He bought a fine farm called Spinello, on the hill of Fiesole, and another with a fine building, called il Cantone, on the plain above S. Salvi on the River Affrico, and a large house in the via de' Ginori, with the money which the duke gave him. Having made a competency, he would not take pains, and cared little for the blame he incurred by leaving unfinished the tomb of Sig. Giovanni, the audience-chamber, the choir and the altar. But having erected the altar and the marble pedestal for his God the Father, and prepared the model, he at length began it, and worked slowly, assisted by his masons.

At this time Benvenuto Cellini, a goldsmith, the most famous of his day, came from France,[1] where he had served King Francis. He had also done some bronze casts, and being introduced to Duke Cosimo, who wished to adorn the city, he was much honoured. The duke employed him to do a bronze Perseus and Medusa about five braccia high, to be placed under one of the arches of the loggia of the piazza. Benvenuto meanwhile was engaged upon other things for the duke; but as one sculptor always envies another, just as one potter envies and harasses another potter, Baccio could not endure the favours bestowed upon Benvenuto. He thought it strange that a goldsmith, who had been accustomed to make medals and small figures, should

[1] In 1545.

now turn to colossal figures. He was unable to conceal his feelings, but he met his match. Thus one day, in the presence of the duke, Baccio said many biting things about Benvenuto, to which the latter, who was equally hot tempered, replied with equal violence, and in discussing art and pointing out each other's defects they frequently came to words before the duke, who gave them perfect liberty to say what they pleased, as it amused him to hear them sharpening their wits on each other. Apart from this he took no notice. This rivalry or rather enmity induced Baccio to press on with his God the Father, but already he did not enjoy so much favour from the duke as formerly, so he courted the duchess. One day, as they were quarrelling as usual, Benvenuto said, "Prepare for another world, Baccio, for I shall drive you out of this one." Baccio answered, "Let me know a day beforehand, so that I may confess and make my will, and not die like a beast, such as you are." The duke was thus amused by their quarrels for many months, but now he imposed silence upon them, lest harm should ensue, and employed them to make a bust of himself to be cast in bronze, in competition. Meanwhile Baccio finished his God the Father, to be placed in the church on a pedestal beside the altar. It was a draped figure, six braccia high. After finishing it he sent to Rome for his pupil, Vincenzio de' Rossi, to do in clay what was lacking in marble at the altar, and made him do two angels holding candelabra at the corners, and most of the reliefs of the predella and pedestal. He then placed everything on the altar and sent for the duke to see him uncover it; but though the duchess, who favoured Baccio, besought him, the duke would not go, being incensed because of all his works Baccio had not finished one, though he had enriched him and bestowed many favours and honours upon him, arousing much ill-humour among the citizens. Yet in the end the duke went, with the idea of assisting Baccio's natural son Clemente, a clever youth, who had made considerable progress in design, as it would fall to him to finish his father's works. At the same time, in 1554, Giorgio Vasari arrived from Rome, where he had been serving Julius III., as the duke proposed to make new buildings and decorate the palace of the piazza and make the large hall. In the following year Giorgio brought from Rome Bartolommeo Ammannati the sculptor, to make the façade opposite the audience-chamber begun by Baccio, with a fountain in the middle, and he immediately began the statues. Baccio recognised that the duke did not want him any more, as he was employing others. Filled with chagrin, he had become so eccentric that no one could speak with him, and he used his son Clemente very strangely. Accordingly Clemente, who had made a large clay head of the duke for the audience-chamber, asked his permission to go to Rome because his father was so strange. The duke granted the permission, but Baccio would give him nothing, although the youth was his right arm in all his work in Florence, and he did not, nevertheless, mind his departure. But that same year, owing to his studies and disorders, Clemente died at Rome, leaving a fine marble bust of Duke Cosimo in Florence which Baccio afterwards placed above the principal door of his house in the via de' Ginori. Clemente also left a dead Christ supported by Nicodemus, a portrait of Baccio, in an advanced state. These meritorious statues Baccio placed in the church of the Servites. The death of Clemente was a great loss to Baccio and to art, as he recognised afterwards. Baccio unveiled the altar of S Maria del Fiore and his God the Father, which was blamed. The altar he left unchanged, but went on with the choir. Many years before a great piece of marble, ten and a half braccia high by three broad, had been excavated at Carrara. On hearing of it, Baccio rode thither and offered the overseer 50 crowns for it as earnest money, and having made the bargain, he returned to Florence, and there induced the duchess to give him a giant to do to be placed on the piazza beside the lion, with a great fountain and Neptune in the middle on a car drawn by sea-horses, to be cut out of this block. After making several models, Baccio showed them to her highness, but the matter had gone no farther at the end of 1559, when the overseer came to demand the rest of his payment, threatening that otherwise he would break up the marble and sell it, as he had many demands. The duke directed Giorgio Vasari to pay the money. Benvenuto and Ammannati, learning that the duke had not given the marble to Baccio, asked him for permission to make a model in competition, and that the marble should be given to the one who did best. The duke did not refuse, and offered this hope. He knew that the ability, judgment and design of Baccio were superior to those of any sculptor who served him if he would only take pains, and he felt confident that the competition would incite Baccio to do better. Indeed, Baccio feared the disfavour of the duke more than anything, and began diligently to make models. From the duchess Baccio obtained permission to go to Carrara to direct the marble to be sent to Florence. On arriving there he so cut the marble that he rendered it impossible for the others to produce any good work in it, such being his purpose. On returning to Florence he had a long dispute with Benvenuto, who told the duke that Baccio had spoiled the marble. At length the duchess succeeded in getting the marble assigned to Baccio, and it was ordained that it should be brought by sea and up the Arno to Signa. In the loggia of the piazza Baccio set up a place to chisel the marble, and there he began some cartoons for paintings to adorn the rooms of the Pitti palace. They were painted by a youth called Andrea del Minga, who manipulated his colours very creditably. The scenes represented the creation of Adam and Eve, their expulsion from Paradise, Noah and Moses with the tables.[1] When completed he gave them to the duchess, whose favour he sought in his disputes. Indeed, if she had not supported him and admired his talents, he would have altogether lost the duke's favour. The duchess also employed Baccio in the garden of the Pitti palace, where she erected a grotto of tufa and pumice-stone, and containing a fountain, where Baccio had caused his pupil, Giovanni Fancelli, to make a large basin and some life-size goats spouting water, and a countryman emptying a cask full of water, for a lake. For these things the duchess continually recommended Baccio to the duke, who at length allowed him to begin a model of the Neptune. So he again sent to Rome for Vincenzio de' Rossi, who had left Florence, to help him. Meanwhile he wanted to finish the dead Christ supported by Nicodemus, which his son Clemente had advanced, because he heard that Michelagnolo had finished one at Rome in a marble block containing four figures, to be placed at his tomb in S. Maria Maggiore. Thus spurred Baccio soon finished it, and went about looking for a place in the principal churches of Florence where he could put it and make a tomb for himself. Not finding one to suit him, he chose a Chapel of the Pazzi in the church of the Servites. The owners, at the duchess's request, granted the place to him without relinquishing their rights or their device, allowing him simply to make a marble altar and place the statues upon it with the tomb below. He then arranged with the friars for the installation. Baccio therefore built the altar and basement of marble, and proposed to bury his father, Michelagnolo, there, who was interred in the same church as well as himself and his wife; but at this time he fell sick, perhaps through labouring too hard at moving

[1] In the Prometheus room of the Pitti palace.

the body, or from the emotions caused thereby. He grew steadily worse, and died in eight days at the age of seventy-two, having been robust and strong up to that time, without experiencing a day's illness. He was honourably buried beside his father in the tomb he had prepared, with this epitaph:

D.O.M.
BACIVS BANDINELL. DIVI IACOBI
EQVES
SVB HAC SERVATORIS IMAGINE.
A SE EXPRESSA CVM IACOBA DONIA
VXORE QVIESCIT AN. S.   MDLIX.

He left both sons and daughters, who inherited much landed property, houses and money. To the world he left the works in sculpture already described, and numerous designs, which are in the possession of his children. Our book contains some which cannot be improved upon. The marble for the giant was more disputed than ever, for Benvenuto was always importuning the duke, and had prepared a small model. On the other hand, Ammannati, having more experience in marble sculpture, thought the work ought to be given to him. Giorgio having to go to Rome with the cardinal, the duke's son, when he assumed the red hat, Ammannati gave him a wax model for the figure and one in wood of the same size as the marble, in order that Giorgio might show it to Michelagnolo to ask his opinion and thus induce the duke to give him the marble. Giorgio readily agreed, and so the duke employed him to fill an arch of the loggia of the piazza and Ammannati to make a full-size model of the giant. On hearing this Benvenuto came in a fury to Pisa, where the duke was, and declared he could not bear competing with an inferior, asking to be allowed to make a large model in the same place. The duke agreed that he should occupy another arch of the loggia, and gave him the materials. While these masters were engaged upon their models and had shut up their apartments so that neither should see what the other was doing, a young Flemish sculptor, Giovan Bologna, entered the lists. He asked Don Francesco, prince of Florence, to allow him to make a model for a giant of the same size. The prince agreed, and Giovan began, not intending to execute the work in marble, but simply to show his ability. He began the model in the convent of St. Croce. With these three Vincenzio Danti, a Perugian sculptor, competed, younger than them all, not to get the marble but to show his spirit and intelligence. He made a model with many good parts of the same size in the house of M. Alessandro di M. Ottaviano de' Medici. The duke went to see the first models, and preferring Ammannati's model to that of Benvenuto, he resolved to give the marble to the former, as the younger and more skilful worker in marble. Giorgio Vasari prompted the duke, for he did many good offices for Ammannati, knowing that he was prepared to take every pains and hoping to see an excellent work speedily finished. The duke would not then see the model of Giovan, not liking to entrust so great a work to him, for he had seen none of his efforts, although many artists and connoisseurs informed him that Giovan's model was in many respects better than the others. Had Baccio been still alive there would have been no contest, for the work would doubtless have been given to him. Death deprived him of this, but added to his glory, the excellence of his Hercules and Cacus shining by contrast with the models of the other masters, who, though praiseworthy, could not add to the beauty of his work.

Seven years after Baccio's death Duke Cosimo finished the audience-chamber for the marriage of Queen Joan of Austria, appointing Giorgio Vasari the director. He endeavoured to remedy the numerous defects which the building would have shown if completed according to its original plan. Thus, by God's grace, the work was completed, and enriched with ornaments of niches, pilasters and statues. As far as possible he made it rectangular and raised a corridor on Tuscan columns, the statue of Leo begun by Baccio being completed by his pupil, Vincenzio de' Rossi. The work was further adorned with friezes full of stucco, with numerous figures and devices. Below the niches, in the divisions of the vaulting, numerous panels were made in stucco, beautifully modelled, the structure being thus greatly embellished. According to the original design, the roof of the hall was only twenty-one braccia high and the audience-chamber only eighteen braccia, leaving a space of three braccia. But I have now raised the old roof twelve braccia, fifteen braccia above the audience-chamber of Baccio and Giuliano, making the present roof thirty-three braccia high. Duke Cosimo certainly showed great spirit in having this work done for that wedding in the space of five months, when less than two-thirds had been completed and that had taken more than fifteen years. Not only did he have all Baccio's work completed, but directed Vasari to make a corridor above, overlooking the piazza and the hall. Thus princes and lords can see all the festivities there without being seen, and can then withdraw to the rooms by private or public staircases. However, many were displeased because the room was not made rectangular, and many would have pulled it down and rebuilt it. But it was thought better to do the work thus, to avoid the appearance of presumption, and not to cast a slur upon Baccio, by showing him to be incapable of correcting the mistakes of others.

To return to Baccio. His talents were always recognised during his life, and they will be still more appreciated and missed after his death. He would have gained more esteem for himself personally and his abilities if he had possessed a more amiable and courteous disposition; but he was just the reverse, and his abusive language lost him all goodwill and obscured his talent, so that men viewed his works askance and never liked them. Although he served many lords, he did it so ungraciously that none of them ever esteemed him. As he always spoke ill of the works of others, no one could endure him, and all who could do so returned his abuse with interest. He made abominable accusations in the courts, and these were retorted upon him. He was always engaged in litigation, and seemed to delight in it. But his designing was so excellent that it obscures all his other defects, it was the thing to which he devoted his chief energies, and it wins him a place among the best artists. I have always valued his works, endeavouring to finish them capably, and, indeed, Baccio deserves eternal fame and honour. I have refrained from speaking of his surname until now. He was variously called Brandini and Bandinelli. The former name is on his engravings. Later on he preferred Bandinelli, and he kept it to the end, saying that his ancestors were the Bandinelli of Siena, who came to Gaiuole and thence to Florence.

GIULIANO BUGIARDINI, Painter of Florence
(1475–1554)

BEFORE the siege of Florence the population had so increased that the quarters outside the gates, with the churches, monasteries and hospitals, formed almost another city of honourable citizens and good artists, mostly less wealthy than those of the city, but less heavily taxed for the gabelle and other charges.

In one of these suburbs outside the Faenza gate Giuliano Bugiardini was born, and he lived there, as his ancestors had done, until 1529, when all the buildings were destroyed. Before that time, while still a youth, he had studied in the garden of the Medici on the piazzi of S. Marco, learning art under Bertoldo the sculptor, and winning the friendship of Michelagnolo. The affection of the latter was inspired rather by Giuliano's diligence and love for art than by any profundity of design in him, and he was a man of an amiable disposition who lived simply, without malignity or envy. His chief fault was a too great love for his own works, which in him was greater than with the generality, possibly because of the labour he bestowed upon them. Michelagnolo used to call him happy, because he was contented with his knowledge, whereas he himself was never fully satisfied with his own works. After studying design in the garden, Giuliano was associated for a while with Buonarrotti, Granacci and Domenico Ghirlandajo in the chapel of St. Maria Novella. Having become a fair master, he worked in Gualfonda with Mariotto Albertinelli, where he finished a panel, now at the door of S. Maria Maggiore of Florence, representing St. Albert, the Carmelite friar, with the devil at his feet in the shape of a woman, a much-admired work.

Before the siege it was customary to carry a draped picture before the catafalque in the burial of noble dead at Florence, which was left in the church as a memorial to the dead and the family. Thus, when Cosimo Rucellai the elder died, his sons Bernardo and Palla proposed as a novelty to have a banner four braccia broad by five high, with draperies beneath bearing the Rucellai arms. The work being given to Giuliano, he made four excellent figures of SS. Cosmo and Damian, St. Peter and St. Paul, executed with the utmost diligence.

Mariotto Albertinelli, observing the diligence of Giuliano in following designs in which he did not change a hair's breadth, and being himself about to abandon painting, left him a panel of Frà Bartolommeo to finish, which was simply designed and shaded with water-colours on the gypsum of the panel, as was his custom. Giuliano executed the work with great diligence, and it was placed in the church of S. Gallo outside the gate. The church and convent being ruined during the siege, it was taken to the hospital of the Preti in via San Gallo, thence to the convent of S. Marco, and ultimately to S. Jacopo tra' Fossi, at the high altar of which it now stands.[1] It represents a dead Christ, the

[1] It is now in the Pitti Gallery.

Magdalene embracing His feet and St. John supporting His head on one knee. St. Peter weeps and St. Paul opens his arms and contemplates his dead Lord. Giuliano executed this panel with such judgment that he deservedly won the greatest praise both then and thereafter. For Cristofano Rinieri he then finished the Rape of Dinah, left unfinished by Frà Bartolommeo, and made a replica, which was sent to France.[1] Being invited to Bologna by some friends, he did some portraits. In a chapel in the new choir of S. Francesco he did an oil-painting of the Virgin and two saints,[2] then much admired, for there were not many masters there. Returning to Florence, he did five pictures of the life of the Virgin for some unknown person, which are now in the house of Maestro Andrea Pasquali, the duke's physician, a very remarkable man. M. Palla Rucellai having given him a panel to do for his altar in S. Maria Novella, Giuliano began a Martyrdom of St. Catherine, but after keeping it in hand for twelve years he did not finish it, not having the invention or knowledge requisite for such a scene. He was troubled where to put the wheels, how to manage the flames burning her, and he would alter one day what he had done on another. Meanwhile, indeed, he did many other things, among them a good portrait of M. Francesco Guicciardini, who had returned from Bologna [3] and was writing his history in his villa at Montici. He also made a portrait of Signora Angiola de' Rossi, sister of the Count of Sansecondo, for Sig. Alessandro Vitelli, her husband, then of the guard of Florence. For M. Ottaviano de' Medici he did a portrait of Pope Clement seated, with Frà Niccolo della Magna standing, borrowed from one by Frà Bastiano del Piombo. He did another of Pope Clement seated, with Bartolommeo Valori kneeling before him and speaking to him, executed with incredible labour and patience. M. Ottaviano had secretly asked him to draw Michelagnolo, and after talking with the great artist, who was fond of his conversation, for two hours, Giuliano said to him, "If you would like to see yourself, come and see how I have caught your expression." Michelagnolo got up and, looking at the portrait, said, laughing, "What the devil have you done? you have put one eye on my temple— look here a moment." After examining it carefully, Giuliano said, "I do not notice, but sit down and I will see if it is so." Buonarroti, who knew how the mistake had come about, im-

---

[1] Painted 1531; now in the Vienna Gallery.
[2] Now in the Gallery, Bologna.
[3] He left Bologna, where he had been governor, in 1534.

mediately sat down sideways, and Giuliano, after looking at
him several times, at length got up and said, "It seems to
me that it is as I have shown it." "It is a natural defect,
then; go on and do not spare your brush or art," said
Buonarroti. When it was finished, Giuliano gave it to M.
Ottaviano with the portrait of Pope Clement by Frà Bastiano, fetched from Rome by Buonarroti. For Cardinal Inno-
cenzo Cibo, Giuliano copied Raphael's portrait of Pope Leo,
Cardinal Giulio de' Medici and Cardinal Rossi, but substi-
tuted Cardinal Cibo for the latter, executing the work with
great diligence. He next portrayed Cencio Guasconi, a beautiful
youth of the time, and then did a tabernacle in fresco for the
villa of Baccio Pedoni at Olmo a Castello, without much design
but with great diligence. Palla Rucellai wishing him to finish
the picture already mentioned, Giuliano resolved to bring
Michelagnolo to see it, and after telling him how with great
labour he had made the fire from heaven breaking the wheel
and killing those about it, and a sun issuing from a cloud
releasing St. Catherine from death, he begged Michelagnolo, who
could not help laughing at his perplexities, to tell him how to
make the eight or ten principal figures of the soldiers in the act
of flight, fallen, wounded and dead, because he did not know
how to foreshorten them in a row in such a narrow space.
Buonarroti, taking compassion on him, picked up a piece of
charcoal and sketched a row of naked figures foreshortened in
various attitudes some falling forward, some backward, some
dead, others wounded, all done with the judgment and excellence
peculiar to him. Giuliano thanked him, and soon after brought
his friend Tribolo to see what Buonarroti had done, but as he
had only drawn the outlines Giuliano could not continue the
work because there were no shadows. To help him Tribolo made
some rough clay models copied from Michelagnolo's design,
giving them the spirit and style that Michelagnolo had imparted
to his design, with the *Gradina*, which is a graduated chisel,
but making them somewhat crude to give greater strength. But
this rough style did not please Giuliano, so when Tribolo had
gone he washed them over with a brush dipped in water until
he had rendered them perfectly smooth, removing the parts
intended to cause sharp shadows and thus utterly ruining all the
excellence of the work. When Tribolo heard of it he laughed at
Giuliano's simplicity. The latter ultimately completed the work
in such a manner that no one would have supposed Michelagnolo
had ever looked at it.

Having become old and poor, with very little work to do, Giuliano made great efforts to produce a Pietà in a tabernacle in rather small figures, to go to Spain. It looked strange to see an old man devoting so much patience to his work out of love for art. On the doors of the tabernacle he did a Night on a black ground, copied from Michelagnolo's in the sacristy of S. Lorenzo, to show the darkness at the Saviour's death. As the Night had nothing to distinguish it except an owl, Giuliano indulged his playful fancies, introducing a lantern for bird-fowling at night, a candle, a night-cap, pillows, bats, and other things suggestive of darkness. When Buonarroti saw it he nearly choked with laughter at such strange fancies. Giuliano, after a well-ordered life, died in 1556, aged seventy-five, and was buried in S. Marco at Florence. One day, when Giuliano was telling Bronzino that he had seen a lovely woman whom he loudly praised, the latter asked, "Do you know her?" "No," he replied, "but she is very beautiful, for you see she is one of my pictures and that is enough."

CRISTOFANO GHERARDI, called DOCENO OF BORGO S. SEPOLCRO, Painter

(1508-1556)

WHILE Raffaello dal Colle of Borgo S. Sepolcro, a pupil of Giulio Romano, who helped him with the Hall of Constantine in the Pope's palace, and in the apartments of the T at Mantua, was painting the picture of the chapel of S. Gilio and Arcanio in the Borgo, with a Resurrection imitated from Giulio and Raphael, an Assumption for the bare-footed friars outside the Borgo, and other works for the Servite friars at Città di Castello, a youth of sixteen called Cristofano Doceno, son of Guido Gherardi, of an honourable family in the city, was studying painting with great profit, aided by natural inclination, and designed and coloured so well and so gracefully that it was a marvel. Raffaello, having seen some animals by him, as dogs, wolves, hares, various birds and fishes, and remarked his pleasant and witty conversation and his eccentric manner of living, was glad to enjoy his friendship and to have him in his shop as a pupil. There Cristofano designed for some time, where he met Rosso, made friends with him, and studied his designs, thinking them of great beauty, for he had only seen Raffaello's. But their studies were interrupted, for when Giovanni de' Turini dal Borgo, then captain of the Florentines, took a company of Florentine citizens and men of Città di Castello for the defence of the city, then besieged by the imperial army of Pope Clement, Cristofano went with them, being led astray by some of his friends. He hoped to have an opportunity of studying the masterpieces of Florence, but was disappointed, as he was stationed in the bastions on the hill outside. At the conclusion of the war Cristofano, being induced by his friends and by his desire to see the paintings and sculptures of the city, joined the guard of Florence, of which Sig. Alessandro Vitelli of Città di Castello was commander. While he was there Sig. Alessandro della Bilia, painter and soldier of Città di Castello, learned from Battista that Cristofano was studying painting, and had a fine picture of his, proposed to send him with Battista and another Battista, also of Città di Castello, to decorate with paintings a garden and loggia which he had begun at Città di Castello. But as he died while the garden was building, the other Battista taking his place, nothing further was done. Giorgio Vasari, having returned from Rome, and being in Florence with Duke Alessandro until Cardinal Ippolito, his patron, should return from Hungary, had had the rooms in the Servite convent to begin some frescoes of the acts of Cæsar in the corner room of the Medici palace where Giovanni da Udine had decorated the vaulting with stucco and painting. Cristofano, having known and liked Giorgio in the Borgo in 1528 when he went to see Rosso, resolved to join him, and to take advantage of this opportunity to devote himself to art more seriously than in the past. Giorgio having associated with him for a year, and finding him likely to become a skilful artist and of a pleasant conversation, grew very fond of him. Being commissioned by Duke Alessandro to make the citadel of Città di Castello in conjunction with Antonio da Sangallo and Pier Francesco da Viterbo, and taking the way of Città di Castello, to repair the walls of the Vitelli garden, he took Cristofano with him, having himself designed the friezes for some rooms and the scenes for a study, and other sketches for the façades of the loggia, all of which he and Bastiano completed. They did it with an excellence and grace that would not have been surpassed by a practical master, and Cristofano, by dint of this experience, became very skilful in design and colour. In 1536, when Charles V. came to Florence, a magnificent reception was prepared, Vasari being charged by Duke Alessandro to decorate the S. Pier Gattolini gate, the façade at the top of the via Maggio at S. Felice in piazza, and the pediment of the door of S. Maria del Fiore, as well as a standard for the castle, fifteen braccia by forty, for which fifty thousand pieces of gold leaf were required. The Florentine painters and others, thinking that the duke favoured Vasari too much, contrived that he should not obtain any master masons, nor any youths or others from the city to assist him in anything. On learning this Vasari sent for Cristofano, Raffaello dal Colle and Stefano Veltroni of Monte Sansovino, his kinsman, and with their assistance and that of other painters he completed the work, in which Cristofano excited universal admiration and was much praised. When it was finished, he remained several days in Florence assisting Vasari in the preparations for the marriage of the duke in the palace of M. Ottaviano de' Medici. Among other things he made the arms of the duchess Margaret of Austria, with the balls, supported by an eagle and some infants, excellently done. On the assassination of the duke a plot was laid in the Borgo to hand over a gate of the city to Piero Strozzi when he came to Sestino. Some exiles of the place wrote to Cristofano asking him to help them. Although he would not agree, he preferred to tear up the letters instead of denouncing them to Gherardo Gherardi, then Duke Cosimo's commissioner in the Borgo, as he should have done. When matters became settled, several Borghesi were banished as rebels, among them Doceno. Alessandro Vitelli, who knew the facts and might have helped him, would not say a word in order to force him to serve him in the garden at Città di Castello, on which much time had been wasted, and at length Cristofano, in despair, went with the other exiles to S. Justino, one and a half miles from the Borgo in the state of the Church, and not far from the Florentine frontier. Although in peril, he there painted a handsome room in a tower for the Abbot Bufolini of Città di Castello, with infants, foreshortened figures, arabesques, festoons and masks. The abbot, being pleased, gave him another room to do. Wishing to make some stucco ornaments there, and not having marble to make the powder, he used white stone from the river, which adheres well. Within these stucco ornaments Cristofano painted in fresco some deeds of the Romans, of great beauty.

Meanwhile Giorgio being engaged upon the screen of the abbey of Camaldoli, and wishing to make a decoration in fresco full of scenes above and two pictures below, would have been glad of Cristofano's assistance, and to make his peace with the duke. But it was not possible, although M. Ottaviano de' Medici begged the duke to relent. Vasari, however, endeavoured to get Cristofano away from S. Giustino, where he was in great peril. Being employed in 1539 to do three panels in oils, with a frieze, and twenty subjects of the Apocalypse in small figures, the monasteries of the order, grotesques and festoons for the monks of Monte Oliveto, in their monastery of S. Michele in Bosco, outside Bologna, at the end of a refectory, Vasari wrote to ask Cristofano to come to Bologna with Battista Cungi, a Borghese who had served Vasari seven years. They reached Bologna before Vasari, who was still at Camaldoli preparing a cartoon for a Deposition from the Cross, afterwards placed at the high altar. They began to prepare the panels, Vasari having arranged with Dattero, a Jew, a friend of M. Ottaviano de' Medici, who had a bank at Bologna, to provide them with what they needed. Dattero, being very courteous, paid them every civility. He often accompanied them, and as Cristofano had a great mark on one eye, and Battista had large eyes, they were taken for Jews.

One morning a cobbler was ordered by Dattero to bring a pair of new shoes to Cristofano, and on reaching the monastery he said to Cristofano, who was standing at the door watching the almsgiving, "Messer, can you tell me where the two Jew painters at work here live?" "Jews or no Jews," said Cristofano, "what do you want with them?" "I have brought these shoes for one of them named Cristofano," replied the man. "I am a better Christian than you," said Cristofano. "As you please," replied the cobbler; "but everyone knows that you are Jews, and your appearance bears it out." "I wager we shall do the work of Christians," rejoined Cristofano.

But to return to the work. On Vasari reaching Bologna the panels were finished in a month, he designing and the others sketching and colouring. The frieze was next attacked, and Cristofano was to do it alone. However, Stefano Veltroni, of Monte Sansovino, Vasari's cousin, who had sketched the picture of the Deposition, arrived from Camaldoli and helped him, producing a marvellous work. Cristofano did the arabesques so well that better could not be seen, though they lacked finish, while Stefano wanted grace and delicacy, his brush not exactly following the lines. But being very patient, he ultimately rendered his arabesques with more care and delicacy. They all worked in rivalry at this frieze, so that Stefano learned finish from Cristofano, and taught Cristofano a better style. Vasari next made one of the large festoons about the windows, representing fruits from Nature. He then directed Cristofano and Stefano to do the rest in the same style on either side of the window, promising a scarlet pair of shoes to the one who should do best. Thus, working in friendly rivalry, they produced beautiful festoons to the smallest details, such as millet seeds, bunches of fennel, etc., so that Vasari gave shoes to both. He made great efforts to induce Cristofano to do a part of the designs for the frieze, but without avail. While Giorgio was himself at work he did the buildings for two panels with more grace, style and masterly judgment than Cristofano would have displayed, and indeed no painter could have accomplished the things he did without study. On finishing these buildings, while Vasari was completing the twenty scenes from the Apocalypse for the frieze, Cristofano did the table utensils in the scene where St. Gregory, a portrait of Clement VII., is eating with the twelve poor men.[1] Beginning the third panel, while Stefano was gilding the frame of the other two, he erected a wooden scaffolding for Vasari to make the three angels appearing to Abraham in the valley of Mamre, on the other side of which Cristofano did some buildings. Being a very careless man, he would sometimes make a platform of stools and chairs and even of pails and pans placed upside down, on which to mount, but one day, as he was stepping back to see what he had done, his foot slipped, his platform was overturned and he fell five braccia, injuring himself, so that it was necessary to let blood and to tend him carefully or he would have died. Even so, he was so careless that one night he allowed the bandages from his arm to come undone, and if Stefano, who slept with him, had not hastened to his assistance, he would have died, as he made a pool of blood in the bed, and it was a hard matter to revive him. Vasari tended him as if he had been his brother, and indeed he needed it, as he had not recovered before the completion of the work. Cristofano then returned to S. Giustino, and there completed some of the rooms of the abbot which he had left unfinished. At Città di Castello he did unaided a panel which had been allotted to his friend Battista, and a lunette over the side door of S. Fiorido, with three figures in fresco.

Giorgio being summoned to Venice by the influence of M. Pietro Aretino to arrange a sumptuous feast for the nobles and lords of the company of the Calza, and the scenery of a comedy by M. Pietro, and being unable to do so much single-

[1] Now in the Accademia, Bologna.

handed sent for Cristofano and Battista Cungi, who reached
Venice after having been carried by the fortune of the sea to
Sclavonia. They found that Vasari had already designed everything, so that they only needed to begin the painting. The
lords of the Calza having taken a large unfinished house at the
end of Canareio, only the principal walls and roof of which
were standing, employed Giorgio to make two rows of seats there,
seventy braccia long and sixteen broad, to accommodate the
ladies. The side walls he divided into four squares of four braccia
broad, containing figures, the niches being between projections
nine braccia high. There were ten niches in all, twenty termini
and eight scenes. The first on the right, in grisaille, represented
Adrian for Venice seated on a rock in the midst of the sea,
surrounded by Neptune, Thetis, Proteus, Nereus, Glaucus, Palæ-
mon, and other sea-gods and nymphs, presenting jewels, pearls
and gold, and other treasures of the deep. Some cupids were
shooting arrows, and others scattering flowers, the remaining
space being filled with lovely palms. The second contained
nude figures of the Rivers Drave and Save, with their vases.
The third represented the corpulent Po with seven sons, for his
seven mouths. The fourth was the Brenta, with other rivers of
Friuli. Opposite the Adria was the isle of Candia, where Jupiter
is seen suckled by a goat and is surrounded by nymphs. Next
it and opposite the Drave was the river Tagliamento, with the
mountains of Cadore. Below this, opposite the Po, were Lake
Benaco and the Mincio. Next to this and opposite the Brenta
were the Adige and Tesino falling into the sea. The pictures
on the right wall were separated by the virtues Liberality,
Concord, Mercy, Peace and Religion, in niches. On the other
wall were Fortitude, Prudence, Justice, a Victory with War
beneath, and Charity. Above were a cornice, architrave and a
frieze, with glass balls full of distilled water and lights behind
to render the whole apartment luminous. The ceiling was
divided into four compartments, ten braccia by eight each,
with a frieze of the breadth of the niches round the cornices
and forming a border of three braccia about the spaces. There
were twenty-three squares in all and a double one over the
stage. They represented the twenty-four hours. The first, of
ten braccia, was Time sending the Hours to their places, accompanied by Æolus, Juno and Iris. Another at the entrance door
had the chariot of Dawn, issuing from the arms of Tithonus,
and scattering roses, the car being drawn by cocks. Another
contained the chariot of the Sun, and the fourth the chariot

of Night drawn by owls. Night, with the moon on her head, was preceded by stars, and surrounded by darkness. Cristofano did the majority of these pictures, and so well as to excite general wonder, especially in the chariot of Night, for which he made sketches in oils, achieving what seemed impossible. In the Adria picture he made the marine monsters with such variety and beauty that people were amazed at them. In fact, in the whole work he showed himself a most skilful painter, especially in the arabesques and foliage.

On finishing this trophy Vasari and Cristofano remained some months in Venice painting the ceiling or soffit of a room for M. Giovanni Cornaro with nine large pictures in oils. Vasari might have remained there a year, at the prayer of Michele Sanmichele, the Veronese architect, but Cristofano dissuaded him, as he did not value the design or the painters there, saying that it was better to return to Rome, the true school of the noble arts, where ability is much better recognised than at Venice. So they both left, as Vasari had no desire to remain, but Cristofano being outlawed could not follow Vasari, and so he returned to S. Giustino, where he was continually employed on work for the abbot, but before long he went on to Perugia upon the occasion of the first visit of Paul III., after the wars with the Peruginese.[1] He acquitted himself very well in some things prepared for the Pope's reception, especially in the door of Frà Ranieri, where he did a large Jupiter enraged, at the wish of the governor Barba, and another of Jupiter appeased, two very fine figures. At the other side he made Atlas with the world on his back, between two women, one holding a sword and the other the scales. These works and others, done by Cristofano for those festivities, led to his employment to decorate some rooms for the citadel then built by the Pope at Perugia, at the desire of M. Tiberio Crispo, then the governor, Lattanzio, a painter of the March, having hitherto worked there. With Lattanzio's assistance and by himself Cristofano did the greater part of the best things there. Other workers were Raffaello dal Colle and Adone Doni of Ascoli,[2] a very skilful painter who did many things in his native place and elsewhere. There was also Tommaso del Papacello, a painter of Cortona. But Cristofano was the best of all, and won the most praise, and thus, through Lattanzio, he acquired the favour of Crispo, who employed him frequently. This Crispo having built a new church at Perugia called S. Maria del Popolo,

In 1539.   [2] Assisi.

originally del Mercato, Lattanzio began a panel in oils, and Cristofano did all the upper part, which is very beautiful. Lattanzio being subsequently appointed bargello of Perugia, Cristofano returned to S. Giustino, where he remained many months working for the Abbot Bufolini. In 1543 Giorgio, having to do a panel in oils for Cardinal Farnese for the grand chancery, and another in the church of S. Agostino for Galeotto da Girone, sent for Cristofano, who came readily, as he wanted to see Rome. He remained there for several months, doing little else but sightseeing. However, he made such progress that, on returning to S. Giustino, he produced such beautiful figures in a hall, for a caprice, that he might have been studying them for twenty years. On Vasari going to Naples in 1545 to do a refectory for the friars of Monte Oliveto, a much greater work than that of S. Michele in Bosco at Bologna, he sent for Cristofano, Raffaello dal Colle and Stefano, who arrived there at the appointed time, except Cristofano, who was sick. However, at Vasari's request, he went as far as Rome, but, being detained by his brother Borgognone, also an exile, who wished to take him to France to serve Colonel Giovanni da Turrino, he lost the opportunity. However, on Vasari's return to Rome in 1546 to do twenty-four pictures, afterwards sent to Naples and placed in the sacristy of S. Giovanni Carbonaro, containing Old Testament subjects and the life of St. John the Baptist, and the organ-shutters of the Piscopio, six braccia high, he employed Cristofano, who executed figures and landscapes of great excellence. Giorgio intended to make use of him for the hall of the chancery, painted from his designs and finished in a hundred days for Cardinal Farnese. But Cristofano fell sick and returned to S. Giustino, so soon as he began to get better. Vasari finished the hall without him, aided by Raffaelo dal Colle, Gian Battista Bagnacavallo of Bologna, the Spaniards, Roviale and Bizzerra, and many other friends and pupils. From Rome Giorgio went to Florence, and proceeding thence to Rimini to do a chapel in fresco and a picture for Abbot Gian Matteo Faettani in the church of the monks of Monte Oliveto, he went through S. Giustino to take Cristofano with him. But Abbot Bufolini, for whom he was painting a room, would not let him go, though he promised Giorgio to send him to Romagna soon. Despite this, he delayed so long that, when Cristofano went, he found that Vasari had finished the work and had also done a panel at the high altar of S. Francesco of Arimini for M. Niccolo Marcheselli and another in the Camaldoline church of Classi for

Father Don Romualdo da Verona, the abbot. Shortly before, about 1550, Giorgio had done the Marriage of Esther in the refectory of the abbey of the black monks of S. Fiore at Arezzo. In the Martelli Chapel in S. Lorenzo at Florence he had done a panel of St. Gismondo, when he was called to Rome to serve Julius III. on his creation. He hoped, by means of Cardinal Farnese, who went to live in Florence at that time, to restore Cristofano to Duke Cosimo's favour, but it was not possible. Thus poor Cristofano remained an exile until 1554, when Vasari was invited to serve the duke, and seized the opportunity to obtain his pardon.

The Bishop de' Ricasoli, wishing to please the duke, had begun to paint in grisaille the three façades of his palace at the end of the Ponte alla Carraia, when M. Sforza Almeni, the duke's favourite chamberlain, resolved to paint his house in the via de' Servi similarly. Not finding painters in Florence to suit him, he wrote to Giorgio Vasari, who had not yet come to Florence, to prepare designs for the façade. Giorgio, who was his good friend and knew how both stood with Duke Alessandro, sent him a beautiful design, embellishing the whole front with rich ornaments representing the life of man from birth to death. M. Sforza was so delighted, and the duke also, that they resolved it should not be begun before Vasari reached Florence. When he at length arrived they welcomed him heartily, and began to discuss who should execute the work. Giorgio, seizing the opportunity, said that no one was so suitable as Cristofano, and that nothing could be done without his assistance. When M. Sforza had reported this to the duke, it was found after careful inquiry that Cristofano's fault had not been so grave as had been represented, and the duke at length pardoned him. On receiving the news at Arezzo, Vasari immediately sent post to Cristofano, who knew nothing of all this, and was beside himself with joy. Acknowledging Vasari to be his best friend, he left Città di Castello on the following morning for the Borgo, and, presenting his letter of liberation to the commissioner, went to his father's house, to the amazement of his mother and brother, who had been pardoned long before. After two days he proceeded to Arezzo, where Giorgio received him more joyfully than if he had been his own brother, the two artists resolving to spend their lives together. Both then travelled to Florence, and Cristofano went to kiss the duke's hand, the prince being astonished at seeing such a good little man when he had expected a bravo. M. Sforza also showed him great favour, and Cristofano began the façade. Here Giorgio assisted him, as he could not yet work in the palace, and designed the scenes, drawing some figures on the lime. But although Vasari retouched much, all the façade, the greater part of the figures, all the ornaments, festoons and large ovals are Cristofano's, and Vasari admitted that he knew more than himself in the management of colours in fresco. If Cristofano had studied art steadily as a youth (for he never prepared designs beforehand), and had pursued art with determination, he would have had no peer, his skill, judgment and memory causing him to produce things without other study, so that he surpassed many who really knew more than he. He executed his work with incredible skill and speed, and when once he had set to work he never raised his head, whatever the time. His conversation was so amusing as he worked that Vasari often worked with him from morning to evening without ever feeling tired. Cristofano finished this façade in a few months, and some weeks he went to the Borgo to see and enjoy his things. I will describe this work, because it may not enjoy a long life, being in an exposed position, and it was scarcely finished before it suffered serious damage by a heavy rain and hail.

It is in three divisions, the first from the bottom, with the door and two windows, the second with the second windows, and the third with the top windows and up to the cornice of the roof. The windows have six lights, forming seven spaces, the whole work being divided by lines from the roof to the ground. Beneath the cornice of the roof is a cornice in perspective, with corbels over a frieze of infants, six of whom are standing, one over the middle of the arch of each window, and holding festoons of fruit, leaves and flowers, passed from hand to hand according to the seasons of life. In the middle of the festoons are other infants in various attitudes. Between the upper windows in the seven spaces he made the seven planets with their signs above them. On the parapet below is a frieze of Virtues in pairs holding large ovals with representations of the seven ages of man, each age with appropriate Virtues, and under the ovals between the spaces of the windows beneath are the three theological and the four moral Virtues. In the frieze above the door are the seven liberal Arts on the right of the ovals containing the seven Ages, and near them are the moral Virtues, the planets, signs and other things. Between the grated windows are active and contemplative life with scenes and statues, Death, Hell and the Resurrection. In a word

Cristofano executed almost alone the cornice, festoons and infants, and the seven signs of the planets. He first did the Moon, as Diana, with a lap full of flowers, like Proserpine, with a moon on her head and the sign of Cancer above. Below the oval representing Infancy there are some nurses suckling infants and women in childbed, executed by Cristofano with much grace. This oval is supported by Will, a beautiful maiden, half naked, standing beside Charity, who suckles children. Below is Grammar teaching children to read. Mercury next follows with the caduceus and his emblem. In the oval is Boyhood with boys, some going to school and some playing. This is supported by Truth, a naked child, a pure and simple maiden, with a male Falsehood at one side with beautiful face but hollow eyes; below the oval is Faith baptising a boy in a shell full of water and holding a cross in her left hand; below is Logic, veiled and with a serpent. The Sun follows as Apollo holding the lyre, with his sign above. The oval contains Adolescence as two youths going together, one climbing with an olive staff a mountain illuminated by the Sun, the other stopping half-way to admire the beauties which Fraud lays before him, hiding her ugly face behind a beautiful mask, and lured by her over a precipice. Sloth supports this oval, represented as a corpulent man, sleepy and naked, like Silenus; and Work, as a robust labourer, has agricultural implements about him. These are in that part of the ornament between the windows containing Hope, with the anchor at her feet. On the parapet below is Music, with various instruments. Venus follows, embracing Love, with her sign above. The oval contains scenes of Youth, a young man seated with books, measuring instruments and other things pertaining to design, with maps, globes and spheres. Behind him is a loggia containing young men singing, dancing and playing, and a banquet of young men engaged in pleasures. This oval is supported on one side by Self-knowledge surrounded by sextants, astrolabes, quadrants and books, and looking in a mirror, and on the other side by Fraud, old and ugly, lean and toothless, who laughs at Knowledge and hides her face behind a beautiful mask. Below the oval is Temperance, a bridle in her hand, and Rhetoric on the parapet in a line with the others. Mars follows, in armour, with many trophies and the sign of Leo above. In the oval beneath is Manhood, as a mature man, between Memory and Will, who offer him a gold basin containing dice, and show him the way of safety to a mountain. This oval is supported by Innocence, a maiden with a lamb at

her side, and accompanied by a smiling Hilarity. Below and
between the windows is Prudence tiring herself at a mirror
and below her on the parapet is Philosophy. Jupiter follows
with his thunderbolts and eagle, and the sign above. The oval
contains Old Age as an old man dressed as a priest and kneeling
before an altar, upon which he places the gold basin containing
a pair of wings. This oval is supported by Pity, who clothes
some naked infants, and Religion with sacerdotal vestments.
Beneath is Fortitude, armed, with one leg on a column, putting
balls into the mouth of a lion. On the parapet below is Astrology.
The last of the planets is Saturn as a melancholy old man
eating his children, and a great serpent biting its tail. Above
is the sign of Capricorn. The oval contains Decrepitude, with
Jupiter receiving a decrepit old man regarded by Felicity and
Immortality, who throw his garments to the world. This oval
is supported by Happiness, standing in the ornament beneath
Justice, who is seated and holds the sceptre with the stork above
the balls, and with arms and laws about her. On the parapet
below is Geometry. Below, about the grated windows and the
door, Leah, in a niche, represents active life, and on the other
side is Industry, with a cornucopia and a pair of spurs. Towards
the door is a scene of smiths, architects and masons before the
gate of Cosmopolis, a city built by Duke Cosimo in the isle of
Elba, with a view of Porto Ferraio. Between this scene and the
frieze containing the liberal arts is Lake Trasimene, surrounded
by nymphs issuing from the water, with tench, pikes, eels and
roach, and beside the lake is Perugia, a nude figure, with a dog
in her hand, pointing to Florence on the opposite side. This
figure is embraced by an Arno, and beneath her is the Contemplative Life, with astrologers and philosophers measuring
the heaven and making the duke's horoscope. In the niche
opposite Leah is Rachael representing the Contemplative Life.
The last scene, between two niches and completing the work,
is Death on a withered horse, with the scythe in his hand,
accompanied by war, pestilence, famine trampling on all
manner of people. In a niche is Pluto, and beneath Cerberus,
while in another is a large figure rising from a tomb. Over
the grated windows Cristofano did some nudes holding the
duke's device, and the ducal arms over the door, the six
balls supported by naked infants flying. In the basement
beneath Cristofano made the device of M. Sforza, triangular
pyramids resting upon three balls with the legend IMMOBILIS.
When the work was finished the duke and M. Sforza showered

praise upon him, and the latter, being courteous and gentle, wished to make him some notable gift for his ability and labour, but Cristofano declined, being contented with his favour, for he always cherished the greatest affection for that lord.

Whilst this work was going forward Vasari stayed in the house of Sig. Bernardetto de' Medici, as he had always done, and Cristofano with him. The latter, seeing how fond his host was of painting, did two scenes in grisaille in the corner of his garden, the Rape of Proserpine, and Vertumnus and Pomona, gods of agriculture. He further adorned them with the most beautiful termini, infants and other decorations. He then began a hall in the new apartments of the palace. This was twenty braccia broad, and as Tasso had not made it more than nine braccia high, it was raised three braccia, making it twelve braccia in all, by Vasari without moving the gabled roof. But before beginning the painting it was necessary to devote some time to repairing the ceiling and other works there. Vasari therefore obtained permission to go to Arezzo, stopping there two months with Cristofano. But he could not rest, as he had to go to Cortona, painting the vaulting and walls of the company of Jesus with Cristofano, who did very well, especially on various sacrifices from the Old Testament in the lunettes between the arches of the vaults. Properly speaking, the whole work was by Cristofano, as Vasari only did some sketches, designed a few things on the lime, and retouched where necessary. On the completion of this large, admirable and well-executed work they both returned to Florence in January 1555, and began to paint the hall of the Elements, Vasari doing the ceiling pictures and Cristofano executing some designs for connecting the friezes, containing heads of unicorns and tortoises with the sail, the duke's device. But he showed his skill best in some festoons of fruit on the lower frieze, of the utmost beauty of colouring, and with masks at intervals with the ropes of the festoons in their mouths, of varied and curious forms, a branch of art in which Cristofano may be said to have excelled all others. On the wall containing the birth of Venus he did some large figures and many small ones in a landscape from Vasari's cartoons, very well executed. On the wall containing the Loves making arrows for Cupid, he did three Cyclops forging Jove's thunderbolts, and on six doors he did six large ovals in fresco with ornaments in grisaille and fine bronze-coloured scenes. In the same hall he painted Mercury and Pluto between the windows. He next did the chamber of the goddess Ops, next this room, painting the four Seasons in fresco on the ceiling and some festoons of marvellous variety and beauty, those of Spring being being full of thousands of flowers; those of Summer with a boundless quantity of fruit and grain, those of Autumn with grapes and vine-tendrils, and those of Winter with turnips, radishes, carrots and dry leaves. In the middle picture containing the car of Ops he painted in oils four magnificent lions drawing it, for he had no peer in drawing animals. In the chamber of Ceres, next this, he did infants and festoons in the corners. In the middle picture, where Vasari had made Ceres seeking Proserpine with a pine-torch and in a chariot drawn by two serpents, Cristofano completed a number of things, as Vasari was sick and had left it unfinished with more beside. Coming to a terrace after the chamber of Jupiter, and next that of Ops, it was resolved to dedicate it to Juno. The stucco ornaments and arrangement of figures being designed by Vasari, he arranged that Cristofano should execute the fresco-work by himself, desiring him to do something fine in his own profession, as the thing had to be seen close up, and the figures were not more than a braccia. Here Cristofano did a Marriage of Juno in an oval of the vaulting, with Hebe, goddess of youth, on one side and Iris on the other, accompanied by a rainbow. In the same vaulting he did three other pictures, two together and a larger one in a line with the oval, containing the marriage, with Juno in a chariot drawn by peacocks. The others contain the goddess of Power and Abundance with a cornucopia. On the walls below, over the two entrance doors, are Juno converting Io, daughter of the River Inachus, into a cow, and Calixtus into a bear. For these works the duke became very fond of Cristofano, seeing him very diligent in working, for every morning Cristofano appeared, and was so engrossed in his work that very often he had not clothes to go away in. In his haste he often put on slippers kept under his bed, which were not a pair, and usually his cloak was the wrong way on. One morning he arrived early, finding the duke and duchess looking at the work, dressed to go hunting, while the court were making ready. They perceived that as usual Cristofano's cloak was on the wrong way, with the hood inside, and both laughed. The duke then said: "Why is your cloak always put on the wrong way about, Cristofano?" "Sire, I do not know," replied the artist. "I wish there was some kind of cloak without back or front, but the same on both sides, because I usually dress myself in the dark, and with one of my eyes I can see nothing. But

let your excellency look at what I paint and not how I dress."
The duke did not answer, but a few days after he had a cloak
made of fine cloth, without back or front, and the same inside
as out, trimming and all. He sent this to Cristofano by a courier
as a gift. Receiving this early one morning, Cristofano examined
it without ceremony, and said to the courier, "The duke is a
sensible man; tell him that it is all right." But Cristofano was
careless about his person, and hated nothing so much as putting
on new clothes. Vasari, who knew his humour, would have new
clothes made secretly, when he needed any, and put them in
his room in the early morning, removing the old ones, so that
Cristofano was obliged to put on the others. It was amusing
to listen to his anger as he put on the new ones. "What folly
is this?" he would say. "Why cannot a man live as he pleases?
Why the devil should these enemies of comfort give themselves
so much trouble?" One morning, when he had put on a pair
of white hose, Domenico Benci, a painter, who also worked in
the palace with Vasari, took Cristofano with other youths to
the Madonna dell' Impruneta. Having spent the day in walking,
dancing and enjoying themselves, they returned after supper.
Cristofano, being tired, went to bed immediately, but he could
only draw off one of his new stockings, his feet being wet.
When Vasari went in to see how he was, he found him asleep
with one stocking on. With the help of a servant he drew it
off, while Cristofano cursed the clothes, Giorgio and the inventors
of such things, which, he said, keep men in chains. He declared
he would go back to S. Giustino, where he lived as he pleased
and was not so pestered, so that it was no small effort to appease
him. He was little addicted to argument, and he liked brevity
in speech, and had a preference for short names. Of a slave of
M. Sforza called M. he exclaimed, "That is a good name, better
than your Giovan Francesco and Giovanni Antonio, which take
an hour to pronounce." He was naturally amiable, and as he
said such things in his Borghese dialect, it was enough to make
sorrow laugh to hear him. On feast days he would spend all
the time at the places where printed legends and pictures were
sold, and if he bought any he would as often as not leave them
where he had picked them up while he turned to look at others.
He would never ride a horse unless compelled, although he was
nobly born and fairly well off. On the death of his brother
Borgognone, when he should have gone to Borgo, Vasari, who
had received a considerable sum of money for his salary, said
to him, "I have a good deal of your money, you ought to

take it with you for your requirements." Cristofano replied, "I do not want money, take it for yourself. I shall be content to remain near you, and to live and die with you." "I am not in the habit of profiting by the labours of others," replied Vasari; "if you do not want it I will send it to your father Guido." "Do not do that," said Cristofano, "for he would be sure to put it to a bad use as he always does." At length he took it and went to Borgo, sick in body and troubled in mind. In a few days his grief at his brother's death, whom he had loved dearly, and a cruel disorder of the reins, caused his death. He received the sacraments, and distributed the money he had brought with him to the members of his house and the poor. It is said that his only cause of grief before his death was that he had left Vasari with too much on his hands in the duke's palace. Not long after the duke heard with sorrow of Cristofano's death, and ordered a marble bust, with the following epitaph, to be made and sent to the Borgo, where it was placed in S. Francesco:

D.O.M.
CHRISTOPHORO GHERARDO
BVRGENSI
PINGENDI ARTE PRAESTANTISS.
QVOD GEORGIVS VASARIVS ARETINVS
HVIVS ARTIS FACILE PRINCEPS
IN EXORNANDO
COSMI FLORENTIN. DVCIS PALATIO
ILLIVS OPERAM QVAM MAXIME
PROBAVERIT
PICTORES HETRVCI POSVERE
OBIIT. A.D. MDLVI.
VIXIT ANN. LVI. M. III. D. VI.

JACOPO DA PONTORMO, Painter of Florence
(1494 – 1557)

THE ancestors of Bartolommeo di Jacopo di Martino, the father of Jacopo da Pontormo, whose Life I now write, came, as some declare, from Ancisa of the Valdarno, famous as the home of the ancestors of M. Francesco Petrarca. But whatever their place of origin, this Bartolommeo was a Florentine, and of the family of the Carucci. He is said to have been a pupil of Domenico del Ghirlandajo, and being a painter of merit, who did many things in Valdarno, he ultimately went to work at Empoli, and took a wife at Pontormo nearby, called Alessandra, daughter of Pasquale di Zanobi and Mona Brigida, his wife. The fruit of this union was Jacopo, born in 1493. But the father dying in 1499, the mother in 1504, and the grandfather in 1506, the boy remained in the charge of Mona Brigida, his grandmother, who kept him several years in Pontormo, and had him taught reading, writing and the elements of Latin grammar. At the age of thirteen she took him to Florence, and put him in the Court of Wards, so that his small property might be taken charge of by that magistracy, as was the custom. After leaving him in the house of a cobbler, a distant relation, Mona Brigida returned to Pontormo, taking Jacopo's sister with her. But Mona Brigida dying soon after, Jacopo was forced to bring this sister to Florence and put her in the house of a relation called Niccolaio, who lived in the via de' Servi. But this child died in 1512 before being married. Jacopo had not been many months in Florence before Bernardo Vettori sent him to stay with Lionardo da Vinci, and then with Mariotto Albertinelli, Piero di Cosimo, and finally, in 1512, with Andrea del Sarto, with whom he did not remain long, for after he had done the cartoons for the arch of the Servites it does not seem that Andrea bore him any good will, whatever the cause may have been.

Jacopo's first work was a little Annunciation for a tailor, his friend. The tailor dying before this was finished, it remained in Jacopo's hands, who was then with Mariotto, who boasted of it, and showed it to all who visited his shop. It happened that Raphael came to Florence, and upon seeing this he marvelled, and foretold Jacopo's future success. Not long after, when Mariotto left Florence to do the panel begun by Frà Bartolommeo at Viterbo, Jacopo, who was young, melancholy and lonely, remained without a master, and went of his own accord to Andrea del Sarto at the time when he had completed the series on St. Philip in the court of the Servites. These greatly pleased Jacopo, as did the style, design and everything else of Andrea. Jacopo therefore tried to imitate him, and before long he made marvellous progress in design and colouring, so that he seemed to have followed art for many years. Andrea having finished an Annunciation for the church of the friars of Sangallo, now destroyed, he gave the predella to Jacopo to do in oils. He made a dead Christ, with two little angels weeping and holding torches. At the sides he did two prophets in circles, executed with the skill of a master. But Bronzino has said that he remembers having heard from Jacopo that Rossi also worked at the predella. Jacopo also assisted Andrea in many pictures and works on which he was continually engaged.

On the elevation of Cardinal Giovanni de' Medici to the papacy as Leo X., the friends of the house in Florence made numerous scutcheons of the Pope in stone, marble, canvas and fresco. The Servite friars, wishing to show their devotion to the house and the Pope, had a stone coat-of-arms of Leo made and placed in the middle of the arch of the first portico of the Nunziata, on the piazza, and soon after directed Andrea di Cosimo,[1] the painter, to gild and decorate it with arabesques, of which he was an excellent master, and with devices of the Medici house, adding figures of Faith and Charity on either side. Andrea, feeling that he could not do so much by himself, resolved to give the figures to others, and calling Jacopo, who was not more than nineteen, he gave them to him, although he had some difficulty to persuade him, as the youth was unwilling at first to undertake a work in a place of such importance. However, he took courage, and although he was not so skilful in fresco as in oils, he accepted the work. While still with Andrea del Sarto, he withdrew to make the cartoons in S. Antonio at the Faenza gate, where he lived, and, that done, he one day took his master to see them. Andrea praised them loudly, but, whether through envy or some other cause, he never regarded Jacopo kindly again. Thus, when Jacopo sometimes went to his shop, it was shut, or he was chased away by the apprentices. Accordingly he withdrew and began to reduce his expenses, for he was very poor, and studied with great assiduity. When Andrea di Cosimo had finished gilding the arms, Jacopo began to finish the rest by himself, and moved by his desire to make a name, and aided by his natural grace and fertility, he executed the work with marvellous quickness, and as perfectly as an old and experienced master. With added courage, he felt he could do a much better work, and he had thought of breaking up the old one and making another after a design of his own. The friars, seeing the work was finished and that Jacopo came no more, went to Andrea and persuaded him to unveil his work. Andrea sought Jacopo to ask if he wished to retouch anything, and not finding him, for he was engrossed upon the new design, and would see no one, he removed the

[1] Andrea di Cosimo Feltrini.

scaffolding and uncovered the work. That same evening, when Jacopo left his house to go to the Servites, it being night, to take down what he had done and set to work on the new design, he found the work unveiled and a crowd regarding it. He sought out Andrea, and wrathfully complained of his acting without him, telling him what he intended to do. Andrea answered, "You do wrong to complain, for your work is so good that I am sure you could not do better, and as you will have no lack of employment, use these designs for something else." His work was of such beauty that for its new style and the sweetness of the heads of the two women and the charm of the infants it was the finest fresco ever seen till then. There are two other infants in the air holding a drapery over the Pope's arms, of unsurpassable beauty, while all the figures have the utmost relief, and their colouring cannot be over-praised. Michelagnolo, on seeing it, and knowing it to be the work of a youth of nineteen, said, "This youth, if he lives and continues to pursue art, will attain to heaven." The men of Pontormo, hearing of Jacopo's renown, sent for him and employed him to do the arms of Pope Leo over a door on the main street, with two lovely infants, but it has been all but destroyed by water. At the carnival of that year there were great rejoicings in Florence over the creation of Leo, and, among other festivities, two were carried out at the expense of two companies of lords and nobles of the city. The head of one of these, called the Diamond, was Sig. Giuliano de' Medici, the Pope's brother, and it was so called because the diamond was the device of Lorenzo the elder, his father. That of the other, with a Branch as device, had Sig. Lorenzo, son of Piero de' Medici, as its head, with a dried laurel branch, with new leaves springing forth, to show the revival of his grandfather's name. M. Andrea Dazzi, who was then professing Greek and Latin at the University of Florence, was charged by the Diamond company to devise something for a triumph. He arranged one like those of the Romans, with three beautiful wooden cars richly painted. The first represented Boyhood, with a row of boys; the second was Manhood, with persons who had done great things at that season of life; the third was Old Age, with men who had done great deeds when old. All the characters were most sumptuously dressed. The architects of these cars were Raffaello delle Viviole, Carota the carver, Andrea di Cosimo the painter, and Andrea del Sarto. The draperies of the figures were designed by Ser Piero da Vinci, Lionardo's father, and Bernardo di Giordano, while Jacopo Pontormo was charged to paint the three cars singlehanded, with scenes in chiaroscuro, representing the transformations of the gods. These are now in the possession of Pietro Paolo Galeotti, an excellent goldsmith. The first car bore the device *Erimus*, the second *Sumus*, the third *Fuimus*. The canzone began: *"Volano gli anni,"* etc.

Sig. Lorenzo, head of the Branch company, having seen these things and desiring to surpass them, gave the charge of all to Jacopo Nardi, a noble and learned man (to whom his native Florence was afterwards much bound). This Jacopo arranged six triumphs, double in number to those of the Diamond. The first, drawn by oxen draped with grass, represented the golden age of Saturn and Janus. At the top of the car were Saturn with the scythe and two-headed Janus holding the keys of the temple of Peace, with Fury bound at his feet, and countless things pertaining to Saturn, beautifully coloured by Pontormo. Six pairs of shepherds accompanied this car, dressed in sable and martin's fur, wearing shoes of antique pattern and with garlands on their heads of many kinds of leaves. The horses on which they rode were without saddles, but covered with the skins of lions, tigers and wolves, the gilded claws of which hung gracefully at the sides. The cruppers had gold cord and the spurs bore the heads of sheep, dogs and other animals. The bridles were made of various kinds of verdure and silver cord. Each shepherd had four footmen dressed as shepherds of a simple kind in other skins, bearing torches made like dry branches and with pine-branches, very beautiful to see. The second car, drawn by two pairs of oxen draped with rich cloth, with garlands at their heads and large beads hanging from their gilt horns, carried Numa Pompilius, second King of the Romans, with the books of religion and all the priestly trappings and necessaries for sacrifice, as he was the first of the Romans to regulate religion and sacrifices. Six priests accompanied the car on handsome mules, their heads covered with cloth hoods embroidered with gold and silver ivy leaves, worked with mastery. They wore ancient sacerdotal vestments, with rich gold borders and fringes, some carrying a censer and some a gold vase or something similar. Their footmen were like Levites, whose torches resembled ancient candelabra. The third car represented the consulship of Titus Manlius Torquatus, consul after the end of the first Carthagenian war, and who governed so that Rome flourished in virtue and prosperity. This car, decorated with many fine ornaments by Pontormo, was drawn by eight fine horses, preceded by six pairs of senators on horseback in togas covered with a gold web, accompanied by lictors with the fasces, axes and other instruments of justice. The fourth car, drawn by buffaloes dressed as elephants, represented Julius Cæsar triumphing for his victory over Cleopatra, on a car painted with his most famous deeds by Pontormo. Six pairs of men-at-arms in rich and shining armour accompanied him, having gold fringes, and with their lances at their sides. Their half-armed footmen carried torches in the form of trophies of different kinds. The fifth car, drawn by winged horses like griffins, had Augustus, the ruler of the universe, accompanied by six pairs of poets on horseback, crowned like Cæsar with laurel and dressed according to their provinces. Each poet bore a scroll inscribed with his name. On the sixth car, drawn by six pairs of heifers richly caparisoned, was the just Emperor Trajan, before whose car, richly painted by Pontormo, rode six pairs of doctors of law, with togas down to their feet and cloaks of ermine, such as they anciently wore. The footmen carrying torches were scribes, copyists and notaries, with books and writings in their hands. After them came the car of the Golden Age, richly made, with many figures in relief by Baccio Bandinelli and beautiful paintings by Pontormo, among which the four cardinal Virtues were much admired. In the midst of the car was a great globe, upon which lay a man, as if dead, his arms all rusted, his back open and emerging therefrom a naked gilded child, representing the Golden Age revived by the creation of the Pope and the end of the Iron Age from which it issued. The dried branch putting forth new leaves had the same signification, although some said that it was an allusion to Lorenzo de' Medici, Duke of Urbino. The gilt boy, the child of a baker, who had been paid 10 crowns, died soon after of the effects. The canzone sung at the masquerade was composed by Jacopo Nardi; the first stanza ran thus:

> Colui che da le leggi alla natura,
> E i varj stati e secoli dispone,
> D'ogni bene è cagione
> E il mal, quanto permette, al mondo dura:
> Onde, questa figura
> Contemplando, si vede
> Come con certo piede
> L'un secol dopo l'altro al mondo viene,
> E muta il bene in mal e'l mal in bene.[1]

[1] He who makes Nature's laws and disposes of principalities and the ages is the source of all good, and when He allows it evil oppresses the world. Hence, in contemplating this figure you may see how surely one age follows another and how the good changes to ill and the ill to good.

From his work for this feast Pontormo won much advantage and more praise than probably any youth of his age had ever obtained in the city. Thus when Pope Leo afterwards came to Florence he was much employed on the preparations. With Baccio da Montelupo, a sculptor of the age, who made a wooden arch at the top of the via del Palagio, from the steps of Badia, he painted some beautiful scenes, which afterwards suffered from the negligence of those who had charge of them. One only remained, a Pallas tuning her instrument to the lyre of Apollo with much grace. The excellence of the other scenes may be judged from this.

In the same festivities Ridolfo Ghirlandajo was charged to embellish the Pope's hall, adjoining the convent of S. Maria Novella, the ancient residence of the pontiffs in the city. Being pressed for time, he was forced to employ assistance. Having decorated all the other rooms, he charged Pontormo to do some frescoes in the chapel [1] where the Pope heard Mass every morning. Jacopo did a God the Father with cherubs, and a Veronica with the face of Christ on a handkerchief, a work that was much admired though done in such haste. In a chapel in S. Raffaello, behind the Archivescovado of Florence, he painted a Madonna and Child between St. Michael and St. Lucy, and two other saints kneeling, and a God the Father surrounded by seraphim in the lunette of the chapel. Maestro Jacopo, a Servite friar, afterwards allotted to him a part of the Servite cloister, a thing he had greatly desired, because Andrea del Sarto had gone to France and left the work there unfinished. Jacopo made the cartoons with great care, but being in poor circumstances, and as he had to live while striving to acquire honour, he did two beautiful figures above the door of the Women's Hospital, behind the church of the hospital of the priests, between the piazza of S. Marco and the via di Sangallo, opposite the wall of the sisters of St. Catherine of Siena. These were Christ as a pilgrim receiving some women into the hospital, a work that has always been deservedly praised. At the same time he painted some pictures in oils for the masters of the mint on the car of the Moneta, which goes in procession every St. John's day, the car being made by Marco del Tasso. Over the door of the company of la Cecilia, on the hill of Fiesole, he did a St. Cecilia in fresco, holding roses, one of the most beautiful frescoes in existence. When Maestro Jacopo, the Servite friar, had seen these works, his desire was greatly kindled, and he hoped to

[1] Done in 1513.

get Pontormo to finish the cloister, thinking that the competition with the other masters who had worked there would spur him to produce something extraordinarily fine. Jacopo did a Visitation in a manner somewhat more elegant than his wont, being moved as much by his desire for honour and glory as for gain. This gave his work much greater beauty, for the women, children, youths and old men are rendered so charming, in such harmonious colouring, that it is a marvel. The flesh-colouring of a boy seated on some steps and that of all the other figures is such that it cannot be surpassed for softness. By these and his other works Jacopo took rank beside Andrea del Sarto and Franciabigio, who had laboured there. He finished the task in 1516, only receiving 16 crowns for it. I remember well that Francesco Pucci allotted to him the altarpiece of a chapel which he had erected in S. Michele Bisdomini, in the via de' Servi. Jacopo executed this with marvellous style and in brilliant colouring. He represents the Virgin seated offering the Infant Jesus to St. Joseph, who is laughing in a wonderfully natural manner. Very beautiful also are the little St. John the Baptist and two other naked boys supporting a canopy. Here also are St. John the Evangelist, a fine old man, and a St. Francis kneeling, with clasped hands, and intently regarding the Virgin and Child, so that he seems to be breathing. No less fine is St. James at the side. It is the finest picture ever produced by this rare painter.[1] I think it was afterwards that he did for Bartolommeo Lanfredini in Lung Arno, between the S. Trinità and the Carraia bridges, in a passage, two graceful boys in fresco above a door supporting a scutcheon. But Bronzino, who deserves credence in these things, declares that they were among the first things executed by Jacopo. If so, Pontormo deserves the more praise, for they are of unequalled beauty.

To continue: Jacopo next did a panel for the men of Pontormo, which was placed in the chapel of the Madonna in their principal church of S. Agnolo. It represents St. Michael and St. John the Evangelist. At this time a youth called Giovanmaria Pichi of Borgo a S. Sepolcro was staying with Jacopo, and did very well, becoming a Servite friar afterwards, while he executed some works in the Pieve at S. Stefano. With Jacopo he painted a large Martyrdom of St. Quentin to be sent to the Borgo, but as Jacopo wished him to win honour, he retouched it, and being unable to leave it, he thus finished the whole, the picture may therefore be called his, so that it is no wonder

[1] Dated 1518.

that it is very beautiful. It is now in the Observantine church of S. Francesco at the Borgo. Another apprentice, Giovanni Antonio Lappoli of Arezzo, mentioned elsewhere, drew himself in a mirror while with Jacopo, who did not think the likeness good, and drew an admirable portrait of him himself. This is now at Arezzo in the house of the youth's heirs. Pontormo also portrayed two of his friends in one picture, one the son-in-law of Becuccio Becchieraio and another whose name I do not know. For Bartolommeo Ginori he did some hangings for use after his death, according to a Florentine custom. In the upper part he did a Virgin and Child on white taffeta, and the arms of the family beneath. In the middle of the hangings, formed of twenty-four pieces of white taffeta, he did two St. Bartholomews, two braccia high. This new style made all the others executed before look poor and insignificant, and led to the large style of to-day which is very light and less costly. At the top of the garden and vineyard of the friars of S. Gallo outside the S. Gallo gate Jacopo did a dead Christ, a weeping Virgin and two cherubs in the air, in a chapel in a line with the entrance. One of the cherubs holds the cup and the other supports Christ's head. On one side is St. John in tears, with his arms open, on the other St. Augustine in the episcopal habit, leaning sadly and thoughtfully on his pastoral staff, contemplating the Saviour's death. For M. Spina, familiar of Giovanni Salviati, he did the latter's arms, who had been created cardinal by Pope Leo,[1] in a court opposite the principal door of the house, with the red hat and two cherubs, of great beauty and much valued by M. Filippo Spina as Pontormo's work. Jacopo also did the wood decoration for some apartments of Pierfrancesco Borgherini in conjunction with other masters, notably the history of Joseph in small figures of great beauty, on two chests. But his best work, which shows his genius in the vivacity of heads, composition of figures, variety of attitudes and beauty of invention, may be seen in this chamber of Borgherini, a Florentine nobleman, on the left of the side entrance. It is a representation in small figures of Joseph in Egypt receiving his father Jacob and all his brethren.[2] Among these figures he introduced Bronzino, his pupil, then a child, at the foot of the scene, seated on some steps, with a basket, a marvellously life-like and beautiful figure. If this picture had been large I venture to say that it would not be possible to match it for grace, perfection and excellence, and artists consider it Jacopo's best work. No wonder then that

[1] In 1517. [2] Now in the National Gallery, London.

Borgherini valued it or that great men wished him to sell it to present to lords and princes.

Pierfrancesco having withdrawn to Lucca because of the siege of Florence, Giovanni Battista della Palla, who desired the ornaments of this room, with other things to be taken to France to present to King Francis in the name of the Signoria, induced the gonfaloniere and Signori to take it and pay the wife of Pierfrancesco. But when he went to the house the lady confronted him. "Do you venture to come here, vile bagman," she said, "to rob the decorations of noblemen and deprive the city of its richest possessions to adorn foreign countries hostile to us? I do not wonder at you, who are a base-born man and the enemy of your country, but I marvel that the magistrates permit such abominable rascality. This bed, which is the object of your lust for money, is my marriage-bed, in honour of which my brother-in-law Salvi had all this decoration prepared, and I honour it in memory of him and for love of my husband, and I will defend it with my life. Leave this house with your baggage, and tell those who sent you that I will not allow any of these things to be removed from their places, and if those who trust in such a vile creature as you wish to present something to King Francis, let them despoil their own houses. If you are so rash as to enter this place again I will teach you the respect due by such as you to the houses of nobles." These words of Madonna Margherita, who was daughter of Ruberto Acciaiuoli, a noble and prudent citizen, being herself a lady of spirit, preserved these treasures for her house.

Giovannimaria Benintendi about the same time decorated an ante-chamber with pictures by various artists, imitating Jacopo's work for the Borgherini. Jacopo, being much encouraged by praise, did an Adoration of the Magi,[1] and by dint of much study and diligence he rendered the heads and other parts varied, beautiful and worthy of all praise. For M. Goro da Pistoia, then secretary of the Medici, he did an admirable three-quarter figure of Cosimo de' Medici the elder,[2] now in the house of M. Ottaviano de' Medici, in the possession of his son M. Alessandro, a youth of holy life, learned, and a worthy son of his father and of Madonna Francesca, daughter of Jacopo Salviati, and aunt of Duke Cosimo. By these works, especially the last, Pontormo had won the friendship of M. Ottaviano, and he was commissioned[3] to paint the two ends of the great hall of Poggio a Caiano, where the two round windows

---

[1] Now in the Pitti Gallery.   [2] Uffizi Gallery.   [3] In 1521.

are, from the ceiling to the floor. Wishing to do better than usual in such a place, and in competition with the other painters engaged there, Jacopo showed himself over anxious, as he kept doing and effacing his things, though he was always making new discoveries for the embellishment of the work. Thus he represented a countryman seated with a pruning-knife in his hand for Vertumnus, executed with great beauty, and some infants there are very life-like and natural. In his Pomona and Diana on the other side he perhaps involved their draperies too much, though the whole work is beautiful and much praised. But meanwhile Leo died, and the work was left unfinished, like many others at Rome, Florence, Loreto and elsewhere, when the world lost that true Mæcenas.

On returning to Florence Jacopo did a St. Augustine seated and giving the benediction, with two beautiful nude infants flying in the air. This is over an altar in the little church of the sisters of St. Clemente in the via di S. Gallo. He also completed a Pietà with some nude angels, a beautiful work, highly valued by the Ragusan merchants, for whom he did it. It contained a fine landscape, mostly copied from a print of Albert Dürer. He also did a Virgin and Child with some cherubs, now in the house of Alessandro Neroni, and another Madonna, different in style, for some Spaniards, which Bronzino was commissioned to buy for M. Bartolommeo Panciatichi at a sale many years after.

In 1522, when the plague broke out in Florence, so that many fled to escape the infection, Jacopo took the opportunity to leave the city. The prior of the Certosa, a house built by the Acciaiuoli, three miles from Florence, wished to have some fresco paintings at the corners of a large and beautiful cloister surrounding a lawn, and gave them to Jacopo, who readily accepted the work, and went there, accompanied by Bronzino only. Enjoying the quiet and solitude so dear to him, Jacopo thought it a good opportunity to study and to embellish and vary his style. Not long before a good number of delicate engravings by Albert Dürer had come to Florence, and among others some scenes of the Passion of Christ, of the utmost perfection in beauty, variety in the costumes and invention. Jacopo proposed to make use of them in the cloister, expecting thus to give satisfaction to himself and to most of the Florentine artists, who with one accord praised these engravings. Jacopo therefore sought to endow his figures with the expressions, vigour and variety possessed by those of Albert, and thus lost the natural sweetness and grace of his first manner, exchanging it for the German style, so that, though his later works are beautiful, his figures lack their former excellence and grace. At the entrance to the cloister he did Christ in the Garden, the darkness illuminated by the moon, so that it seems almost daylight. As Christ prays, Peter, James and John are sleeping, a marvellous imitation of Dürer. Not far off, Judas is bringing the Jews, with a curious expression like that of all the soldiers, who are done in the German style, so that they excite our compassion for the artist, who took such pains to learn what others avoid, abandoning a good style which pleased everyone. Was not Pontormo aware that Germans and Flemings come to learn the Italian style which he made such efforts to shake off as if it was bad? Next this is Christ led before Pilate, the Saviour displaying the humility of His innocence abandoned to wicked men, and Pilate's wife her compassion and fear of the divine judgment, and, as she pleads for Christ to her husband, she regards Him with a pitying wonder. Pilate is surrounded by soldiers, German in costume and expression, and anyone who did not know the artist might suppose this the work of an ultramontane. It is true that in the distance there is a servant of Pilate mounting some steps, carrying a basin and jug to wash his master's hands, very life-like, and showing something of Jacopo's old style. For a Resurrection in another corner Jacopo had the caprice to change his colouring, his brain always evolving new things, and he made it so sweet and good that if he had adopted another style than the German the work would have been most beautiful, the soldiers who are lying asleep in various attitudes, like death, seeming unsurpassable. He continued in another corner with Christ bearing the Cross, followed by the people of Jerusalem, the two naked thieves going before, between the executioners, some of whom are on foot and some mounted, with ladders, the title of the cross, hammers, nails, ropes and other tools. Behind a hillock is the Virgin with the Maries weeping as they regard Christ, who has fallen to the ground, while the Jews are beating Him and Veronica offers Him the handkerchief, accompanied by old and young women weeping at the Saviour's sufferings. This scene proved much better than the others, perhaps because Jacopo recognised the harm done to his style by his study of German work, or because he had been warned by friends. Some naked Jews and heads of old men are finely executed in fresco, although he has preserved the German style for the whole. In the other corners he continued with the Crucifixion and Deposition from the Cross. But he left them, intending to do these last, and did instead a Deposition in the same style, but with harmonious colouring. Besides a beautiful Magdalene kissing Christ's feet, two old men representing Joseph of Arimathea and Nicodemus, although in the German style, have the most beautiful expression imaginable, with downy beards and soft colouring.

As the quiet of the Certosa pleased Jacopo, he devoted several years to this work, and when the plague was over and he had returned to Florence, he continued to frequent the place, and obliged the friars in many ways. Among other things he did the portrait of a lay brother then living, and aged one hundred and twenty, over a door leading into the chapel, so well executed and so life-like that it alone excuses Pontormo for his fancies when in that lonely place far from men. For the prior's chamber he did a Nativity, with a light on Christ's face in the darkness, thrown by Joseph holding a lantern, of the same order of ideas that he derived from the German prints. Let no one blame Jacopo for imitating Albert Dürer, because many painters have done it and do so still. But he did wrong in adopting that stiff style for everything, the draperies, expression and attitudes, which should be avoided when borrowing the ideas, as he had a graceful and beautiful modern style. For the guest-chamber he did a large canvas in oils, without apparent effort, of Christ with Cleophas and Luke, of life-size,[1] and, as he followed his genius, it proved a marvellous success, for among the servants he introduced the portraits of some friars whom I have known, making marvellous likenesses.

Bronzino, while his master was thus engaged, pursued his study of painting, being encouraged thereto by Pontormo, who loved his pupils. Without ever having seen colouring in oils, he did a fine nude St. Laurence on the gridiron on the wall over the cloister door leading to the church, showing signs of the excellence to which he afterwards attained, and delighting Jacopo, who already foresaw his future success. Not long after, Ludovico di Gino Capponi having returned from Rome, and having brought the chapel in S. Felicità which Brunnellesco erected for the Barbadori, on the right on entering the church, resolved to have it richly decorated. He accordingly consulted his friend M. Niccolo Vespucci, a knight of Rhodes, who, being a friend of Jacopo, praised his genius, so that Ludovico allotted the chapel to him. He built a screen and shut off the chapel

[1] Painted in 1528; now in the Uffizi, Florence.

for three years. On the vaulting he did God the Father surrounded by the four Patriarchs, and at the four circles at the
angles he did the Evangelists, giving one to Bronzino. I must
add that Pontormo hardly ever made use of his apprentices,
or allowed them to touch his own work, but when he did, usually
for purposes of instruction, he let them do the whole alone, as
Bronzino did here. In his works in the chapel Jacopo appears to
have returned to this first manner, but not in the picture, as
he devised a novelty, executing it in such level colouring that it
is hard to distinguish the lights from the half-tints, and the
half-tints from the shadows. It represents a dead Christ being
carried to the sepulchre, with the Virgin and the other Maries, in
an utterly different style from the first, showing how his brain
was seeking for new fancies and was not content with holding fast to one. The composition and colouring are altogether
different from the painting of the vaulting, and the four Evangelists, in a different style, are much better. On the window
wall are the Virgin, and the angel annunciating, showing his
curious ideas and how he never rested content. While he was
engaged upon this work he would not allow even the patron
to see it, in order that he might do it in his own way, and when
it was finally uncovered, without his friends knowing anything
about it, all Florence marvelled. For a chamber of the same
Ludovico he did a Madonna in the same style, and represented
a daughter of his, a very beautiful maiden, as St. Mary Magdalene. Near the monastery of Boldrone, at the junction of the
Cestello road with the one that mounts the hill to Cercina, two
miles from Florence, he did in a tabernacle Christ on the Cross,
the Virgin weeping, St. John the Evangelist, St. Augustine and
St. Julian, all in the German style, for he had not yet rid himself
of the fancy, and not unlike those done at the Certosa. For the
nuns of St. Anna at the S. Friano gate he did a panel of the
Virgin and Child, St. Anne behind, St. Peter, St. Benedict, and
other saints.[1] The predella in small figures represents the Signoria of Florence going in procession, with drums, fifes, mace-
bearers, commendatories, and the rest of the household, because
the panel was commissioned by the captain of the palace. While
Jacopo was engaged upon this, Silvio Passerini, cardinal of
Cortona, was sent to Rome, with Alessandro and Ippolito de'
Medici, by Clement VII., and Ottaviano the Magnificent, to
whom the Pope recommended them, employed Pontormo to
paint their portraits[2]; he did excellent ones, although he did not

---

[1] Painted 1543; now in the Louvre.   [2] In 1524.

depart much from his German style. With Ippolito he drew a
favourite dog called Rodon, making it appear alive.[1] He also
drew Bishop Ardinghelli, afterwards cardinal, and for his friend
Filippo del Migliore he painted a Pomona in his house in the
via Larga, where he seems to be attempting to throw off his
German style somewhat. Gio. Battista della Palla, observing
Jacopo to be daily becoming more famous and not having
succeeded in getting his paintings and those of others to send
to King Francis, resolved to send the king something by Pontormo, as he knew his Majesty desired it. He at length succeeded
in inducing him to do a fine Resurrection of Lazarus, one of his
best works, and it was sent among others to King Francis.
The heads were very beautiful, and Lazarus reviving from the
dead is marvellous, having the green about the eyes and dead
flesh at the ends of his feet and hands. In a picture of one and
a half braccia for the nuns of the hospital of the Innocenti, he
did the history of the eleven thousand martyrs crucified in a
wood by order of Diocletian,[2] containing a cavalry battle and
fine nudes, and some cherubs in the air shooting arrows at the
executioners. The emperor is also surrounded by some fine nudes
going to their death. This picture, admirable in every part, is
now greatly valued by Don Vincenzio Borghini, master of the
hospital, and a former friend of Jacopo. He made one like it
for Carlo Neroni, with the martyrs only and the angel baptising, and Carlo's portrait. At the time of the siege of Florence
he drew the portrait of Francesco Guardi, dressed as a soldier,
a fine work. On the cover of this work Bronzino painted Pyg-
malion praying Venus to make his statue live, as we read in
the poets. At this time, after long toil, Jacopo obtained what he
had long desired, a house of his own, where he could live as
he pleased, for he bought one in the via della Colonna, opposite
the nuns of S. Maria degli Angeli. When the siege was over,
Pope Clement directed Ottaviano de' Medici to have the hall
of Poggio a Caiano completed. Franciabigio and Andrea del
Sarto being dead, the care of it was entirely entrusted to Pontormo. After making his scaffolding, he began on the cartoons,
but in the midst of his ceaseless fancies he did not begin to
work. This might not have happened if Bronzino had been near,
but he was then working at Imperiale, a place of the Duke of
Urbino, near Pesaro, and although daily summoned by Jacopo
he could not leave his post. When he had decorated a vaulting

---

[1] Possibly the man with the dog in the Pitti Gallery.
[2] Now in the Pitti Gallery, with a replica in the Uffizi.

at Imperiale with a fine nude cupid, the Prince Guidobaldo, who knew the youth's skill, commanded him to paint his portrait. But as the prince wished to be painted in some armour which he was expecting from Lombardy, Bronzino was forced to stay longer than he intended. Meanwhile he painted the case for a harpsichord, which greatly delighted the prince. Bronzino afterwards completed the portrait, greatly to the satisfaction of the prince.

Jacopo wrote so many times that at length Bronzino went, but could not succeed in inducing his master to make anything but cartoons, in spite of the entreaties of Ottaviano the Magnificent and Duke Alessandro. One of these cartoons, most of which are now in the house of Ludovico Capponi, represents Hercules crushing Antæus, another Venus and Adonis, and a sheet of nudes playing ball. Sig. Alfonso Davalo, Marquis of il Guasto, having obtained a cartoon of a *Noli me tangere* by means of Frà Niccolo della Magna, by Michelagnolo, tried every way to induce Jacopo to execute it in painting, for Buonarroti had said that no one could do it better. This work, when completed, was considered marvellous for the grandeur of Michelagnolo's design and the colouring of Jacopo. When Sig. Alessandro Vitelli, then captain of the guard at Florence, had seen it, he made Jacopo do him another from the same cartoon and had it placed in his house at Città di Castello. It being seen how highly Michelagnolo esteemed Pontormo and how excellently the latter executed the designs of the former, Bartolommeo Bettini induced his friend Michelagnolo to make a cartoon of a nude Venus with a cupid kissing her, to be painted by Pontormo and put in the middle of a room of his, in the lunettes of which Bronzino had begun to paint Dante, Petrarch and Boccaccio, intending to represent the other Tuscan lyric poets there. Jacopo executed this cartoon at his ease, in a style known to all the world, so that I need not stop to praise it. These designs led Pontormo to consider the style of Michelagnolo, and he resolved to imitate it so far as he was able. He then saw his mistake in letting slip such work as that of Poggio a Caiano, and he blamed for it a long sickness and finally the death of Pope Clement, which stopped everything there. Jacopo had done a portrait of Amerigo Antinori, a youth very popular in Florence at that time. The portrait being universally praised, Duke Alessandro intimated to Jacopo that he desired a large one of himself. For greater convenience Jacopo made the portrait on a half-sheet of paper with as much care as an illumination, and besides being a good likeness it contains every requisite of a good painting. From this, which is now in Duke Cosimo's wardrobe, Jacopo copied another portrait of the duke holding a pen and drawing a woman's head. The duke gave this to Signora Taddea Malespina, sister of the Marchioness of Massa. The duke, wishing to reward Jacopo, told his servant Niccolo da Montaguto to get him to ask what he wanted and it would be granted. But so great was the pusillanimity, respect or modesty of this man that he only asked for enough money to redeem a mantle which he had pawned. When the duke heard this he laughed, and gave him 50 gold crowns and the offer of a pension, though Niccolo had hard work to make him accept it.

Jacopo having finished the Venus from Bettini's cartoon with marvellous success, it was not given to Bettini for the price which Jacopo had promised, but was taken out of Jacopo's hands by some fortune-hunters, almost by force, out of spite to Bettini, and then presented to Duke Alessandro, the cartoon being restored to Bettini. When Michelagnolo heard this he was sorry for his friend and bore a grudge against Jacopo, who, though he received 50 crowns from the duke, cannot be said to have defrauded Bettini, for he had only obeyed his prince's command. But some say it was Bettini's fault for wanting too much. With this money Pontormo had a chance of repairing his house. He began to build, but he did not do anything of importance. Thus, though some say he intended to spend a great deal for his state and make a convenient and artistic abode, yet it has rather the appearance of the dwelling of a fantastic and solitary man than a well-considered house. The room where he slept and sometimes worked was approached by a wooden ladder which he drew up after him, so that no one could come up without his knowledge or permission. But what aroused more dissatisfaction was that he would only work when he wished, and being often requested to do things by noblemen, and notably on one occasion by M. Ottaviano de' Medici, he would not serve them, but would then begin something for some plebeian instead at a low price. Thus Rossino, a clever mason, received from him in payment for some building a beautiful Madonna, upon which Jacopo took as much pains as the mason did over his work. Rossino also succeeded in obtaining from Jacopo a fine portrait of Cardinal Giulio de Medici, copied from one by Raphael, and also a beautiful crucifix. But though Ottaviano bought this from Rossino as a work of Jacopo, it is certain that it is by Bronzino, who did it by himself while with Jacopo at the Certosa, although it remained in Pontormo's possession, I do not know why. These three paintings are now in the house of M. Alessandro de' Medici, Ottaviano's son. But although these proceedings and this solitary life of Pontormo's are blameworthy, it is easy to excuse him, and he might well do the works which he liked and leave the others without blame. No artist is bound to work except when and for whom he pleases, and he alone suffers from his course of action. As for solitude, I have always heard that it is the friend of study, but even if it were not, I do not think that we ought to blame one who, without offending God and his neighbour, lives after his own fashion in the way best suited to his temperament.

But to return to the works of Jacopo. Duke Alessandro having restored the villa of Careggi, built by Cosimo de' Medici the elder, two miles from Florence, and executed the decoration of the fountain and the labyrinth in the middle of an open court, directed that the two loggias facing it should be painted by Jacopo with assistance, in order that it might be done more quickly, and so that the conversation would render him more cheerful and make him work without troubling his brain with various fancies. The duke himself sent for Jacopo, and asked him to finish the work as soon as possible. Jacopo therefore sent for Bronzino, and in the five compartments of the vaulting made him do figures, namely Fortune, Justice, Victory, Peace and Fame, and at the sixth Jacopo himself did a Love. He then designed some cherubs in the oval of the vaulting with various animals, foreshortened from below all except one being coloured by Bronzino, who did excellently. While Jacopo and Bronzino were engaged upon these figures, Jacone, Pierfrancesco di Jacopo and others did the surrounding decoration, and so the whole work was soon finished, to the delight of the duke, who wished to have the other loggia painted. But there was not time, for the work being finished on 13 December, 1536, the duke was assassinated by his kinsman Lorenzino on 6 January following. On the succession of Duke Cosimo, followed by the successful affair of Montemurlo, the work of Castello was begun, as related in the Life of Tribolo. The duke, to please Donna Maria, his mother, directed Jacopo to paint the first loggia on the left on entering the palace. Here, after designing the ornaments, he gave it to Bronzino to execute and to the others who had worked at Careggi. He then shut himself up and continued the work at his ease, endeavouring to surpass the work at

Careggi, which he had not done entirely by himself. He could easily do so, for he received 8 crowns a month from the duke, whom he drew, young as he was, at the beginning of the work, with Donna Maria, his mother. The scaffolding having stood for five years, and no one being able to see what Jacopo had done, the lady became angry and one day commanded that it should be pulled down. But Jacopo had been warned, and obtaining some days' grace he retouched where he thought it necessary. He then devised a canvas to cover it when the quality were not there so that the air should not damage it, as had happened at Careggi. Great expectations had been raised, as it was thought that Jacopo would have surpassed himself and produced a stupendous work. However, the work did not altogether realise these expectations, for, although many particulars are good, the figures are out of proportion and their attitudes seem strange and ill regulated. But Jacopo excused himself by saying that he did not like the place, because, being outside the city, it was exposed to the fury of the soldiers and other accidents. However, the air and time are gradually destroying it, as he did it in oils on dry lime. In the middle of the vaulting he did Saturn with the sign of Capricorn, and Mars Hermaphroditus in the signs of Leo and Virgo, with some flying cherubs like those at Careggi. He then did large female figures, almost nude, of Philosophy, Astrology, Geometry, Music, Arithmetic and a Ceres, with small circular scenes in various tints appropriate to the figures. But although all this labour did not give great satisfaction, at least much less than was expected, the duke expressed himself as pleased, and employed Jacopo at every opportunity, for the artist was much esteemed by the people for his numerous beautiful works in the past.

The duke having brought to Florence the Flemings Giovanni Rosso and Niccolo,[1] excellent masters of arras, to teach the art to the Florentines, directed that gold and silk hangings should be made for the council chamber of the Two Hundred, at a cost of 60,000 crowns, and that Jacopo and Bronzino should prepare cartoons of the history of Joseph. Jacopo having done one of the Death of Joseph announced to Jacob, and another of Joseph and Potiphar's wife, the duke and the masters did not like them, thinking them strange and unsuitable for the medium, and so Jacopo did no more. Returning to his accustomed work, he did a Madonna, presented by the duke to Don . . ., who took it to Spain. The duke, following in the footsteps of his ancestors, has

[1] John Rost and Nicholas Kercker.

always sought to decorate his city, and he now resolved to paint the principal chapel of the magnificent church of S. Lorenzo, erected by Cosimo de' Medici the elder. He gave this to Jacopo either of his own notion or by means of M. Pierfrancesco Ricci, major-domo, as is said. Jacopo was delighted, because of the importance of the work, he being well advanced in years and feeling that he had such an opportunity to display his talents. Some say that when he heard the work had been allotted to him, notwithstanding that Francesco Salviati, a famous painter, was in Florence and had decorated the audience-chamber of the palace of the Signoria, he declared he would show how designing and painting in fresco should be done, that other painters were commonplace, and similar insolent speeches. But as I always knew him to be a modest man who spoke well of all, as a good artist should, I do not believe he ever uttered such boasts, which are the sayings of vain and presumptuous men without talent or character. I would have preferred not to mention this except that I believe it to be my duty as a veracious historian. If such reports were circulated, they were spread abroad by the malicious, for Jacopo was always modest.

Having shut himself up alone in the chapel, Jacopo kept the place closed for eleven years, so that not a living soul entered it except himself. It is indeed true that some youths who were drawing in the sacristy of Michelagnolo climbed on to the roof, as boys will, and lifting the tiles and gilt bosses saw everything. When Jacopo heard it he took it very ill, but made no other sign except to cover up everything with more diligence than ever. Some say that he harassed and annoyed the youths greatly. He expected to surpass all the painters, even perhaps Michelagnolo, so it was said. In the upper part he did the creation of Adam and Eve, the Fall, the expulsion from Paradise, Tilling the Soil, the Sacrifice of Abel, the Death of Cain, the Blessing of the Seed of Noah, and the designing of the Ark. He decorated the lower walls, which are fifteen braccia square, with the Flood, containing a mass of drowned bodies, and Noah speaking with God, the general resurrection of the dead, with a universal and general confusion such as will probably take place on the last day. Opposite the altar, between the windows, is a row of nudes forming a ladder from the earth to paradise, many dead being there, and two of them clothed except the legs and arms, and holding lighted torches, forming the ends. At the top and in the middle he did Christ in majesty surrounded by nude angels, and raising the dead for judgment. I have never been able to understand the meaning of this scene, but I know that Jacopo was an ingenious man and associated with the learned. I mean what he intended by Christ raising the dead, with God the Father beneath him creating Adam and Eve. At one corner are the Evangelists, nude figures with books in their hands, and I do not think he has anywhere observed the order of the scene, measure, time, variety of the heads, changes in the flesh-tints, or any rule, proportion or perspective. The whole is full of nudes, arranged, designed and coloured after his fashion, with so much melancholy as to afford little pleasure to the observer, for even I, though a painter, do not understand it, and it seems to me that in this labour of eleven years Jacopo has sought to bewilder both himself and those who see the work.[1] It contains some torsos with their shoulders turned forward and sides, done with marvellous study and labour, and Jacopo made clay models for nearly all. However, the work is not in his usual style, and everyone feels it to be without measure, the torsos being mostly large and the legs and arms small, not to speak of the heads, which lack that singular grace and excellence which he used to give and which afford such pleasure in his other paintings. He seems indeed to have taken pains with some parts and neglected others of more importance. Thus, whereas he hoped to surpass all artists, he fell far short of his own previous efforts, and so we see that when men wish to force Nature they ruin their natural endowments. But we cannot fail to pity him, for artists are prone to error like other men, and even Homer is said to have sometimes slept, while all of Jacopo's works contain some good parts, no matter how much he forced Nature. He died shortly before finishing this work, some say of grief and dissatisfaction with himself, but the truth is, he was old and worn out in making portraits, clay models and fresco-work, and he fell into a dropsy, of which he died at the age of sixty-five. After his death many beautiful designs, cartoons and clay models were found in his house, and a fine Madonna in good style, apparently executed many years before. It was subsequently sold by his heirs to Piero Salviati. Jacopo was buried in the first cloister of the church of the Servites, below his own Visitation, being followed by all the painters, sculptors and architects. He was a frugal and temperate man, rather wretched in his manner of life and clothing, and he almost always lived alone, without anyone to serve or cook for him. However, in his last years, he adopted Battista Naldini, a youth of good intelligence, who took as much

[1] It was uncovered in 1558, but all whitewashed over in 1738.

care of Jacopo as the latter would permit. Under Jacopo he made
considerable progress in design, and excited the highest expectations. Pontormo's friends, especially at the end of his life, were
Pierfrancesco Vernacci and Don Vincenzio Borghini, with whom
he relaxed occasionally and dined with them. But he always
cherished a great affection for Bronzino, who returned it, being
grateful for the benefits received. Jacopo had strange notions,
and was so fearful of death that he never allowed it to be mentioned, and he avoided dead bodies. He never went to feasts or
to other places where crowds collected for fear of being crushed,
and he was solitary beyond belief. Sometimes when he went to
work he would fall into such deep thought that he came away
at the end of the day without having done anything but think.
This frequently occurred while he was engaged at S. Lorenzo, as
may readily be believed, for when he had made up his mind he
was not deterred by anything from carrying out what he had
proposed, like a clever and skilful man.

SIMONE MOSCA, Sculptor and Architect
(1492 – 1553)

No one except Simone Mosca of Settignano has ever equalled
the beautiful works of the Greeks and Romans in bases, capitals,
friezes, cornices, festoons, trophies, masks, candelabra, birds,
arabesques, or other such carvings. In our own day he has shown
by his genius that his predecessors in that work had not been
able to imitate the excellence of the ancients or to adopt the true
method of carving, for their works tend to be dry and crude in
the turning of foliage, while he has made them rich and bold,
with the finest leaves, flowers and fruits, not to speak of the
birds gracefully carved in his festoons, so that we may say that
he alone, with all respect to the others, has been able to rid
marble of the hardness frequently given to it by sculptors, and
made his things appear real; and we may say the same of his
cornices and other similar works, executed with grace and
judgment.

Having studied design with great success in his childhood,
and then become skilful in carving, he was taken to Rome by
Maestro Antonio da Sangallo, who recognised his genius. There
he began by doing some capitals and bases, and a frieze of

foliage for the Florentine church of S. Giovanni, and some works for the palace of Alessandro, first Cardinal Farnese. He spent feast days and his spare time in drawing the antiquities of the city, and before long he drew and made plans more gracefully and clearly than Antonio himself. He studied ancient foliage, the turns of the leaves, and, selecting the best things, he became in a few years so universal that he could do anything alone, as we see by some arms for the church of S. Giovanni in Strada Giulia, in one of which he made a large lily, the ancient device of the commune of Florence, with a background of leaves and vine-tendrils of marvellous design. Before long, when Antonio da Sangallo was directing the marble ornament for a chapel and tomb of M. Agnolo Cesis, afterwards built in 1550 in S. Maria della Pace, he employed Simone to do a part of some pilasters and bases full of friezes. Simone acquitted himself so well that his work may be distinguished from the rest by its grace and perfection. Better altars for sacrifice in the antique style cannot be seen than those he did for the basement here. Sangallo, when doing a well-head in the cloister of S. Piero ad Vincola, employed Mosca to adorn the shaft with some beautiful masks. Returning in the summer to Florence with a good name among artists, Simone did the festoons and other carving for Bandinelli's Orpheus in the court of the Medici palace, for which Benedetto da Rovezzano made the pedestal, although one festoon is only sketched. After doing several things in macigno, which I need not mention, Simone proposed to return to Rome, but was prevented by the sack. So he took a wife and remained in Florence, where he accepted everything, for he had no income. In those days Pietro de Subisso, an Aretine master mason, came to Florence. He constantly employed a number of workmen, as all the buildings of Arezzo passed through his hands. Among many other things Simone did for him a macigno chimneypiece for a hall, and a laver of no great value in Arezzo, in the house of the heirs of Pellegrino da Fossombrone, citizen of Arezzo, originally built by M. Piero Geri, a famous astrologer, from designs by Andrea Sansovino, and sold by his nephews. Simone rested his chimneypiece upon two pilasters, making two niches in the thickness on the fireside. Over the pilasters he put an architrave, frieze and cornice, and a slab above with festoons and the arms of the family. He executed the work with such mastery that although of macigno it looked finer than marble, and it was easier to work than marble, being rather sandy. On the pilasters he made trophies in half-relief and bas-relief, of unequalled beauty and quaintness, with helmets, shoes, targes and other armour. He also introduced masks, marine monsters and other graceful fancies made to look like silver. The frieze between the architrave and the cornice contains finely turned foliage, full of birds so well made that they seem to be flying, and their little legs, no larger than nature, cut in the stone, are marvellous to see, and appear impossible to do ; indeed the work is a veritable miracle. In a festoon he made leaves and fruit, cut with such diligence that they seem almost to surpass Nature. It also contains fine masks and chandeliers, and although Simone need not have devoted so much labour upon work for which he was very poorly paid, his love for art and his delight in work made him do so. But he did not do the same with the laver there, which, though beautiful, is not remarkable. At the same time he assisted Piero di Sobisso, who did not know much, in designs for constructions, plans of houses, doors, windows and other matters of his profession. At the corner of the Albergotti, below the school and studium of the commune, is a fine window designed by him, and there are two in the house of Ser. Bernardino Serragli at Pellicceria. At the corner of the friar's palace there is an escutcheon by him of Clement VII. in macigno. A macigno chapel of the Corinthian order, erected in the black monk's abbey of S. Fiore at Arezzo for Bernardino di Cristofano da Giuovi, was designed and partly executed by him. He wanted the patron to have the altarpiece there done by Andrea del Sarto, and then by Rosso, but one thing and another prevented it. At length he turned to Giorgio Vasari, when difficulties again presented themselves. The artist endeavoured, however, to manage it. The chapel being dedicated to St. James and St. Christopher, he wanted a Virgin and Child, and St. Christopher with the Christ-child on his shoulder. It was impossible to make a giant of six braccia in a picture of four. But as Giorgio wished to oblige Bernardino he made a design thus. He placed the Madonna in the clouds with the sun behind her back. On the ground knelt St. Christopher with one leg in the water, while the Virgin placed the Christ-child, holding the globe, on his shoulder. He distributed St. James and the other saints so as not to interfere with this. The design pleased Bernardino, who would have had it executed, but he died and his heirs have done nothing. While Simone was engaged upon this chapel, Antonio da Sangallo passed through Arezzo, after fortifying Parma, and went to Loreto to finish the chapel of the Virgin, where he had assembled Tribolo, Raffaello Montelupo, Francesco da Sangallo

the younger, Girolamo da Ferrara, Simone Cioli and other workmen to finish what Andrea Sansovino had left incomplete. He
induced Simone to go with him, giving him charge not only of
the carving, but of the architecture and other ornaments. In
this commission Mosca did admirably, executing many things
perfectly with his own hands, especially some marble infants
over the doors. Some are by Simone Cioli, but the best are
Mosca's, and are of rare excellence. He also did the marble
festoons about the work with much grace, worthy of all praise,
so it is no wonder that artists have come from distant places to
see them. Antonio, recognising his worth, employed him on
important things, intending one day, when the opportunity
served, to reward him and show him how much he appreciated
his merits. When Paul III. succeeded Clement VII. and ordained
that Antonio should do the unfinished well-head at Orvieto, he
took Mosca there to finish it. He encountered some difficulties,
especially in the ornamentation of the doors, for the mouth of
the well being round and hollow rendered it difficult to adapt
square doors to the stone ornament. But Simone's genius over-
came this, and he executed the work with so much grace and
perfection that no one would have supposed there had been any
difficulty. He made the finish of macigno and filled in with
bricks, with some beautiful white stone slabs and other ornaments flush with the doors. He made the arms of the Pope there
in marble, where the balls of Clement VII. were to have been,
with great success, turning the balls into lilies, converting the
Medici arms into those of the Farnese, although this royal and
magnificent work had been conceived by Clement, to whom no
reference was made in this final and most important part, but
such is the way of the world.

While Simone was finishing the well, the wardens of S. Maria,
the Duomo of Orvieto, wished to finish the marble chapel, of
which the marble basement had been executed by Michele Sanmichele of Verona. They accordingly desired Simone to do it,
recognising in him an excellent artist. An agreement was
made,[1] and, as Simone liked the Orvietans, he brought his
family to live there, and then set to work with his mind at
ease, being greatly honoured by all in the city. As an example
he did some pilasters and friezes, and recognising his excellence
they ordained for him a provision of 200 gold crowns a year,
and so he completed the work. In the middle he arranged
a beautiful marble half-relief of the Adoration of the Magi,

[1] In 1538.

executed by his friend Raffaello da Montelupo, sculptor of
Florence. The decoration consists of pedestals, two and a half
braccia broad, on either side of the altar, on which are pilasters
five braccia high, with the Adoration of the Magi between them.
The two pilasters nearest this are decorated with candlesticks
and friezes of arabesques, masks, figures and foliage. In the
predella beneath, above the altar and between the pilasters, is
a half-length angel holding an inscription, with festoons above,
between the capitals of the pilasters, where the architrave,
frieze and cornice project, of the same breadth as the pilasters.
Above the middle is an arch adorning the relief, containing
several angels. Above it is a cornice from one pilaster to another,
forming a top to the whole work. In this is a God the Father
in half-relief and two Victories at the sides. The whole is finely
composed and richly carved, with its delicate perforations and
the excellence of every part of the capitals, cornices, masks,
festoons and candlesticks completing this admirable work.

While Simone was staying at Orvieto his fifteen-year-old
son Francesco, surnamed "il Moschino," being, as it were, born
with the chisel in his hand, and with such high genius that he
gracefully executed whatever he wished, did the angels holding
the inscription for this work, under his father's supervision, the
God the Father, the angels in the arch and the Victories at the
sides, the excellence of which amazed everyone. Thus when the
chapel was finished the wardens engaged Simone to do another
like it on the opposite side, to fill up the space of the high-
altar chapel, and without changing the architecture to vary the
figures and put a Visitation in the middle, to be done by Moschino. This was agreed, and father and son began the task.[1]
Meanwhile Mosca proved of great help to the city in preparing
designs for houses and many other edifices, doing, among other
things, the plan and façade of the house of M. Raffaelo Gualtieri,
father of the bishop of Viterbo, and of M. Felice, both noble
and virtuous lords. He also did plans for houses for the counts
of Cervara. In many places near Orvieto, and especially for
Sig. Piero Colonna of Stripicciano, he did models for many
buildings. When the Pope built the citadel of Perugia, where
the houses of the Baglioni were, Antonio Sangallo sent for
Mosca to make the ornaments, and so he designed the doors,
windows, chimneypieces, and such things, including two fine
escutcheons of the Pope. M. Tiberio Crispo, the castellan, whom
Simone had served in this work, sent him to Bolsena, where he

[1] In 1550.

made for him a beautiful abode in the highest part of the village, overlooking the lake, partly on old foundations and partly new, with handsome steps and many stone ornaments. M. Tiberio, being appointed castellan of the castle of St. Angelo soon after, brought Mosca to Rome to restore the rooms of the castle. Among other things he did two escutcheons of the Pope over the arches forming the ends of the new loggia facing the country, the mitre and keys being beautifully perforated, and the festoons and masks marvellous.

Returning to Orvieto to finish the chapel, Mosca worked there during Paul's life, and made it even more excellent than the first, for he was so fond of art that he could never work enough, and sought to do the impossible, moved more by his desire for glory than for gold, for he was better pleased at doing good work than in winning wealth.

On the election of Pope Julius III. in 1550, who wished to attack S. Pietro, Mosca came to Rome and approached the deputies of the fabric to obtain some marble capitals, chiefly for the sake of Giovandomenico,[1] his son-in-law. Giorgio Vasari having found Mosca, of whom he was very fond, in Rome, whither he had been called to serve the Pope, tried every means to obtain work for him. The old Cardinal di Monte, when he died, had instructed his heirs to make a marble tomb in S. Pietro a Montorio, and Pope Julius, his heir and nephew, gave orders that this should be done, entrusting the work to Vasari, who wanted Mosca to do something remarkable for it. But after Giorgio had prepared models, the Pope consulted Michelagnolo before making up his mind. That artist advised the Pope not to trouble about carvings because, although they enrich work, they confuse the figures, and a relief is much better if well done, harmonising better with the statues. His Holiness followed this advice, and Mosca was dismissed because Vasari could not employ him, and the tomb was finished without carving, coming out much better than it would have done with it.

On returning to Orvieto, Simone was directed to design two large marble tabernacles for the crossing at the end of the church. In one of these Raffaello da Montelupo did a nude figure of Christ bearing the Cross, in marble, and in the other Moschino did a nude St. Sebastian. For the same church Moschino did St. Peter and St. Paul of the same size, considered good statues. Meanwhile the chapel of the Visitation was so far advanced

[1] His surname was Bersuglia or Versuglia.

during Mosca's life that it only lacked two birds, and even these would have been done, but M. Bastiano Gualtieri, bishop of Viterbo, kept him employed to do a marble ornament of four pieces, which was sent to France to the cardinal of Lorraine, who valued it highly, for it was marvellously beautiful, full of foliage, and executed with such diligence that it was considered Simone's best work. He died in 1554, soon after finishing it, aged fifty-eight, to the detriment of the church of Orvieto, in which he was honourably buried. Francesco Moschino being elected in his place by the wardens, did not care for the task, and left it to Raffaello Montelupo. Proceeding to Rome, he finished two graceful marble figures of Mars and Venus for M. Roberto Strozzi; they are now in the court of his house in Banchi. He then did a relief of small figures representing Diana bathing with her nymphs and converting Actæon into a stag, who is torn to pieces by his own dogs. He came to Florence and presented it to Duke Cosimo, whom he longed to serve. The duke praised the work, and gratified Moschino's desire, for he is always ready to employ men of genius. The duke gave him work in the opera of the Duomo at Pisa, where he has done an angel and Virgin, four braccia high, Adam and Eve with the apple, a God the Father with cherubs, all in marble, in the chapel of the Nunziata, erected by Stagio di Pietrasanta, with the carving and other things, all of which have brought Moschino name and fame. As this chapel is nearly finished, the duke has directed that he shall begin the chapel of the Incoronata opposite, at the left immediately on entering the church. Moschino acquitted himself very well in the things allotted to him for the apparatus for the marriage of Queen Joanna and the illustrious Prince of Florence.

GIROLAMO and BARTOLOMMEO GENGA, and GIOVAMBATTISTA SAN MARINO, Girolamo's Son-in-law

(1476 – 1551; 1518 – 1558; 1506 – 1554)

GIROLAMO, who came from Urbino, was put by his father, at the age of ten, to the art of wool, which he greatly disliked, and he used secretly to draw with charcoal and a writing-pen. Some friends of his father, observing this, advised him to take the

boy away and make him a painter; so he was put with some
mediocre masters at Urbino. But, seeing his good style, his
father put him, when fifteen, with Luca Signorelli of Cortona,
a famous master of the day, with whom he remained several
years, and whom he followed to the March of Ancona, Cortona
and many other places where he worked, especially Orvieto.
In the Duomo there Luca decorated a chapel of the Virgin
with numerous figures, upon which Girolamo was constantly
engaged, for he was one of Luca's best pupils. Leaving Luca,
he joined Perugino, a celebrated painter, with whom he remained
about three years, studying perspective, which he mastered so
well as to become excellent, as his works in painting and architecture show. At this time Raphael was with Perugino and
much beloved by him. Girolamo left Pietro and went to Florence,
where he studied a while. He then proceeded to Siena, spending
several months with Pandolfo Petrucci, in whose house he
painted many rooms, admirable for their excellent design and
charming colouring, so that Pandolfo became very fond of him.

On Pandolfo's death Girolamo returned to Urbino,[1] where
Duke Guidobaldo kept him some time to paint horse-trappings,
then in use, in company with Timoteo da Urbino,[2] a painter
of some fame and considerable experience. With him Girolamo
decorated a chapel of St. Martin in the Vescovado for Giovam-
piero Arrivabene of Mantua, then bishop of Urbino, with a
life-like portrait of the bishop, both artists displaying great
talent. The duke also employed Genga more especially to make
apparatus and scenery for comedies, in which he succeeded
admirably, owing to his knowledge of perspective and the
principles of architecture. He proceeded thence to Rome, and
in S. Caterina da Siena in the Strada Giulia did a Resurrection,
showing himself a rare master, as is testified by the good design,
firm attitude of the figures, foreshortening and colouring, as
artists who have seen it know. While in Rome he measured
the antiquities, and his heirs possess writings by him upon
these. Duke Guido died about this time, and Francesco Maria,
who succeeded, recalled Genga at the time when he married
Leonora Gonzaga, daughter of the Marquis of Mantua, to make
triumphal arches and scenery for comedies for her reception.
Genga did so well that he won the highest renown, and Urbino
resembled a Rome in triumph through his skill. When the duke
was expelled, Girolamo followed him to Mantua, as he had done
at previous exiles, and settled with his family at Cesena. At the

high altar of S. Agostino there he did an oil-painting of an Annunciation, with God the Father below, and under that the Virgin and Child between the four Doctors of the Church, a beautiful and valuable work.[1] He did an Annunciation with many angels, prophets and apostles in fresco in a chapel on the right of S. Francesco at Forli, which displays his marvellous genius. For M. Francesco Lombardo, a physician, he did the Story of the Holy Spirit, finished in 1512, and other works in the Romagna, which brought him honour and rewards. When the duke returned to his state Girolamo went with him, and was employed as architect to restore the old palace and add a tower on the Monte dell' Imperiale above Pesaro. He decorated the palace with pictures representing the exploits of the duke, executed by Francesco da Forli, Raffaello dal Borgo,[2] well-known painters, and by Camnillo Mantovano, who excelled in landscapes. The young Florentine Bronzino also worked there, as related in Pontormo's Life. The Dossi of Ferrara being invited there, a chamber was allotted to them; but as their work did not please the duke, it was destroyed and repainted by the others. Genga made the tower one hundred and twenty feet high, with thirteen wooden staircases, so well arranged in the wall that one moves from floor to floor with ease, and the tower is rendered marvellously strong. The duke wishing to fortify Pesaro, for which he called in Pierfrancesco da Viterbo, a famous architect, Girolamo always took part in the discussions, in which his judgment commanded respect, so that I may venture to say that the design of the fortress is more his than anyone else's, though he attached little value to that kind of architecture. The duke, perceiving his genius, determined to erect the present palace at Imperiale near the old one. It is a beautiful structure, full of chambers, colonnades and courts, loggias, fountains and pleasant gardens, so that all princes passing that way go to see it, and among them Paul III. when he went to Bologna with his court, who was greatly delighted. The duke also employed Genga to restore the court of Pesaro and the park, where he erected an imitation ruin of great beauty and a staircase similar to that of the Belvedere at Rome. He restored the fortress of Gradara and the court of Castel Durante, all the works of this great genius being excellent. He also did the corridor above the garden of the court of Urbino, and an enclosed court with stones perforated with great diligence. From his design the bare-footed

---

[1] Now in the Brera, Milan.
[2] Francesco Minzocchi and Raffaello dal Colle.

friars' convent at Monte Baroccio was begun, and S. Maria
delle Grazie at Sinigaglia, both interrupted by the duke's death.
From his design the Vescovado of Sinigaglia was begun about
the same time, and his model may still be seen. He did sculptures
and clay and wax figures of considerable beauty, which are
now in the house of his nephews at Urbino. At Imperiale he did
some clay angels, of which he made plaster casts and put them
over the doors of the apartments decorated with stucco in the
new palace. For the bishop of Sinigaglia he did some curious
drinking-vessels in wax, to be executed in silver, and some other
fine ones for the duke's sideboard, more carefully finished. He
was a clever designer of masques and costumes, as was seen
in the duke's time, whose rewards he richly deserved. On the
accession of the present Duke Guidobaldo, his highness made
Genga begin the church of S. Giovanni Battista at Pesaro,[1]
executed from Genga's model by his son Bartolommeo. It is
a beautiful building in every part, for Genga imitated the
antique, making it the finest church in those parts, equalling
the most admired ones in Rome. From Genga's design Bartolommeo Ammannati, a young Florentine sculptor, executed the
tomb of Duke Francesco Maria in S. Chiara at Urbino, a beautiful thing in spite of its simplicity and the trifling cost. Genga
also brought Battista Franco, a Venetian painter, to decorate
the great chapel of the Duomo of Urbino, where the still unfinished decoration of the organ was being executed from his
design. Soon after he went to Mantua, as the cardinal there
had written to the duke to ask him to send Girolamo to restore
the Vescovado. He executed this work to the satisfaction of
the cardinal, who got him to make a model of a façade for the
Duomo. Genga made it in such a way that he may be said to
have surpassed all his contemporaries, for it displays grandeur,
proportion, grace and fine composition.

Being now an old man, Genga went to live at a villa of his
in the territory of Urbino, called le Valle, for rest from his
labours. To avoid being idle, he there did a Conversion of
St. Paul in hæmatite, the figures and horses being of considerable size and in fine attitudes, and executed with the utmost
care. It is in the possession of his heirs, who value it highly.
While resting there he fell sick of a severe fever and died after
receiving the sacraments on 11 July, 1551, aged about seventy-
five, to the grief of his wife and children. The body was taken
to Urbino and honourably buried in the Vescovado before the

[1] In 1515.

chapel of St. Martin, which he had painted, amid the sorrow of
his relations and all the citizens.

Girolamo was a good man of whom no evil is reported. He
was an excellent musician as well as a painter, sculptor and
architect. He could converse well, and his society was agreeable
and entertaining. He displayed the utmost courtesy and affection to his relations and friends, and founded the house of the
Genghi at Urbino, with honour, reputation and wealth. He
left two sons, one of whom followed in his footsteps and practised architecture, in which he would have become excellent
had he lived. The other, who devoted himself to family cares,
still survives.

Francesco Menzochi of Forli was a pupil of Genga, as has
been said. While a child he began to draw by himself, copying
a picture by Marco Parmigiano of Forli in the Duomo there,
representing the Virgin, St. Jerome and other saints, then considered the best of modern paintings. He also imitated the
works of Rondinino [1] da Ravenna, a more excellent painter
than Marco, who had just before done a beautiful panel for the
high altar of the Duomo of a Last Supper, and a dead Christ
in the lunette above, with a predella of small figures of the
history of St. Helena.[2]

Thus, when Genga went to paint the chapel of St. Francesco
at Forli for M. Bartolommeo Lombardino, Frencesco went to
stay with him and learn, and he continued to serve him throughout his life, at Urbino and at Imperiale, doing excellently, being
much valued and loved by Genga. Many panels in different
parts of Forli show his skill, especially three in S. Francesco
and some scenes in fresco in a hall of the palace. He did many
works for the Romagna. In Venice he painted four large pictures
in oils for the Patriarch Grimani, for the ceiling of a salon in
his house, representing the story of Psyche, and considered
very beautiful. They surround an octagon done by Francesco
Salviati. But he displayed his highest powers in the chapel of
the Sacrament in the church of Loreto, representing angels
standing about the body of Christ, and two scenes on the walls,
one of Melchisedec, the other the Fall of the Manna, executed
in fresco. In the decorated ceiling he did fifteen scenes of the
Passion, nine painted and six in half-relief, so rich and well
designed that they brought him great honour, and he had to
do another chapel of the same size before leaving, dedicated
to the Conception. He decorated the vaulting with rich stucco,

[1] i.e. Rondinello.   [2] Painted in 1506; now in the Forli Gallery.

and taught his son Pietro Paolo the work. This Pietro has since done him much honour, having become very skilful in the profession. On the walls Francesco did a Nativity and the Presentation of the Virgin, and above the altar St. Anne, the Virgin and Child, with two angels crowning the Virgin. Indeed, his works are praised by artists as well as his character and life. He lived quietly as a Christian and enjoyed the fruits of his labours.

Another pupil of Genga, Baldassarre Lancia of Urbino,[1] after studying many things and making fortifications, notably for the Signoria of Lucca, where he spent some time, came to serve Duke Cosimo similarly in his fortifications for Florence and Siena, and he produced many ingenious things, working honourably and skilfully, and receiving great rewards from the duke. Many others served Genga, but as they did not achieve great excellence, I need not mention them.

In 1518 a son Bartolommeo was born to Girolamo at Cesena, whither the father had followed the exiled duke. He brought the boy up well, and as he grew sent him to learn grammar, in which he made considerable progress. When he was eighteen, his father, perceiving that he was fonder of design than letters, taught him himself for about two years, at the end of which he sent him to study design and painting at Florence, which he recognised as the true studio of artists, owing to the countless works there by famous masters, both ancient and modern. While there Bartolommeo made the friendship of Giorgio Vasari and of Bartolommeo Ammannati the sculptor, from whom he learned much. After spending three years at Florence he returned to his father, then engaged upon the building of S. Giovan. Battista at Pesaro. On seeing his designs his father concluded that Bartolommeo would succeed far better in architecture than in painting. Accordingly he detained him for some months, teaching him perspective, and then sent him to Rome to see the marvellous ancient and modern buildings. All of these he measured during the four years he spent there, and made great progress. On returning to Urbino, he passed through Florence to see his brother-in-law Francesco Sanmarino, engineer of Duke Cosimo. Sig. Stefano Colonna of Palestria, then the duke's general, having heard his worth, tried to retain him by a good provision, but as Bartolommeo was under great obligations to the Duke of Urbino, he would not serve another, and entering the duke's service was much valued by him. Not long after,

[1] 1510-71.

when the duke married Vittoria Farnese, Bartolommeo was charged to make the apparatus for the wedding. He rendered it sumptuous, among other things making a fine triumphal arch in the Borgo of Valbuona, which could not be surpassed, and showed how much he had learned at Rome. When the duke, as general of the Signoria of Venice, had to go to Lombardy to inspect the fortresses, he took Bartolommeo with him, and employed him in choosing sites and preparing plans for fortresses, notably at the S. Felice gate at Verona.

While they were in Lombardy, the King of Bohemia passed through that province on his way back from Spain, and being received by the duke he saw the fortresses. They pleased him, and he made the acquaintance of Bartolommeo, whom he wanted to take to Bohemia to fortify his lands, promising a good provision. But as the duke refused to let him go, the matter fell through. Soon after returning to Urbino Bartolommeo lost his father, and the duke appointed him in his place to superintend all the buildings of the state, sending him to Pesaro, where he took up the building of S. Gio. Battista with Girolamo's model. Meanwhile he made a beautiful suite of rooms in the court of Pesaro, above the Strada de' Mercanti, where the duke now lives, with richly decorated doors, stairs and chimneys, of which he was an excellent architect. When the duke saw this he desired him to do another suite in the court of Urbino, almost all on the side facing S. Domenico. When finished this proved the most beautiful and ornate suite in the palace. The lords of Bologna having asked for him from the duke for a few days, the permission was readily granted, and Bartolommeo went to serve them, greatly pleasing them and receiving many favours. For the duke he made a beautiful model for a seaport at Pesaro. This was taken to the house of Count Giovan Jacomo Lionardi, then the duke's ambassador at Venice, to be examined by artists who frequented the count's apartments and discussed various matters with him. When the model was shown and explained by Genga, all present proclaimed the beauty of the work and the genius of the master. But when he returned to Pesaro the work was not carried out because new matters of great importance distracted the duke's attention. At this time Genga designed the church of Monte l'Abate and S. Pier in Mondavio, which was executed by Don Pier Antonio Genga, so that I do not think it can be surpassed, considering its small scale.

On the creation of Pope Julius III., who appointed the Duke

of Urbino captain-general of the Church, his excellency went to Rome with Genga. As the Pope wished to fortify Borgo, Genga prepared some fine designs at the duke's request, which are now in the duke's possession. Bartolommeo's fame being thus spread abroad, the Genoese asked his help for some of their fortifications while he was at Rome, but the duke would not permit it then or afterwards when they again made the request on his return to Urbino. Towards the end of his life two knights were sent to Pesaro by the Grand Master of Rhodes to beg the duke to send them Bartolommeo to fortify the island of Malta against the Turks, and make two cities by uniting several scattered villages. They begged the duke for two months without success, although assisted by the duchess and others; but at length he granted the request at the instance of a good Capuchin father of whom the duke was very fond, the friar representing it as a Christian act to be much commended. Bartolommeo, who had never received a higher honour, set out with the knights on 20 January, 1558, but being delayed in Sicily by the fortune of the sea, they did not reach Malta before 14 March, where the grand master received them gladly. When shown what to do, Bartolommeo made fortifications of the utmost excellence, so that he seemed a new Archimedes to the grand master and the knights, who made him rich presents and greatly esteemed him. After making the model for a city, some churches and the palace and residence of the grand master in beautiful style, Bartolommeo fell sick of his last illness. One day in July, which is a very warm month there, he was put to take the air between two doors, and before long this brought on terrible pains and a violent dysentery, so that he died in seventeen days, to the grief of the master and all those noble and valiant knights, who thought they had found a man after their own heart. When the Duke of Urbino received the news he was overcome by grief, and resolved to show his affection to the five children, whom he took into his especial care and protection. Bartolommeo was an ingenious deviser of masques and excellent in the apparatus for comedies and scenes. He was fond of composing sonnets and other morsels of prose and verse, especially in *ottava rima*, in which he displayed considerable merit. He died in 1558, aged forty.

As Gio. Battista Bellucci of S. Marino was son-in-law of Girolamo Genga, I have thought it well to write what I have to say about him in this place, chiefly in order to show that great minds succeed in everything they wish, however late they take up difficult tasks. Moreover, study joined to natural inclination has often produced marvels. Gio. Battista was born at S. Marino on 27 September, 1506, of Bartolommeo Bellucci, a man of good family. After he had learned the elements of letters his father sent him when eighteen to learn business at Bologna with Bastiano di Ronco, a merchant of the art of wool. After remaining there about two years, he returned to S. Marino, sick of quartan fever, which lasted two years. When he recovered he began business for himself, and so continued until 1535. At this time his father married him to a daughter of Guido Peruzzi, an honourable man of Cagli. As she died soon after, Gio. Battista went to Rome to find his brother-in-law Domenico Peruzzi, who was squire to Sig. Ascanio Colonna, with whom he remained two years as a gentleman and then returned to Pesaro. It happened that Girolamo Genga was then working there, and perceiving the young man to be virtuous and able, he gave him a daughter to wife and brought him to his house. Gio. Battista, being very fond of architecture and carefully studying the works of his father-in-law, began to acquire the methods of building and to study Vitruvius, and thus by what he taught himself, and what he learned from Genga, he became a good architect, especially in fortifications and other military matters. His wife dying in 1541, leaving two children, he remained a widower until 1543. At that time, in September, Sig. Gustamante, a Spaniard, was at S. Marino, sent by the emperor to the republic on some affairs, and he discovered Gio. Battista's excellence as an architect and warmly recommended him to Duke Cosimo as an engineer. He served the duke in all the fortifications of his dominions as the need arose, and among other things he completed the citadel of Pistoia,[1] begun many years before, winning great praise, although it is not very large. He then built a strong mole at Pisa, and as his methods pleased the duke he did the walls at the hill of S. Miniato outside Florence, from the S. Niccolo gate to the S. Miniato gate, with a bulwark on either side of the gate, and enclosing the church and monastery of S. Miniato, making a fortress at the top which dominates the whole city and the country to the east and south. This work earned great admiration. He also prepared many plans for fortifications in the duke's dominions and made clay models, which are in the duke's possession. Being an able and studious man, Gio. Battista wrote a small book on the method of fortifying.[2] This useful work is

---

[1] In 1544.
[2] *Trattato della Fortificazione*, published at Venice in 1598.

now in the possession of M. Bernardo Puccini, a Florentine nobleman, who learned much about architecture and fortifications from his friend the author. Gio. Battista, having designed several bastions for the walls of Florence in 1554, some of which were begun, he accompanied Sig. Garzia of Toledo to Monte Alcino, where he made mines under a bulwark and blew it up, but was hit in the side by a shot. He soon recovered, and going secretly to Siena took a plan of the city and of the earthworks which the Sienese had made at the Camollia gate. He showed this plan to the duke and the Marquis of Marignano, and demonstrated that it would not be difficult to take them or to press towards Siena. This was seen on the night that Siena was taken by the marquis,[1] who was then accompanied by Gio. Battista, by the duke's direction. The marquis became much attached to him, and as he needed his judgment and skill in the camp for the war of Siena, he induced the duke to send him as captain of a large company of infantry. The duke thus employed him both as a soldier and as an architect. Being sent by the marquis to Aiuolo, a fortress in Chianti, he was shot in the head while establishing his batteries. He was carried by the soldiers to the Pieve of S. Paolo of the Bishop da Ricasoli, and died in a few days. His children buried him honourably at S. Marino.

Gio. Battista merits great praise, because it was marvellous that he should have attained to such excellence in a profession which he only took up at the age of thirty-five, and if he had begun earlier he would probably have been a marvel. He was somewhat obstinate, so that it was a hard matter to make him change his mind. He was very fond of reading history, on which he set the highest value, and himself laboriously wrote a relation of events of most importance. His death caused great sorrow to the duke and his numerous friends, and when his son Gianandrea went to kiss the duke's hands he was graciously received for his father's sake. Gio. Battista was forty-eight when he died.

[1] 17 April, 1555.

MICHELE SAN MICHELE, Architect of Verona
(1484 – 1559)

MICHELE was born at Verona in 1484, and learned the elements of architecture from his father Giovanni and his uncle Bartolommeo, both excellent architects. At sixteen he went to Rome, leaving his father and two clever brothers, one of whom named Jacopo studied letters, and the other, Don Cammillo, was a regular and general canon of that order. He studied ancient architecture with such diligence, measuring and carefully observing everything, that in a short time he became famous not only in Rome, but in all the neighbourhood. Thus the Orvietans made him the architect of their famous church,[1] with a good salary, and this led him to go to Monte Fiascone for the building of their principal church. In both these places he left good architecture, and in S. Domenico at Orvieto a fine tomb was made from his design,[2] I think for one of the Petrucci, a Sienese noble, which cost a great sum of money. In the same place he made countless designs for private houses, and won a name for good judgment and excellence. Thus Pope Clement determined to employ him on important matters in the war then raging in Italy, and granted him a good provision to go with Antonio Sangallo to visit the most important places in the states of the Church and erect fortifications where necessary, especially at Parma and Piacenza, which were farthest from Rome and most exposed to the dangers of war. After they had done this to the Pope's satisfaction, Michele desired to see his home, his relations and friends, after so many years, and, even more, the fortresses of the Venetians. After remaining some days at Verona, he visited the fortress of Trevisi, and then proceeded to Padua on the same errand. The Venetian rulers being suspicious of this, imagining that he intended to do them some harm, had him arrested at Padua, and, being imprisoned, he underwent a long examination. Finding him innocent, they released him, and requested him to enter their service with a good salary. He excused himself because he was bound to the Pope, and giving good promises, he left them; but before long, by means of his prayers and the urgent solicitations of the Signoria, the Pope was induced to grant him permission to go and serve the Re-

[1] In 1509.   [2] 1518 to 1522.

public, his natural lords. While there he displayed his judgment and knowledge by constructing a fine and powerful bastion at Verona,[1] although the task seemed very difficult, and it greatly pleased the Signory and the Duke of Urbino, then their captain-general. Proposing next to fortify Legnago and Porto, important places of the dominion on either side of the River Adige, united by a bridge, they instructed San Michele to make a model to show how it could be done. They and the duke were greatly pleased with his design, and therefore he executed it, making a fort of unmatched strength, as all who have seen it know. He then fortified Orzinuovo in the Bresciano, a port similar to Legnago. Being demanded by Francesco Sforza, the last Duke of Milan, he obtained permission from the Signoria, but only for three months. He went and inspected all the fortresses of that state and directed what he thought necessary to be done, to the great satisfaction of the duke, who gave him 500 crowns, and thanked the Venetian Government.

Before returning to Venice, San Michele went to see the strong city of Casale di Monferrato, constructed by Matteo S. Michele, his kinsman, an excellent architect, and a marble tomb by Matteo in S. Francesco there. He had no sooner returned home than he was sent with the Duke of Urbino to inspect Chiusa, an important fortress and pass above Verona, and then to Friuli, Bergamo, Vicenza, Peschiera and other places, on which he returned detailed reports to his Government. They then sent him to fortify the cities and places of Dalmatia, and he diligently restored where he thought it necessary. As he could not do all, he left his nephew, Gian. Girolamo, there, who, having fortified Zara strongly, raised the marvellous stronghold of S. Niccolo at the mouth of the port of Sebenico.

Meanwhile Michele had hastened to Corfu and restored the fortress, doing the like in Cyprus and Candia, although he was soon forced to return owing to the fear of losing the island in the ensuing Turkish wars. This was after he had inspected the Venetian fortresses in Italy, when he went with all speed to Canea, Candia, Retimo, Settia, and especially Canea and Candia, which he entirely rebuilt and rendered impregnable. When Napoli di Romania was afterwards besieged by the Turks, its successful resistance was due to the diligence of Michele in fortifying it and the valour of Agostino Clusoni of Verona, the captain. On the conclusion of the war Michele went with M. Tommaso Mozzenigo chief admiral, to fortify Corfu anew.

[1] In 1522.

They returned to Sebenico, where the diligence of Gian. Girolamo in making the fort of S. Niccolo was much praised.

Returning to Venice, Michele received the thanks of the
republic for his services. They gave him the charge of constructing a fortress on the Lido at the mouth of the port of
Venice,[1] saying that, as he had done work so far away, it was
only right that he should do one of such importance, which
would be always in sight of the senate and rulers. It was
expected he would show every diligence in laying safe foundations in that marshy soil, surrounded by the sea and washed
by the tides, making it handsome and strong. He made his
model, and was requested to execute it without delay. Accordingly, after receiving what he needed from the Government, he
filled in his foundations, drove a double row of piles, and made
excavations with the aid of many men skilled in those waters,
but the more he laboured with pumps and other machinery
for keeping out the water, the more it rose up from below,
because the place is in the sea. One morning, in order to make
a supreme effort, he gathered together all the able-bodied men
he could collect and by incredibly swift action he was able to
overcome the waters long enough to lay the first stones on his
piles in the presence of many signors. The stones being very large,
formed an admirable foundation. He then continued rapidly,
keeping the water out, a thing many had regarded as impossible. The foundations being laid, Michele built a marvellous
fortress upon them after they had been allowed to rest for
some time, the exterior being of rustic-work in large Istrian
stone, which is extremely hard and resists the weather. Thus
this fortress, for its site, beauty and extraordinary cost, is one
of the most remarkable in Europe, and equals in majesty the
most famous structures of the Romans. It seems cut from a
single stone out of the solid rock, owing to the great blocks
which form it and the skill with which they are joined, not to
speak of the decorations, of which it would be impossible to
say too much. Inside Michele made a piazza with pilasters and
arches in the rustic order, which would have been marvellous
if finished. On the completion of this great work some malignant spirits assured the Signoria that, although it was handsome
and well-devised, it would be useless, and even dangerous, in
an emergency, for it would be destroyed by the weight of its
own artillery. The Signoria therefore thought it prudent to
cause a great quantity of the heaviest artillery in the arsenal

[1] In 1544.

to be taken thither, and fired off all the pieces simultaneously, making a noise like the crack of doom and a fire like Mongibello or Hell. The building, however, remained firm, establishing the reputations of Michele and confounding the objectors, who had caused such general alarm that pregnant women had left the city.

Michele next fortified Marano, a place of no small importance in the lagoons, with speed and diligence. His fame, and that of his nephew, Gio. Girolamo, being spread about, they both received several invitations from Charles V. and King Francis of France. But although honourable conditions were offered to them, they refused to leave their own rulers to serve strangers, and continued their work of inspecting and restoring the Venetian fortresses.

Michele worked especially hard to fortify his native Verona, making the unequalled city gates, besides other things. He did the Porta Nuova in the rustic Doric order,[1] a structure the massiveness of which harmonises with the strength of the place, being built of *tufa* and flints, with rooms inside for the guard, and several other conveniences not previously found in such structures. It is square and open at the top, the horse entrance defended by two large bastions on either side; a costly and magnificent work, that no one expected to see equalled in the future as it was not in the past. But a few years later Michele did another gate, commonly called del Palio,[2] which is in no wise inferior. Indeed, by these two gates the Venetian rulers equalled the buildings of ancient Rome. The exterior of the latter gate is in the Doric order, with projecting columns, eight in all, placed in pairs, with the arms of the rectors of the city between them, forming a large front, with polished bosses and beautiful decoration. The door space is square, of a new, curious and beautiful architecture. Above is a rich Doric cornice, and over this there was to have been a front to form a parapet for artillery, as we see by the model. The interior contains large rooms for the soldiers and other conveniences. On the city side Michele made a handsome loggia, the exterior in the Doric and rustic order, and the interior rustic, with large pilasters with columns round outside and square within in half-relief, with Doric capitals and no bases, and surmounted by a carved Doric cornice along the entire length of the loggia within and without. In fine, the work is marvellous, and Sig. Sforza Pallavicino, governor-general of the Venetian armies, well said that nothing

[1] In 1541-2.   [2] Completed 1557.

to equal it could be found in Europe. It was Michele's last miracle, for he had hardly completed the first order when he died. The work will never be completed because, as usually happens with great things, some malignant spirits depreciated it, for they could not produce nearly so fine a thing themselves. Michele also did the fine S. Zeno gate at Verona,[1] but its beauty is obscured by that of the other two, though it would be remarkable anywhere else. He also made a bastion near the gate, and the one lower down, opposite S. Bernardino, and another opposite the Campo Marzio, called dell' Acquaio, larger than all the others, at the point where the Adige enters the city. At Padua he did the Cornaro and S. Croce bastions, which are of marvellous size and built in a style introduced by him of making them angular instead of round, the exterior points forming an obtuse angle which can easily be defended from the flanking bastions or from the gateway. He also introduced the method of making bastions with a front and two sides, the side ones to defend the ditch and curtains, with open embrasures, and the middle one to attack the enemy from. This has been generally followed, the old method of underground casemates being abandoned, because the smoke and other things prevented the manipulation of the artillery, while they weakened the foundations of the tower and walls. Michele made two fine gates at Legnago. At Peschiera he founded the fortress, and did many things at Brescia, executing everything with such diligence and solidity that none of his erections has moved a hair's breadth. Finally he restored the fortress of Chiusa above Verona, making convenient passages to enter without passing through the fortress, and so that by raising a bridge no one can enter or approach the narrow path cut in the rock. On returning from Rome he made the beautiful Ponte Nuovo at Verona, at the order of M. Giovanni Emo, then podestà, a marvellous work for its strength. Michele excelled not only in fortifications but also in private buildings, temples, churches and monasteries, as we see in Verona and elsewhere, notably in the ornate Guareschi Chapel in S. Bernadino in the Corinthian order.[2] He made this entirely of soft white stone called *bronzo*, from the sound it gives when worked. After marble this is the finest stone yet discovered, as it is flawless and unspoiled by blemishes. Owing to its materials, and the carving by excellent masters, this chapel is considered the finest of its kind in Italy, as Michele has so arranged the round work that the altars, with their fonts and cornices, and

[1] 1540.   [2] Now Pellegrini; erected in 1557.

the door space, all form a perfect curve, like the exit made by
Brunelleschi for the church of the Angeli at Florence, a task
of great difficulty. In a gallery above, encircling the chapel,
Michele made beautiful columns, capitals, foliage, grotesques,
pilasters and other carved work with incredible diligence. The
square outside door in the Corinthian order resembles an ancient
one which he is said to have seen in Rome. Michele left it unfinished, and whether through avarice or ignorance it was given
to others to complete. They ruined it, to the chagrin of Michele,
who lived to see it done. He sometimes complained to his
friends that he had not thousands of ducats to redeem this
monument from the avarice of a woman who ruined it through
her anxiety to spend as little as possible.

Michele designed the beautiful round church of the Madonna
di Campagna near Verona,[1] although the weakness and ignorance
of the directors of the work have subsequently ruined many
parts, and they would have done worse, only Bernardino Brugnoli, a kinsman of Michele, who had charge of it, made a complete
model from which the structure is now being built. For the friars
of S. Maria in Organo, monks of Mount Oliveto at Verona,
he designed a façade for their church in the Corinthian order. After
it had reached a certain height under Paolo S. Michele, it
remained so owing to the great expenses incurred by the monks
on other things, but chiefly owing to the death of Don Cipriano
of Verona, a man of holy life and much authority in the order,
of which he was twice general, and who had begun it. In S.
Giorgio of Verona, a convent of the regular priests of St. Giorgio
in Alega, Michele made the cupola, a beautiful work, which
proved successful, although many thought that the buttresses
were too feeble to bear such a weight; but they were subsequently
strengthened by Michele so that there is no longer any danger.
In the same convent he designed and founded a handsome
campanile of squared stone, partly *tufa* and partly of a harder
kind, of which he completed a large part, and which is now being
continued by his nephew Bernardino.

Luigi Lippomani, bishop of Verona, having decided to complete the campanile of his church begun one hundred years
before, obtained a beautiful design from Michele, who took into
consideration the retention of the old work and the costs which
the bishop would bear. But M. Domenico Porzio, a Roman, the
bishop's vicar, who knew little of building, though otherwise a
worthy man, gave the work to one who understood nothing

[1] Built 1559 to 1586.

about it. Accordingly he made it of unsquared mountain stone, introducing the steps into the thickness of the walls, so that anyone might have foretold the fall of the building which ensued, and it was predicted by Frà Marco de' Medici of Verona, who has always been fond of architecture among his severer studies. But he was answered: "Frà Marco may be learned in letters, philosophy and theology, but he has not sounded the depths of architecture so that we can put faith in him." When the campanile had been raised as high as the bells, it cracked in four places, so that after an expenditure of many thousand crowns on its construction it became necessary to pay three hundred crowns to the builders to pull it down, in order that its fall might not destroy everything about it. Such is the fate of those who forsake excellent masters for bunglers.

On Monsignor Luigi being elected bishop of Bergamo, Agostino Lippomano succeeding him as bishop of Verona, they employed Michele to make a model of the campanile and begin it. He therefore began the work which is now proceeding slowly under Girolamo Trivisani, a Dominican, who succeeded Lippomano. The model is of great beauty, the steps being so arranged as not to weaken the structure. For the Veronese Counts della Torre Michele made a beautiful round chapel, with an altar in the middle, in their villa of Fumane, and in the Santo of Padua he erected a fine tomb for M. Alessandro Contarini, procurator of S. Marco and proveditore of the Venetian fleet,[1] in which Michele showed his conception of the true methods of constructing such work, departing from the usual fashion, which in his judgment partakes more of the altar and chapel than of the tomb. It is of solid composition, and, as is fitting for a soldier, is decorated with a Thetis and two prisoners by Alessandro Vittoria, considered good figures, and a marble bust of Alessandro by Danese da Carrara. Below are other ornaments of prisoners, trophies and military spoils. In Venice he made a much-admired model for the monastery of the nuns of S. Biagio Catoldo.

When it was proposed to rebuild the lazar-house for the plague-stricken at Verona, the old one being destroyed with other buildings in the suburbs, Michele prepared a design of incredible beauty, and so the work was begun near the river, a little outside the esplanade. However, this design, now in the possession of the heirs of Luigi Brugnoli, Michele's nephew, was not entirely carried out owing to bad judgment and meanness,

[1] Who died 1553; the tomb was made in 1555.

as it was much reduced by the authorities, because of the death of some nobles who had presided at the work at its beginning and whose spirit was equal to their rank. Michele also did the handsome palace of the Counts of Canossa at Verona, built by Monsignor di Baius, Count Ludovico Canossa, celebrated by all the writers of his day. For the same count Michele built another sumptuous palace at Grezano in the Veronese territory. He restored the façade of the Counts Bevilacqua and all the rooms of their castle of Bevilacqua. In Verona he did the much-admired house and façade of the Lavezzoli,[1] and in Venice he built the sumptuous palace of the Cornari, near S. Paolo, and restored another palace of the Cornari house at S. Benedetto all' Albore for M. Giovanni Cornari, his great friend.[2] He secured the employment of Giorgio Vasari to paint nine oil-paintings for the ceiling of a magnificent room of carved and richly gilded wood. He further restored the house of the Bragadini, opposite S. Marina, making it convenient and ornate. In the same city he founded and raised above the ground the marvellous palace of M. Girolamo Grimani on the Grand Canal near S. Luca.[3] Death prevented him from finishing it, and the other architects employed by that nobleman greatly changed his design. Near Castelfranco the famous palace of the Soranzi was built under Michele's direction by the family, and it is considered the handsomest and most convenient villa-residence yet erected in those parts.[4] In the territory of Piombino he made the Cornaro house and other private buildings, which it would take too long to describe, it being sufficient to mention the principal ones. He also made two handsome doors at Verona, one for the palace of the rectors and captain, the other for the Podestà palace,[5] both admirable, although the latter, which is Ionic with double columns and intercolumns highly decorated, and victories in the angles, appears somewhat dwarfed where it is, being without a pedestal, and very broad owing to the doubling of the columns, but this was the wish of M. Giovanni Delfini, who had it done. When Michele was enjoying the ease, honour and reputation in his county, which his labours had brought him, an event took place which brought his life to a close. But to make matters more clear, and that Michele's works may be better appreciated, I will first say something of his nephew, Gian. Girolamo.

---

[1] Now Pompei, about 1530, which contains the Museo Civico.
[2] The former Mocenigo and the latter Cornaro Spinelli.
[3] Now the Court of Appeal.
[4] Demolished.
[5] The former in the present Tribunale, the latter made in 1532.

He was the son of Paolo, Michele's brother, and being a youth of fine spirit his uncle taught him most carefully in architecture, and became so fond of him that he wished to have him at his side in all works of importance, especially fortifications. He thus became so excellent that any difficult task might safely be entrusted to him in fortifications, of which he was most fond. The Venetian rulers, recognising his talents, put him among the number of their architects, young as he was, with a good provision, and sent him from place to place to inspect and repair their fortresses and execute his uncle's designs. He showed great judgment in the fortification of Zara, and in the marvellous stronghold of S. Niccolo in Sebenico, which is considered one of the best and strongest private forts in existence. From his uncle's design he restored the great fortress of Corfu,[1] considered the key to Italy in that direction. Here he made the two large towers on the land side much stronger than before, with casemates flanking the ditch in the modern style introduced by Michele. He then enlarged the moat and cut down a hill which seemed to command the fortress. At one corner he made a strong place where the people of the island could stay in safety during a siege, without danger of being taken by the enemy, whereby he won so much credit that the Government granted him a provision equal to that of his uncle, judging him even superior to Michele in the art of fortifying. It was very gratifying to Michele to see his own skill developed in his nephew at a time when age was depriving him of his power to travel. Besides his judgment in choosing sites, Gian. Girolamo showed great industry in making designs and models in relief to show the Government the smallest details. This diligence greatly pleased them, for they saw the work without having to leave Venice constantly to visit the distant possessions of the state. That they might be better seen, they kept them in the doge's palace, and they not only defrayed the expenses of such models, but lavished many favours on their author. Gian. Girolamo might have served many lords, with rich provisions, but he would never leave the Venetians. By the advice of his father and uncle, he married a noble Veronese maiden of the Frascatori, intending to establish himself in those parts. But he had not been many days with his beloved Madonna Ortensia when he was summoned to Venice and sent in haste to Cyprus, to inspect the places and direct the officials to provide for all emergencies. He spent three months there, drawing and describing everything for the benefit

[1] He was at Corfu in 1548.

of his Government. But his zeal for his duties made him careless of his life, and he fell sick of a fever in that burning climate and died in six days, though some said he had been poisoned. However, he died content in serving his rulers and in being employed on important work, for they confided more in his skill in fortifying than in that of any other engineer. When he perceived that his sickness was mortal, he gave all his designs and descriptions to his brother-in-law, Luigi Brugnoli, an architect then engaged in fortifying Famagosta, the key of the realm, to be taken to the Signoria.

When the news of Gian. Girolamo's death reached Venice, every member of the senate sorrowed for the loss of so devoted a servant of the republic. Gian. Girolamo was forty-five at his death, and his brother-in-law buried him honourably in S. Niccolo, at Famagosta, and returning to Venice presented the plans and descriptions to the Signoria. That done, he was sent to complete the fortification of Legnago, where he had been engaged for many years in executing Michele's designs. He died there soon after, leaving two sons, who are skilful in design and architecture. Bernardino the elder has now charge of many undertakings, such as the campanile of the Duomo and that of S. Giorgio, and the Madonna di Campagna, in which he displays his excellence, and especially in the principal chapel of S. Giorgio at Verona, of composite order, which the Veronese consider unequalled in Italy for its composition, grandeur, design and work. It follows the curve of the niche and is of the Corinthian order, with composite capitals, double columns in relief and pilasters behind. He also carved the front with great mastery, so that Barbaro, patriarch-elect of Aquileia, who has written on architecture, marvelled at the work when he saw it on returning from the Council of Trent, and after examining it several times he confessed that it could not be surpassed, and this shows the quality of Bernardino's genius.

To return to Michele. The death of Gian. Girolamo, in whom his line became extinct, caused him great grief, which brought on a malignant fever of which he died in a few days, to the sorrow of his country and her rulers. His death took place in 1559, and he was buried in the Carmelite church of S. Tommaso, in the tomb of his ancestors. M. Niccolo San Michele the physician has recently begun to erect a fine marble tomb there.

Michele was a man of irreproachable life, and always honourable. He was gay by nature, but could be grave on occasion. He feared God, and was so religious that he would do nothing before he had heard Mass and performed his devotions, while before beginning anything of importance he would first go and sing the Mass of the Holy Spirit, or that of the Virgin. He was open and courteous with his friends, whom he made free of his possessions. I will relate an instance of his delicacy which, I believe, is known to few except myself. When I last parted from him in Venice he said, "You must know, M. Giorgio, that in my youth I was at Monte Fiascone, where I fell in love with the wife of a mason, who responded to my passion, without anyone being aware of it. I have now heard that the poor woman is left a widow, with a daughter, whom she declares to be mine, though I do not believe it. I want you to take her these 50 gold crowns from me that she may make a provision for her daughter suitable to her station." When I visited the good woman she freely confessed that Michele was not the father of her daughter; however, I paid her the money, which was as welcome to her as 500 crowns would have been to another.

Michele was so courteous that no sooner did he know what his friends wanted than he endeavoured to gratify them, even if it cost him his life, and no one ever did him a service without receiving double in return. Giorgio Vasari having made a design for him at Venice with his utmost diligence, of Lucifer and his followers conquered by St. Michael, falling from heaven into a terrible hell, Michele did nothing but simply thank him at parting; but when Giorgio returned to Arezzo soon after he found that Michele had sent his mother some beautiful robes, as if he had been a rich lord, and a courteous letter, for her son's sake. The Venetian rulers frequently offered to increase his provision, but he refused, asking that it might be given to his nephews. In fine, he was so gentle, courteous and amiable that he deserved the affection of the great, of the Cardinal de' Medici, afterwards Clement VII., of Cardinal Alessandro Farnese, afterwards Paul III., of the divine Michelagnolo, of Francesco Maria, Duke of Urbino, and countless Venetian senators and nobles. In Verona he enjoyed the friendship of Frà Marco de' Medici, and many others whom I need not mention.

I will now take this opportunity to speak of some Veronese painters now living who are worthy of mention. The first is Domenico del Riccio,[1] who did three façades in the isolated house of Fiorio della Seta, on the Ponte Nuovo, at Verona. In one over the river are battles of marine monsters, in the second battles of centaurs and many rivers, in the third are two scenes

[1] Called Brusasorci.

in colours, the first over the door of a feast of the gods and the other over the river of the wedding of Benaco and the nymph Carida, representing Lake Garda, where the Mincio rises. The same house contains a large frieze, with coloured triumphs, executed with great skill, in a good style. In the house of M. Pellegrino Ridolfi, at Verona, he painted the coronation of the Emperor Charles V. and his riding through Bologna with the Pope in great pomp. He painted in oils the principal picture of the church, newly erected by the Duke of Mantua near the castle, representing the Martyrdom of St. Barbara, executed with great finish and judgment. The duke was induced to entrust this work to him from having seen a panel he had done in the chapel of St. Margaret, in the Duomo of Mantua, in competition with Paolino, who did that of St. Anthony, Paolo Farinato, who did that of St. Martin, and Battista del Moro, who did that of the Magdalene. All four had been brought there by Cardinal Ercole of Mantua to decorate the church, restored by Giulio Romano. Domenico did other works in Verona, Vicenza and Venice, but let these suffice. He was a worthy and clever artist, an excellent musician as well as a painter, and one of the first members of the Philharmonic Academy of Verona. His son Felice will not be inferior to him, as, although young, he has displayed considerable excellence in a panel, in the church of the Trinity, of the Madonna, and six life-size saints. It is indeed no wonder, for he learned art in Florence, staying in the house of Bernardo Canigiani, a Florentine noble, friend of his father Domenico.

At this time there lived in Verona, Bernardino, called l'India, who besides many other works decorated the ceiling for a room in the house of Count Marc' Antonio del Tiene with the fable of Psyche, and another chamber for Count Girolamo da Canossa with fine inventions. Another famous young painter, Eliodoro Forbicini, was skilful in all manner of painting, but especially in grotesques, as we see in the two rooms just mentioned and in other places. Battista da Verona,[1] as he is known outside his own country, after learning the elements of painting from an uncle at Verona, placed himself with the admirable Titian at Venice and became an excellent painter. With Paulino he decorated, while still young, a hall at Tiene, in the Vicenza territory, in the palace of the commissary Portesco, with countless figures, which brought them both credit and reputation. These two did many things in fresco in the palace of la Soranza at Castelfranco, both being sent to work there by Michele San

[1] Battista Farinati, called Zelotti, 1532–92.

Michele, who loved them like sons. They also decorated the façade of the house of M. Antonio Cappello, on the Grand Canal at Venice, and then did the ceiling of the Council Chamber of the Ten, dividing the pictures between them. Not long after Battista was summoned to Vicenza, where he did many works, and finally painted the façade of the Monte della Pietà with a quantity of nude figures larger than life-size, in divers attitudes and well designed, and in a marvellously short time. If he did so much in a life of less than thirty years we may imagine what he might have become.

Paulino, also a Veronese painter,[1] is now in good repute at Venice, and though not over thirty he has produced admirable works. He was the son of a sculptor, born in Verona, and learned the elements of painting from Giovanni Caroto of Verona. In conjunction with Battista he painted the hall at Tiene, as already mentioned, and then worked with him at Soranza. At Masiera, near Asolo in the Trevisano,[2] he painted the fine house of Sig. Daniello Barbaro, patriarch-elect of Aquileia. In the refectory of the monastery of S. Nazzaro of the black monks, at Verona, he did a large canvas of the banquet given to Christ by Simon the leper,[3] when the sinner anointed His feet, with a number of portraits, rare perspectives, and two most natural dogs under the table, and some cripples in the background, admirably done. In the hall of the council at Venice there is an oval by Paulino, larger than all the others there, in the middle of the ceiling, representing Jupiter putting to flight the vices, symbolising the action of that supreme council. He also painted the ceiling of the church of S. Sebastiano,[4] a most rare work, and the picture of the principal chapel, with some others to adorn it, and the organ-shutters, all most admirable. In the hall of the Great Council he represented Frederick Barbarossa presented to the Pope, with numerous figures in varied costumes, forming a beautiful representation of the attendants of the emperor and the Venetian senate, many of the nobles and senators of the republic being portraits; indeed, this work deserves universal praise for its grandeur, design and varied attitudes. Paulino next decorated the ceilings of some chambers of the Council of Ten with foreshortened figures of great beauty. He painted the façade of a merchant's house between S. Maurizio and S. Moisè, a beautiful work, which, however, is gradually being destroyed by the sea air. For Cammillo Trivisani he painted a loggia and a

---

[1] Paolo Veronese, 1528–88.
[2] The Villa Maser, painted in 1560.
[3] Now in the Turin Gallery.
[4] Commissioned in 1555.

chamber in fresco at Murano which were much admired, and at the end of a large apartment at S. Giorgio Maggiore, Venice, he painted the Marriage at Cana in oils, on canvas,[1] a marvellous work for its size, the number of figures, the variety of the costumes and the invention, and if I remember rightly it contains more than one hundred and fifty heads, all different and executed with great diligence. The procurators of S. Marco employed him to paint some corner circles in the ceiling of the Nicene library, left to the Signoria by Cardinal Bessarione, and very rich in Greek books. The Government promised a reward to the one who should do best in painting this, in addition to the usual payment, and the work was divided among the foremost painters then in Venice. When the finished paintings had been examined they placed a golden chain round Paulino's neck, for he was judged to have done the best. The picture which obtained this prize for him was Music, a representation of three young women, the most beautiful playing a large viol da gamba and regarding the keyboard, listening with her ear down. One of the others is playing the lute, while the third is singing from a book. Near them is a wingless cupid playing a harpsichord, to show that music gives birth to love, or rather that love is always associated with music, and that is why the cupid is wingless. He there introduces Pan, the god of shepherds, as described by the poets, with his pipes, an instrument as it were dedicated to him by the famous pastoral poets. Paulino did two other pictures in the same place, one of Arithmetic and some philosophers, clothed in the antique style, and one of Honour, seated, to whom sacrifices and crowns are offered; but as this young man is not yet thirty-two and at the height of his powers, I will say no more of him at present.

Another Veronese, Paolo Farinato, was a skilful painter. While pupil of Niccolo Ursino he did many works in Verona, but his chief ones are frescoes in the house of the Fumanelli representing various scenes suggested by M. Antonio, a member of the family, and a physician famous through all Europe. He did two large paintings in the principal chapel of S. Maria in Organo, the Massacre of the Innocents and Constantine ordering children to be brought in order that he may bathe in their blood and cure himself of leprosy. The niche of the chapel contains two large scenes by him, though smaller than the first: Peter walking on the water, and St. Gregory's banquet to the poor. All these admirable works contain a great number of figures, executed

[1] Commissioned 1562; now in the Louvre.

with design, study and diligence. There is a panel of S. Martin
by him in the Duomo of Mantua. He did it in competition with
his other compatriots, as already related. This is the end of the
Life of the excellent Michele San Michele and the other famous
men of Verona, worthy of all praise for their excellence in art
and their many talents.

GIOVANNANTONIO DA VERZELLI, called SODOMA, Painter

(1477-1549)

THE actions of men would produce marvellous results if they
knew how to avail themselves of their opportunities to become
rich, through the favours of the great and by labouring in
their youth to aid their good fortune by ability. The contrary,
however, is too often seen, for men frequently trust to fortune
only, and they are usually disappointed, as we see every day
by experience, while mere ability without good fortune is of
little avail. If Giovannantonio had possessed talent equal to his
good fortune, such as he might have acquired by study, he would
not have passed his old age in wretchedness after an extravagant
and bestial career. Being invited to Siena by some merchants,
agents of the Spanocchi, his good or bad fortune left him a while
without competitors there. This apparent benefit proved harmful
to him in the long run, because he slept as it were, neglected
to study, and did most of his things without models, his only
method of study being to draw some famous things of Jacopo
dalla Fonte and little else. He began by doing several portraits
in that bright colouring which he had brought from Lombardy,
and he made many friends in Siena, rather because the people
are well disposed to strangers than because he was a good
painter. His manner of life was licentious and dishonourable,
and as he always had boys and beardless youths about him of
whom he was inordinately fond, this earned him the name of
Sodoma[1]; but instead of feeling shame he gloried in it, writing
stanzas and verses on it, and singing them to the accompaniment
of the lute. He loved to fill his house with all manner of curious
animals: badgers, squirrels, apes, catamounts, dwarf asses, Barbary racehorses, Elba ponies, jackdaws, bantams, turtle-doves

[1] The name was not given before 1513.

and similar creatures, in fact, all that came into his hands. In addition to these he had a raven, which he had taught to speak so well that it imitated his voice, especially in answering the door, and many mistook it for its master. The other animals were so tame that they were always about him, with their strange gambols, so that his house resembled a veritable Noah's ark. This strange life and his paintings, which certainly contained some good points, earned him such a reputation among the Sienese, that is to say among the common people, for the nobles knew better, that many considered him a great man. Thus when Frà Domenico da Leccio, a Lombard, became general of the monks of Monte Oliveto, Sodoma went to visit him at Monte Oliveto da Chiusuri, the principal house of the order, fifteen miles from Siena, and persuaded the general to allow him to complete the life of St. Benedict,[1] of which Luca Signorelli had done part of a wall. He did this for a small sum, and the expenses of his apprentices and mixers of colours. It is unnecessary to describe his follies there, but they so amused the friars that they dubbed him *il Mattaccio*.[2] But to return to the work. After he had done some scenes without skill or finish, the general complained, and Sodoma said that his brush danced according to the tune of money, and if the general would spend more he would do better work. The general having promised better payment, Sodoma did the three remaining scenes at the corners with far more study and finish than the others, and far greater success. One is St. Benedict leaving Norcia and his parents to go and study at Rome; the second is St. Maur and St. Placidus as children offered to God by their parents; the third represents the Goths burning Monte Cassino. To spite the general and the monks, he painted the last scene of Fiorenzo the priest, St. Benedict's enemy, bringing harlots to dance and sing about the monastery, in order to tempt the brethren. Like the bad man he was, he represented the women naked, and altogether offensive and ugly, and he would not allow any of the monks to see him working, as he would have been stopped. When the scene was uncovered, the general determined to have it destroyed, but Sodoma, after much idle talk, seeing his anger, draped all his figures and rendered the scene the best in the series. Under each of the scenes he made two medallions, to represent all the generals of the order, and as he had not their portraits, he drew most of them from fancy and some of the old friars then in the

---

[1] In 1505, 1506.
[2] A strong and more opprobrious form of *Matto*, a fool.

monastery, including Frà Domenico, the general who had given him the work. But as some of these heads subsequently lost their eyes, and others were damaged, Frà Antonio Bentivogli wisely had them all removed. While Sodoma was engaged on these scenes a Milanese noble assumed the habit in that house. He wore a yellow cloak with black trimmings, as was then customary, and after he had entered the order the general gave this cloak to Sodoma, who drew himself in it, with the help of a looking-glass, and introduced the portrait in the scene where St. Benedict as a child repairs the broken sieve of his nurse, with a raven, a baboon,[1] and other animals at his feet. On completing this work he painted the Miracle of the Five Loaves and Two Fishes, and other figures in the refectory of the monastery of St. Anna,[2] of the same order, five miles from Monte Oliveto. He then returned to Siena, where he painted the façade of the house of M. Agostino de' Bardi of Siena, at la Postierla, containing some praiseworthy things, but most of it has been destroyed by the weather.

About this time Agostino Chigi, a famous and wealthy Sienese merchant, arrived in Siena, and made Sodoma's acquaintance through his follies and his reputation as a good painter. He took Sodoma with him to Rome, where Julius II. was then having painted the papal chambers of the Vatican built by Nicholas V., and he induced the Pope to employ Sodoma. As Perugino, who was doing the vaulting of a room near the Borgia tower, worked slowly, being an old man, and could not do all that had originally been arranged, Sodoma was set to paint another chamber next to Perugino's.[3] Here he decorated the vaulting with cornices, foliage and friezes, and then did some meritorious frescoes in circles. But as he did not progress, being addicted to his bestial pursuits, and Raphael of Urbino being brought to Rome by Bramante the architect, the Pope, recognising his superiority, commanded that neither Perugino nor Sodoma should do further work there, but that everything should be destroyed. Raphael, however, who was modesty itself, allowed the work of his old master to remain, and of Sodoma's work he only destroyed, the filling in and the figures of the circles and squares, leaving the friezes and other ornaments which still surround the Justice, Philosophy, Poetry and Theology of Raphael. But the worthy Agostino, unaffected by the rebuff which Sodoma had received, employed him to paint the story of Alexander and Roxana in a principal room communicating with the great hall,

[1] Actually a badger.   [2] St. Anna in Creta, commissioned in 1503.
                              [3] In 1508.

in his palace of Trastevere.[1] Here he introduced a number of cupids unlacing Alexander's cuirass and removing his shoes, helmet and vest, while others scatter flowers on the bed and perform similar offices. Near the room he made a Vulcan forging arrows, then much admired. If Sodoma, who had good parts and many natural advantages, had attended to his studies, as any other man would, he might have achieved greatness. But he thought of nothing but pleasure, worked when he pleased, and only cared about dressing himself grandly, wearing brocaded doublets, cloaks embroidered with gold, rich cuffs, collars and such trifles, like a mountebank, which all greatly amused Agostino.

When Leo X. succeeded Julius II., the new Pope delighted in strange and thoughtless figures such as Sodoma, and that artist was much rejoiced, especially as he had a grudge against Julius for the shame done to him. Accordingly he did a nude Lucretia stabbing herself[2] for the new Pope. He succeeded in making a beautiful body and a breathing head, for fortune sometimes helps the foolish and thoughtless, and through M. Agostino, who was intimate with the Pope, he presented the picture to His Holiness, who made him a knight and rewarded him. Sodoma, therefore, thinking himself a great man, gave up working except when compelled by necessity. But on Agostino going on his affairs to Siena, and taking Sodoma with him, the latter was obliged to paint for lack of funds, and accordingly he did a Deposition from the Cross, the Virgin fainting, and an armed man turning his back, his face being reflected in a polished helmet lying on the ground.[3] This work, considered one of the best he ever did, was placed on the right-hand on entering S. Francesco. In the cloister next the church he did a Christ at the Column, with many Jews surrounding Pilate, with columns in perspective forming a court.[4] He introduced his own portrait as a beardless man with long hair, then the fashion. Soon after he did some pictures for Jacopo the Sixth, lord of Piombino,[5] and some other things on canvas, while staying in his house. This Jacopo procured him many small animals from his island of Elba, which Sodoma took to Siena.

While Sodoma was staying at Florence a monk of the Brandolini, abbot of Monte Oliveto outside the S. Friano gate,

[1] The Farnesina, in 1514.
[2] In 1518.
[3] Now in the Siena Gallery, probably painted in 1502.
[4] Siena Gallery, about 1507.
[5] Sodoma worked for him in 1538.

employed him to paint some pictures in fresco on the wall of
the refectory. But owing to his follies he did them very badly,
and was mocked by those who had expected good work from
him. Meanwhile, having brought a barbary horse with him, he
entered him for the race of St. Bernaba and, as fate willed, he
won. The boys who used to call out the name of the victor after
the trumpet had sounded asked him what they should cry, and
when he replied, "Sodoma, Sodoma," they repeated the name.
But when some reverend men heard their shouts they began to
say, "What ribaldry is this? Why is such a name shouted in our
city?" So before long poor Sodoma, his horse and a baboon he
had with him were stoned by the boys and the mob. Having
collected many prizes during several years, which had been
won by his horses, he boasted greatly about them, would show
them to all who visited his house, and frequently display them
at his windows.

But to return to his works. For the company of St. Bastiano in
Camollia, behind the church of the Umiliati, he painted a processional banner in oils of a nude St. Sebastian bound to a tree,
resting on his right leg, the left being foreshortened, and raising
his head to an angel which is crowning him, a really beautiful
and admirable work. On the reverse are the Virgin and Child,
and below them St. Sigismund, St. Roch and some flagellants
kneeling. It is said that some merchants of Lucca offered the
men of the company three hundred gold crowns for this work,
but they would not deprive their city of such a rare painting.
Indeed, whether by study or good fortune, Sodoma did some
things excellently, though they were very few. In the sacristy
of the friars of the Carmine is a fine picture of the Nativity of
the Virgin with some nurses, and at a corner near the piazza
de' Tolomei he did for the art of the shoemakers a Virgin and
Child, St. John, St. Francis, St. Roch and St. Crispin, their patron
holding a shoe, the heads and all the rest of the figures being
excellent. In the company of St. Bernardino da Siena, next S.
Francesco, he did some frescoes in competition with Girolamo
del Pacchia, painter of Siena, and Domenico Beccafami, namely
the Presentation of the Virgin at the Temple, the Visitation,
Assumption and Coronation.[1] In the corners of the same chapel
he did a saint in episcopal habit, St. Louis and St. Anthony of
Padua, and best of all St. Francis raising his head to regard a
little angel who seems to be speaking to him, the saint's head
being marvellous. In a hall of the palace of the Signoria at Siena

[1] The Coronation in 1532; the rest in 1518.

Sodoma painted [1] some tabernacles full of columns, cherubs and other ornaments. The tabernacles contain figures, one of St. Victor armed in the ancient style and holding a sword; at his side St. Ansano is baptising, and next him is a St. Benedict, all being of great beauty. In the bottom of the palace, where salt is sold, he painted a Resurrection with soldiers about the sepulchre, and two little angels with heads considered very beautiful. Over a door farther along is a Virgin and Child with two saints painted in fresco. [2] At S. Spirito he painted the chapel of St. James for the Spanish nation, representing St. Nicholas of Tolentino on the right and St. Michael killing Lucifer on the left of an ancient image of the Virgin, and in a lunette above he made the Virgin investing a saint with the sacerdotal habit, and surrounded by angels. Above all these figures, which are in oils, he did in a lunette a St. James on a galloping horse, with drawn sword, and many Turks wounded and slain below him. At the sides of the altar he painted in fresco St. Anthony the abbot and a nude St. Sebastian at the column, considered meritorious.

In the duomo of the same city, at an altar on the left of the entrance, there is an oil-painting of the Virgin and Child between St. Joseph and St. Calixtus, considered a beautiful work, and showing much more diligence in the colouring than is usual with Sodoma. For the company of the Trinità he painted a handsome bier, and did another for the company of la Morte, which is considered the finest in Siena. I think it is the finest to be found anywhere, because, besides being truly admirable, such things are rarely done with much diligence or at great cost. In the chapel of St. Catherine of Siena in S. Domenico he painted two scenes, [3] on either side of the tabernacle, containing the head of the saint made of silver, the one on the right representing the saint fainting in the arms of the sisters, receiving the stigmata from Christ, who is in the air. Baldassarre Peruzzi, the Sienese painter, said that he had never seen fainting better represented than here by Sodoma. We may say as much of Sodoma's design of this painting, preserved in our book of designs. On the left an angel is bringing the saint the Host, and she raises her head and sees Christ and the Virgin in the air, while two sisters stand behind her. In another scene on the right wall is painted a criminal going to execution who despaired of his salvation, but the saint prayed for him and her prayers were answered, so that when the man's head was cut off his soul was seen mounting to heaven, thus affording an example of the

[1] 1529-34.   [2] In 1530.   [3] In 1526.

power of the intercession of the saints. This scene contains a large number of figures, but no one need wonder if they are not of absolute perfection, for I have heard that Sodoma's slothfulness was such that he never made drawings or cartoons for such works, but drew them with his brush on the lime, as we see he has done here. He also painted a God the Father on the arch before the chapel. The other scenes of the chapel he did not finish, partly through his own fault, for he would only work when in the mood and partly because he was not paid.[1] Below is a God the Father with a Virgin beneath, and St. Dominic, St. Sigismund, St. Sebastian and St. Catherine. In St. Agostino he painted an Adoration of the Magi [2] on a panel on the right on entering the church, considered a good work, for besides the Virgin, which is much admired, and the first of the Magi and some horses, there is a life-like head of a shepherd between two trees. Over a door called S. Vienno, in the city, he did a Nativity in a large tabernacle, with angels in the air, and a finely foreshortened infant on the arch, done in high relief, to show that the Word has become flesh. In this work Sodoma introduced himself as an old man, bearded, holding a brush with which he has painted the word *Feci*. In the chapel of the commune in the piazza at the foot of the palace he painted in fresco a Virgin and Child supported by cherubs, St. Ansano, St. Victor, St. Augustine and St. James.[3] In a pyramid above he did a God the Father surrounded by angels. This work shows that he was becoming careless about art, and losing the excellence of his earlier period, when he endowed his heads with a better air and rendered them beautiful and gracious. We see this because some works done long before this possess another style and another grace, for example the divine and graceful Pietà in fresco on a wall over the door of Captain Lorenzo Mariscotti over the Postierlà. An oil-painting of a Madonna also, painted for M. Enea Savini of la Costerella, is much admired, and so is a canvas done for Assuero Rettori of S. Martino, of Lucretia stabbing herself, supported by her father and husband, with fine attitudes and graceful heads.

Perceiving that the devotion of the Sienese was entirely attracted by the talents and excellent works of Domenico Beccafami, and having no house or income in Siena, while he had almost spent everything, and being old and poor, Sodoma departed to Volterra almost in despair. By good fortune he

---

[1] They were finished by Francesco Vanni in 1593. [2] In 1536.
[3] Commissioned in 1537.

found M. Lorenzo di Galeotto de' Medici, a rich and honoured
noble, with whom he hoped to remain a long while. In the house
of M. Lorenzo he painted on canvas the Chariot of the Sun
guided by Phæton and falling into the Po. But it is clear that
he did the work as a pastime, and it was executed carelessly
with little consideration. Becoming tired of Volterra and of his
patron's house, for he loved his liberty, Sodoma went to Pisa, and
through the influence of Battista del Cervelliera did two pictures
in the duomo for M. Bastiano della Seta, the warden. These were
placed in a niche behind the high altar, next to those of Sog-
liano and Beccafami. One is a Dead Christ with the Virgin and
other Maries, and the other Abraham sacrificing Isaac.[1] But as
the work did not turn out very well, the warden, who had intended
to employ Sodoma to do some panels for the church, dismissed
him, for men who do not study lose in old age the natural excellence of their youth and are usually left with a mediocre skill
and style. At this same time Sodoma finished a panel which he
had already begun in oils for S. Maria della Spina, of the Virgin
and Child, with the Magdalene and St. Catherine kneeling before
her, and St. John, St. Sebastian and St. Joseph standing at the
sides, all the figures being much better than the two pictures of
the duomo.[2] Having nothing more to do at Pisa, he went to
Lucca, where he did a Madonna at some steps leading to a
dormitory of S. Ponziano, a house of the friars of Monte Oliveto,
for an abbot whom he knew. That done, he returned to Siena
weary, poor and old, dying soon after, for he fell sick, and
having no one to care for him, he went to the great hospital
and there ended his life in a few weeks.

While young and famous he married a lady of good family
at Siena, and had a daughter by her in the first year. But his
bestiality disgusted her and she refused to see him again, living
on what she earned and her dowry, supporting with patience
the bestiality and follies of this man whom the monks of Monte
Oliveto so aptly called Mattaccio.

Riccio of Siena,[3] Sodoma's pupil and a skilful painter, having
married his master's daughter, who had been well brought up
by her mother, inherited all the artistic possessions of his
father-in-law. He has done many fine works in Siena and elsewhere, and has decorated a chapel with fresco and stucco on
the left on entering the duomo of Siena. He now lives at Lucca,

[1] Dated 1541.
[2] Painted in 1542, now in the Museo Civico, Pisa.
[3] Bartolommeo Negroni.

where he has produced many admirable works and is continuing to do so. Another youth, called Giomo del Sodoma, was also a pupil of Giovann Antonio, but as he died young he had little opportunity of displaying his merit, and it is unnecessary to say more of him. Sodoma lived seventy-five years, and died in 1554.[1]

BASTIANO, called ARISTOTILE DA SAN GALLO, Painter and Architect of Florence

(1481 – 1551)

WHEN Pietro Perugino in his old age painted the high-altar picture of the Servites at Florence, he had with him as a pupil Bastiano, nephew of Giuliano and Antonio di S. Gallo. But the youth did not remain long with him, for having seen Michelagnolo's oft-mentioned cartoon in the Medici palace, the style so pleased him that he would never return to Pietro's shop, thinking his style, by comparison, to be dry, slight and unworthy of imitation. Among those who studied the cartoon, for it was the school of painters for some time, Ridolfo Ghirlandaio was considered the best, and so Bastiano chose him as a friend, to learn colouring of him, and they became very intimate. However, Bastiano continued to study the cartoon, copying the nudes in it, and he also drew a group of figures which none of those who worked there had ever previously drawn entirely. By means of hard study he was able to reproduce the vigour, attitudes and muscles of the figures, which Buonarotto had placed in difficult postures. As Bastiano spoke gravely, slowly and sententiously, the artists dubbed him Aristotile, which became him the better, as he greatly resembled an ancient portrait of that great philosopher. But to return to the cartoon. Bastiano always valued it, and when the original was destroyed he would not allow his reproduction to be copied for any money, and only showed it to his dearest friends as a favour. However, in 1542, his friend Giorgio Vasari persuaded him to copy it in oils in grisaille, and the copy was sent by Monsignor Giovio to King Francis of France, who valued it greatly and richly rewarded San Gallo. Vasari hoped by this means to preserve the memory of the work, as drawings are easily damaged.

[1] He died 15 February, 1549.

As Aristotile, like all his house, delighted in architecture in his youth, he measured the plans of buildings and carefully studied perspective. In this his brother, Giovan Francesco, afforded him great assistance, for he was architect of S. Pietro under Giuliano Leni, the provveditore. His brother having brought Aristotile to Rome, employed him to keep accounts in a great factory of furnaces, kilns, works and ovens, which brought him much gain. Bastiano remained there some time doing nothing but draw in Michelagnolo's chapel and frequenting Raphael's house, having received an introduction from M. Gianozzo Pandolfini, bishop of Troia.

Raphael having designed a palace for the bishop, to be erected in the via di S. Gallo at Florence, Giovan Francesco went to execute it, displaying the utmost diligence. But the work was interrupted by his death in 1530, and by the siege of Florence. Aristotile, who had long before returned to Florence, was made head of the work, as Giuliano Leni had advanced him a great sum of money on the security left by his brother at Rome. By the advice of Luigi Alamanni and Zanobi Buondelmonti, his friends, Bastiano devoted a part of this money to buying a site for a house behind the convent of the Servites, near Andrea del Sarto, which he built, intending to take a wife and settle there. Being fond of perspective, which he had studied at Rome under Bramante, Bastiano seemed to care for nothing else. However, besides many portraits, he painted the Fall and the expulsion from Paradise, in oils. These were copied from Michelagnolo's on the vaulting of the chapel at Rome, and consequently they were little praised. However, he won great praise for a triumphal arch which he made, in conjunction with Francesco Granacci, for the visit of Pope Leo to Florence, opposite the door of the Badia, with many scenes. For the festivities in celebration of the marriage of Duke Lorenzo de' Medici he proved of great assistance, especially in making scenery for comedies for Franciabigio and Ridolfo Grillandai, who had charge of everything. He then painted several Madonnas in oils, partly his own and partly copied from others, including one like Raphael's in the Popolo at Rome, where the Virgin is covering the Child with a veil. It is now in the possession of Filippo dell' Antello. The heirs of M. Ottaviano de' Medici possess another, with the portrait of Lorenzo copied by Aristotile from Raphael. He did many other pictures at the same time, which were sent to England. But perceiving that he lacked invention, and that painting requires study and a good foundation in design, without which he could not become excellent, Bastiano resolved to make architecture and perspective his profession, and painted scenery for comedies at every opportunity that presented itself, for he was fond of such work. The bishop of Troia having set to work again on his palace in the via di S. Gallo once more, Aristotile had charge of it and completed it to his great praise.

Having become very friendly with his neighbour, Andrea del Sarto, from whom he learnt to do many things perfectly in perspective, Bastiano was employed at the numerous festivities of the companies of nobles, Florence being then tranquil. Thus he and Andrea did the scenery for the amusing comedy Mandragola,[1] performed by the company of la Cazzuola in the house of Bernardino di Giordano at the corner of Monteloro. Not long after Bastiano did another perspective for another comedy by the same author in the house of Jacopo the smith. In these scenes, which gave great delight, especially to Alessandro and Ipolito de' Medici, then in Florence in the ward of Silvio Passerini, cardinal of Cortona, Aristotile acquired such a name that it became his principal profession, and some say he earned his name because he was as eminent in perspective as Aristotle in philosophy. But when in 1527 the joy of Florence was turned into sorrow and travail by wars and discords, as so frequently happens, the Medici being driven out and the plague and siege following, artists were in little request, and Aristotile remained at home engaged upon his studies and fancies. But when Duke Alessandro came to rule the city, the youths of the company of the Children of the Purification, opposite S. Marco, arranged a tragi-comedy about Tamar, taken from the Book of Kings, composed by Giovan Maria Primerani. For this Aristotile made one of the most beautiful scenes ever beheld, and as the comedy was good and well played it greatly pleased the duke and his sister, so that they released the author from prison to make another comedy. For this Aristotile made fine scenery and a perspective full of colonnades, niches, tabernacles, statues and other things not used before, in the loggia of the garden of the Medici on the piazza of S. Marco. These gave great pleasure and much enriched that branch of painting. The comedy dealt with the imprisonment and release of Joseph. The duke being greatly pleased, directed that a comedy should be played on his marriage with Margaret of Austria, with scenery by Aristotile, in the company of the weavers in the via de S. Gallo

[1] By Niccolò Machiavelli.

next the house of Ottaviano de' Medici. This was executed by Aristotile with every possible diligence.

Lorenzo di Pier Francesco de' Medici, who composed the comedy, had charge of the scenery and music, and as he was absorbed by his purpose to kill the duke, whose favourite he was, he thought the comedy would present a favourable opportunity. Thus at the point where the steps of the perspective ended, and the scene forms a wall of eighteen braccia high round the court to enclose a capacious room, with a ceiling above for the singers, he wished to make another gallery for the instruments, which cannot be so easily moved, and the space where the wall had been pulled down in front was to be covered with canvas painted in perspective with buildings. All this pleased Aristotile, because it enriched the scene, and left the musicians' gallery free. But he did not wish the beam supporting the roof which projected from the wall to be sustained by anything less than a strong arch, while Lorenzo only proposed to place small supports, in order not to impede the music. But Aristotile, recognising that this was a trap to destroy a number of people, refused to agree, for indeed Lorenzo simply intended to kill the duke in the fall. Not being able to oppose Lorenzo, Aristotile intended to resign, when Giorgio Vasari, who though young was then in the service of the duke and of Ottaviano de' Medici, hearing the dispute between the two as he was painting the scenery, and intervening dexterously, heard both, and then showed how it would be possible to manage without an arch, or impeding the music, by putting two beams of fifteen braccia each along the wall clamped by iron bands to other rafters upon which the middle king-post should rest, where it would be just as safe as with an arch. But Lorenzo would not listen either to Aristotile, who approved, or to Giorgio, who proposed, and cavilled at everything, thus disclosing his evil intent. Giorgio perceiving that a great disaster might ensue, involving the death of three hundred persons, said that he would inform the duke, who would send and provide for everything. When Lorenzo heard this he feared discovery, and allowed Aristotile to follow Vasari's advice. This scene was the finest yet made by Aristotile. He introduced many side scenes in relief, and a marble triumphal arch in the middle full of reliefs and statues, with receding streets and many other things executed with rich invention and incredible diligence.

After Lorenzo had slain Duke Alessandro, Duke Cosimo succeeded in 1539, and soon after married the incomparable

lady Leonora di Toledo, who may be compared with the most
famous women of antiquity, and perhaps preferred before them.
For the wedding, which took place on 27 June, 1539, Aristotile
surpassed himself in a scene representing Pisa, in the great
court of the Medici palace containing the fountain. It would be
impossible to assemble a greater variety of windows, doors,
façades of palaces, streets and receding distances, all in perspective. He also represented the leaning tower, the cupola and
round church of S. Giovanni, with other things of the city. Of
the steps and their realism I will say nothing, in order not to
repeat myself. It had eight faces with square sides, very artistic
in its simplicity, and imparting grace to the perspective above,
so that nothing better of its kind could be desired. He next
devised an ingenious wooden lantern like an arch behind the
buildings, and a sun a braccia high made of a crystal ball filled
with distilled water, with two lighted torches behind, illuminating the sky of the scenery and the perspective, so that it
looked like a veritable sun. It was surrounded by golden rays
covering the curtain, and was managed by a windlass, so as to
rise to the meridian in the middle of the play, and sink in the
west at its end. Antonio Landi, a Florentine noble, wrote the
comedy and, Gio. Battista Strozzi, a clever youth, directed the
interludes and music. But as much was written about these
accessories of the comedy at the time, I will content myself by
saying that, besides certain persons who did some paintings,
everything was carried out by Gio. Battista Strozzi, Tribolo
and Aristotile. Under the scenery of the comedy, the side walls
were divided into painted squares, eight braccia by five, each
surrounded by an ornamentation $1\frac{2}{3}$ braccia broad, forming a
frieze with a cornice towards the painting, making four circles
in a cross with two Latin mottoes for each story, and the others
containing appropriate devices. Above was a frieze of blue
baize except about the proscenium, and over this a canopy
covering the whole court. In the frieze above each scene were
the arms of the most famous families related to the Medici.
Beginning from the east, the first subject nearest the stage, by
Francesco Ubertini, called Il Bacchiacca, was Cosimo's return
from exile, with the device of two doves on a gold branch, and
Duke Cosimo's arms in the frieze. The next, by the same hand,
was Lorenzo's visit to Naples, the device a pelican, and the
arms those of Duke Lorenzo, namely the Medici and Savoy.
The third, painted by Pier Francesco di Jacopo di Sandro, was
the visit of Leo X. to Florence, the device a right arm, and

the arms those of Duke Giuliano, namely the Medici and Savoy. In the fourth, by the same hand, was the taking of Biegrassa [1] by Sig. Giovanni, the device Jove's thunderbolts, and the arms those of Duke Alessandro, namely Austria and the Medici. The fifth contained Pope Clement crowning Charles V. at Bologna, the device a serpent biting its tail, the arms those of France and the Medici. This was by Domenico Conti, pupil of Andrea del Sarto, who did not display much skill, for he lacked the assistance of some youths which he hoped to have, as all artists, whether good or bad, were employed. Thus the laugh was turned against him, for he had at other times presumed to ridicule others. The sixth and last scene on that side was by Bronzino, and represented the dispute between Duke Alessandro and the Florentine exiles at Naples before the emperor, with the River Sebete and many figures, the finest picture of the series. The device was a palm, and the arms those of Spain. Opposite the return of Cosimo was the happy birth of Duke Cosimo, the device a phœnix, and the arms the red lily of Florence. Next this was the elevation of Cosimo to be duke, the device Mercury's wand, and the arms those of the castellan of the fortress. This was designed by Francesco Salviati, but as he was obliged to leave Florence, it was excellently finished by Carlo Portelli of Loro. The third contained three rash envoys of Campana driven from the Roman senate for their insolent demands, as Livy relates in the twentieth book of his history, an allusion to the three cardinals who vainly sought to remove Duke Cosimo from the government. The device was a winged horse, and the arms those of the Salviati and Medici. The next contained the capture of Monte Murlo, the device an Egyptian horn owl on the head of Pyrrhus, and the arms those of the Sforza and Medici. This was painted by Antonio di Donnino, an artist who depicted vigorous movement, and the background contains a skirmish of cavalry that is far better than the works of some others reputed skilled artists. The next shows Duke Alessandro invested by the emperor, the device a magpie with maple leaves in its mouth, and the frieze containing the arms of the Medici and Toledo, all by the hand of Battista Franco of Venice. The last of the series represented the marriage of Duke Alessandro at Naples, the device two crows, the ancient symbol of marriage, and the arms those of Don Petro di Toledo, viceroy of Naples. This scene by Bronzino surpassed all the others as

[1] Abbiategrasso between Milan and Mortara, taken by Cosimo's father, Giovanni delle Bande Neri, in 1524.

much as his first. Over the loggia Aristotile devised a frieze with other scenes and arms, which was much admired, and pleased the duke, who rewarded him richly. From this time Aristotile did scenery every year for the comedies played at the carnival, having become so skilled in that branch that he proposed to write upon it and to teach it. However, this proved more difficult than he had thought, and he gave it up, especially as the governor of the palace got him to employ Bronzino and Francesco Salviati to make perspectives, as will be said in the proper place.

As many years passed without his being employed, Aristotile went to Rome to visit his cousin, Antonio da San Gallo. He was cordially welcomed, and immediately asked for employment on some buildings, with a provision of ten crowns a month. Antonio then sent him to Castro, where he remained for some months, doing a great part of the walls for Paul III. from Antonio's designs. Aristotile had been brought up with Antonio, and was inclined to be familiar with him, but they say that Antonio kept him at a distance, because he could never accustom himself to use the you, but always said thou, even before the Pope, lords and nobles, as all Florentines do in the old-fashioned way to everyone, as if they were from Norcia, without accommodating themselves to the modern style. Antonio disliked this, accustomed as he was to being treated with deference by cardinals and other great men. Aristotile, becoming tired of Castro, begged Antonio to let him return to Rome, to which his cousin readily agreed, stipulating, however, that he should treat him with more respect, especially in the presence of the great.

One carnival year, when Ruberti Strozzi was entertaining some noble friends at a banquet, Aristotile prepared the scenery for a comedy in the great hall, as best he could in so narrow a place. It was so beautiful that Cardinal Farnese, among others, was amazed, and employed him to do one in a middle hall adjoining the garden in his palace of S. Giorgio, where the chancery is, hoping to retain him in his service. Accordingly Aristotile executed this to the best of his ability, delighting the cardinal and artists. The cardinal having commissioned M. Curzio Franzipani to satisfy Aristotile, M. Curzio, like a discreet man, wished to avoid an excessive payment, and asked Perino del Vaga and Giorgio Vasari to value the work. Perino was delighted, because he hated Aristotile, and took it ill that he had received that work, which he thought due to himself, because he was in the cardinal's service. He was filled with fear and jealousy, as the cardinal had not only employed Aristotile, but Vasari also, giving him 1000 crowns for painting the hall of *Parco maiori* in the chancery, in one hundred days. Perino, therefore, intended to put so low a valuation on Aristotile's perspective that he should repent of having done it. Aristotile, however, having learned the names of the valuers, went to visit Perino, and began by thee-ing him, as was his custom, for they had been friends in their youth. Perino, already in a bad temper, flew in a rage, and almost disclosed what he intended to do. Aristotile told everything to Vasari, who promised that he would see he did not suffer wrong. When Perino and Giorgio met to decide the matter, Perino, as the elder, began to disparage the work, saying that Aristotile had received money in advance, and his assistants were paid, and he had already received more than enough. He added, "If I had done it, it would have been utterly different, with different scenes, but the cardinal is always favouring someone who brings him little honour." Giorgio, perceiving that Perino was more anxious to rave against the cardinal and Aristotile than to recognise the labours and ability of a good artist, said quietly, "Although I do not know much about such work, I have seen some by competent hands, and this seems well executed, and worth much and not little as you say, and I do not think it right that those who work hard for several weeks, including nights, should only be paid like those who work by day without the toil of body and mind, simply imitating, whereas Aristotile has used his brain. Even if you could have made more scenes and ornaments, you might not have done them with more grace, for Aristotile in such painting is judiciously considered by the cardinal to be a much better master than you. But take heed lest in the long run you do more harm to art and talent than to Aristotile, and even more to yourself in giving way to your chagrin, for those who see the work will not blame it, but our bad judgment, and perhaps our malignity. Those who seek to aggrandise their own things by blaming or underestimating the good works of others will ultimately be known to God and man as the malignant, ignorant, bad men they are. Consider, too, that you have all the work at Rome, and what you would think if others valued your works at the same rate as you value theirs. Be kind to this poor old man, and see how unreasonable you are." These friendly words brought Perino to a better state of mind, and Aristotile was satisfied. With this money, and what was sent from France for his picture, added

to his provisions, he returned joyfully to Florence, although his
friend Michelagnolo intended to employ him on the building
which the Romans proposed to erect at the Capitol.

Aristotile returned to Florence in 1547, and on going to kiss
the hands of Duke Cosimo begged him to employ him on the
numerous buildings begun. The duke received him kindly, as
he always did men of ability, and ordained for him a provision
of 10 crowns a month, telling him that he should be employed
as occasion arose. On this provision Aristotile lived quietly for
some years, and died on 31 May, 1551, aged seventy. He was
buried in the church of the Servites. Our book contains some
of his designs, and some are owned by Antonio Particini,
including several fine sheets in perspective.

Two friends of Aristotile flourished at the same time, of whom
I will write a short notice, because they deserve a place among
the rare geniuses for their admirable works. One was Jacone,
and the other Francesco Ubertini, surnamed Il Bachiacca.
Jacone did not produce much, spending his time in argument,
and contenting himself with the little that his fortune and
sloth brought him, which was much less than he needed. But
as he associated a great deal with Andrea del Sarto, his design
was good and bold, the posture of his figures being original and
fantastic, as he tried to make them different from others in
every respect; and indeed he designed fairly, and imitated the
good when he liked. In Florence, while still young, he did
several Madonnas, many of which were sent to France by
Florentine merchants. In S. Lucia, in via de' Bardi, he did a
God the Father, Christ, the Virgin Mary, and other figures. At
Montici, at a corner of the house of Ludovico Capponi, he did
two figures in grisaille about a tabernacle. In S. Romeo he
painted a Virgin and two Saints on a panel. Hearing the praises
of the façades of Polidoro and Maturino done in Rome, he went
to that city unknown to anyone, and stayed many months,
painting portraits, and making such progress in art that he
became a creditable painter. Thus the knight Buondelmonti
employed him to paint in grisaille his house, opposite S. Trinità,
on the edge of the Borgo S. Apostolo. Here Jacone did scenes
of the life of Alexander the Great, executed with such grace
and design that many believe the designs were by Andrea del
Sarto. Indeed, from this one might have expected great results
from Jacone. But as he was always intent on having a good
time, and preferred going to feasts and banquets with his
friends to studying, he lost rather than gained ground. I do

not know whether it was laughable or pitiful, that he was in the company of friends or rather a troop, who, under pretext of behaving like philosophers, lived like swine, never washed their hands, face, head, or beard, did not clean their house, only made their bed once in two months, covered their table with drawing-sheets, and only drank from the flask or bottle, a manner of living which they considered very fine. But as the exterior is the only index we have of the interior, I consider that their minds must have been as dirty and bestial as they appeared externally. At the feast of S. Felice in Piazza, when the Annunciation was represented, as described elsewhere, being produced in 1525 by the company of the Orciuolo, Jacone made a fine double triumphal arch standing alone, with eight columns, pilasters, frontispieces, finished by Piero da Sesto, a skilled woodworker. He did nine scenes for it, the better ones painted by himself, and the others by Francesco Ubertini Bachiacca. They were taken from the Old Testament, and mostly related to Moses.

Being taken to Cortona by a Scopetine friar, his kinsman, Jacone painted two oil-pictures in the Madonna outside the city, one of the Virgin with St. Roch, St. Augustine, and other saints, the other the Coronation of the Virgin with two saints below, and St. Francis receiving the stigmata, both very beautiful works. Returning to Florence, he did an apartment for Bongianni Capponi, and others for him in the villa of Montici. When Jacopo Pontormo painted the loggia in the villa of Careggi for Duke Alessandro, as related in his Life, Jacone assisted him with the arabesques and other things. He was then employed on small matters which I need not mention. The conclusion is that Jacone wasted the best time of his life on follies, on vain considerations and in speaking ill of one and another.

At that time the art of design in Florence was confined to a coterie of persons who thought more of enjoying themselves than of work. Their occupation was to gather in the shops and other places, and there malignantly criticise the works of others who lived like honourable men, and were excellent. Chief among this circle were Jacone, Piloto the goldsmith, and Tasso the carpenter, but Jacone was the worst, for he was always slandering someone. Thus it is not surprising that much harm originated in the company, and Piloto was killed by a youth for his evil tongue. Their manners and habits did not please decent people, as they most of them, I will not say all, behaved like wool-beaters and such folk, loafing round the walls and carousing in taverns. One day, when Giorgio Vasari was returning from Monte Oliveto, outside Florence, from a visit to the abbot, the virtuous Don Miniato Pitti, he found Jacone with a great part of his mob at the corner of the Medici. Jacone, half-jesting and half in earnest, intended to say something offensive to Giorgio, and when the latter rode into the midst of them Jacone exclaimed, "Well, Giorgio, how is your lordship?" "Very well, Jacone," answered Giorgio. "I was once poor like you, and now I have 3000 crowns or more. You thought me a simpleton, now the friars and priests admire me. I once served among you, now I have a servant to wait on me and look after my horse. I once wore the clothes of a poor painter, now I am dressed in velvet; I went on foot, now I ride on horseback, so I am doing very well, Jacone. God be with you." When poor Jacone realised all this he was confused, and said never a word, considering his own wretchedness, and how the deceiver often comes off worse than the deceived. At length Jacone died of exhaustion in a hovel in a small street or alley called Codarimessa in 1533, having fallen sick, and being poor, uncared for, and unable to use his legs.

Francesco d'Ubertino, called Bacchiacca,[1] was a diligent painter, and although the friend of Jacone, he lived a well-ordered life. He was also a friend of Andrea del Sarto, who greatly assisted him. He excelled chiefly in small figures, which he finished with great patience, as we see in the predella in S. Lorenzo at Florence, under the picture of Sogliani, and in another predella in the chapel of the Crucified, excellently done. In the chamber of Pier Francesco Borgherini, already mentioned, he did many small figures for chests and chair-backs in conjunction with others,[2] which may be distinguished from the others by their different style. For the antechamber of Giovan Maria Benintendi he did two fine pictures of small figures, the finer of which represents the Baptism of Christ,[3] containing also more figures. He did various others, which were sent to France and England. Finally he entered the service of Duke Cosimo, for he was an admirable animal-painter, and filled the duke's scriptorium with all manner of birds and rare plants, divinely executed in oils. He next did cartoons of all the months of the year, with countless small figures, for a beautiful arras of silk and gold, executed with

[1] 1494–1557.
[2] Two are in the National Gallery, representing the story of Joseph.
[3] This seems to be in the Berlin Gallery.

unsurpassed skill and diligence by Marco, son of Maestro John
Rost, a Fleming. Bachiacca next painted in fresco the grotto of
a fountain at the Pitti, and finally designed the embroidery for
the hangings of a bed, full of scenes of small figures, the richest
work of its kind to be seen, containing pearls and other valuable
things, the work of Antonio Bachiacca, Francesco's brother, an
admirable embroiderer. Francesco died before the completion
of this, the marriage-bed of the prince of Florence, Don Francesco
Medici, and Joan of Austria, and so Giorgio Vasari completed it.
Francesco died at Florence in 1557.

BENVENUTO GAROFALO and GIROLAMO DA CARPI, Ferrarese Painters, and other Lombards
(1481 – 1559; 1501 – 1568)

IN this part of the Lives I will gather together all the best painters,
sculptors and architects of our day in Lombardy, after Mantegna, Costa, Boccaccino of Cremona and Francia, as I cannot
write each Life in detail, and I think it sufficient to mention their
works, a thing I should never have undertaken to do, or to pass
judgment, if I had not first seen them. Therefore as from 1542
to the present year, 1566, I had not travelled all through Italy
to see these works, which have multiplied so in this space, I
wanted to see and judge for myself, being near the end of these
labours of mine. Therefore, on the completion of the wedding
of my master, Don Francesco Medici, prince of Florence and
Siena, with Queen Joan of Austria,[1] over which I have been fully
occupied for two years, on the ceiling of the principal hall of
their palace, I determined, regardless of expense or time, to
revisit Rome, Tuscany, part of the March, Umbria, Romagna,
Lombardy and Venice with her dominion to see the old things
once more and the many new ones done since 1542. As I have
noted the most memorable things, I will now fill up the gaps,
in order that I may not do wrong to the talents of many nor fail
in the sincerity expected of those who write such impartial
histories, without departing from my arrangement, and I will
then write of some who are still living, and producing excellent
works, as is due, I think, to the merit of rare and gifted artists.
To begin with the Ferrarese, Benvenuto Garofalo was born

[1] In 1565.

at Ferrara in 1481 of Piero Tisi, whose ancestors were Paduans. He was so inclined to painting that he did nothing but draw while still a child, when going to school to read. His father, who considered painting frippery, tried in vain to distract him, but perceiving that it was necessary to second Nature, for his son did nothing but draw day and night, he put him with Domenico Panetti [1] at Ferrara, a painter of some repute at the time, though his style was dry and laboured. Benvenuto spent some time with Domenico, but one day, when on a visit to Cremona, he saw a Christ on the Throne, in the midst of four saints giving the benediction, in the principal chapel of the duomo, among other things of Boccaccino Boccacci, a Cremonese painter who had decorated the tribune in fresco. Pleased by the work, he joined Boccaccino through the influence of some friends. That artist was then engaged upon scenes from the life of the Virgin there, as related in his Life, in competition with Altobello,[2] who was doing some admirable scenes of Jesus Christ opposite. After spending two years at Cremona, making great progress under the instruction of Boccaccino, Benvenuto went to Rome in the year 1500 at the age of nineteen. There he joined Giovanni Baldini, a Florentine painter of considerable skill, who had many fine drawings of various famous masters, upon which Benvenuto continually worked when he had time, chiefly at night. Having thus spent fifteen months, and visited with delight the things of Rome, he went to Mantua for a while,[3] after having run through several places in Italy. There he stayed two years with Lorenzo Costa the painter, serving him with such affection that at the end of the time Lorenzo introduced him to Francesco Gonzaga, marquis of Mantua. But Benvenuto had not been there long before he was forced to return to Ferrara, where his father had fallen sick. He remained there for four years, doing many things, some by himself and some in conjunction with Dossi.

In 1505 M. Jeronimo Sagrato, a Ferrarese noble living in Rome, sent for him, and Benvenuto returned willingly, chiefly to see the miracles of Raphael and the chapel painted by Michelagnolo. But on reaching Rome he was overcome by despair at seeing the grace and vigour of Raphael's paintings and Michelagnolo's profundity of design.[4] He cursed the style of Lombardy, and what he had learned with so much pains at Mantua, and would willingly have rid himself of it had he been able. But as he

[1] 1460–1512.   [2] Altobello da Melone.   [3] Probably about 1511.
[4] But the Sistine Chapel was not begun before 1508.

could not, he resolved to unlearn, and become a pupil after having been a master so many years. Accordingly he began to draw from the best and most difficult things, and to study that much-admired style with all possible diligence, and he did little else for two whole years. In this way he so far changed his bad style into a good one that artists esteemed him, and, what was more, he became the friend of Raphael, who obligingly taught him many things, always assisting and favouring him.

If Benvenuto had followed the style of Rome he would doubtless have done things worthy of his genius. But being compelled by some chance to return to Lombardy he promised Raphael, on taking leave, to return to Rome, as the master advised, for Raphael assured him that he could give him more work of importance than he wanted. Accordingly, when Benvenuto had finished the business which brought him to Ferrara, he prepared to return to Rome. But Alfonso, duke of Ferrara, set him to paint a small chapel in the castle with other artists. His departure was next interrupted by the courtesy of M. Antonio Costabili, a prominent noble of Ferrara, who employed him to do an oil-painting at the high altar of the church of S. Andrea. That done, Benvenuto was forced to do another in S. Bertolo, a Cistercian convent, representing an Adoration of the Magi, which was much admired. He then did one in the duomo full of various figures, and two others for the church of S. Spirito, one of the Virgin and Child in the air, with others below, and the other a Nativity.[1]

While thus engaged he was plunged in sorrow whenever he thought of Rome, and he determined to return. However, his plan was spoiled by the death of his father, when he found himself with a marriageable sister and a brother of fourteen on his shoulders, and his affairs in disorder. He was thus forced to make up his mind to remain in his native place, and so, having parted company with the Dossi, who had worked with him till then, he painted a Resurrection of Lazarus by himself in a chapel in S. Francesco, full of various figures in vigorous attitudes coloured charmingly, which won him praise. In another chapel there he painted the Massacre of the Innocents,[2] with marvellous vigour in the movements of the soldiers and other figures, the various emotions being admirably expressed, such as the fear of the mothers and nurses, the dead children, the cruelty of the

---

[1] These three works are in the Pinacoteca, Ferrara; the first, from S. Andrea, is by Dosso Dossi.
[2] In 1519.

murderers, and many other things which afforded great delight. It is true that for this work Benvenuto made clay models to obtain the lights and shadows, and a lay figure with movable joints which could be draped in any manner, things never before practised in Lombardy. More important still, he drew every detail from life, knowing well how essential it is to imitate and observe Nature. For the same church he finished the altarpiece of a chapel,[1] and on a wall he painted in fresco Christ taken in the Garden. In S. Domenico in that city he painted two panels in oils, the Miracle of the Cross and St. Helena, and St. Peter Martyr [2] with a number of excellent figures, where he seems to have departed considerably from his first style, displaying more vigour and less effort. For the nuns of St. Salvestro he did Christ on the Mount speaking with His Father,[3] with the three Apostles sleeping below. For the nuns of St. Gabriello he did an Annunciation, and for those of S. Antonio a Resurrection for the high altar. For the high altar of the Jesuit church of S. Girolamo he did Christ in the manger with a choir of angels in a cloud, considered most beautiful.[4] S. Maria del Vado contains a beautifully designed and coloured panel by him of the Ascension, with the Apostles standing amazed below.[5] In the church of S. Giorgio, a house of the monks of Monte Oliveto outside the city, he painted an Adoration of the Magi, one of his very best works. All these paintings afforded great delight to the Ferrarese, so that he was employed to paint countless pictures for their private houses and monasteries, and for the villages and villas round about. Among others he did a Resurrection at Bondeno, and in the refectory of S. Andrea he painted in fresco several subjects connecting the Old and New Testaments, displaying much ingenuity.[6] But as his works are countless, it is sufficient that I have mentioned the best.

Girolamo da Carpi having learned the elements of painting from Benvenuto, they together painted the façade of the house of the Muzzarelli in the Borgo Nuovo, partly in grisaille and partly in colours, with imitations of bronze. They also painted the exterior and interior of the palaces of Copara, a pleasure-resort of the Duke of Ferrara. Benvenuto did many other things for the duke both by himself and in conjunction with other painters. After being long resolved not to take a wife, he finally

[1] 1520-4.   [2] 1536.
[3] Now in the Berlin Gallery.   [4] Now in the Dresden Gallery.
[5] Now in the Chigi Gallery, Rome.
[6] The Adoration of the Magi from Monte Oliveto and the frescoes from S. Andrea are now in the Pinacoteca, Ferrara.

married at the age of forty-eight, being separated from his brother and become tired of living alone. Hardly a year passed before he fell grievously sick, lost the sight of one eye and was in danger of losing the other. But he made a vow to God that he would ever afterwards wear grey clothing, and his eye was spared by God's grace, so that in his sixty-fifth year he could work with marvellous diligence and polish. Thus when the duke of Ferrara once showed to Paul III. Benvenuto's Triumph of Bacchus,[1] five braccia long, and the Calumny of Apelles, executed at that age from designs by Raphael, pictures which are over the duke's chimneypiece, the Pope was amazed that an old man with only one eye could have produced works so grand and so beautiful. Benvenuto worked ceaselessly every feast day for twenty years for the love of God in the convent of the nuns of St. Bernardino, doing many works of importance in oils, tempera and fresco. This was a marvellous thing, and a proof of his sincere and sterling nature, for he had no competitor there, and yet he devoted as much care and pains as if the place had been frequented. These works are composed with merit, with good expressions, not involved, and in a sweet and beautiful style.

Benvenuto taught his numerous pupils with great care but with no results, and instead of the gratitude which he might at least have expected from them experienced only sorrow, and he used to say that he had never had any enemies except his pupils and apprentices. In 1550 the trouble with his eyes returned, and he became totally blind. He lived on for nine years, supporting this visitation with patience and submitting to the will of God. At length at the age of seventy-eight he rejoiced at death, thinking he had lived too long in darkness and hoping to enjoy eternal light. He died on 6 September, 1559, leaving a son called Girolamo, a very amiable man, and one daughter.

Benvenuto enjoyed an excellent character, loved his jest, was pleasant in conversation and patient in adversity. In his youth he was fond of fencing, loved to play the lute, and was the warmest of friends. He was intimate with Giorgione, Titian and Giulio Romano, and very friendly to all artists, as I can bear witness, for he received me with great kindness on the two occasions that I was at Ferrara. He was honourably buried in the church of S. Maria del Vado, and his virtues were celebrated by the talented in verse and prose. As I could not get his portrait,

[1] Now in the Dresden Gallery.

I have prefaced this chapter with that of Girolamo da Carpi,[1] whose Life I am about to write.

This Girolamo was of Ferrara, and a pupil of Benvenuto. He was first employed by Tommaso his father, a painter of scutcheons, to make cornices and angles and such things by the dozen. As he made some progress under Benvenuto, he hoped his father would take him away from his mechanical pursuits. But as Tommaso did not, being intent only on gain, Girolamo resolved to leave him. Accordingly he went to Bologna, where he was well received by the nobles. Having made some portraits which were good likenesses, he acquired such a reputation that by his gains he was better able to assist his father than when in Ferrara.

At this time a *Noli me tangere* of Correggio was brought to the house of the Counts Ercolani at Bologna, executed with incredible skill and tone. The style so captivated Girolamo that, not satisfied with copying this picture, he went to Modena to see other works by Correggio. There one of these works in especial filled him with wonder, a large picture of the Virgin and the Child espousing St. Catherine, St. Sebastian and other figures, with such beautiful heads that they seem to have been made in Paradise, while finer hair or hands or more charming and natural colouring could not be desired.[2] M. Francesco Grillenzoni, doctor, the owner of the picture and a great friend of Correggio, granted Girolamo permission to copy this picture, and this he did with the utmost diligence. He also copied the picture of St. Peter Martyr painted by Correggio[3] for a company of seculars, who value it greatly as it deserves, for besides other things it contains a lovely Christ-child in His Mother's lap, which seems to breathe, and a St. Peter Martyr. He further copied a small picture by the same master of no less beauty, belonging to the company of St. Bastiano. The copying of all these works greatly improved Girolamo's style, completely transforming it. From Modena he went to Parma, where he heard some of Correggio's work was, and copied the paintings in the tribune of the Dumo, namely the finely foreshortened Virgin rising into heaven surrounded by a multitude of angels, the Apostles looking on, and four saints in niches, St. John the Baptist with a lamb, St. Joseph, St. Bernard degli Uberti, cardinal and bishop of the city, and another bishop, patrons of the city, which he considered an extraordinary work. In S. Giovanni Evangelistà he studied the figures by Correggio

---

[1] Girolamo Bianchi, 1501–68.   [2] Now in the Louvre.
[3] Dresden Gallery.

in the principal chapel in the Coronation of the Virgin, St. John
the Evangelist, the Baptist, St. Benedict, St. Placidus, and a
multitude of angels, and the marvellous figures in the chapel of
St. Joseph in S. Sepolcro, a divine painting. As those who are
fond of a style and carefully study it acquire it at least in part,
so that many even become more excellent than their masters,
Girolamo acquired the manner of Correggio strongly. Thus on
returning to Bologna he always imitated him, studying only
that style and the picture there said to be by Raphael. I learned
all these particulars from Girolamo himself, who was my friend,
at Rome in 1550, when he lamented that he had spent his youth
and his best years at Ferrara and Bologna and not in Rome, or
some other place where he would doubtless have made greater
progress. It was no small detriment to his art that he was too
much devoted to his amours and to playing the lute when he
might have been studying painting. On returning to Bologna
he painted the portrait of M. Onofrio Bartolini of Florence, then
studying in the city, and who afterwards became Archbishop of
Pisa. This head, now in the possession of M. Nofri's heirs, is very
beautiful and graceful.

At this time one Maestro Biagio,[1] a painter, was working in
Bologna, and, seeing the rise of Girolamo, he feared he would be
supplanted and lose his profits. Accordingly he took an opportunity of making Girolamo's friendship, and they became such
close companions that they began to work together, and so
continued a while. This was prejudicial to Girolamo's earnings and
to his art as well, for, like Biagio, he began to borrow everything
from the designs of others and no longer took pains with his work.

A monk named Antonio, of the monastery of S. Michele in
Bosco outside Bologna, having painted a life-size St. Sebastian
in oils at Scaricalasino in a convent of the same order of Monte
Oliveto, and some figures in fresco in the garden of S. Scolastica
in the principal Monte Oliveto, the abbot of Ghiaccino, who had
made him spend the year at Bologna, wanted him to paint the
new sacristy of their church. But Frà Antonio did not feel
equal to such a work, and perhaps did not relish the labour, as
is frequently the case with such men, and he so contrived that
the work should be allotted to Girolamo and Biagio, who painted
it all in fresco, making angels and cherubs in the divisions of
the vaulting, and at the end a Transfiguration in great figures,
after Raphael's in S. Pietro a Montorio. On the walls they did
saints containing some good parts. But Girolamo, perceiving

[1] Biagio Pupini.

that his association with Biagio was ruining him, separated from him on completing this work, and began by himself. His first work done thus was a panel in the chapel of St. Sebastian in S. Salvadore in which he did far better. On learning of the death of his father he returned to Ferrara, where he only did a few portraits and insignificant works.

In the meantime Titian had come to Ferrara to do some things for Duke Alfonso in a room or study where Gian Bellino had previously worked, and where Dosso had done a Bacchanal with figures of such merit that it alone would earn him the name of an excellent painter. By means of Titian and others Giolamo approached the duke's court, requesting permission to copy Titian's portrait of Duke Ercole as a specimen of his skill. He did so well that it looked like the original, and was sent to France. Girolamo .then married and had children, perhaps earlier than was prudent. In S. Francesco at Ferrara he painted the four Evangelists at the angles of the vaulting, figures of considerable merit. In the same place he made a frieze about the church, a rich and grand work, full of half-length figures and cherubs charmingly entwined. In the same church he did a panel of St. Anthony of Padua and other figures, and another of the Virgin in the air with two angels, placed at the altar of Signora Giulia Mazzarella, who was finely portrayed by Girolamo. In S. Francesco, at Rovigo, he did the Descent of the Holy Spirit, a work admirable for its composition and the beauty of the heads. In S. Martino at Bologna he painted a panel of the Magi with fine heads and figures. In Ferrara, in conjunction with Garofalo, he did the façade of the house of Signor Battista Muzzarelli, as already related, and the palace of Coppara, a villa of the duke twelve miles from Ferrara.[1] In Ferrara he did the façade of Piero Soncini on the piazza towards the fish-market, representing the taking of Goletta by Charles V. In the Carmelite church of S. Polo in the same city Girolamo painted a St. Jerome in oils with two other saints of life-size, and in the duke's palace he did a life-size figure representing Chance, possessing vivacity, motion, grace and good relief. He also did a recumbent nude Venus of life-size, with Love beside her, sent to King Francis of France at Paris, and I, who saw it in Ferrara in 1540, can vouch for its excellence. He began, and in great part finished, the decoration of the refectory of S. Giorgio, a house of the monks of Monte Oliveto at Ferrara, which has been completed recently by Pellegrino Pellegrini, a

[1] 1535; destroyed by a fire at the palace in 1808.

Bolognese painter. But a recital of all the pictures that he did
for nobles and lords would occupy too much of this story, and
I will only speak of two fine ones: one of marvellous beauty,
after a Correggio, in the possession of the knight Boiardo[1] in
Parma, of the Virgin putting a shirt on the Christ-child, and
the other after a picture by Parmigiano in the vicar's cell in
the Certosa of Pavia, finished with as much care as a miniature.

As Girolamo also delighted in architecture, he designed many
buildings for private individuals, and served Cardinal Ippolito
of Ferrara in this respect, who had bought the garden of the
cardinal of Naples at Montecavallo in Rome, surrounded by
numerous vineyards. Girolamo was taken by the cardinal to
Rome, and served him not only in the buildings but also in
the truly regal woodwork of the garden, to the amazement of
all. Indeed, I do not know of anyone who could surpass him
in wood, his work being afterwards covered with beautiful
verdure. He made various temples adorned with the finest
ancient statues in Rome, some of which were entire, and some
restored by Valerio Cioli, a Florentine sculptor, and others.
By these works Girolamo acquired a great reputation at Rome,
and the cardinal, who was very fond of him, introduced him
in 1550 to the service of Pope Julius III., who made him architect of the Belvedere, giving him rooms there and a good
provision. But as it was impossible to please the Pope in such
matters, especially as he understood little of design, and disliked in the evening what had pleased him in the morning, and
as Girolamo was always at odds with some old architects who
objected to a new and little-known man being set over them,
he resolved to withdraw, knowing their enmity, and being himself of a cold nature. He therefore returned to Montecavallo
to the service of the cardinal. For this action Girolamo was praised
by many, as life is too serious to be always contending with one
and another, and, as he said, it is better to enjoy peace of mind
with bread and water than have worry and honour. Having
made a picture of the cardinal which seemed excellent to me,
and being already worn out, Girolamo returned with his patron
to Ferrara to enjoy quiet at home with his wife and children,
leaving the hopes of fortune to his rivals, who won from the
Pope no more than he. While he was in Ferrara, a part of the
castle was burned by some accident,[2] and Duke Ercole commissioned Girolamo to restore it. He did very well, although

[1] Baiardo; the original now in the National Gallery.
[2] In 1554.

the country lacks stone for the ornaments, and he deserved the liberal reward he received from the duke for his labours. At length, after doing these and many other works, Girolamo died in 1556, aged fifty-five, and was buried in the church of the Angeli beside his wife. He left two daughters and three sons: Giulio, Annibale, and another. He was a man of cheerful disposition and pleasant conversation. In working he was somewhat slow; his stature was medium, and he particularly delighted in music and amours, perhaps more than was seemly. His buildings were continued by Galasso Ferrarese the architect, a man of great skill and judgment, who might have displayed much more ability had he been employed on great works, if we may judge by his designs.

Another Ferrarese, and an excellent sculptor, was Maestro Girolamo,[1] who, while living in Ricanati, has done many things in marble at Loreto after Andrea Contucci, his master, and executed numerous ornaments about the Virgin's chapel there. After Tribolo left there, on finishing the principal marble relief behind the chapel, representing the angels carrying the chapel to the wood of Loreto, Girolamo remained at work on the spot from 1534 to 1560, doing many works, the first being a seated prophet $3\frac{1}{2}$ braccia high, an excellent figure, placed in a niche on the west. As it gave satisfaction he was employed to do all the other prophets, except the one on the east, and outside towards the altar, done by Simone Cioli of Settignano, also a pupil of Andrea Sansovino. The others are executed with diligence, study and great skill. For the chapel of the Sacrament he did the bronze candelabra, about 3 braccia high, full of foliage and figures, and marvellously well cast. A brother of his, skilful in such founding, did many other things with him at Rome, notably a large bronze tabernacle for Paul III. for the Paolina Chapel of the Vatican.

Among the Modenese there have always been excellent artists, as we see by the four pictures not mentioned hitherto because the master is unknown. They were executed one hundred years ago in the city, and are very beautiful for the time and diligently done. The first is at the high altar of S. Domenico and the others at the chapels in the screen of the church. A painter called Niccolo[2] now lives there, who in his youth did many ornaments in fresco about the shambles of considerable beauty, and the beheading of SS. Peter and Paul at the high altar of S. Piero, a house of the black monks, the soldier executioner

[1] Girolamo Lombardi.   [2] Niccolò dell' Abbate, 1512-72.

being copied from a similar head by Correggio in S. Giovanni Evangelistà at Parma. As Niccolo is more excellent in fresco than in other painting, I hear that he has done some fine ones in France under M. Francesco Primaticcio, abbot of S. Martino, from whose designs he has done many works,[1] besides many others executed in Modena and Bologna.

Gio. Battista,[2] Niccolo's rival, has done much in Rome and elsewhere, and especially at Perugia, where he did many excellent paintings of the life of St. Andrew in the chapel of Sig. Ascanio della Cornia in S. Francesco. In competition with him, Niccolo Arrigo, a Fleming,[3] master of stained-glass windows, did an oil-painting of the Magi in the same place which would be very meritorious were it not confused and over-coloured, thus destroying the distances. He did better in a window of the chapel of St. Bernardino in S. Lorenzo of that city, designed and painted by him. But to come back to Battista. On returning to Modena he did two large scenes, of great excellence, relating to SS. Peter and Paul, on the walls of the same S. Piero where Niccolo painted his panel.

Modena also contains sculptors worthy of a place among the good artists, as besides Modanino, mentioned elsewhere, they have Il Modana, who has done some excellent clay figures of life-size in a chapel of St. Domenico at Modana, and in the middle of the dormitory of the black monks of S. Piero a Virgin, St. Benedict, St. Justina and another, all most realistically coloured like marble, while the air of the heads, the draperies and proportion are admirable. In the dormitory of S. Giovanni Evangelistà at Parma he did the same figures,[4] and in S. Benedetto at Mantua he did a number of figures in relief,[5] of life-size, for the façade and for several niches under the portico, of such beauty that they resemble marble.

Prospero Clemente of Modena is a skilful sculptor, as we may see in his tomb of Bishop Rangone in the duomo of Reggio,[6] containing a life-size effigy of the bishop seated, with two finely executed cherubs, done for Signor Ercole Rangone. Under the vaulting of the duomo at Parma is his tomb of the Blessed Bernardo degli Uberti, cardinal and bishop of the city, finished in 1548, and much admired. Many other excellent artists have flourished there at various times, as besides Cristofano Castelli,[7]

---

[1] At Fontainebleau. Mostly destroyed in 1738. What remains has been much restored.
[2] Gio. Batt. Ingoni (died 1608).   [3] Enrico Palladeni of Malines.
[4] In 1561; now in the Accademia, Parma.
[5] In 1559.   [6] In 1566.   [7] Casetti.

who did a fine panel in the duomo in 1499, and Francesco
Mazzuoli, whose Life has been written, there were many more.
Francesco having done some things in the Madonna della
Steccata, leaving the work unfinished at his death, Giulio
Romano made a coloured drawing, which may be seen there
by anyone, and directed that Michelagnolo Anselmi, a Sienese
by birth but a naturalised Parmesan, and a good sculptor,
should execute the work, which was a Coronation of the Virgin.
He acquitted himself excellently, and obtained a large niche to
do for large pictures opposite his former work. There he completed an Adoration of the Magi, with a number of fine figures,
as related in the Life of Mazzuoli, and he also did the Wise
Virgins on the flat part of the arch, with a decoration of copper
bosses. But he died while a third of the work remained undone,
and this was supplied by Bernardo Soiaro [1] of Cremona, as I
shall relate presently. The same city also contains by him the
chapel of the Conception in S. Francesco and a celestial glory
in the chapel of the Cross in S. Pier Martire.

Jeronimo Mazzuoli, Francesco's cousin, completed the work
left unfinished in the chapel of the Madonna, painting an arch
and doing the bosses. In the niche opposite the principal door
he painted the Descent of the Holy Spirit, and on another
arch the Nativity, which was shown to me in 1566 before it
was uncovered, and it afforded me great pleasure as a really
fine work in fresco. The large middle tribune of the same church,
painted by Bernardo Soiaro of Cremona, will be a fine work
when completed, worthy of the others there, the decoration
having been begun by Francesco, while the design of the church
is due to Bramante.

The Mantuan artists, as related in the Life of Giulio Romano,
spread their influence throughout Lombardy, where able men
have not since been lacking and their works are known to be
good and admirable, and although Giovan Battista Bertano,
chief architect of the Duke of Mantua, has made many
magnificent apartments in the castle, and above the aqueducts
and the corridor, decorated with stucco and paintings, mostly
executed by Fermo Guisoni, Giulio's pupil, and by others, as
will be related, yet they do not equal Giulio's. The same Giovan
Battista has done an admirable oil-painting of the Martyrdom
of St. Barbara in her church in the duke's castle, executed from
his design by Domenico Brusasorci. Having studied Vitruvius,
he has written on the Ionic volute and issued a work upon it.

[1] Bernado Gatti, ob. 1575.

For his house at Mantua he made a column of a single stone at the principal door, the one opposite being set out to scale with all the measurements of that order, marked, i.e. as the ancient palm, inch, foot and braccia, so that anyone may see whether they are correct or not. In S. Piero, the duomo of Mantua, of which Giulio Romano was the architect, restoring it in a new form, he had a picture done for each chapel by various painters, two of them from his design by Fermo Guisoni, namely St. Lucy with two infants and a St. John the Evangelist. He had a similar one done for Ippolito Costa of Mantua of St. Agatha with her hands bound between two soldiers, who are cutting off her breasts. Battista d' Agnolo del Moro of Verona painted, as already related, the altar-picture, of St. Mary Magdalene in the same church, and Jeronimo Parmigiano did that of St. Thecla. For Paolo Farinato of Verona he had that of St. Martin painted, and St. Margaret by Domenico Brusasorci. Giulio Campo of Cremona did that of St. Jerome, and the best of all, though all are good, is a Temptation of St. Anthony by a demon in the shape of a woman, by Paolo Veronese.

But the Mantuans have never possessed a more skilful painter than Rinaldo, a pupil of Giulio, who did a panel in S. Agnese there representing the Virgin in the air, St. Augustine and St. Jerome, figures of great beauty, but death cut him off all too early. In a handsome study full of ancient marble statues and busts of Sig. Cesare Gonzaga, he employed Fermo Guisoni to paint the genealogy of the Gonzaga house, which is remarkably well done, especially in the air of the heads. Besides this the Sig. Cesare has some fine paintings, such as Raphael's Madonna with the cat, and a Virgin gracefully washing the Infant Jesus. In another study made for medals, decorated in ebony and ivory by Francesco da Volterra, who is unequalled in such work, there are some small antique bronze figures of unsurpassable beauty. In fact, since I last saw Mantua to the present year, 1566, when I again visited it, it has become more ornate and beautiful than ever, while artists are always multiplying there.

Giovan Battista of Mantua, the engraver and sculptor mentioned in the Lives of Giulio Romano and Marcantonio of Bologna, had two sons who engrave divinely on copper, and what is more remarkable, a daughter called Diana, a gentle and graceful child whom I have seen, who also engraves remarkably, her beautiful works amazing me. I must not forget that in S. Benedetto at Mantua, a famous monastery of black

monks restored by Giulio Romano, many Mantuan artists and
other Lombards have done fine work, besides those mentioned
in Giulio's Life. It also contains works of Fermo Guisoni, namely
a Nativity, two of Girolamo Mazzuola, three of Lattanzio Gam-
bardo of Brescia, and three others of Paolo Veronese, the best
of all. In the same place, at the end of the refectory, there is a
fine Last Supper by Frà Girolamo,[1] a lay brother, copied from
Lionardo's at Milan so well that I was amazed. I am glad to
mention this, because when I saw the original at Milan in 1566
it was in such a bad state that it showed no more than a series
of confused images, so that the piety of the good father remains
to testify to Lionardo's genius. In the mint at Milan there is
a copy of a portrait of a smiling woman by Lionardo done by
the friar, and of a young St. John the Baptist, very well imitated.

Cremona, as I said in the Life of Lorenzo di Credi and elsewhere, has at various times produced excellent painters, and I
have already related how, when Boccaccino Boccacci painted
the niche of the duomo there and the life of the Virgin, Bonifacio
Bembi was a good painter, and Altobello[2] did many frescoes
of the life of Jesus Christ with better design than Boccaccino.
Altobello next painted a chapel in S. Agostino there in a graceful and beautiful style, as all may see. In the court of the
palace at Milan he made a figure armed in the ancient style,
better than any of the others executed there about the same
time. When Bonifazio died, leaving the stories of Christ unfinished, Giovann. Antonio Licino of Pordenone, called de'
Sacchi in Cremona, completed them with a series of five scenes
from the Passion, with large figures, magnificent colouring and
foreshortenings possessing force and vivacity. These things
taught the Cremonese the right methods of painting in oils as
well as in fresco, for in the same duomo there is a fine picture
by Pordenone on a panel in the middle of the church. This
style was imitated later by Camillo, Boccaccino's son, in painting the principal chapel of St. Gismondo outside the city, and
other works, doing far better than his father. But being a
slow worker and rather easygoing he only produced small and
unimportant things.

One who most successfully imitated the good style, being
aided by the competition of the others, was Bernardo de' Gatti,
surnamed Il Soiaro, said by some to be of Vercelli, by others
called a Cremonese. Be that as it may, he painted a fine picture
for the high altar of S. Piero, of the regular canons, and the

[1] Frà Girolamo Monsignori.   [2] Altobello Melone.

Miracle of the Five Loaves and Two Fishes in the refectory,[1] but
he retouched it so much *a secco* that it has lost its beauty. In
a vault in S. Gismondo outside Cremona he did an Ascension,
a charming thing beautifully coloured. In S. Maria in Campagna
at Piacenza, opposite the St. Augustine of Pordenone and in
competition with him, he did a mounted St. George killing the
dragon, with vigour, movement and fine relief. He was then
employed to do the tribune left unfinished by Pordenone, painting the life of the Virgin in fresco, and although Pordenone's
prophets, sibyls and infants are marvellously beautiful, yet
Soiaro did so well that the whole work seems by one hand.
Similarly some little altar-pictures of his at Vigevano deserve
great praise for their excellence. At length, in Parma, he finished
the niche in the Madonna della Steccata interrupted by the
death of Michelagnolo of Siena, and as he acquitted himself
well the Parmesans gave him the principal tribune in the
middle of the church, where he is painting an Assumption in
fresco, which is expected to prove admirable.

When Boccaccino was still alive, though old, Cremona possessed another painter called Galeazzo Campo, who painted the
rosary of the Virgin in a large chapel in S. Domenico and the
façade at the back of S. Francesco, works of merit. He had
three sons, Giulio, Antonio and Vincenzio. But although Giulio
learned the elements of art from his father, he followed the
better style of Soiaro, and studied some heads by Francesco
Salviati done at Rome for arras and sent to Duke Pier Luigi
Farnese at Piacenza. His first works as a youth in Cremona
were four great scenes of the Martyrdom of St. Agatha, in her
church, which equalled the skill of a practised master. After
doing some things in St. Margherita he painted the façades of
several palaces in grisaille, with good design. He painted in oils
the high-altar picture of S. Gismondo, outside Cremona,[2] very
beautiful for the number and variety of the figures, and equal
to the works of the other artists who had previously painted
there. He then did several frescoes on the vaulting, notably
the Descent of the Holy Spirit, the Apostles being gracefully
and artistically foreshortened from below. In the church of la
Passione in Milan, of regular canons, he painted a crucifix in
oils with some angels, the Virgin, St. John and the other Maries.
For the nuns of St. Paolo at Milan he did four scenes from the
life of St. Paul,[3] being assisted by his brother Antonio Campo,
who also painted a chapel of the new church of the nuns of

St. Caterina at the Ticinese gate, designed by Il Lombardino,[1] representing St. Helena seeking for the Cross, a work of considerable merit. Vincenzio also, who like Antonio learned of Giulio, is a youth of good promise. Besides these two brothers Giulio had as pupils Lattanzio Gambaro of Brescia and others. But the one who did him most honour was Sofonisba Anguisciola of Cremona, with her three sisters, the virtuous daughters of Sig. Amilcare Anguisciola and Signora Bianca Punzona, both noble families of Cremona. Of this Signorina Sofonisba, of whom I said a little in the Life of Properzia of Bologna, as I knew no more then, I have this year seen a picture in her father's house at Cremona, most carefully finished, representing her three sisters playing at chess, in the company of an old lady of the house, making them appear alive and lacking speech only. In another she has portrayed her father between his daughter Minerva, distinguished in painting and letters, and his son Asdrubale, also breathing likenesses. At Piacenza the archdeacon's house contains two other fine pictures by her, one a portrait of the archdeacon and the other of Sofonisba herself, both speaking likenesses. She was afterwards taken by the Duke of Alva to serve the Queen of Spain,[2] where she now is, enjoying a good provision and much honoured, and has produced many marvellous portraits. Her fame led Pope Pius IV. to request a portrait by her of the Queen of Spain. She executed this with the utmost diligence and sent it to Rome with the following letter:

"HOLY FATHER,

"I have learned from your Nuncio that you desired a portrait of my royal mistress by my hand. I considered it a singular favour to be allowed to serve your Holiness, and I asked Her Majesty's permission, which was readily granted, seeing the paternal affection which your Holiness displays to her. I have taken the opportunity of sending it by this knight. It will be a great pleasure to me if I have gratified your Holiness's wish, but I must add that, if the brush could represent the beauties of the queen's soul to your eyes, they would be marvellous. However, I have used the utmost diligence to present what art can show, to tell your Holiness the truth. And so I humbly kiss your most holy feet. Madrid, September 16, 1561.

"Your Holiness's most humble servant,

"SOFONISBA ANGUISCIOLA."

[1] i.e. Cristofano Lombardi.
[2] Isabella of Valois, third wife of Philip II., in 1559.

To this the Pope replied as follows, for he thought the portrait marvellous, and sent back gifts worthy of Sofonisba's talent: "*Pius Papa IV. Dilecta in Christo filia.* We have received the portrait of our dear daughter the Queen of Spain, which you have sent. It has given us the utmost satisfaction both for the person represented, whom we love like a father for the piety and the good qualities of her mind, and because it is well and diligently executed by your hand. We thank you and assure you that we shall treasure it among our choicest possessions, and commend your marvellous talent which is the least among your numerous qualities. And so we send you our benediction. May God save you. *Dat. Rome die* 15 *Octobris* 1561." This testimony is sufficient to show the ability of Sofonisba. A sister of hers named Lucia has left no less fame at her death by means of some paintings which are equally beautiful and valued, as we see by an excellent portrait by her at Cremona of Sig. Pietro Maria the physician. Even better is another portrait by this gifted lady of the Duke of Sessa of the utmost excellence and vivacity. The third sister, Europa, is still a child full of grace and talent, and from speaking with her and seeing her designs, I think she will not be inferior to the others. She has painted many portraits of nobles in Cremona, which are natural and very good, and has sent to Spain a portrait of her mother which greatly pleased Sofonisba, and those of the court who saw it. Anna, the fourth sister, though quite little, is also studying design with great profit. I know not what more I can say, except that it suffices to possess natural ability, and aid it by study as these noble and gifted sisters have done, so that the house of Sig. Amilcare, the worthy father of an honourable family, seems to me to be the home of painting and of every excellence. However, if women can so well produce living men, what marvel that they can paint them!

But to return to Giulio Campo, whose pupils these ladies were. Among other things he did an organ-cover for the cathedral with great diligence, and a number of figures of the history of Esther and Ahasuerus, with the impaling of Haaman, while the same church contains a graceful picture of his at the altar of St. Michael.[1] But as he is still living, I will say no more of his, works at present. Other Cremonese are Geremia the sculptor mentioned in the Life of Filareto, who did a large marble work in S. Lorenzo, a house of the monks of Monte Oliveto, and Giovanni Pedoni, who has done many things

[1] Painted in 1566.

in Cremona and Brescia, especially in the house of Sig. Eliseo Raimondo.

Brescia also has possessed many excellent in design. Among them Jeronimo Romanino [1] has done countless works there, including a picture in S. Francesco of considerable merit, with shutters, painted in tempera within and without. There is another oil-painting by him of great beauty in close imitation of Nature. More able than he was Alessandro Moretto,[2] who painted the translation of St. Faustin and Jovita with accompanying figures under the arch of the Brusciata gate. In S. Nazzaro at Brescia he did some works of merit, and others in S. Celso,[3] also a charming panel in S. Piero in Oliveto. In the mint of Milan there is a Conversion of St. Paul by him containing very natural heads and well-draped figures. He was fond of imitating cloths of gold and silver, velvet, damask and other kinds, with which he carefully draped his figures. His heads are vigorous, in Raphael's style, though of very inferior excellence. His son-in-law, Lattanzio Gambaro,[4] learned art under Giulio Campo, and is now the best painter in Brescia. By him are the high-altar picture of the black monks of St. Faustino, the vaulting and walls and other paintings in the church. The high-altar picture in S. Lorenzo is also his, and so are two scenes on the walls and the vaulting. He also painted the façade of his house, with fine inventions, and the interior. In this house, between S. Benedetto and the Vescovado, I saw, when last in Brescia, two handsome portraits by him of Alessandro Moretto, his father-in-law, a fine head of an old man, and that of his wife. If his other works equalled these he might be numbered among the foremost artists. But as his works are countless, and he is still alive, this notice must suffice.

Many works of Giangirolamo Bresciano [5] may be seen in Milan and Venice, and the mint contains four very fine representations of nights and fires. In the house of Tommaso da Empoli there is a very fine Nativity at night,[6] and some similar fancies, in which he excelled. But as he only did such things and no large works, I can say no more of him except that he was imaginative and fantastic, and his works deserve much praise.

Girolamo Muziano of Brescia,[7] having spent his youth in

[1] 1485–1566.   [2] Alessandro Bonvicino, 1498–1555.
[3] SS. Nazzaro and Celso is one church.
[4] 1541–74.   [5] Girolamo Savoldo, 1480–1550.
[6] At page 16 above Vasari attributes it to Lorenzo Lotto.
[7] 1528–90.

Rome, has done many fine works of figures and landscapes, two oil-paintings in the principal church of S. Maria at Orvieto, and some prophets in fresco, all good works, while his engravings are well designed. I say no more, because he is still alive in the service of Cardinal Ippolito da Este, in his buildings and restorations at Rome, Tigoli and elsewhere. Finally Francesco Richino, another Brescian painter, has recently returned from Germany. Besides many paintings in various places, he has done two in oils in S. Pier Oliveto at Brescia executed with study and great diligence. The brothers Cristofano and Stefano of Brescia [1] have a great reputation among artists for their ability in perspective, and among other things they have represented a corridor of double twisted columns on the flat ceiling of S. Maria dell' Orto at Venice, like those of the Porta Santa at S. Pietro in Rome. They form a superb corridor for the church with cross-vaulting, and it is seen in the middle of the church finely foreshortened, amazing those who see it, as the flat ceiling looks deep, and there is a variety of cornices, masks, festoons and other things forming a rich decoration to the work, which deserves the highest praise for its novelty and the diligence of its execution. As this greatly pleased the senate, they employed the brothers to do a similar small ceiling in the library of S. Marco, which is admirable. They have been recently summoned to their native Brescia to do the same for a magnificent hall begun on the piazza many years before, at great cost, erected above a theatre of large columns with a passage beneath. The hall is seventy-two paces long, thirty-five broad, and thirty-five braccia high at the highest point, although it seems much more, being isolated, with no other building near. The brothers were employed on the ceiling with great success, making the roof of rafters bound by large iron clamps and covered with lead, forming a ceiling like an inverted boat, the whole constituting a rich work. This great space, indeed, only contains three oil-paintings, ten braccia each, done by Titian with the greatest beauty and proportion, but it would be much enriched by the addition of many more, as in other respects the hall is constructed with great judgment.

Having hitherto spoken of the artists of design of the cities of Lombardy, I think it well to say something of Milan, the capital of the province, which has not hitherto been noticed, although it has been referred to several times. To begin with Bramantino,[2] mentioned in the Life of Pier della Francesca,

---

[1] Cristofano and Stefano Rosa.   [2] Bartolommeo Suardi, 1455-1536.

I find that he has done many more things than those mentioned above, and it certainly did not seem likely that so
celebrated an artist, who introduced good design to Milan,
should have produced so few works as those noted. After painting some chambers in Rome for Pope Nicholas, and completing
for the pediment of the door of S. Sepolcro a foreshortened
Christ resting in the lap of the Virgin, with the Magdalene and
St. John, an admirable work, he painted a Nativity in fresco
on a wall of the court of the mint at Milan. In S. Maria di Brera
he painted the Nativity of the Virgin on the screen, and some
prophets on the shutters of the organ, finely foreshortened
from below, and a receding perspective admirably arranged.
I am not surprised at this, because he thoroughly understood
architecture. I remember having seen a fine book in the hands
of Valerio Vincentino containing the antiquities of Lombardy,
drawn and measured by Bramantino, and the plans of many
noble edifices, which I copied from the book when a boy. It
contained the Lombard church of S. Ambrogio at Milan, full
of sculpture and paintings in the Byzantine style, with an apse
of large size, but not well designed. This church was restored
by Bramante, who made a stone portico at one side, with
columns resembling clipped trees, both novel and varied. It
also had a drawing of the ancient portico of S. Lorenzo in the
same city, built by the Romans, a large and beautiful work,
but the church is in the Gothic style. The same book had a
drawing of S. Ercolino, which is very ancient and full of marble
incrustation and stucco, very well preserved, and some large
granite tombs; also the church of S. Piero in Ciel d'oro at Pavia,
containing the body of St. Augustine in the sacristy, the tomb
being full of small figures by the hands, I think, of Agnolo and
Agostino of Siena. It had a drawing of the brick tower built
by the Goths, a fine structure containing figures six braccia
high still in a good state of preservation. It is said that Boethius
died in this tower and was buried in S. Piero in Ciel d'oro, now
called S. Agostino, where the saint's tomb may still be seen,
with an inscription by Aliprando, who restored it in 1222. The
book also contained drawings by Bramantino of the ancient
round church of S. Maria in Pertica, erected of spoils by the
Lombards, and now containing the bones of the slain French
and others who fell at Pavia when King Francis was taken prisoner
by Charles V. Leaving the designs, I say that Bramantino
painted the façade of the house of Giovanbattista Latuate at
Milan with a lovely Madonna between two prophets, and on

the façade of Sig. Bernardo Scacalarozzo he painted four meritorious giants in imitation bronze, with other works at Milan, which brought him praise because he was the first painter in the good style there, and led to Bramante's excellence in architecture by the good style of his buildings in perspective; for the first things studied by Bramante were these of Bramantino, and under that influence S. Satiro was erected, which pleases me as a very rich work, ornate within and without with columns, double corridors and other ornaments, including a handsome sacristy full of statues. But it chiefly merits praise for the middle tribune, the beauty of which, as related in Bramante's Life, led Bernardino da Trevio [1] to follow the same method in the duomo of Milan, and to study architecture, although painting was his first profession; and he had done four scenes of the Passion in a cloister of the monastery of le Grazie, and some others in grisaille. By him Agostino Busto, a sculptor, called Bambaia, was advanced and greatly helped. He is mentioned in the Life of Baccio da Montelupo, and did some works in S. Marta, a nunnery at Milan. Although it is difficult to obtain leave to enter the place, I managed to see the tomb of Gaston de Foix, who died at Pavia,[2] in several pieces of marble, with ten reliefs of small figures most carefully finished, descriptive of the deeds, battles and sieges of that lord, and of his death and burial. In short it is a marvellous production, and I stood lost in wonder that such delicate and marvellous work could be made by the hands; for the tomb contains extraordinary carving of trophies, arms of all kinds, chariots, artillery, and many other instruments of war, with the effigy of the lord in armour, of life-size and joyful aspect at having died in the moment of victory. It is a shame that this work, which is worthy of a place among the marvels of art, should be unfinished and allowed to remain in pieces without being put together, and I am not surprised that some of the pieces have been stolen, sold, and set up in other places. It is true that undutifulness and ingratitude are so rife that not one of the number benefited by Monseigneur de Foix has ever thought of preserving his memory from this disgrace. There are some works in the duomo by this Agostino, and the tomb of the Biraghi in S. Francesco, with many others of great

---

[1] Bernardino Zenale.
[2] He was slain at the battle of Ravenna in 1512. The effigy and some fragments of the tomb are preserved in the Castello at Milan. Other fragments are in the Ambrosiana, Milan, Turin and elsewhere. There is a sketch of the whole monument in the Victoria and Albert Museum.

beauty in the Certosa of Pavia. A rival of his, Cristofano Gobbo,[1] did many things for the façade of the Certosa and in the church, of such excellence that he may be numbered among the best sculptors then in Lombardy, and the Adam and Eve by him, on the eastern façade of the duomo of Milan, are considered remarkable and equal to any by other masters there.

About the same time another sculptor named Angelo il Ciciliano flourished in Milan. On the same side he did a Magdalene in the air with four cherubs, of great beauty, and not inferior to Cristofano's. The latter also studied architecture, and among other things did the portico of S. Celso at Milan, finished after his death by Tofano, called Il Lombardino,[2] who, as related in the Life of Giulio Romano, did many churches and palaces in Milan, notably the monastery, façade and church of the nuns of St. Caterina at the Ticinese gate, and many similar structures. By his influence Silvio da Fiesole [3] was employed to decorate a door of the duomo, between the north and west, containing the life of the Virgin, his work being a beautiful marriage. The fine Marriage at Cana opposite is by the hand of Marco da Gra,[4] a sculptor of some skill. A studious sculptor called Francesco Brambilari continued this series, and has almost finished a Descent of the Holy Spirit of great beauty. He has also done a marble scroll and a marvellous group of infants and foliage for the duomo, to take a statue of Pope Pius IV. de' Medici of Milan. If they had the same opportunities for study here as there are at Rome and Florence, these artists would become marvellous. They are indeed much indebted to Leone Leoni of Arezzo, who, as I shall relate, has spent much time and money in bringing plaster casts of antiquities to Milan for himself and the other artists.

But to return to the Milanese painters. After Lionardo had painted the Last Supper there many tried to imitate it, among them Marco d' Uggiono and others mentioned in his Life. Cesare da Sesto,[5] also a Milanese, imitated it very well; and besides the works mentioned in the Life of Dosso he did a large picture, which is in the mint at Milan, representing Christ baptised by John, a very rich and beautiful painting. By the same hand is an Herodias with the head of John the Baptist on a charger, done with great art. He also painted a panel in S. Rocco outside the Roman gate of a youthful saint, and did some other pictures which are much praised.

[1] Cristofano Solari, fl. 1490–1522.　　[2] Cristofano Lombardi.
[3] Silvio Cosini.　　[4] Marco Ferreri.　　[5] 1480–1521.

Gaudenzio,[1] painter of Milan, who was considered a clever painter in his life, did the high-altar picture in S. Celso and the Passion of Christ in fresco in a chapel of S. Maria delle Grazie, with life-size figures in curious attitudes. He then did a panel below this in competition with Titian, but in spite of his efforts he did not surpass the works of the other artists there. Bernardino del Lupino,[2] who has been mentioned above, painted the façade, loggias, halls and chambers of the house of Sig. Gianfrancesco Rabbia, near S. Sepolcro in Milan, with the Metamorphoses of Ovid and other fables, containing good and beautiful figures produced with delicacy. For the Monasterio Maggiore he painted the entire front of the high altar[3] with various scenes, and did a Christ at the Column in a chapel and many other works which all possess merit. This is the end of the Lives of various Lombard artists.

[1] Gaudenzio Ferrari, 1481–1546.   [2] Bernardino Luini, 1475–1532.
[3] In 1529.

END OF VOL. 3

CONTENTS OF VOLUME FOUR

PART III—*continued*